1000 Recipes
Baking

igloobooks

Published in 2013
by Igloo Books Ltd
Cottage Farm
Sywell
NN6 0BJ
www.igloobooks.com

LEO002 0613
2 4 6 8 10 9 7 5 3
ISBN 978-1-78197-172-7

Food photography and recipe development: PhotoCuisine UK
Front and back cover images © PhotoCuisine UK

Printed and manufactured in China

1000 Recipes
Baking

CONTENTS

CAKES AND BAKES

SERVES 6

Provençal Tart

PREPARATION TIME 10 MINUTES

COOKING TIME 25 MINUTES

INGREDIENTS

250 g / 9 oz all-butter puff pastry
4 tbsp olive oil
1 red onion, finely chopped
2 cloves garlic, crushed
1 small aubergine, cubed
1 red pepper, cubed
150 g / 5 oz mushrooms, sliced
2 large eggs
100 ml / 3.5 fl. oz / ⅓ cup double (heavy) cream
100 g / 3 ½ oz goat's cheese, sliced
6 anchovy fillets in oil, drained

- Preheat the oven to 220°C (200° fan), gas 7. Roll out the pastry on a floured surface and use it to line a 23 cm loose-bottomed tart case.
- Line the pastry case with cling film and fill with baking beans then bake for 10 minutes or until golden brown.
- Remove the baking beans and clingfilm and return to the oven for 5 minutes to cook the base.
- Meanwhile, heat the oil in a frying pan and fry the onion for 5 minutes. Add the garlic and vegetables and cook for 20 minutes, stirring occasionally.
- Lower the oven temperature to 180°C (160° fan), gas 4. Beat the eggs and cream together with a fork to combine, then stir in the vegetable mixture and season.
- Scrape it into the pastry case and arrange the goat's cheese and anchovies on top.
- Bake the tart for 25 minutes. Leave to cool, then serve.

Smokey Mediterranean Vegetable Tart

2

- Add a teaspoon of smoked paprika to the beaten egg and add a cubed green pepper for a more smoky and piquant Mediterranean flavour.

MAKES 12

Brioche Cream Buns

PREPARATION TIME 2 HOURS 30 MINUTES

COOKING TIME 10-12 MINUTES

INGREDIENTS

250 g / 9 oz / 1 ¼ cups butter, cubed
400 g / 14 oz / 2 ⅔ cups strong white bread flour
2 ½ tsp easy blend dried yeast
4 tbsp caster (superfine) sugar
1 tsp fine sea salt
4 large eggs, plus 3 extra yolks

TO FINISH:
1 egg, beaten
4 tbsp sugar nibs
300 ml / 10 ½ fl. oz / 1 ¼ whipped cream

- Rub the butter into the flour then stir in the yeast, sugar and salt. Beat the whole eggs and yolks together and stir into the dry ingredients.
- Knead the dough on a lightly oiled surface with 2 plastic scrapers for 10 minutes until smooth.
- Leave the dough to rest in a lightly oiled bowl, covered with oiled clingfilm, for 2 hours.
- Divide the dough into 12 balls and transfer them to a greased baking tray.
- Cover with oiled clingfilm and leave to prove for 2 hours or until doubled in size.
- Meanwhile, preheat the oven to 220°C (200° fan), gas 7.
- Once risen, brush the tops with beaten egg and sprinkle with sugar nibs then bake for 10 - 15 minutes.
- Transfer the rolls to a wire rack and leave to cool completely before splitting and filling with whipped cream.

Brioche Whisky Cream Buns

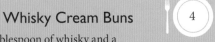

4

- Add a tablespoon of whisky and a tablespoon of icing (confectioners) sugar to the double cream for a sweet alcoholic twist to this tea time classic.

MAKES 6

Almond Cakes

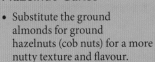

Hazelnut Cakes 6

- Substitute the ground almonds for ground hazelnuts (cob nuts) for a more nutty texture and flavour.

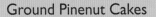

Ground Pinenut Cakes 7

- For a fresh nutty taste substitute the almonds for pinenuts. Grind the pinenuts and mix with the flour to stop the nuts sticking together.

PREPARATION TIME 20 MINUTES

COOKING TIME 20-25 MINUTES

INGREDIENTS

55 g / 2 oz / ⅓ cup self-raising flour, sifted
1 tsp baking powder
55 g / 2 oz / ½ cup ground almonds
110 g / 4 oz / ½ cup caster (superfine) sugar
110 g / 4 oz / ½ cup butter, softened
2 large eggs

- Preheat the oven to 190°C (170° fan), gas 5 and oil a 6-hole silicone tartlet mould or 6 individual tartlet tins.
- Combine all of the ingredients in a bowl and whisk together for 2 minutes or until smooth.
- Divide between the tins and bake for 20 – 25 minutes.
- Test with a wooden toothpick, if it comes out clean, the cakes are done.
- Transfer the cakes to a wire rack to cool before serving.

SERVES 8

Almond and Honey Cake

PREPARATION TIME 25 MINUTES

COOKING TIME 30-35 MINUTES

....

INGREDIENTS

55 g / 2 oz / / ⅓ cup self-raising flour, sifted
55 g / 2 oz / ½ cup ground almonds
55 g / 2 oz / ½ cup caster (superfine) sugar
110 g / 4 oz / ⅓ cup honey
110 g / 4 oz / ½ cup butter, softened
2 large eggs
1 tsp almond essence

FOR THE TOPPING

4 tbsp runny honey
60 g / 2 oz flaked (slivered) almonds

- Preheat the oven to 190°C (170° fan), gas 5 and grease and line a 23 cm round cake tin.
- Combine the flour, ground almonds, sugar, honey, butter, eggs and almond essence in a bowl and whisk together for 2 minutes or until smooth.
- Scrape the mixture into the prepared tin and bake for 30 – 35 minutes.
- Test with a wooden toothpick, if it comes out clean, the cake is done.
- Mix the honey and almonds together and spoon it on top of the cake.
- Return the cake to the oven for 5 minutes or until the honey melts into the cake and the almonds turn golden.
- Transfer the cake to a wire rack to cool.

Almond Honey and Orange Blossom Cake **9**

- Add 1 tsp of orange blossom to the cake batter at the same as the almond essence. This will give the cake a subtle floral orange note.

10

SERVES 8-10

Almond Loaf Cake

PREPARATION TIME 5 MINUTES

COOKING TIME 45 MINUTES

....

INGREDIENTS

225 g / 8 oz / 1 cup butter, softened
225 g / 8 oz / 1 cup caster (superfine) sugar
4 large eggs, beaten
125 g / 4 ½ oz / ¾ cup self-raising flour
100 g / 3 ½ oz / 1 cup ground almonds

- Preheat the oven to 180°C (160° fan), gas 4 and grease and line a large loaf tin with greaseproof paper.
- Cream the butter and sugar together until well whipped then gradually whisk in the eggs, beating well after each addition.
- Fold in the flour and ground almonds then scrape the mixture into the tin.
- Bake the cake for 45 minutes or until a skewer inserted in the centre comes out clean.
- Turn the loaf out onto a wire rack and leave to cool before slicing.

Almond and Lemon Loaf Cake **11**

- After creaming the butter, sugar and eggs together add the zest and juice of one lemon to the batter mix. This will give the cake a fresh lemon taste.

12

MAKES 6 Strawberry Meringue Cakes

- Preheat the oven to 190°C (170° fan), gas 5 and oil a 6-hole silicone tartlet mould or 6 individual tartlet tins.
- Combine the flour, baking powder, sugar, butter and eggs in a bowl and whisk together for 2 minutes.
- Divide between the tins and bake for 20 – 25 minutes. Test with a wooden toothpick, if it comes out clean, the cakes are done.
- Turn the cakes out onto a large baking tray and spread the tops with strawberry jam.
- Whisk the egg whites until stiff, then gradually whisk in half the sugar until the mixture is shiny.
- Fold in the remaining sugar then spoon the meringue on top of the cakes, allowing it to ooze down the sides.
- Return the cakes to the oven and cook for 10 minutes.
- Leave the cakes to cool before topping them with sliced strawberries and nuts.

Raspberry Meringue Cakes

 13

- Substitute the strawberry jam for raspberry and use the same quantity of fresh raspberries whole instead of the sliced strawberries for a sharper tasting meringue cake.

PREPARATION TIME 10 MINUTES

COOKING TIME 30-35 MINUTES

INGREDIENTS

110 g / 4 oz / ⅔ cup self-raising flour, sifted
1 tsp baking powder
110 g / 4 oz / ½ cup caster (superfine) sugar
110 g / 4 oz / ½ cup butter, softened
2 large eggs
6 tbsp strawberry jam
400 g / 14 oz strawberries, sliced
2 tbsp toasted flaked (slivered) almonds
2 tbsp pistachio nuts, chopped

FOR THE MERINGUE

4 large egg whites
110g / 4 oz / ½ cup caster (superfine) sugar

14

SERVES 8 Summer Fruit Frangipane Tart

- Preheat the oven to 200°C (180° fan), gas 6.
- To make the pastry, rub the butter into the flour until the mixture resembles fine breadcrumbs.
- Stir in the sugar and add enough cold water to bring the pastry together into a pliable dough.
- Chill the dough for 30 minutes then roll out on a floured surface. Use the pastry to line a 24cm round loose-bottomed tart case.
- Prick the pastry with a fork, line with greaseproof paper and fill with baking beans or rice.
- Bake for 10 minutes then remove the paper and beans.
- Return to the oven for 8 minutes to crisp.
- Whisk together the almonds, butter, sugar, eggs and flour until smoothly whipped and spoon the mixture into the pastry case.
- Press a ring of strawberries around the edge of the frangipane, then stud the centre with raspberries and redcurrants.
- Bake the tart for 25 minutes or until the frangipane is cooked through. Leave to cool completely.
- Cut the remaining strawberries in half and pile them in the centre of the tart with the left over raspberries and redcurrants.

PREPARATION TIME ?? MINUTES

COOKING TIME ?? MINUTES

INGREDIENTS

150g / 5 ½ oz / 1 ½ cups ground almonds
150g / 5 ½ oz / ⅔ cup butter, softened
150g / 5 ½ oz / ⅔ cup caster (superfine) sugar
2 large eggs
2 tbsp plain (all purpose) flour
4 tbsp apricot jam
200 g / 7 oz / 1 ⅓ cups strawberries
200 g / 7 oz / 1 ⅓ cups raspberries
100 g / 3 ½ oz / ⅔ cup redcurrants

FOR THE PASTRY

200g / 7 oz / 1 ⅓ cups plain (all purpose) flour
100g / 3 ½ oz / ½ cup butter, cubed
50g / 1 ¾ oz / ¼ cups caster (superfine) sugar

15

SERVES 6

Grape Clafoutis

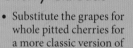

Cherry Clafoutis

16

- Substitute the grapes for whole pitted cherries for a more classic version of the clafoutis.

Shiny Fruit Clafoutis

17

- For a shiny more sumptuous finish warm 4 tablespoons of apricot jam in a pan, add a little water if necessary to thin. Strain through a sieve and using a pastry brush glaze the tart for a professional patisserie style finish.

Prune Clafoutis

18

- Substitute the grapes for pitted prunes.

PREPARATION TIME 10 MINUTES

COOKING TIME 35-40 MINUTES

INGREDIENTS

75 g / 2 ½ oz / ⅓ cup caster (superfine) sugar
75 g / 2 ½ oz / ⅓ cup butter
300 ml / 10 ½ fl. oz / 1 ¼ cups whole milk
2 large eggs
50 g / 1 ¾ oz / ⅓ cup plain (all purpose) flour
2 tbsp ground almonds
1 lemon, zest finely grated
300 g / 10 ½ oz / 2 cups mixed seedless grapes

- Preheat the oven to 190°C (170° fan), gas 5.
- Melt the butter in a saucepan and cook over a low heat until it starts to smell nutty.
- Brush a little of the butter around the inside of a 20 cm round pie dish then add a spoonful of caster (superfine) sugar and shake to coat.
- Whisk together the milk and eggs with the rest of the butter.
- Sift the flour into a mixing bowl with a pinch of salt and stir in the ground almonds, lemon zest and the rest of the sugar.
- Make a well in the middle of the dry ingredients and gradually whisk in the liquid, incorporating all the flour from round the outside until you have a lump-free batter.
- Arrange the grapes in the prepared pie dish, pour over the batter and transfer to the oven immediately.
- Bake the clafoutis for 35 – 45 minutes or until a skewer inserted in the centre comes out clean.
- Serve warm or at room temperature.

19

SERVES 8

Apple and Cinnamon Loaf Cake

- Preheat the oven to 170°C (150° fan), gas 3 and line a large loaf tin with non-stick baking paper.
- Sieve the flour, cinnamon and baking powder into a mixing bowl and add the sugar, butter and eggs.
- Beat the mixture with an electric whisk for 4 minutes or until smooth and well whipped.
- Fold in the chopped apples and scrape the mixture into the loaf tin.
- Bake for 55 minutes or until a skewer inserted comes out clean.
- Transfer the cake to a wire rack and leave to cool completely.

PREPARATION TIME 10 MINUTES

COOKING TIME 55 MINUTES

INGREDIENTS

300 g / 10 ½ oz / 2 cups self-raising flour
2 tsp ground cinnamon
2 tsp baking powder
250 g / 9 oz / 1 ½ cups light brown sugar
250 g / 9 oz / 1 ¼ cups butter, softened
5 large eggs
2 eating apples, cored and chopped

Pear and Cinnamon Loaf

20

- Use 2 pears instead of apples for a different texture and flavour. Conference pears or similar work well in this recipe.

21

SERVES 8

Apple and Poppy Seed Cake

- Preheat the oven to 170°C (150° fan), gas 3 and butter a round baking dish.
- Sieve the flour and baking powder into a mixing bowl and add the brown sugar, butter, eggs and half the poppy seeds.
- Beat the mixture with an electric whisk for 4 minutes or until smooth and well whipped.
- Sprinkle the rest of the poppy seeds and the caster (superfine) sugar over the base of the baking dish and arrange the apple slices on top.
- Spoon the cake mixture on top of the apple and bake for 45 minutes or until a skewer inserted comes out clean.
- Leave the cake to cool for 20 minutes before turning out onto a serving plate.

PREPARATION TIME 15 MINUTES

COOKING TIME 45 MINUTES

INGREDIENTS

300 g / 10 ½ oz / 2 cups self-raising flour
2 tsp baking powder
250 g / 9 oz / 1 ½ cups dark brown sugar
250 g / 9 oz / 1 ¼ cups butter, softened
5 large eggs
2 tbsp poppy seeds
1 tbsp caster (superfine) sugar
3 eating apples, cored and sliced

Pear and Almond Upside-Down Cake

22

- Subsitute the apples for sliced pears and sprinkle with 4 tbsp of flaked (slivered) almonds for a nutty fruity

23

SERVES 8

Apple and Cider Loaf Cake

PREPARATION TIME 10 MINUTES

COOKING TIME 55 MINUTES

INGREDIENTS

300 g / 10 ½ oz / 2 cups self-raising flour
2 tsp baking powder
250 g / 9 oz / 1 ½ cups light brown sugar
250 g / 9 oz / 1 ¼ cups butter, softened
4 large eggs
100 ml / 3 ½ fl. oz / ⅓ cup dry cider
2 eating apples, coarsely grated

- Preheat the oven to 170°C (150° fan), gas 3 and line a large loaf tin with non-stick baking paper.
- Sieve the flour and baking powder into a mixing bowl and add the rest of the ingredients.
- Beat the mixture with an electric whisk for 4 minutes or until smooth and well whipped.
- Scrape the mixture into the loaf tin and bake for 55 minutes or until a skewer inserted comes out clean.
- Transfer the cake to a wire rack and leave to cool completely.

Pear and Perry Loaf Cake

24

- Use pears (varieties such as Conference lend themselves well to this recipe) and Perry instead of cider for a different take on this classic loaf cake.

25

SERVES 8

Banana and Walnut Loaf Cake

PREPARATION TIME 10 MINUTES

COOKING TIME 55 MINUTES

INGREDIENTS

3 very ripe bananas
110 g / 4 oz / ½ cup soft light brown sugar
2 large eggs
120 ml / 4 fl. oz / ½ cup sunflower oil
225 g / 8 oz / 1 ½ cup plain (all-purpose) flour
1 tsp bicarbonate of soda
75 g / 2 ½ oz / ⅔ cup walnuts, chopped

- Preheat the oven to 170°C (150° fan), gas 3 and line a long thin loaf tin with non-stick baking paper.
- Mash the bananas roughly with a fork then whisk in the sugar, eggs and oil.
- Sieve the flour and bicarbonate of soda into the bowl and add the chopped walnuts. Stir just enough to evenly mix all the ingredients together.
- Scrape the mixture into the loaf tin and bake for 55 minutes or until a skewer inserted comes out clean.
- Transfer the cake to a wire rack and leave to cool completely.

Banana and Hazelnut Loaf

26

- Use the same quantity of chopped hazelnuts (cob nuts) instead of the walnuts to help bring out the fruity notes of the banana in this delicious loaf cake.

SERVES 6-8 (27)

Apple and Vanilla Pie

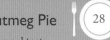

Apple and Nutmeg Pie (28)

- For a more autumnal taste to this delicious pie use _ teaspoon of freshly grated nutmeg instead of the vanilla pod.

Apple, Pear and Vanilla Pie (29)

- Use half pear and half apple for a more fruity and delicious variation of this classic pie.

PREPARATION TIME 45 MINUTES

COOKING TIME 35-45 MINUTES

INGREDIENTS

125 g / 4 ½ oz / ½ cup caster (superfine) sugar
2 tbsp plain (all purpose) flour
1 vanilla pod, seeds only
900 g / 2 lb bramley apples, peeled and chopped
1 egg, beaten

FOR THE PASTRY

300 g / 11 oz / 2 cups plain (all purpose) flour
150 g / 5 ½ oz / ⅔ cup butter, chilled

- Sieve the flour into a mixing bowl. Dip the chilled butter in the flour then grate it into the bowl and mix evenly.
- Add enough cold water to bring it together into a pliable dough then chill for 30 minutes.
- Preheat the oven to 190°C (170 fan), gas 5 and butter a 23 cm round pie tin.
- Mix the sugar, flour and vanilla seeds together then add the apples and mix together.
- Roll out half the pastry on a floured surface and use it to line the pie tin.
- Pack the apples into the pastry case and brush around the top of the pastry with beaten egg.
- Roll out the other half of the pastry and lay it over the apples. Press down round the outside to seal.
- Crimp the edges and trim away any excess pastry.
- Make a couple of holes in the top with a knife and brush with beaten egg then bake for 35 – 45 minutes – the pastry should be crisp and golden brown on top and starting to shrink away from the edge of the tin.

SERVES 8 · 30

Gluten and Dairy Free Banana Loaf Cake

PREPARATION TIME 10 MINUTES

COOKING TIME 55 MINUTES

INGREDIENTS

3 very ripe bananas
110 g / 4 oz / ½ cup caster (superfine) sugar
2 large eggs
120 ml / 4 fl. oz / ½ cup sunflower oil
175 g / 6 oz / 1 ¼ cups rice flour
50 g / 1 ¾ oz / ⅓ cup ground almonds
2 tsp baking powder

- Preheat the oven to 170°C (150° fan), gas 3 and line a medium loaf tin with non-stick baking paper.
- Mash the bananas well with a fork then whisk in the sugar, eggs and oil.
- Sieve the rice flour and baking powder into the bowl and add the ground almonds. Stir just enough to evenly mix all the ingredients together.
- Scrape the mixture into the loaf tin and bake for 55 minutes or until a skewer inserted comes out clean.
- Transfer the cake to a wire rack and leave to cool completely.

Nutty Gluten and Dairy Free Banana Loaf Cake

  31

- Try ground hazelnuts (cob nuts) for a more classic nutty taste and texture to this delicious and tasty loaf.

SERVES 8 · 32

Banana and Chocolate Chip Loaf Cake

PREPARATION TIME 10 MINUTES

COOKING TIME 55 MINUTES

INGREDIENTS

3 very ripe bananas
110 g / 4 oz / ⅓ cup dark brown sugar
2 large eggs
120 ml / 4 fl. oz / ½ cup sunflower oil
225 g / 8 oz / 1 ½ cup plain (all purpose) flour
1 tsp bicarbonate of soda
75 g / 2 ½ oz / ½ cup chocolate chips

- Preheat the oven to 170°C (150° fan), gas 3 and line a loaf tin with non-stick baking paper.
- Mash the bananas roughly with a fork then whisk in the sugar, eggs and oil.
- Sieve the flour and bicarbonate of soda into the bowl and add the chocolate chips. Stir just enough to evenly mix all the ingredients together.
- Scrape the mixture into the loaf tin and bake for 55 minutes or until a skewer inserted comes out clean.
- Transfer the cake to a wire rack and leave to cool completely.

Banana, Rum and Fudge Chip Loaf Cake

 33

- Use fudge chips instead of chocolate chips for a more toffee like taste, add 1-2 tablespoons of rum to taste for a more grown up loaf cake.

Mini Berry Cupcakes

MAKES 36

- Preheat the oven to 190°C (170° fan) / 375F / gas 5 and line a 36 hole cupcake tin with paper cases.
- Combine the flour, sugar, butter, eggs and vanilla extract in a bowl and whisk together for 2 minutes or until smooth.
- Divide the mixture between the paper cases and press a berry into the top of each one.
- Transfer the tin to the oven and bake for 10 – 15 minutes.
- Test with a wooden toothpick, if it comes out clean, the cakes are done.
- Transfer the cakes to a wire rack and leave to cool completely.

PREPARATION TIME 35 MINUTES

COOKING TIME 10-15 MINUTES

INGREDIENTS

110 g / 4 oz / 1 cup self-raising flour, sifted
110 g / 4 oz / ½ cup caster (superfine) sugar
110 g / 4 oz / ½ cup butter, softened
2 large eggs
1 tsp vanilla extract
18 raspberries
18 blackberries

Blueberry and Peach Cupcakes

- Take 36 blueberries and use as you would the raspberries using 2 per muffin. Chop 2 peaches into cubes and use one cube per muffin for a sweet, fruity muffin.

Cake Breton

SERVES 8

- Preheat the oven to 180°C (160° fan), gas 4 and butter a 23 cm round spring-form cake tin.
- Put the prunes and brandy in a food processor and pulse until pureed. Rub the butter into the flour with a pinch of salt then stir in the sugar.
- Beat 5 of the egg yolks and stir them into the dry ingredients. Bring the mixture together into a soft dough and divide it in two.
- Press one half into the bottom of the cake tin to form an even layer. Spread the prune mixture on top, leaving a clear border round the outside.
- Roll out the other half of the dough between 2 sheets of greaseproof paper then peel away the paper and lay it on top of the prunes.
- Press it into the edges to form an even layer.
- Brush the top of the gateau with the final egg yolk then score a tartan pattern on top with a fork.
- Bake the gateau for 40 – 45 minutes or until golden brown and cooked through.
- Cool completely before unmolding and cutting into slices.

PREPARATION TIME 15 MINUTES

COOKING TIME 40-45 MINUTES

INGREDIENTS

250 g / 9 oz / 1 ¼ cups soft, stoneless prunes
4 tbsp brandy
250 g / 9 oz / 1 ¼ cups butter, cubed
250 g / 9 oz / 1 ⅔ cups plain (all purpose) flour
250 g / 9 oz / 1 ¼ cups caster (superfine) sugar
6 large egg yolks

37

MAKES 1 LOAF # Carrot, Cheese and Walnut Loaf

Parsnip, Parmesan and Pinenut Bread

38

- Use parsnip instead of carrot, Parmesan instead of cheddar and coarsely chopped pinenuts instead of the walnuts.

Potato, Cheese and Walnut Bread

39

- Take the same weight in par cooked potato as you would the carrot.

Carrot. Blue Cheese and Walnut Bread

40

- A good quality blue cheese broken into small chunks combined with the walnut makes a delicious festive style savoury loaf cake.

PREPARATION TIME 2 HOURS 30 MINUTES

COOKING TIME 35-45 MINUTES

INGREDIENTS

400 g / 14 oz / 2 ⅔ cups strong white bread flour, plus extra for dusting
½ tsp easy blend dried yeast
1 tbsp caster (superfine) sugar
1 tsp fine sea salt
100 g / 3 ½ oz / ¾ cup carrot, grated
100 g / 3 ½ oz / 1 cup Cheddar cheese, grated
100 g / 3 ½ oz / ¾ cup walnuts, roughly chopped

- In a large bowl, mix together the flour, yeast, sugar and salt. Stir the grated carrot, cheese and walnuts into 280 ml of warm water.
- Stir it into the dry ingredients then knead the mixture on a lightly oiled surface with your hands for 10 minutes or until the dough is smooth and elastic.
- Leave the dough to rest in a lightly oiled bowl, covered with oiled clingfilm, for 1 – 2 hours.
- Punch the dough with your fist to knock out the air then knead it for 2 more minutes.
- Roll the dough with your hands into a fat sausage, then turn it 90⁰ and roll it tightly the other way. Tuck the ends under and transfer the dough to the tin, keeping the seam underneath.
- Cover the tin loosely with oiled clingfilm and leave to prove somewhere warm for 45 minutes.
- Preheat the oven to 220⁰C (200⁰ fan), gas 7.
- Transfer the tin to the top shelf of the oven then quickly throw a small cupful of water onto the floor of the oven and close the door.
- Bake for 35 – 40 minutes or until the loaf sounds hollow when you tap it underneath. Transfer the bread to a wire rack and leave to cool completely before slicing.

SERVES 8 Pineapple Upside-Down Cake

- Preheat the oven to 170⁰C (150⁰ fan), gas 3 and butter a 23 cm round cake tin.
- Sieve the flour and baking powder into a mixing bowl and add sugar, butter and eggs.
- Beat the mixture with an electric whisk for 4 minutes or until smooth and well whipped.
- Spread the jam over the base of the cake tin and arrange the pineapple rings on top.
- Spoon in the cake mixture and bake for 35 minutes or until a skewer inserted comes out clean.
- Leave the cake to cool for 20 minutes before turning out onto a serving plate.

PREPARATION TIME 15 MINUTES

COOKING TIME 35 MINUTES

INGREDIENTS

300 g / 10 ½ oz / 2 cups self-raising flour
2 tsp baking powder
250 g / 9 oz / 1 ¼ cups caster (superfine) sugar
250 g / 9 oz / 1 ¼ cups butter, softened
5 large eggs
4 tbsp raspberry jam
4 canned pineapple rings, drained

Banana Upside-Down Cake

- Use 3 ripe bananas sliced into half centimetre thickness instead of the pineapple for a delicious twist to this classic upside-down cake.

MAKES 9 Chocolate Brownies

- Preheat the oven to 170⁰C (150⁰ fan), gas 3 and oil and line a 20 cm x 20 cm / 8" x 8" square cake tin.
- Melt the chocolate, cocoa and butter together in a saucepan, then leave to cool a little.
- Whisk the sugar and eggs together with an electric whisk for 3 minutes or until very light and creamy.
- Pour in the chocolate mixture and sieve over the flour, then fold everything together until evenly mixed.
- Scrape into the tin and bake for 35 – 40 minutes or until the outside is set, but the centre is still quite soft, as it will continue to cook as it cools.
- Leave the brownie to cool completely before cutting into 9 squares.

PREPARATION TIME 25 MINUTES

COOKING TIME 15-20 MINUTES

INGREDIENTS

110 g / 4 oz milk chocolate, chopped
85 g / 3 oz / ¾ cup unsweetened cocoa powder, sifted
225 g / 8 oz / 1 cup butter
450 g /15 oz / 2 ½ cups light brown sugar
4 large eggs
110 g / 4 oz / ⅔ cup self-raising flour

Double Chocolate Brownies

- Instead of using one type of chocolate chip use half milk or dark and half white for an extra sweet take on this delicious tray bake.

45

SERVES 8-10

Cherry and Honey Cake

PREPARATION TIME 10 MINUTES

COOKING TIME 35-40 MINUTES

INGREDIENTS

300 g / 10 ½ oz / 2 cups self-raising flour
2 tsp baking powder
125 g / 4 ½ oz / ½ cup caster (superfine) sugar
125 g / 4 ½ oz / ⅓ cup runny honey
250 g / 9 oz / 1 ¼ cup butter, softened
5 large eggs
150 g / 5 oz / 1 cup cherries, halved and stoned

- Preheat the oven to 170⁰C (150⁰ fan), gas 3 and line a 23 cm round spring form cake tin with greaseproof paper.
- Sieve the flour and baking powder into a mixing bowl and add the sugar, honey, butter and eggs.
- Beat the mixture with an electric whisk for 4 minutes or until smooth and well whipped.
- Arrange the cherries in the prepared cake tin then spoon the cake mixture on top.
- Bake for 35 – 40 minutes or until a skewer inserted in the centre comes out clean.
- Transfer the cake to a wire rack and leave to cool completely.

Apricot and Honey Cake

 46

- Use the same weight in apricots as you would cherries, stone halve and quarter each apricot.

47

SERVES 8

Black Cherry Brulee Tart

PREPARATION TIME 20 MINUTES

COOKING TIME 15-20 MINUTES

INGREDIENTS

200 g / 7 oz / 1 ⅓ cups black cherries, pitted
28 g / 1 oz / 2 tbsp caster (superfine) sugar

FOR THE PASTRY

200g / 7 oz / 1 ⅓ cups plain (all purpose) flour
100g / 3 ½ oz / ½ cup butter, cubed

FOR THE CUSTARD

4 large egg yolks
75 g / 2 ½ oz / ⅓ cup caster (superfine) sugar
1 tsp vanilla extract
2 tsp cornflour
450 ml / 16 fl. oz / 1 ¾ cups whole milk

- Preheat the oven to 200⁰C (180⁰ fan), gas 6.
- To make the pastry, rub the butter into the flour and add just enough cold water to bind.
- Chill for 30 minutes then roll out on a floured surface. Use the pastry to line a 24 cm round cake tin.
- Prick the pastry with a fork, line with clingfilm and fill with baking beans or rice and bake for 10 minutes. Cook for another 8 minutes to crisp.
- Arrange the black cherries in the pastry case. To make the custard, whisk together the egg yolks, sugar, vanilla extract and cornflour. Heat the milk almost to a simmer then gradually whisk it into the egg mixture.
- Cook the mixture until it thickens, stirring constantly. Pour on top of the cherries.
- Leave to cool completely then refrigerate for at least an hour. Sprinkle the top with caster (superfine) sugar and caramelise it under a very hot grill.

Prune Brulee Tart

 48

- Use the same weigh in prunes as you would cherries for a more grown up tart.

49

SERVES 6

Cherry Clafoutis

Cherry and Chocolate Clafoutis

50

- Follow the recipe above but substitute 20g/ _ oz of the flour for cocoa powder for a rich chocolate taste.

Raspberry Clafoutis

51

- Instead of cherries why not use the same weight in raspberries for a delicious take on this classic dessert.

PREPARATION TIME 10 MINUTES

COOKING TIME 35-45 MINUTES

INGREDIENTS

300 g / 10 ½ oz / 2 cups cherries, stoned
2 tbsp kirsch
75 g / 2 ½ oz / ⅓ cup butter
75 g / 2 ½ oz / ⅓ cup caster (superfine) sugar
300 ml / 10 ½ fl. oz / 1 ¼ cups whole milk
2 large eggs
50 g / 1 ¾ oz / ⅓ cup plain (all purpose) flour
2 tbsp ground almonds

- Preheat the oven to 190°C (170° fan), gas 5.
- Put the cherries in a bowl with the kirsch and leave to marinate for 30 minutes.
- Melt the butter in a saucepan and cook over a low heat until it starts to smell nutty.
- Brush a little of the butter around the inside of a 20 cm quiche dish then add a spoonful of caster (superfine) sugar and shake to coat.
- Whisk together the milk and eggs with the rest of the butter.
- Sift the flour into a mixing bowl with a pinch of salt and stir in the ground almonds and the rest of the sugar.
- Make a well in the middle of the dry ingredients and gradually whisk in the liquid, incorporating all the flour from round the outside until you have a lump-free batter.
- Arrange the cherries in the prepared baking dish, pour over the batter and transfer to the oven immediately.
- Bake the clafoutis for 35 – 45 minutes or until a skewer inserted in the centre comes out clean.
- Leave to cool and serve warm or at room temperature.

MAKES 12

Chocolate Sponge Squares

PREPARATION TIME 10 MINUTES

COOKING TIME 45-50 MINUTES

INGREDIENTS

150 g / 6 oz / 1 cup self-raising flour
28 g / 1 oz / ¼ cup unsweetened cocoa powder
2 tsp baking powder
175 g / 6 oz / ¾ cup caster (superfine) sugar
175 g / 6 oz / ¾ cup butter
3 eggs

TO DECORATE

12 silver dragees
sugar-coated cake decorations

- Preheat the oven to 180°C (160 fan), gas 4 and grease and line a 30 cm x 23 cm cake tin.
- Put all of the cake ingredients in a large mixing bowl and whisk them together with an electric whisk for 4 minutes or until pale and well whipped.
- Scrape the mixture into the tin and level the top with a spatula.
- Bake for 30 - 35 minutes. The cake is ready when a toothpick inserted in the centre comes out clean.
- Transfer the cake to a wire rack to cool completely before cutting into 12 squares and topping each one with a silver dragee.

Chocolate and Coffee Squares

- Add 2 tablespoons of espresso or very strong coffee to the batter mix for a more grown up take on this delicious cake.

MAKES 1 LOAF

Chestnut Bread with Pine Nuts and Raisins

PREPARATION TIME 2 HOURS 30 MINUTES

COOKING TIME 35-40 MINUTES

INGREDIENTS

200 g / 7 oz / 1 ⅓ cups chestnut flour
200 g / 7 oz / 1 ⅓ cups strong white bread flour, plus extra for dusting
½ tsp easy blend dried yeast
1 tbsp caster (superfine) sugar
1 tsp fine sea salt
2 tbsp olive oil
100 g / 3 ½ oz / ¾ cup pine nuts
100 g / 3 ½ oz / ½ cup raisins
2 tbsp runny honey

- In a large bowl, mix together the flours, yeast, sugar and salt. Stir the oil, pine nuts and raisins into 280 ml of warm water and stir it into the dry ingredients.
- Knead the mixture on a lightly oiled surface with your hands for 10 minutes or until the dough is smooth and elastic.
- Leave the dough to rest in a lightly oiled bowl, covered with oiled clingfilm, for 1 – 2 hours or until doubled in size.
- Transfer the dough to an oiled roasting tin and push it out with your fingers to fill the bottom.
- Cover again with oiled clingfilm and leave to prove for 1 hour or until doubled in size.
- Meanwhile, preheat the oven to 220°C (200° fan), gas 7.
- Bake for 35 – 40 minutes or until the loaf sounds hollow when you tap it underneath. Transfer the bread to a wire rack and brush with honey; then leave to cool.

Chestnut Bread with Cranberry and Almond

- Use chopped dried cranberries instead of raisins and chopped almonds instead of the pine nuts.

56

SERVES 8

Rhubarb and Chestnut Loaf Cake

- Preheat the oven to 170⁰C (150⁰ fan), gas 3 and line a large loaf tin with non-stick baking paper.
- Sieve the flours and baking powder into a mixing bowl and add the sugar, butter and eggs.
- Beat the mixture with an electric whisk for 4 minutes or until smooth and well whipped then fold in the rhubarb.
- Scrape the mixture into the loaf tin and bake for 55 minutes or until a skewer inserted in the centre comes out clean.
- Transfer the cake to a wire rack and leave to cool completely.

PREPARATION TIME 10 MINUTES

COOKING TIME 55 MINUTES

INGREDIENTS

200 g / 7 oz / 1 ⅓ cups self-raising flour
100 g / 3 ½ oz / ⅔ cup chestnut flour
2 tsp baking powder
250 g / 9 oz / 1 ½ cups light brown sugar
250 g / 9 oz / 1 ¼ cups butter, softened
5 large eggs
2 sticks rhubarb, chopped

Rhubarb, Chestnut and Chocolate Loaf Cake

57

- Add 2 tbsp of chocolate chips to the mix, at the same time as you add the rhubarb.

58

SERVES 8

Chocolate and Cherry Summer Pudding

- Put the cherries in a bowl with the sugar and kirsch and leave to macerate for 2 hours. Line a pudding basin with clingfilm.
- Put the cherries in a sieve and collect the juice.
- Dip the bread in the cherry juice and use it to line the pudding basin, saving one slice for the lid.
- Bring the cream to a simmer then pour it over the chocolate and stir gently to emulsify.
- Fold the cherries into the chocolate ganache and spoon it into the pudding basin.
- Top with the last slice of soaked bread then cover the basin with clingfilm.
- Put a small board on top of the pudding basin and weigh it down with a can, then leave it to chill in the fridge for at least 4 hours.
- Invert the pudding onto a plate and peel away the clingfilm.

PREPARATION TIME 15 MINUTES

INGREDIENTS

300 g / 10 ½ oz / 2 cups cherries, stoned and halved
4 tbsp caster (superfine) sugar
1 tbsp kirsch
6 slices white bread, crusts removed
250 ml / 9 fl. oz / 1 cup double cream
250 g / 9 oz dark chocolate (minimum 60 % cocoa solids), chopped

White Chocolate and Raspberry Summer Pudding

59

- Use white chocolate instead of dark and measure soak the equivalent cherry weight in raspberries and soak in Framboise instead of kirsch.

60

MAKES 9

Chocolate and Pine Nut Brownies

Chocolate and Hazelnut Brownies

61

- Hazelnuts make a great alternative to pine nuts and give this decadent brownie an extra nutty quality. Roughly chop the hazelnuts (cob nuts) and method above.

Chocolate and Fudge Brownies

62

- If you fancy a change from chocolate and nuts then use chocolate and mini fudge pieces. These little sweet nuggets give a delicious extra chewy texture to the brownie.

PREPARATION TIME 25 MINUTES

COOKING TIME 35-40 MINUTES

INGREDIENTS

110g / 4 oz milk chocolate, chopped
85 g / 3 oz / ¾ cup unsweetened cocoa powder, sifted
225 g / 8 oz / 1 cup butter
450 g / 15 oz / 2 ½ cups light brown sugar
4 large eggs
110 g / 4 oz / ⅔ cup self-raising flour
85 g / 3 oz / ⅔ cup pine nuts

- Preheat the oven to 170°C (150° fan), gas 3 and oil and line a 20 cm x 20 cm / 8" x 8" square cake tin.
- Melt the chocolate, cocoa and butter together in a saucepan, then leave to cool a little.
- Whisk the sugar and eggs together with an electric whisk for 3 minutes or until very light and creamy.
- Pour in the chocolate mixture and sieve over the flour, then fold everything together with the pine nuts until evenly mixed.
- Scrape into the tin and bake for 35 – 40 minutes or until the outside is set, but the centre is still quite soft, as it will continue to cook as it cools.
- Leave the brownie to cool completely before cutting into 9 squares.

MAKES 12

Mini Chocolate Orange Loaf Cakes

- Preheat the oven to 180⁰C (160⁰ fan) / 350F / gas 4 and line 12 mini loaf cake tins with cases.
- Beat the egg in a jug with the oil and the orange juice and zest until well mixed.
- Mix the flour, cocoa, baking powder, sugar, hazelnuts (cob nuts) and chocolate in a bowl, then pour in the egg mixture and stir just enough to combine.
- Divide the mixture between the paper cases, then bake in the oven for 20 – 25 minutes.
- Test with a wooden toothpick, if it comes out clean, the cakes are done.
- Transfer the cakes to a wire rack and leave to cool completely.

PREPARATION TIME 25 MINUTES

COOKING TIME 20-25 MINUTES

INGREDIENTS

1 large egg
120 ml / 4 fl. oz / ½ cup sunflower oil
120 ml / 4 fl. oz / ½ cup orange juice
1 tbsp orange zest, finely grated
375 g / 12 ½ oz / 2 ½ cups self-raising flour, sifted
55g / 2 oz / ½ cup unsweetened cocoa powder, sifted
1 tsp baking powder
200 g / 7 oz / ¾ cup caster (superfine) sugar
75 g / 2 ½ oz / ⅔ cup hazelnuts (cob nuts) (cob nuts), chopped
110 g / 4 oz dark chocolate (minimum 60% cocoa solids), chopped

Chocolate, Coffee and Hazelnut Mini Loaf Cakes

64

- For a richer tasting mini loaf cake use 120ml/ 4fl.oz strong coffee instead of the orange juice.

65

SERVES 8

Light Fruit Cake

- Preheat the oven to 180⁰C (160⁰ fan), 355F, gas 4 and line a loaf tin with non-stick baking paper.
- Sieve the flour into a mixing bowl and rub in the butter until it resembles fine breadcrumbs then stir in the sugar, dried fruit, cherries and lemon zest.
- Lightly beat the egg with the milk and stir it into the dry ingredients until just combined.
- Scrape the mixture into the loaf tin and bake for 55 minutes or until a skewer inserted comes out clean.
- Transfer the cake to a wire rack and leave to cool completely.

PREPARATION TIME 15 MINUTES

COOKING TIME 55 MINUTES

INGREDIENTS

225 g / 8 oz / 1 ½cups self raising flour
100 g / 3 ½ oz / ½ cup butter, cubed
100 g / 3 ½ oz / ½ cup caster (superfine) sugar
100 g / 3 ½ oz / ⅔ cup mixed dried fruit
8 glace cherries, quartered
1 tsp grated lemon zest
1 large egg
75 ml / 2 ½ fl. oz / 1 ⅓ cups whole milk

Rich Fruit Cake

66

- By using dark muscovado sugar and a tablespoon of brandy added to the base cake mixture this cake will take on a richer, fruitier flavour.

67

SERVES 8

Chocolate and Pear Tarte Tatin

PREPARATION TIME 10 MINUTES

COOKING TIME 20-25 MINUTES

....

INGREDIENTS

2 tbsp butter
2 tbsp dark brown sugar
6 pears, peeled, cored and halved
250 g / 9 oz all-butter puff pastry
100 g / 3 ½ oz dark chocolate (minimum 60 % cocoa solids), chopped

- Preheat the oven to 220°C (200° fan), gas 7.
- Heat the butter and sugar in an ovenproof frying pan and add the pears. Cook over a very low heat for 5 minutes, turning occasionally, until they start to soften.
- Arrange the pears, cut side up and leave to cool a little.
- Roll out the pastry on a floured surface and cut out a circle the same size as the frying pan.
- Lay the pastry over the pears and tuck in the edges, then transfer the pan to the oven and bake for 25 minutes or until the pastry is golden brown and cooked through.
- Meanwhile, melt the chocolate in a microwave or bain marie.
- Using oven gloves, put a large plate on top of the frying pan and turn them both over in one smooth movement to unmold the tart.
- Drizzle the melted chocolate between the pears and serve immediately.

68

MAKES 12

Chocolate Sponge with Apricots

PREPARATION TIME 10 MINUTES

COOKING TIME 30-35 MINUTES

....

INGREDIENTS

150 g / 6 oz / 1 cup self-raising flour
28 g / 1 oz / ¼ cup unsweetened cocoa powder
2 tsp baking powder
175 g / 6 oz / ¾ cup caster (superfine) sugar
175 g / 6 oz / ¾ cup butter
3 eggs

TO DECORATE

300 ml / 10 ½ fl. oz / 1 ¼ cups double cream
1 can apricot slices, drained

- Preheat the oven to 180°C (160 fan), gas 4 and grease and line 2 x 20 cm round cake tins.
- Put all of the cake ingredients in a large mixing bowl and whisk them together with an electric whisk for 4 minutes or until pale and well whipped.
- Divide the mixture between the tins and level the top with a spatula.
- Bake for 30 - 35 minutes. The cakes are ready when a toothpick inserted in the centre comes out clean.
- Transfer the cakes to a wire rack to cool completely.
- Whip the double cream until thick and spoon half of it onto the first cake. Top with two thirds of the apricot slices then position the second cake on top.
- Spread the rest of the cream over the top of the cake and decorate with the remaining apricot slices.

Chocolate and Strawberry Gateau

SERVES 10-12

- Preheat the oven to 180°C (160° fan), 355F, gas 4 and grease and line 2 x 20 cm round cake tins.
- Whisk all of the cake ingredients. Divide the mix between the tins and bake for 30 - 35 minutes.
- The cakes are ready when a toothpick inserted in the centre comes out clean.
- Transfer the cakes to a wire rack to cool completely.
- Measure ¼ of the cream into a saucepan and bring to a simmer. Pour it over the chopped chocolate and stir until smooth.
- Whip the rest of the cream until thick. Fold ⅔ strawberry slices into the cream and use the strawberry cream to sandwich the 2 cakes together.
- Pour the slightly cooled chocolate glaze over the cakes and spread it round the sides with a palette knife.
- Put the cake in the fridge for 1 hour to set before decorating with the reserved strawberries.

PREPARATION TIME 10 MINUTES

COOKING TIME 45-50 MINUTES

INGREDIENTS

150 g / 6 oz / 1 cup self-raising flour
28 g / 1 oz / ¼ cup cocoa powder
2 tsp baking powder
175 g / 6 oz / ¾ cup caster sugar
175 g / 6 oz / ¾ cup butter
3 eggs

TO DECORATE

400 ml / 14 fl. oz / 1 ⅔ cups
double cream
100 g / 3 ½ oz milk chocolate, chopped
300 g / 10 ½ oz strawberries, sliced
milk chocolate curls

Chocolate Cake and Plum Terrine

70

SERVES 8

Banana and Coconut Tart

71

SERVES 8

PREPARATION TIME 2 HOURS
30 MINUTES

COOKING TIME 45 MINUTES

INGREDIENTS

225 g / 8oz / 1 cup butter, softened
225 g caster / 8 oz / 1 cup caster (superfine) sugar

4 large eggs, beaten
225 g / 8 oz / 1 ½ cups self-raising flour
1 tbsp unsweetened cocoa powder
75 g dark chocolate, melted

FOR THE FILLING

400 ml / 14 fl. oz / 1 ⅔ cups
double cream
8 ripe plums, stoned and sliced

- Preheat the oven to 180°C (160° fan), 355F, gas 4 and grease and line a large loaf tin with greaseproof paper.
- Cream the butter and sugar together until well whipped then gradually whisk in the eggs, beating well after each addition.
- Sift over and fold in the flour and cocoa powder, then fold in the melted chocolate. Scrape the mixture into the tin and bake for 45 minutes or until a skewer inserted in the centre comes out clean.
- Turn the loaf out onto a wire rack and leave to cool.
- Line the tin with clingfilm. Slice the cake horizontally into 3 even layers and put the top one back into the tin.
- Whip the cream until thick and spoon half of it into the tin. Top with half of the plums then lay the middle cake layer on top and press down.
- Spoon over the rest of the cream and top with the remaining plum slices before adding the final cake layer.
- Refrigerate for 2 hours to firm up. Turn out of the tin and cut into 8 slices to serve.

PREPARATION TIME 20 MINUTES

COOKING TIME 15-20 MINUTES

INGREDIENTS

3 bananas, sliced
2 tbsp caster (superfine) sugar
3 tbsp desiccated coconut
1 pre-made pastry case

FOR THE CUSTARD

4 large egg yolks
75 g / 2 ½ oz / ⅓ cup caster (superfine) sugar
1 tsp vanilla extract
2 tsp cornflour
450 ml / 16 fl. oz / 1 ¾ cups whole milk
3 tbsp desiccated coconut

- Preheat the oven to 200°C (180° fan), 390F, gas 6.
- To make the custard, whisk together the egg yolks, sugar, vanilla extract and cornflour.
- Heat the milk with the desiccated coconut almost to a simmer then then gradually whisk it into the egg mixture.
- Scrape the custard back into the saucepan and cook over a medium heat until the mixture thickens, stirring constantly.
- Pour it into the pastry case and arrange the bananas on top. Mix together the caster (superfine) sugar and desiccated coconut and sprinkle it over the top then place the tart in the oven for 10 minutes to brown the top.
- Leave to cool before slicing.

72

SERVES 8-10

Coconut Cake with Redcurrant Compote

PREPARATION TIME 5 MINUTES

COOKING TIME 45-55 MINUTES

INGREDIENTS

225 g / 8 oz / 1 cup butter, softened
225 g / 8 oz / 1 cup caster (superfine) sugar
4 large eggs, beaten
225 g / 4 ½ oz / 1 ½ cups self-raising flour
100 g / 3 ½ oz / 1 cup desiccated coconut

FOR THE COMPOTE

100 g / 3 ½ oz / ⅔ cup redcurrants
4 tbsp caster (superfine) sugar

- Preheat the oven to 180°C (160° fan), 355F, gas 4 and grease and line a 23 cm round cake tin with greaseproof paper.
- Cream the butter and sugar together then gradually whisk in the eggs, beating well after each addition.
- Fold in the flour and coconut then scrape the mixture into the tin.
- Bake the cake for 45 - 55 minutes or until a skewer inserted in the centre comes out clean.
- Meanwhile, put the redcurrants in a small saucepan with the sugar. Cover and cook gently for 5 minutes then remove the lid, give it a stir and cook for a few more minutes until the redcurrants start to burst and the juices thicken.
- Leave the cake to cool for 20 minutes before serving warm with the compote spooned over the top.

Coconut Cake with Gooseberry Compote

73

- Use tart gooseberries instead of the redcurrants. Check the tartness and add an extra tbsp of sugar to taste if necessary.

74

MAKES 12

Flower Cupcakes

PREPARATION TIME 20 MINUTES

COOKING TIME 15-20 MINUTES

INGREDIENTS

110 g / 4 oz / ⅔ cup self-raising flour, sifted
110 g / 4 oz / ½ cup caster (superfine) sugar
110 g / 4 oz / ½ cup butter, softened
2 large eggs
1 tsp vanilla extract
110 g / 4 oz / ½ butter, softened
225 g / 8 oz / 2 ¼ cups icing (confectioner's) sugar
2 tbsp milk
a few drops of food dye
sugar flowers to decorate

- Preheat the oven to 190°C (170° fan), 375F, gas 5 and line a 12-hole cupcake tin with paper cases.
- Combine the flour, sugar, butter, eggs and vanilla extract in a bowl and whisk together until smooth.
- Divide the mixture between the paper cases, then bake for 15 – 20 minutes.
- Test with a wooden toothpick, if it comes out clean, the cakes are done.
- Transfer the cakes to a wire rack and leave to cool.
- To make the buttercream, beat the butter with a wooden spoon until light and fluffy then beat in the icing (confectioners) sugar a quarter at a time. Use a whisk to incorporate the milk then whisk until smooth.
- Divide the buttercream into separate bowls and stir in the food colourings of your choice.
- Spread the buttercream onto the cakes and decorate each one with a sugar flower.

Flower Essence Cupcakes

75

- For extra depth of flavour you could add a few drops of flower essence such as rose to your buttercream before piping.

76

SERVES 6

Fresh Fruit Sponge Pudding

Dried Fruit Sponge Pudding

77

- Substitute the fruit with 4 dried apricots, 55g/1oz raisins and 55g/1oz prunes. Soak the fruit in hot water for 5 minutes and cut into quarters before adding to the mixture.

Brandy and Fruit Sponge Pudding

78

- For a more grown up pudding add 3 tablespoons of brandy to the dried fruit sponge mixture before baking.

PREPARATION TIME 15 MINUTES

COOKING TIME 30-35 MINUTES

INGREDIENTS

110 g / 4 oz / ⅔ cup self-raising flour, sifted
110 g / 4 oz / ½ cup caster (superfine) sugar
110 g / 4 oz / ½ cup butter, softened
2 large eggs
1 tsp vanilla extract
2 plums, cut into eighths
55 g / 1 oz / ⅓ cup raspberries
55 g / 1 oz / ⅓ cup seedless black grapes

- Preheat the oven to 190°C (170° fan), 375F, gas 5 and butter a small baking dish.
- Combine the flour, sugar, butter, eggs and vanilla extract in a bowl and whisk together for 2 minutes or until smooth.
- Arrange half of the fruit in the baking dish and spoon in the cake mixture.
- Top with the rest of the fruit then bake for 30 – 35 minutes.
- Test with a wooden toothpick, if it comes out clean, the cake is done.
- Serve warm with custard or cream.

79

SERVES 8

Fig and Honey Tarte Tatin

PREPARATION TIME 10 MINUTES

COOKING TIME 20-25 MINUTES

INGREDIENTS

2 tbsp butter, softened and cubed
4 tbsp runny honey
8 figs, quartered
250 g / 9 oz all-butter puff pastry

- Preheat the oven to 220°C (200° fan), 430F, gas 7.
- Dot the butter over the base of a large ovenproof frying pan and drizzle with honey.
- Arrange the fig quarters on top in a single snug layer.
- Roll out the pastry on a floured surface and cut out a circle the same size as the frying pan.
- Lay the pastry over the figs and tuck in the edges, then transfer the pan to the oven and bake for 25 minutes or until the pastry is golden brown and cooked through.
- Using oven gloves, put a large plate on top of the frying pan and turn them both over in one smooth movement to unmold the tart.

Fig and Maple Syrup Tarte Tatin **80**

- Maple syrup makes a great alternative to honey and gives a richer flavour to the tarte tatin.

81

MAKES 12

Chocolate Ganache Mini Loaf Cakes

PREPARATION TIME 20 MINUTES

COOKING TIME 15-20 MINUTES

INGREDIENTS

110 g / 4 oz / ⅔ cup self-raising flour, sifted
110 g / 4 oz / ½ cup caster (superfine) sugar
2 tbsp cocoa powder
110 g / 4 oz / ½ cup butter, softened
2 large eggs

FOR THE GANACHE

100 ml / 3 ½ fl. oz / ½ cup double cream
100 g / 3 ½ oz milk chocolate, chopped
1 tbsp butter, softened

- Preheat the oven to 190°C (170° fan), 375F, gas 5 and oil a 12-hole silicone mini loaf cake mould.
- Combine the flour, sugar, cocoa, butter and eggs in a bowl and whisk together for 2 minutes or until smooth.
- Divide the mixture between the moulds, then transfer the mould to the oven and bake for 15 – 20 minutes.
- Test with a wooden toothpick, if it comes out clean, the cakes are done.
- Transfer the cakes to a wire rack and leave to cool completely.
- Heat the cream to simmering point then pour it over the chocolate and stir until smooth.
- Add the butter and blend it in with a stick blender.
- When the ganache has cooled to a spreadable consistency, spread it on top of the cakes with a palette knife.

Chocolate and Espresso Ganache Mini Loaf Cakes **82**

- Add 3 tbsp of espresso or very strong coffee to the ganache mixture to create a deeper flavoured ganache topping.

SERVES 8

Rhubarb Loaf Cake

- Preheat the oven to 170°C (150° fan), 340F, gas 3 and line a large loaf tin with non-stick baking paper.
- Sieve the flour and baking powder into a mixing bowl and add the sugar, butter and eggs.
- Beat the mixture with an electric whisk for 4 minutes or until smooth and well whipped then fold in the rhubarb.
- Scrape the mixture into the loaf tin and bake for 55 minutes or until a skewer inserted comes out clean.
- Transfer the cake to a wire rack and leave to cool completely.

PREPARATION TIME 10 MINUTES

COOKING TIME 55 MINUTES

INGREDIENTS

300 g / 10 ½ oz / 2 cups self-raising flour
2 tsp baking powder
250 g / 9 oz / 1 ¼ cups caster (superfine) sugar
250 g / 9 oz / 1 ¼ cups butter, softened
5 large eggs
2 sticks rhubarb, chopped

Rhubarb and Lemon Loaf Cake 84

- Adding the zest of one lemon and 2 tablespoons of lemon juice your cake will have an added citrus fresh taste in the mouth.

MAKES 12

Chocolate and Hazelnut Mini Loaf Cakes

- Preheat the oven to 180°C (160° fan) / 350F / gas 4 and line 12 mini loaf cake tins with cases.
- Beat the egg in a jug with the milk and oil until well mixed.
- Mix the flour, cocoa, baking powder, sugar, hazelnuts (cob nuts) and chocolate in a bowl, then pour in the egg mixture and stir just enough to combine.
- Divide the mixture between the paper cases, then bake in the oven for 20 – 25 minutes.
- Test with a wooden toothpick, if it comes out clean, the cakes are done.
- Transfer the cakes to a wire rack and leave to cool completely.

PREPARATION TIME 25 MINUTES

COOKING TIME 20-25 MINUTES

INGREDIENTS

1 large egg
120 ml / 4 fl. oz / ½ cup milk
120 ml / 4 fl. oz / ½ cup sunflower oil
375 g / 12 ½ oz / 2 ½ cups self-raising flour, sifted
55g / 2 oz / ½ cup cocoa powder, sifted
1 tsp baking powder
200 g / 7 oz / ¾ cup caster (superfine) sugar
75 g / 2 ½ oz / ⅔ cup hazelnuts (cob nuts), chopped
110 g / 4 oz dark chocolate (minimum 60% cocoa solids), chopped

Chocolate and Almond Mini Loaf Cakes 86

- For a different nutty taste try using 75g/2fl.oz flaked (slivered) almonds instead of the hazelnuts (cob nuts).

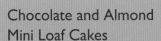

87

SERVES 8

Rich Chocolate Tart

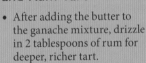

Rich Chocolate and Rum Tart

88

- After adding the butter to the ganache mixture, drizzle in 2 tablespoons of rum for deeper, richer tart.

Rich Chocolate and Gold Leaf Tart

89

- Once the tart is finished and set add a little gold leaf to the ganache topping for decadent look and finish.

PREPARATION TIME 25 MINUTES

COOKING TIME 15-20 MINUTES

INGREDIENTS

250 ml / 9 fl. oz / 1 cup double cream
250 g / 9 oz dark chocolate (minimum 60 % cocoa solids), chopped
55 g / 2 oz / ¼ cup butter, softened

FOR THE PASTRY
100 g / 3 ½ oz / ½ cup butter, cubed
200 g / 7 oz / 1 ⅓ cup plain (all purpose) flour
55 g / 2 oz / ¼ cup caster (superfine) sugar
1 egg, beaten

- Preheat the oven to 200⁰C (180⁰ fan), 390F, gas 6.
- To make the pastry, rub the butter into the flour and sugar and add the egg with just enough cold water to bind.
- Wrap the dough in clingfilm and chill for 30 minutes then roll out on a floured surface.
- Use the pastry to line a 23 cm loose-bottomed tart tin and trim the edges.
- Prick the pastry with a fork, line with clingfilm and fill with baking beans or rice.
- Bake for 10 minutes then remove the clingfilm and baking beans and cook for another 8 minutes to crisp.
- Heat the cream to simmering point then pour it over the chocolate and stir until smooth.
- Add the butter and blend it in with a stick blender.
- Pour the ganache into the pastry case and level the top with a palette knife.
- Leave the ganache to cool and set for at least 2 hours before cutting and serving.

90

SERVES 8

Grape and Mascarpone Tart

- Preheat the oven to 200°C (180° fan), 390F, gas 6.
- To make the pastry, rub the butter into the flour and add just enough cold water to bind.
- Chill for 30 minutes then roll out on a floured surface. Use the pastry to line a cake tin.
- Prick the pastry with a fork, line with clingfilm and fill with baking beans or rice.
- Bake for 10 minutes then remove the clingfilm and baking beans.
- Brush the inside of the pastry case with beaten egg and cook for another 8 minutes to crisp.
- Whisk the mascarpone with the icing (confectioners) sugar and vanilla extract until smooth.
- When the pastry case has cooled to room temperature, spoon in the filling and level the top.
- Cut the grapes in half and arrange in alternating lines.

PREPARATION TIME 20 MINUTES

COOKING TIME 15-20 MINUTES

INGREDIENTS

450 g / 1 lb / 2 cups mascarpone
100 g / 3 ½ oz / 1 cup icing (confectioners) sugar
1 tsp vanilla extract
a small bunch red seedless grapes
a small bunch green seedless grapes

FOR THE PASTRY

200g / 7 oz / 1 ⅓ cups plain (all purpose) flour
100g / 3 ½ oz / ½ cup butter, cubed
1 egg, beaten

Summer Berry and Mascarpone Tart

91

- Use a mix of summer berries such as strawberries, raspberries and blueberries for a colourful topping to this delicious tart.

92

MAKES 12

Custard Tarts with Marsala Sultanas

- Bring the Masala almost to a simmer then take the pan off the heat and pour it over the sultanas. Cover and leave to macerate overnight.
- Preheat the oven to 200°C (180° fan), 390F, gas 6.
- To make the pastry, rub the butter into the flour and add just enough cold water to bind.
- Chill for 30 minutes then roll out on a floured surface. Cut out 12 circles with a pastry cutter, rerolling the trimmings as necessary, and use them to line a 12-hole cupcake tin.
- Whisk the custard ingredients together in a jug and ¾ fill the pastry cases.
- Bake the tarts for 15 – 20 minutes or until the custard has set and the pastry is crisp.
- Serve warm or at room temperature with a sprinkling of icing (confectioners) sugar and the sultanas spooned over.

PREPARATION TIME 45 MINUTES

COOKING TIME 15-20 MINUTES

INGREDIENTS

100 ml / 3 ½ fl. oz / ½ cup Marsala
150 g / 5 ½ oz / ¾ cup golden sultanas
icing (confectioners) sugar to dust

FOR THE PASTRY

200g / 7 oz / 1 ⅓ cups plain (all purpose) flour
100g / 3 ½ oz / ½ cup butter, cubed

FOR THE CUSTARD

2 large egg yolks
55 g / 2 oz / ¼ cup caster (superfine) sugar
1 tsp vanilla extract
2 tsp cornflour
225 ml / 8 fl. oz / ¾ cup cream

Custard Tarts with Sweet Sherry Sultanas

93

- If you find Marsala difficult to find or not to your taste, a sweet sherry will work just as well in these delicious tarts.

94

MAKES 1

Pound Cake

PREPARATION TIME 5 MINUTES

COOKING TIME 45-55 MINUTES

....

INGREDIENTS

450 g / 1 lb / 2 cups butter, softened
450 g / 1 lb / 2 cups caster (superfine) sugar
8 large eggs, beaten
450 g / 1 lb / 3 cups self-raising flour

- Preheat the oven to 180°C (160° fan), 355F, gas 4 and grease and line a 4 lb loaf tin, or 2 x 2 lb loaf tins, with greaseproof paper.
- Cream the butter and sugar together until well whipped then gradually whisk in the eggs, beating well after each addition.
- Fold in the flour then scrape the mixture into the tin.
- Bake the cake for 45 - 55 minutes or until a skewer inserted in the centre comes out clean.
- Turn the loaf out onto a wire rack and leave to cool before slicing.

Raisin Pound Cake

95

- For a fruity taste to this traditional cake stir in 110g/ 4 oz raisins when you fold in the flour and bake as instructed above.

96

MAKES 12

Lemon Buttercream Cupcakes

PREPARATION TIME 1 HOUR

COOKING TIME 15-20 MINUTES

....

INGREDIENTS

110 g / 4 oz / ⅔ cup self-raising flour, sifted
110 g / 4 oz / ¾ cup caster (superfine) sugar
110 g / 4 oz / ½ cup butter, softened
2 large eggs
1 lemon, zest finely grated
55 g / 2 oz / ¼ cup butter, softened
225 g / 8 oz / 2 ¼ cup icing (confectioners) sugar
1 tbsp lemon juice
yellow sugar sprinkles

- Preheat the oven to 190°C (170° fan), 375F, gas 5 and line a 12-hole cupcake tin with paper cases.
- Combine the flour, sugar, butter, eggs and lemon zest in a bowl and whisk together until smooth.
- Divide the mixture between the paper cases, then bake for 15 – 20 minutes.
- Test with a wooden toothpick, if it comes out clean, the cakes are done.
- Transfer the cakes to a wire rack and leave to cool.
- To make the icing, beat the butter with a wooden spoon until light and fluffy then beat in the icing (confectioners) sugar a quarter at a time.
- Add the lemon juice then use a whisk to whip the mixture for 2 minutes or until smooth and light.
- Spoon the icing onto the cakes and swirl with the back of the spoon. Decorate with the sugar sprinkles.

Lime Buttercream Cupcakes

97

- Substitute the same quantity of lemon for lime for and added extra citrus twist to these delicious cupcakes.

Lemon Curd Tart

St Clements Curd Tart 99

- For an orange and lemon twist use the juice and zest of one lemon and 2 large navel oranges and follow the recipe insturctions above.

Lime Curd Tart 100

- Use the zest and juice of 6 limes to make this delicious tart even fresher and more zingy in flavour.

PREPARATION TIME 55 MINUTES

COOKING TIME 15-20 MINUTES

....

INGREDIENTS

2 tsp cornflour
4 lemons, zest and juice
4 large eggs, beaten
225 g / 8 oz / 1 cup butter
175 g / 6 oz / ¾ cup caster (superfine) sugar

FOR THE PASTRY
100 g / 3 ½ oz / ½ cup butter, cubed
200 g / 7 oz / 1 ⅓ cups plain (all purpose) flour
55 g / 2 oz / ¼ cup caster (superfine) sugar
1 egg, beaten

TO DECORATE
1 lemon, zest finely pared
2 slices lemon

- Preheat the oven to 200⁰C (180⁰ fan), 390F, gas 6.
- To make the pastry, rub the butter into the flour and sugar then add the egg with just enough cold water to bind.
- Wrap the dough in clingfilm and chill for 30 minutes then roll out on a floured surface.
- Use the pastry to line a 24 cm loose-bottomed tart tin and trim the edges.
- Prick the pastry with a fork, line with clingfilm and fill with baking beans or rice.
- Bake for 10 minutes then remove the clingfilm and baking beans and cook for another 8 minutes to crisp.
- Meanwhile, dissolve the cornflour in the lemon juice and put it in a saucepan with the rest of the ingredients.
- Stir constantly over a medium heat to melt the butter and dissolve the sugar. After 6 or 7 minutes the mixture should thicken. Continue until it starts to bubble then spoon it into the pastry case and level with a palette knife.
- Leave to cool completely before decorating with the lemon zest and slices.

101

MAKES 12

Lemon Madeleines

PREPARATION TIME 1 HOUR
30 MINUTES

COOKING TIME 10-15 MINUTES

INGREDIENTS

110 g / 4 oz / ½ cup butter
55 g / 2 oz / ⅓ cup plain (all purpose) flour
1 lemon, zest finely grated
55 g / 2 oz / ½ cup ground almonds
110 g / 4 oz / 1 cup icing (confectioners) sugar
3 large egg whites

- Heat the butter until it foams and starts to smell nutty then leave to cool.
- Combine the flour, lemon zest, ground almonds and icing (confectioners) sugar in a bowl and whisk in the eggs whites.
- Pour the cooled butter into the bowl and whisk into the mixture until evenly mixed.
- Leave the cake mixture to rest in the fridge for an hour.
- Preheat the oven to 170°C (150° fan), 325F, gas 3 and oil and flour a 12-hole Madeleine mould.
- Spoon the mixture into the moulds, then transfer the tin to the oven and bake for 10 – 15 minutes.
- Test with a wooden toothpick, if it comes out clean, the cakes are done.
- Transfer the cakes to a wire rack to cool for 5 minutes before serving.

Orange Madeleines

 102

- Swap the zest of the lemon for the zest of half a large navel orange for a different take on this classic recipe.

103

SERVES 10

Chocolate and Almond Marble Loaf

PREPARATION TIME 10 MINUTES

COOKING TIME 45-50 MINUTES

INGREDIENTS

100 g / 3 ½ oz / ⅔ cup self-raising flour
1 tsp baking powder
50 g / 1 ¾ oz / ½ cup ground almonds
150 g / 5 ½ oz / ⅔ cup caster (superfine) sugar
150 g / 5 ½ oz / ⅔ cup butter
3 large eggs
2 tbsp cocoa powder
4 tbsp flaked (slivered) almonds

- Preheat the oven to 180°C (160° fan), 355F, gas 4 and grease and line a loaf tin with greaseproof paper.
- Sieve the flour and baking powder into a mixing bowl then add the ground almonds, sugar, butter and eggs and whisk with an electric whisk for 4 minutes or until pale and well whipped.
- Divide the mixture into 2 bowls. Mix the cocoa powder with 2 tbsp hot water until smooth and stir it into one of the bowls.
- Spoon the mixtures into the tin, alternating between chocolate and plain, then draw a knife down the centre to marble.
- Sprinkle with flaked (slivered) almonds and bake for 45 - 50 minutes. The cake is ready when a toothpick inserted in the centre comes out clean.
- Transfer the cake to a wire rack to cool completely.

Chocolate and Pistachio Marble Loaf Cake

104

- Grind the pistachios up until they resemble the rough texture of the ground almonds and use 4 tbsp of chopped pistachios to top the cake before baking.

105

SERVES 8

Green Tea and Raspberry Loaf Cake

- Preheat the oven to 170°C (150° fan), 340F, gas 3 and line a large loaf tin with non-stick baking paper.
- Sieve the flour, matcha and baking powder into a mixing bowl and add the sugar, butter and eggs.
- Beat the mixture with an electric whisk for 4 minutes or until smooth and well whipped.
- Fold in the raspberries and scrape the mixture into the loaf tin.
- Bake for 55 minutes or until a skewer inserted in the centre comes out clean.
- Transfer the cake to a wire rack and leave to cool completely.

PREPARATION TIME 10 MINUTES

COOKING TIME 55 MINUTES

INGREDIENTS

300 g / 10 ½ oz / 2 cups self-raising flour
2 tbsp matcha green tea powder
2 tsp baking powder
250 g / 9 oz / 1 ¼ cups caster (superfine) sugar
250 g / 9 oz / 1 ¼ cups butter, softened
5 large eggs
75 g / 2 ½ oz / ½ cup raspberries

Green Tea and Cherry Loaf Cake   106

- Take 75g/2 _ oz fresh pitted cherries instead of the raspberries for a slightly firmer fruit texture to the loaf cake.

107

SERVES 8

Chocolate Orange Loaf Cake

- Preheat the oven to 180°C (160° fan), 355F, gas 4 and grease and line a large loaf tin with greaseproof paper.
- Cream together the butter, sugar and orange zest until well whipped then gradually whisk in the eggs, beating well after each addition.
- Sift over and fold in the flour and cocoa powder.
- Scrape the mixture into the tin and bake for 45 minutes or until a skewer inserted in the centre comes out clean.
- Turn the loaf out onto a wire rack and leave to cool completely before decorating with candied peel.

PREPARATION TIME 15 MINUTES

COOKING TIME 45 MINUTES

INGREDIENTS

225 g / 8 oz / 1 cup butter, softened
225 g / 8 oz / 1 cup caster (superfine) sugar
1 orange, zest finely grated
4 large eggs, beaten
225 g / 8 oz / 1 ½ cups self-raising flour
1 tbsp unsweetened cocoa powder
55 g / 1 oz / ⅓ cup candied orange peel

Chocolate, Coffee and Orange Cake   108

- After incorporating the eggs add 2 tablespoons of strong coffee of espresso to the cake mixture for a richer fuller flavoured cake.

109

MAKES 9

Summer Berry Chocolate Brownies

Winter Berry Chocolate Brownies

110

- Swap summer berries such as raspberries and strawberries for winter favourites such as blackberry, loganberry and blueberry.

Fudge and Cherry Chocolate Brownies

111

- Swap in mini fudge pieces and sour cherries for decadent sweet yet sour brownies.

PREPARATION TIME 25 MINUTES

COOKING TIME 35-40 MINUTES

INGREDIENTS

110g / 4 oz dark chocolate (minimum 60 % cocoa solids), chopped
85 g / 3 oz / ¾ cup unsweetened cocoa powder, sifted
225 g / 8 oz / 1 cup butter
450 g /15 oz / 2 ½ cups light brown sugar
4 large eggs
110 g / 4 oz / ⅔ cup self-raising flour
175 g / 6 oz / 1 ¼ cups mixed berries

- Preheat the oven to 170⁰C (150⁰ fan), gas 3 and oil and line a 20 cm x 20 cm / 8" x 8" square cake tin.
- Melt the chocolate, cocoa and butter together in a saucepan, then leave to cool a little.
- Whisk the sugar and eggs together with an electric whisk for 3 minutes or until very light and creamy.
- Pour in the chocolate mixture and sieve over the flour. Reserve some of the berries for decoration and add the rest to the bowl, then fold everything together until evenly mixed.
- Scrape into the tin and bake for 35 – 40 minutes or until the outside is set, but the centre is still quite soft, as it will continue to cook as it cools.
- Leave the brownie to cool completely before cutting into 9 squares.

112

MAKES 12

Mini Green and Fruit Tea Loaf Cakes

- Preheat the oven to 180°C (160° fan) / 350F / gas 4 and oil a 12-hole silicone mini loaf cake mould.
- Beat the egg in a jug with the oil and milk until well mixed.
- Mix the flour, baking powder and sugar in a bowl, then pour in the egg mixture and stir just enough to combine.
- Divide the mixture in half and flavour each half with either the matcha powder or the fruit tea.
- Fill 6 holes of the muffin mould with each mixture, then bake in the oven for 20 – 25 minutes.
- Test with a wooden toothpick, if it comes out clean, the cakes are done.
- Transfer the cakes to a wire rack and leave to cool completely.

PREPARATION TIME 25 MINUTES

COOKING TIME 20-25 MINUTES

INGREDIENTS

1 large egg
120 ml / 4 fl. oz / ½ cup sunflower oil
120 ml / 4 fl. oz / ½ cup milk
375 g / 12 ½ oz / 2 ½ cups plain (all purpose) flour
2 tsp baking powder
200 g / 7 oz / ¾ cup caster (superfine) sugar
½ tbsp matcha green tea powder
1 tbsp loose leaf fruit tea

Mini Coffee and Hazelnut Loaf Cakes

113

- Swap the matcha green tea for instant coffee powder and add 4 tablespoons of ground hazelnuts (cob nuts) for a rich coffee nutty taste.

114

MAKES 6

Milk Chocolate Fondants

- Oil 6 mini pudding basins and dust the insides with cocoa.
- Melt the chocolate, butter and sugar together in a saucepan, stirring to dissolve the sugar.
- Leave to cool a little then beat in the eggs and egg yolks and fold in the flour.
- Divide the mixture between the pudding basins and chill them for 30 minutes.
- Preheat the oven to 180°C (160° fan), 350F, gas 4 and put a baking tray in to heat.
- Transfer the fondants to the heated baking tray and bake in the oven for 8 minutes.
- Leave the fondants to cool for 2 minutes, then turn them out of their moulds and serve immediately.

PREPARATION TIME 50 MINUTES

COOKING TIME 8 MINUTES

INGREDIENTS

2 tbsp unsweetened cocoa powder
150 g / 6 oz milk chocolate, chopped
150 g / 6 oz / ⅔ cup butter, chopped
85 g / 3 oz / ⅓ cup caster (superfine) sugar
3 large eggs
3 egg yolks
1 tbsp plain (all purpose) flour

Milk Chocolate and Pistachio Fondants

115

- Add 4 tablespoons of roughly chopped pistachios for an extra decadent fondant.

116

SERVES 8

Peach Cake with Lemon Thyme Sugar

PREPARATION TIME 15 MINUTES

COOKING TIME 55 MINUTES

....

INGREDIENTS

225 g / 8 oz / 1 ½ cups self-raising flour
100 g / 3 ½ oz / ½ cup butter, cubed
100 g / 3 ½ oz / ½ cup caster (superfine) sugar
1 large egg
75 ml / 2 ½ fl. oz / ⅓ cup whole milk
4 peaches, halved and stoned

FOR THE LEMON THYME SUGAR

1 tbsp lemon thyme leaves
60 g / 2 oz / ¼ cup caster (superfine) sugar

- Preheat the oven to 180°C (160° fan), 355F, gas 4 and butter a round baking dish.
- First make the lemon thyme sugar. Bruise the thyme leaves with a mortar and pestle then add half the sugar and pound again. Stir in the rest of the sugar and set aside.
- Sieve the flour into a mixing bowl and rub in the butter until it resembles fine breadcrumbs then stir in the sugar.
- Lightly beat the egg with the milk and stir it into the dry ingredients until just combined.
- Scrape the mixture into the baking dish and level the surface then press in the peach halves, cut side up.
- Bake the cake for 55 minutes or until a skewer inserted comes out clean.
- Transfer the cake to a wire rack and sprinkle with the lemon thyme sugar then leave to cool completely.

Peach Cake with Lavender Sugar **117**

- Use edible lavender flowers for a more aromatic but delicious cake. Follow recipe above using 1 tablespoon of lavender instead of the lemon thyme.

118

SERVES 8

Golden Syrup Cake

PREPARATION TIME 15 MINUTES

COOKING TIME 30 MINUTES

....

INGREDIENTS

110 g / 4 oz / ⅔ cup self-raising flour, sifted
110 g / 4 oz / ½ cup soft brown sugar
110 g / 4 oz / ½ cup butter, softened
2 large eggs
1 tsp vanilla extract
225 g / 8 oz / ⅔ cup golden syrup

- Preheat the oven to 190°C (170° fan), 375F, gas 5 and butter a shallow baking dish.
- Combine the flour, sugar, butter, eggs and vanilla extract in a bowl and whisk together for 2 minutes or until smooth.
- Spoon the golden syrup into the baking dish and level the surface and spoon the cake mixture on top.
- Bake the cake for 30 minutes then leave to cool in the dish for 10 minutes.
- Wearing oven gloves, put a large plate on top of the dish then turn them both over in one smooth movement to unmould the cake.
- Serve warm with cream or ice cream.

Black Treacle Cake **119**

- For a deeper, richer flavour use 175g/6 oz golden syrup and 50 g/ 2 fl. oz of black treacle.

120

SERVES 10

Coffee and Almond Sponge

Chocolate and Hazelnut Cake

121

- Use 2 tablespoons of cocoa powder instead of the coffee and swap the hazelnuts (cob nuts) for the almonds for a deliciously decadent cake.

Green Tea and Almond Cake

122

- Use the same quantity of Matcha green tea as you would espresso coffee for a delicate and delicious cake.

PREPARATION TIME 10 MINUTES

COOKING TIME 35-40 MINUTES

....

INGREDIENTS

200 g / 7 oz / 1 ⅓ cups self-raising flour
200 g / 7 oz / ¾ cup caster (superfine) sugar
200 g 7 oz / ¾ cup butter
4 eggs
1 tsp baking powder
1 tbsp instant espresso powder

TO DECORATE

200 g / 7 oz / ¾ cup butter, softened
400 g / 14 oz / 4 cups icing (confectioners) sugar
1 tbsp instant espresso powder
100 g / 3 ½ oz / 1 ⅓ cups flaked (slivered) almonds, toasted
6 chocolate coated coffee beans

- Preheat the oven to 180°C (160° fan), 355F, gas 4 and grease and line 2 x 20 cm round loose-bottomed cake tins.

- Put all of the cake ingredients in a large mixing bowl and whisk them together with an electric whisk for 4 minutes or until pale and well whipped.

- Divide the mixture between the 2 tins and bake for 35 – 40 minutes. The cakes are ready when a toothpick inserted in the centre comes out clean.

- Transfer the cakes to a wire rack to cool completely.

- To make the buttercream, whisk the butter with an electric whisk then gradually add the icing (confectioners) sugar and espresso powder. Whisk until smooth and well whipped. If the mixture is too stiff add a tablespoon of warm water.

- Use half of the buttercream to sandwich the 2 cakes together and spread the rest over the top and sides with a palette knife. Draw lines across the top of the cake with the back of a fork.

- Press the almonds onto the side of the cake with your hands and decorate the top with coffee beans.

123

SERVES 8

Clementine Upside-Down Cake

PREPARATION TIME 15 MINUTES

COOKING TIME 35 MINUTES

....

INGREDIENTS

300 g / 10 ½ oz / 2 cups self-raising flour
2 tsp baking powder
250 g / 9 oz / 1 ¼ cups caster (superfine) sugar
250 g / 9 oz / 1 ¼ cups butter, softened
5 large eggs
4 tbsp golden syrup
4 clementines, thinly sliced

- Preheat the oven to 170⁰C (150⁰ fan), gas 3 and butter a 23 cm round cake tin.
- Sieve the flour and baking powder into a mixing bowl and add sugar, butter and eggs.
- Beat the mixture with an electric whisk for 4 minutes or until smooth and well whipped.
- Spread the golden syrup over the base of the cake tin and arrange the clementine slices on top and up the sides of the tin.
- Spoon in the cake mixture and bake for 35 minutes or until a skewer inserted in the centre comes out clean.
- Leave the cake to cool for 20 minutes before turning out onto a serving plate.

Lemon Upside-Down Cake

124

- This cake works well with very thinly sliced lemons. Use 2 unwaxed lemons cut very thinly and lightly coat in 2 tablespoons of sugar and follow as per recipe above.

125

MAKES 12

Marmalade Sponge Squares

PREPARATION TIME 10 MINUTES

COOKING TIME 30-35 MINUTES

....

INGREDIENTS

175 g / 6 oz / 1 ¼ cups self-raising flour
2 tsp baking powder
175 g / 6 oz / ¾ cup caster (superfine) sugar
175 g / 6 oz / ¾ cup butter
3 eggs
4 tbsp marmalade

TO DECORATE

1 - 2 tsp orange juice
100 g / 3 ½ oz / 1 cup icing (confectioners) sugar
orange rind and leaves

- Preheat the oven to 180⁰C (160⁰ fan), 355F, gas 4 and grease and line a 30 cm x 23 cm cake tin.
- Put all of the cake ingredients in a large mixing bowl and whisk them together with an electric whisk for 4 minutes or until pale and well whipped.
- Scrape the mixture into the tin and level the top with a spatula.
- Bake for 30 - 35 minutes. The cake is ready when a toothpick inserted in the centre comes out clean.
- Transfer the cake to a wire rack to cool completely.
- Stir the orange juice into the icing (confectioners) sugar drop by drop until you reach a spreadable consistency.
- Spread the icing over the cake and cut into squares then decorate with the orange rind and leaves.

Apricot Sponge Squares

126

- Swap the marmalade for apricot jam for a sweeter less tart sponge cake.

Orange Drizzle Cake

SERVES 10 **127**

- Preheat the oven to 180°C (160 fan), gas 4 and grease and 20 cm round cake tin.
- Put all of the cake ingredients in a large mixing bowl and whisk them together with an electric whisk for 4 minutes or until pale and well whipped.
- Scrape the mixture into the tin and level the top with a spatula.
- Bake for 35 - 40 minutes. The cake is ready when a toothpick inserted in the centre comes out clean.
- While the cake is cooking, stir the caster (superfine) sugar with the orange juice until dissolved.
- When the cake comes out of the oven, spoon the orange drizzle all over the surface and leave it to cool in the tin.

PREPARATION TIME 10 MINUTES

COOKING TIME 35-40 MINUTES

INGREDIENTS

150 g / 5 ½ oz / 1 cup self-raising flour
150 g / 5 ½ oz / ⅔ cup caster (superfine) sugar
150 g / 5 ½ oz / ⅔ cup butter
3 eggs
1 tsp baking powder
1 tbsp orange zest
2 tbsp orange juice

FOR THE DRIZZLE

100 g / 3 ½ oz / ½ cup caster (superfine) sugar
50 ml / 1 ¾ fl. oz / ¼ cup orange juice

Lemon Drizzle Cake   128

- For a sharper but delicious tasting cake swap the orange juice and zest for lemon.

Orange and Cinnamon Treacle Tart

SERVES 8 **129**

- To make the pastry, rub the butter into the flour and add just enough cold water to bind.
- Chill for 30 minutes.
- Meanwhile, put the sugar in a saucepan with 200 ml water and stir over a low heat until dissolved. Add the orange slices then simmer for 25 minutes.
- Preheat the oven to 200°C (180° fan), 390F, gas 6.
- Roll out the pastry on a floured surface and use it to line a rectangular tart tin.
- Heat the golden syrup with the orange zest and juice until runny then stir in the breadcrumbs and cinnamon.
- Spoon the filling into the pastry case and top with the candied orange slices.
- Bake for 25 – 30 minutes or until the pastry is cooked through underneath.

PREPARATION TIME 45 MINUTES

COOKING TIME 50-55 MINUTES

INGREDIENTS

350 g / 12 ½ oz / 1 cup golden syrup
1 orange, zest and juice
150 g / 5 ½ oz / 2 cups white breadcrumbs
1 tsp ground cinnamon

FOR THE PASTRY

200g / 7 oz / 1 ⅓cups plain (all purpose) flour
100g / 3 ½ oz / ½ cup butter, cubed
1 egg, beaten

FOR THE CANDIED ORANGE SLICES

400 g / 14 oz / 1 ¾ cups caster (superfine) sugar
2 oranges, sliced

Orange and Mixed Spice Tart   130

- For a more spicy taste to this festive tart add 1 teaspoon of mixed spice instead of the cinnamon.

131

SERVES 8

Apricot and Rosemary Frangipane Tart

Peach and Lemon Thyme Frangipane Tart

132

- Replace the apricots with 6 peaches and 1 tablespoon of finely chopped Lemon Thyme for a fresh take on this French classic.

Apricot, Cinnamon and Vanilla Frangipane Tart

133

- Follow the above recipe but add half a teaspoon of vanilla extract and half a teaspoon of ground cinnamon to the frangipane mix before baking.

PREPARATION TIME 30 MINUTES

COOKING TIME 35 MINUTES

INGREDIENTS

225 g / 8 oz puff pastry
150g / 5 ½ oz / 1 ½ cups ground almonds
150g / 5 ½ oz / ⅔ cup butter, softened
150g / 5 ½ oz / ⅔ cup caster (superfine) sugar
2 large eggs
2 tbsp plain (all purpose) flour
8 apricots, stoned and halved
1 tbsp rosemary leaves

- Preheat the oven to 200°C (180° fan), gas 6.
- Roll out the pastry on a floured surface and use it to line a 24cm round loose-bottomed tart case.
- Prick the pastry with a fork, line with greaseproof paper and fill with baking beans or rice.
- Bake for 10 minutes then remove the paper and baking beans.
- Whisk together the almonds, butter, sugar, eggs and flour until smoothly whipped and spoon the mixture into the pastry case.
- Press the apricots into the frangipane, cut side up and sprinkle over the rosemary.
- Bake the tart for 25 minutes or until the frangipane is cooked through and the pastry is crisp underneath. Leave to cool completely.

134

SERVES 8

Pear and Almond Tart

- Preheat the oven to 200°C (180° fan), 390F, gas 6.
- Whisk together the almonds, butter, sugar, eggs and flour until smoothly whipped and spoon the mixture into the pastry case.
- Press the pear quarters into the frangipane and bake the tart for 25 minutes or until the frangipane is cooked through.
- Heat the apricot jam until runny and brush it over the pears then sprinkle with flaked (slivered) almonds.

PREPARATION TIME 45 MINUTES

COOKING TIME 25 MINUTES

INGREDIENTS

150 g / 5 ½ oz / 1 ½ cups ground almonds
150 g / 5 ½ oz / ⅔ cup butter, softened
150 g / 5 ½ oz / ⅔ cup caster (superfine) sugar
2 large eggs
2 tbsp plain (all purpose) flour
1 pastry case
4 pears, cored and quartered
4 tbsp apricot jam
2 tbsp flaked (slivered) almonds

Pear, Raspberry and Almond Tart   **135**

- Add 100g/ 3 _ oz of fresh raspberries and press with the pears into the frangipane bake.

136

SERVES 8

Pear and Honey Upside-Down Cake

- Preheat the oven to 170°C (150° fan), gas 3 and butter a 23 cm round cake tin.
- Sieve the flour and baking powder into a mixing bowl and add the sugar, butter and eggs.
- Beat the mixture with an electric whisk for 4 minutes or until smooth and well whipped.
- Spread the honey over the base of the cake tin and arrange the pears on top, cut side down.
- Spoon in the cake mixture and bake for 35 minutes or until a skewer inserted comes out clean.
- Leave the cake to cool for 20 minutes before turning out onto a serving plate.

PREPARATION TIME 15 MINUTES

COOKING TIME 35 MINUTES

INGREDIENTS

300 g / 10 ½ oz / 2 cups self-raising flour
2 tsp baking powder
250 g / 9 oz / 1 ¼ cups caster (superfine) sugar
250 g / 9 oz / 1 ¼ cups butter, softened
5 large eggs
150 g / 5 ½ oz / ½ cup runny honey
4 pears, peeled, cored and halved

Pear and Maple Syrup Upside-Down Cake   **137**

- Spread 150ml/ 5 _ fl. oz of maple syrup over the base of the cake tin instead of the honey for a slightly stronger, richer tasting cake.

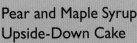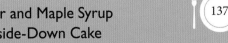

138

MAKES 12

Chocolate and Pistachio Cupcakes

PREPARATION TIME 20 MINUTES

COOKING TIME 15-20 MINUTES

INGREDIENTS

110 g / 4 oz / ⅔ cup self-raising flour, sifted
28 g / 1 oz cocoa powder
110 g / 4 oz / ½ cup caster (superfine) sugar
110 g / 4 oz / ½ cup butter, softened
2 large eggs
1 tsp almond essence

TO DECORATE

225 g / 8 oz / 2 ¼ cups icing (confectioners) sugar
½ tsp almond essence
3 tbsp pistachio nuts, chopped

- Preheat the oven to 190°C (170° fan), 375F, gas 5 and line a 12-hole cupcake tin with paper cases.
- Combine the flour, sugar, butter, eggs and vanilla extract in a bowl and whisk together for 2 minutes or until smooth.
- Divide the mixture between the paper cases, then transfer the tin to the oven and bake for 15 – 20 minutes.
- Test with a wooden toothpick, if it comes out clean, the cakes are done.
- Transfer the cakes to a wire rack and leave to cool completely before peeling off the papers.
- To make the icing, sieve the icing (confectioners) sugar into a bowl and add the almond essence. Stir in enough hot water, drop by drop, to form a spreadable icing and spoon it over the cakes.
- Sprinkle with chopped pistachios and leave the icing to set.

139

SERVES 8

Lemon and Lime Tart

PREPARATION TIME 45 MINUTES

COOKING TIME 50-55 MINUTES

INGREDIENTS

2 lemons, juiced
4 limes, juiced
175 g / 6 oz / ¾ cup caster (superfine) sugar
2 tsp cornflour
4 large eggs, beaten
225 g / 8 oz / ¾ cup double cream

FOR THE PASTRY

100 g / 3 ½ oz / ½ cup butter, cubed
100 g / 3 ½ oz / ⅔ cup plain (all purpose) flour
100 g / 3 ½ oz / ⅔ cup wholemeal flour
55 g / 2 oz / ¼ cup caster (superfine) sugar
1 egg, beaten

TO DECORATE

1 lemon, zest finely pared
1 lime, zest finely pared

- Preheat the oven to 200°C (180° fan), 390F, gas 6.
- To make the pastry, rub the butter into the flours and sugar then add the egg with just enough cold water to bind.
- Wrap the dough in clingfilm and chill for 30 minutes then roll out on a floured surface.
- Use the pastry to line a 24 cm loose-bottomed tart tin and trim the edges.
- Prick the pastry with a fork, line with clingfilm and fill with baking beans or rice.
- Bake for 10 minutes then remove the clingfilm and baking beans and cook for another 8 minutes to crisp.
- Reduce the oven temperature to 170°C (150° fan), 340F, gas 3.
- Stir the lemon and lime juices into the caster (superfine) sugar and cornflour to dissolve, then whisk in the eggs and cream.
- Strain the mixture into the pastry case and bake for 25 – 30 minutes or until just set in the centre.
- Leave to cool completely before decorating with the lemon and lime zest.

140

SERVES 8

Poppy Seed Cake

- Preheat the oven to 180°C (160° fan), 355F, gas 4 and line a 23 cm round cake tin with non-stick baking paper.
- Sieve the flour into a mixing bowl and rub in the butter until it resembles fine breadcrumbs then stir in the sugar and poppy seeds.
- Lightly beat the egg with the milk and stir it into the dry ingredients until just combined.
- Scrape the mixture into the tin and bake for 55 minutes or until a skewer inserted comes out clean.
- Transfer the cake to a wire rack and leave to cool completely.

PREPARATION TIME 15 MINUTES

COOKING TIME 55 MINUTES

INGREDIENTS

225 g / 8 oz / 1 ½ cups self raising flour
100 g / 3 ½ oz / ½ cup butter, cubed
100 g / 3 ½ oz / ½ cup caster (superfine) sugar
2 tbsp poppy seeds
1 large egg
75 ml / 3 ½ fl. oz / ⅓ cup whole milk

141

SERVES 10

Pumpkin Pie

PREPARATION TIME 55 MINUTES

COOKING TIME 1 HOUR 10 MINUTES

INGREDIENTS

600 g / 1 lb 5 oz pumpkin or butternut squash, peeled, deseeded and cubed

2 large eggs
150 ml / 5 ½ fl. oz / ⅔ cup maple syrup
150 ml / 5 ½ fl. oz / ⅔ evaporated milk
1 tsp mixed spice
1 pastry case, sweet

- Preheat the oven to 200°C (180° fan), 390F, gas 6.
- Put the pumpkin in a roasting tin and cover with foil then bake for 30 minutes.
- Drain the pumpkin of any excess liquid then puree it in a food processor.
- Add the eggs, maple syrup, evaporated milk and spice and pulse until smoothly combined.
- Reduce the oven temperature to 180°C (160° fan), 355F, gas 4.
- Pour the pumpkin mixture into the pastry case and bake for 30 - 40 minutes or until just set in the centre.
- Leave to cool completely before slicing.

142

SERVES 6

Pear and Almond Sponge

PREPARATION TIME 10 MINUTES

COOKING TIME 30-35 MINUTES

INGREDIENTS

85 g / 3 oz / ½ cup self-raising flour, sifted
28 g / 1 oz / ¼ cup ground almonds
110 g / 4 oz / ½ cup caster sugar

110 g / 4 oz / ½ cup butter, softened
2 large eggs
½ tsp almond essence
2 pears, peeled, cored and diced
icing (confectioners) sugar to dust

- Preheat the oven to 190°C (170° fan), 375F, gas 5 and grease and line a 23 cm round cake tin.
- Combine the flour, ground almonds, sugar, butter, eggs and almond essence in a bowl and whisk together for 2 minutes or until smooth.
- Fold in the chopped pears and spoon into the prepared tin then bake for 30 – 35 minutes.
- Test with a wooden toothpick, if it comes out clean, the cake is done.
- Transfer the cake to a wire rack and leave to cool completely before dusting with icing (confectioners) sugar.

143

SERVES 8

Fig and Honey Loaf Cake

PREPARATION TIME 15 MINUTES

COOKING TIME 55 MINUTES

INGREDIENTS

225 g / 8oz / 1 ½ cups self raising flour
100 g / 3 ½ oz / ½ cup butter, cubed
85 g / 3 oz / ⅓ cup caster (superfine) sugar
6 fresh figs, chopped
1 large egg
75 ml / 3 ½ fl. oz / ⅓ cup whole milk
3 tbsp runny honey
2 fresh figs, sliced

- Preheat the oven to 180°C (160° fan), 355F, gas 4 and line a loaf tin with non-stick baking paper.
- Sieve the flour into a mixing bowl and rub in the butter until it resembles fine breadcrumbs then stir in the sugar and chopped figs.
- Lightly beat the egg with the milk and honey and stir it into the dry ingredients until just combined.
- Scrape the mixture into the loaf tin and arranged the sliced figs on top.
- Bake for 55 minutes or until a skewer inserted comes out clean.
- Transfer the cake to a wire rack and leave to cool completely.

Prune and Honey Loaf Cake

144

- Substitute 6 figs for 8 chopped prunes for an equally delicious sticky loaf cake.

145

SERVES 8

Oven-Dried Plum Tart

PREPARATION TIME 2 HOURS

COOKING TIME 35-45 MINUTES

INGREDIENTS

150 g / 5 ½ oz / 1 ½ cups ground almonds
150 g / 5 ½ oz / ⅔ cup butter, softened
150 g / 5 ½ oz / ⅔ cup caster (superfine) sugar
2 large eggs
2 tbsp plain (all purpose) flour

FOR THE PASTRY

200 g / 7 oz / 1 ⅓ cups plain (all purpose) flour
100 g / 3 ½ oz / ½ cup butter, cubed
50 g / 1 ¾ oz / ¼ cup caster (superfine) sugar

FOR THE OVEN-DRIED PLUMS

900 g / 2 lb plums, stoned and halved
3 tbsp runny honey

- Preheat the oven to 140°C (120° fan), 280F, gas 1. Spread the plums out on a baking sheet, cut side up and brush with honey. Dry out in the oven for 2 hours then leave to cool.
- Increase the oven temperature to 200°C (180° fan), 390F, gas 6.
- Meanwhile, make the pastry. Rub the butter into the flour until the mixture resembles fine breadcrumbs.
- Stir in the sugar and add enough cold water to bring the pastry together into a pliable dough.
- Chill the dough for 30 minutes then roll out on a floured surface. Use the pastry to line a rectangular tin.
- Whisk together the almonds, butter, sugar, eggs and flour until smoothly whipped and spoon the mixture into the pastry case.
- Arrange the oven-dried plums on top and bake for 25 minutes or until cooked through.

Oven-Dried Apricot Tart

146

- Replace the plums with the same amount of apricots.

MAKES 12

147

Fig and Orange Muffins

Fig and Lemon Muffins 148

- For a sharper tasting muffin use the zest of two lemons instead of the oranges.

Prune and Orange Muffins 149

- Using 8 prunes halved and quartered will give a slightly firmer but sweet tasting muffin.

PREPARATION TIME 25 MINUTES

COOKING TIME 20-25 MINUTES

INGREDIENTS

1 large egg
120 ml / 4 fl. oz / ½ cup sunflower oil
120 ml / 4 fl. oz / ½ cup milk
375 g / 12 ½ oz / 2 ½ cups self-raising flour, sifted
1 tsp baking powder
200 g / 7 oz / ¾ cup caster (superfine) sugar
1 orange, zest finely grated
4 fresh figs, chopped

- Preheat the oven to 180⁰C (160⁰ fan), gas 4 and line a 12-hole muffin tin with greaseproof paper.
- Beat the egg in a jug with the oil and milk until well mixed.
- Mix the flour, baking powder, sugar and orange zest in a bowl.
- Pour in the egg mixt¾ cup ure and stir just enough to combine then fold in the figs.
- Divide the mixture between the paper cases and bake for 20 – 25 minutes.
- Test with a wooden toothpick, if it comes out clean, the cakes are done.
- Transfer the muffins to a wire rack and leave to cool completely.

150

MAKES 6

Plum Tartlets

PREPARATION TIME 15 MINUTES

COOKING TIME 25-35 MINUTES

INGREDIENTS

110 g / 4 oz / ½ cup butter, cubed and chilled
110 g / 4 oz / ⅔ cup plain (all purpose) flour
110 g / 4 oz / ⅔ cup stoneground wholemeal flour
450 g / 1 lb plums, halved and stoned
450g / 1 lb / 1 ¼ cup plum jam (jelly)

- Preheat the oven to 200°C (180° fan) / 400F / gas 6.
- Rub the butter into the flours until the mixture resembles fine breadcrumbs.
- Stir in just enough cold water to bring the pastry together into a pliable dough.
- Roll out the pastry on a floured surface and cut out 6 circles then use them to line 6 tartlet tins.
- Arrange the halved plums in the pastry case and spoon over the jam.
- Bake for 25 – 35 minutes or until the pastry is crisp and the jam has melted around the plums.

Apricot Tartlets

151

- Use apricots instead of plums and apricot jam instead of plum jam for a golden delicious tartlet.

152

MAKES 12

Raspberry Sponge Squares

PREPARATION TIME 10 MINUTES

COOKING TIME 30-35 MINUTES

INGREDIENTS

175 g / 6 oz / 1 ¼ cup self-raising flour
2 tsp baking powder
175 g / 6 oz / ¾ cup caster (superfine) sugar
175 g / 6 oz / ¾ cup butter
3 eggs
200 g / 7 oz / 1 ⅓ cups raspberries
icing (confectioners) sugar to dust

- Preheat the oven to 180°C (160 fan), gas 4 and grease and line a square cake tin.
- Put the flour, baking powder, sugar, butter and eggs in a mixing bowl and whisk them together with an electric whisk for 4 minutes or until pale and well whipped.
- Arrange the raspberries in the bottom of the cake tin and spoon over the cake mixture.
- Bake for 30 - 35 minutes. The cake is ready when a toothpick inserted in the centre comes out clean.
- Transfer the cake to a wire rack to cool completely before dusting with icing (confectioners) sugar and cutting into squares.

Strawberry Sponge Squares

153

- Use 200g/ 7 oz of fresh strawberries for a summer twist to this sponge classic.

MAKES 6 # Redcurrant Tartlets

- Preheat the oven to 200°C (180° fan) / 400F / gas 6.
- Rub the butter into the flour until the mixture resembles fine breadcrumbs.
- Stir in just enough cold water to bring the pastry together into a pliable dough.
- Roll out the pastry on a floured surface and cut out 6 circles then use them to line 6 tartlet tins.
- Divide the redcurrant jelly between the pastry cases and bake for 20 – 25 minutes or until the pastry is crisp.
- Arrange the redcurrants on top while the tarts are still warm then leave to cool.

PREPARATION TIME 20 MINUTES

COOKING TIME 20-25 MINUTES

INGREDIENTS

110 g / 4 oz / ½ cup butter, cubed and chilled
225 g / 8 oz / 1 ½ cups plain (all purpose) flour
300 g / 10 ½ oz / ¾ cup redcurrant jelly (jell-o)
300 g / 10 ½ oz / 2 cups redcurrants

Blackcurrant Tartlets 155

- For a darker but equally delicious looking and tasting tart use blackcurrants instead of redcurrants.

SERVES 8 # Rhubarb Frangipane Tart

- Preheat the oven to 200°C (180° fan), 390F, gas 6.
- To make the pastry, rub the butter into the flour until the mixture resembles fine breadcrumbs.
- Stir in the sugar and add enough cold water to bring the pastry together into a pliable dough.
- Chill the dough for 30 minutes then roll out on a floured surface. Use the pastry to line a 24cm round loose-bottomed cake tin.
- Prick the pastry with a fork, line with greaseproof paper and fill with baking beans or rice.
- Bake for 10 minutes then remove the paper and baking beans. Return to the oven for 8 minutes to crisp.
- Mix together the remaining ingredients and spoon the mixture into the pastry case.
- Bake the tart for 25 minutes or until the frangipane is cooked through.

PREPARATION TIME 45 MINUTES

COOKING TIME 35-45 MINUTES

INGREDIENTS

150 g / 5 ½ oz / 1 ½ cups ground almonds
150 g / 5 ½ oz / ⅔ cup butter, softened
150 g / 5 ½ oz / ⅔ cup caster (superfine) sugar
2 large eggs
2 tbsp plain (all purpose) flour
3 sticks rhubarb, chopped

FOR THE PASTRY
200 g / 7 oz / 1 ⅓ cup plain (all purpose) flour
100 g / 3 ½ oz / ½ cup butter, cubed
50 g / 1 ¾ oz / ¼ cup caster (superfine) sugar

Raspberry Frangipane Tart 157

- For a sweeter tasting tart use 175g/ 6 oz of fresh raspberries in this delicious tasting recipe.

Rhubarb and Custard Tart

Rhubarb, Nutmeg and Custard Tart

159

- Add _ teaspoon of nutmeg to the custard recipe for a slightly spiced tasting tart.

Rhubarb and Raisin Custard Tart

160

- To add a little sweetness to this tart add four tablespoons of raisins to the custard base mix.

PREPARATION TIME 40 MINUTES

COOKING TIME 40-50 MINUTES

....

INGREDIENTS

3 sticks rhubarb, chopped
4 tbsp caster (superfine) sugar
icing (confectioners) sugar to dust

FOR THE PASTRY
200g / 7 oz / 1 ⅓ cups plain (all purpose) flour
100g / 3 ½ oz / ½ cup butter, cubed

FOR THE CUSTARD
4 large egg yolks
75 g / 2 ½ oz / ⅓ cup caster (superfine) sugar
1 tsp vanilla extract
2 tsp cornflour
450 ml / 16 fl. oz / 1 ¾ cups whole milk

- Preheat the oven to 200°C (180° fan), 390F, gas 6.
- Put the rhubarb in a roasting tin and sprinkle with sugar then bake for 20 minutes or until tender.
- Meanwhile, make the pastry. Rub the butter into the flour and add just enough cold water to bind.
- Chill for 30 minutes then roll out on a floured surface. Use the pastry to line a rectangular tart tin.
- Prick the pastry with a fork, line with clingfilm and fill with baking beans or rice.
- Bake for 10 minutes then remove the clingfilm and baking beans and cook for another 8 minutes to crisp.
- Reduce the oven temperature to 170°C (150° fan), 340F, gas 3.
- Whisk together the custard ingredients and pour into the pastry case. Arrange the rhubarb on top.
- Bake the tart for 25 – 35 minutes or until the custard is just set in the centre.
- Leave to cool completely before dusting with icing (confectioners) sugar.

161

SERVES 8

Summer Fruit Meringue Roulade

- Preheat the oven to 180°C (160° fan), 355F, gas 4 and line a Swiss roll tin with non-stick baking paper.
- Whisk the egg whites with the cream of tartar until stiff then whisk in the caster (superfine) sugar a tablespoon at a time.
- Spread it onto the Swiss roll tray in an even layer with a palette knife and bake for 15 minutes.
- Leave to cool completely.
- Whip the double cream until it just holds its shape.
- Sprinkle a large sheet of greaseproof paper with icing (confectioners) sugar and turn the meringue out onto it.
- Spread the meringue with cream and sprinkle over the berries then roll it up, using the greaseproof paper to help you.
- Dust with more icing (confectioners) sugar before serving.

PREPARATION TIME 20 MINUTES

COOKING TIME 15 MINUTES

INGREDIENTS

4 large egg whites
a pinch cream of tartar
200 g / 7 oz / ¾ cup caster (superfine) sugar
300 ml / 10 ½ fl. oz / 1 ¼ cups double cream
200 g / 7 oz / 1 ⅓ cups mixed berries
icing (confectioners) sugar for dusting

Tropical Fruit Meringue Roulade 162

- Use 200g/ 7 oz of mixed tropical fruit such as mango, pineapple and banana instead of the berries for a colourful and exotic tasting roulade.

163

SERVES 10-12

Rose and Mint Cheesecake

- Preheat the oven to 180°C (160° fan), 355F, gas 4.
- Whisk together the filling ingredients until smooth.
- Spoon the cheesecake mixture into the pastry case, levelling the top with a palette knife.
- Bake the cheesecake for 40 – 50 minutes or until the centre is only just set.
- Leave to cool completely in the tin.
- Brush the rose petals and mint leaves with a thin layer of egg white and dip them in the caster (superfine) sugar. Leave to dry on a wire rack for 2 hours.
- Decorate the tart with the leaves and petals and serve.

PREPARATION TIME 45 MINUTES

COOKING TIME 1 HOUR 10 MINUTES

INGREDIENTS

FOR THE FILLING

600 g / 1 lb 5 oz / 2 ¾ cups cream cheese
250 ml / 9 fl. oz / 1 cup whole milk
175 g / 6 oz / ¾ cup caster (superfine) sugar
2 large eggs
1 egg yolk
2 tbsp plain (all purpose) flour
2 tsp rose water
2 tbsp rose petal jam
1 tbsp mint leaves, finely shredded
square 30 cm pastry case

FOR THE CRYSTALLISED PETALS AND LEAVES

12 fresh rose petals
8 fresh mint leaves
1 egg white, beaten
3 tbsp caster (superfine) sugar

Rose and Apricot Cheesecake 164

- For a fruity yet floral tasting cheesecake use 3 dried apricots very finely diced in the filling mix instead of the fresh mint leaves.

165

MAKES 6

Cranberry Sponges

PREPARATION TIME 10 MINUTES

COOKING TIME 20-25 MINUTES

....

INGREDIENTS

175 g / 6 oz / 1 ¼ cups self-raising flour

2 tsp baking powder

175 g / 6 oz / ¾ cup caster (superfine) sugar

175 g / 6 oz / ¾ cup butter

3 eggs

200 g / 7 oz / 1 ⅓ cups cranberries

- Preheat the oven to 180⁰C (160 fan), gas 4 and grease and 6 individual cake tins.
- Put the flour, baking powder, sugar, butter and eggs in a mixing bowl and whisk them together with an electric whisk for 4 minutes or until pale and well whipped.
- Fold in the cranberries and divide the mixture between the tins.
- Bake for 20 - 25 minutes. The cakes are ready when a toothpick inserted comes out clean.
- Transfer the cakes to a wire rack to cool completely.

Sour Cherry Sponges

 166

- Sour cherries work well in this recipe if you don't want to use the cranberries, use the same quantities indicated in the recipe above just remember to chop the cherries up a little.

167

MAKES 12

Apricot Cupcakes

PREPARATION TIME 10 MINUTES

COOKING TIME 15-20 MINUTES

....

INGREDIENTS

110 g / 4 oz / ⅔ cup self-raising flour, sifted

110 g / 4 oz / ½ cup caster (superfine) sugar

110 g / 4 oz / ½ cup butter, softened

2 large eggs

1 tsp vanilla extract

12 canned apricot halves, drained

- Preheat the oven to 190⁰C (170⁰ fan), 375F, gas 5 and line a 12-hole cupcake tin with paper cases.
- Combine the flour, sugar, butter, eggs and vanilla extract in a bowl and whisk together for 2 minutes or until smooth.
- Divide the mixture between the paper cases and press an apricot half into each one.
- Transfer the tin to the oven and bake for 15 – 20 minutes.
- Test with a wooden toothpick, if it comes out clean, the cakes are done.
- Transfer the cakes to a wire rack and leave to cool completely.

Peach Cupcakes

 168

- Use canned peaches cut into quarters for slightly sweeter but equally delicious tasting cupcakes.

169

SERVES 8

Treacle Tart

Treacle and Ginger Tart   170

- Adding a tablespoon of ground ginger to this delicious classic will add a little warmth to every mouthful.

Treacle and Lemon Tart   171

- Add the zest of one lemon to the tart filling mixture for a fresher more acidic taste.

PREPARATION TIME 25 MINUTES

COOKING TIME 25-30 MINUTES

INGREDIENTS

250 g / 9 oz puff pastry
350 g / 12 ½ oz / 1 cup golden syrup
2 lemons, zest and juice
175 g / 6 oz / 2 ⅓ cups white breadcrumbs

- Preheat the oven to 200°C (180° fan), 390F, gas 6.
- Roll out the pastry on a floured surface and use it to line a round tart tin. Trim the edges and reserve any off-cuts.
- Heat the golden syrup with the lemon zest and juice until runny then stir in the breadcrumbs.
- Spoon the filling into the pastry case and level the top.
- Roll out the pastry off-cuts and cut them into thin strips. Twist each strip and lay it across the tart in a lattice pattern, securing the ends with a dab of water.
- Bake for 25 – 30 minutes or until the pastry is cooked through underneath.

MAKES 6

Strawberry and Custard Tartlets

PREPARATION TIME 45 MINUTES

COOKING TIME 15-20 MINUTES

....

INGREDIENTS

200 g / 7 oz / 1 ⅓ cups strawberries,
sliced

FOR THE PASTRY

200g / 7 oz / 1 ⅓ cups plain (all
purpose) flour

100g / 3 ½ oz / ½ cup butter, cubed

FOR THE CUSTARD

2 large egg yolks

55 g / 2 oz / ¼ cup caster (superfine)
sugar

1 tsp vanilla extract

2 tsp cornflour

225 ml / 8 fl. oz / ¾ cup whole milk

- To make the pastry, rub the butter into the flour and add just enough cold water to bind.
- Chill for 30 minutes.
- Preheat the oven to 200°C (180° fan), 390F, gas 6.
- Roll out the pastry on a floured surface and use it to line 6 tartlet cases, rerolling the trimmings as necessary.
- Arrange the strawberry slices in the pastry cases.
- Whisk the custard ingredients together in a jug and ¾ fill the pastry cases.
- Bake the tarts for 15 – 20 minutes or until the custard has set and the pastry is crisp.

Raspberry and Custard Tarts 173

- Use 200g/ 7 oz of fresh raspberries instead of the strawberries for a slightly more acidic but delicious tasting tart.

174

SERVES 8

Summer Fruit Loaf Cake

PREPARATION TIME 15 MINUTES

COOKING TIME 55 MINUTES

....

INGREDIENTS

225 g / 8oz / 1 ½ cups self raising
flour

100 g / 3 ½ oz / ½ cup butter, cubed

85 g / 3 oz / ⅓ cup caster (superfine)
sugar

100 g / 3 ½ oz / ⅔ cup raspberries

100 g / 3 ½ oz / ⅔ cup blackberries

55 g / 2 oz / ⅓ cup redcurrants

1 large egg

75 ml / 2 ½ fl. oz / ⅓ cup whole milk

- Preheat the oven to 180°C (160° fan), 355F, gas 4 and line a loaf tin with non-stick baking paper.
- Sieve the flour into a mixing bowl and rub in the butter until it resembles fine breadcrumbs then stir in the sugar and fruit.
- Lightly beat the egg with the milk and stir it into the dry ingredients until just combined.
- Scrape the mixture into the loaf tin and bake for 55 minutes or until a skewer inserted in the centre comes out clean.
- Transfer the cake to a wire rack and leave to cool completely.

Winter Fruit Loaf Cake 175

- Use a mix of blackberries, raisins and prunes for a denser but equally delicious tasting loaf cake.

176

MAKES 12 Raspberry and Redcurrant Mini Loaves

- Preheat the oven to 190°C (170° fan), 375F, gas 5 and oil a 12-hole silicone mini loaf cake mould.
- Combine the flour, sugar, butter, eggs and vanilla in a bowl and whisk together for 2 minutes or until smooth. Fold in the fruit.
- Divide the mixture between the moulds, then transfer the mould to the oven and bake for 15 – 20 minutes.
- Test with a wooden toothpick, if it comes out clean, the cakes are done.
- Transfer the cakes to a wire rack and leave to cool completely.

PREPARATION TIME 10 MINUTES

COOKING TIME 15-20 MINUTES

INGREDIENTS

110 g / 4 oz / ⅔ cup self-raising flour, sifted
110 g / 4 oz / ½ cup caster (superfine) sugar
110 g / 4 oz ½ cup butter, softened
2 large eggs
1 tsp vanilla extract
75 g / 2 ½ oz / ½ cup raspberries
75 g / 2 ½ oz / ½ cup redcurrants

Raspberry, Redcurrant and Vanilla Mini Loaf

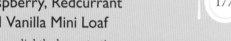

177

- For a slightly deeper tasting sponge at _ teaspoon of vanilla extract and the seeds of half a fresh vanilla pod to the cake batter mix.

178

MAKES 6 Summer Berry and Mascarpone Tartlets

- Preheat the oven to 200°C (180° fan), 390F, gas 6.
- To make the pastry, rub the butter into the flour and add just enough cold water to bind.
- Chill for 30 minutes then roll out on a floured surface. Use the pastry to line 6 tartlet cases.
- Prick the pastry with a fork, line with clingfilm and fill with baking beans or rice.
- Bake for 10 minutes then remove the clingfilm and baking beans.
- Brush the inside of the pastry cases with beaten egg and cook for another 8 minutes to crisp.
- Whisk the mascarpone with the icing (confectioners) sugar and vanilla extract until smooth.
- When the pastry cases have cooled to room temperature, spoon in the filling and level the tops.
- Arrange the fruit on top of the filling and serve.

PREPARATION TIME 45 MINUTES

COOKING TIME 18 MINUTES

INGREDIENTS

450 g / 1 lb / 2 cups mascarpone
100 g / 3 ½ oz / 1 cup icing (confectioners) sugar
1 tsp vanilla extract
12 strawberries, halved
12 raspberries
100 g / 3 ½ oz / ⅔ cup blueberries
6 sprigs redcurrants

FOR THE PASTRY

200g / 7 oz / 1 ⅓ cups plain (all purpose) flour
100g / 3 ½ oz / ½ cup butter, cubed
1 egg, beaten

Summer Berry and Crème Fraiche Tartlets

179

- Swap the mascarpone for crème fraiche for a slightly different take on this French classic.

180

MAKES 1 LARGE OR 2 SMALL

Tea Leaf Pound Cake

Lavender Pound Cake 181

- Use edible lavender flowers instead of the tea leaves for a more aromatic cake.

Lemon and Stem Ginger Pound Cake 182

- Swap the tea leaves for finely chopped stem ginger and add the zest of one unwaxed lemon to the cake batter mix, follow recipe as above.

PREPARATION TIME 20 MINUTES

COOKING TIME 45-55 MINUTES

INGREDIENTS

55 g / 2 oz / ⅓ cup good quality tea leaves
450 g / 1 lb / 2 cups butter, softened
450 g / 1 lb / 2 cups caster (superfine) sugar
8 large eggs, beaten
450 g / 1 lb / 3 cups self-raising flour
2 tbsp granulated sugar

- Preheat the oven to 180°C (160° fan), 355F, gas 4 and grease and line a 4 lb loaf tin, or 2 x 2 lb loaf tins, with greaseproof paper.
- Soak the tea leaves in warm water for 5 minutes.
- Cream the butter and caster (superfine) sugar together until well whipped then gradually whisk in the eggs, beating well after each addition.
- Fold in the flour and half of the tea leaves then scrape the mixture into the tin.
- Bake the cake for 45 - 55 minutes or until a skewer inserted in the centre comes out clean.
- Turn the loaf out onto a wire rack and leave to cool.
- Meanwhile, dry the rest of the tea leaves with kitchen paper and mix them with the granulated sugar. Sprinkle in a line along the top of the cake.

Blackcurrant and Redcurrant Tartlets

MAKES 6

183

- Preheat the oven to 200°C (180° fan), 390F, gas 6.
- To make the pastry, rub the butter into the flour and sugar then add the egg with just enough cold water to bind.
- Wrap the dough in clingfilm and chill for 30 minutes then roll out on a floured surface.
- Use the pastry to line 6 tartlet tins and trim the edges.
- Prick the pastry with a fork, line with clingfilm and fill with baking beans or rice.
- Bake for 10 minutes then remove the clingfilm and baking beans and cook for another 8 minutes to crisp.
- Mix the blackcurrants and redcurrants with the redcurrant jelly and spoon the mixture into the tartlet cases. Return them to the oven for 10 minutes.
- Leave the tartlets to cool for 10 minutes before dusting with icing (confectioners) sugar and serving with the passion fruit sorbet.

Kumquat Tartlets

184

- Swap the berries for chopped kumquats and use marmalade instead of redcurrant jelly to bind for a sharp tasting tartlet. Serve with vanilla ice cream if desired.

PREPARATION TIME 45 MINUTES

COOKING TIME 25-30 MINUTES

INGREDIENTS

200 g / 7 oz / 1 ⅓ cups blackcurrants
200 g / 7 oz / 1 ⅓ cups redcurrants
100 g / 3 ½ oz / ⅓ cup edcurrant jelly (jell-o)

FOR THE PASTRY

100 g / 3 ½ oz / ½ cup butter, cubed
200 g / 7 oz / 1 ⅓ cups plain (all purpose) flour
55 g / 2 oz / ¼ cup caster (superfine) sugar
1 egg, beaten

TO SERVE

icing (confectioners) sugar to dust
6 scoops passion fruit sorbet

Chocolate Layer Cake

SERVES 10-12

185

- Preheat the oven to 180°C (160° fan), 355F, gas 4 and grease and line 3 x 20 cm round cake tins.
- Whisk together all of the cake ingredients with an electric whisk for 4 minutes or until well whipped.
- Divide the mixture between the tins and bake for 30 - 35 minutes.
- The cakes are ready when a toothpick inserted comes out clean.
- Transfer the cakes to a wire rack to cool completely.
- Bring the cream almost to a simmer then pour it over the chopped chocolate and stir until smooth.
- Add the butter and blend it in with a stick blender.
- When the ganache has cooled to a spreadable consistency, use it to sandwich the cakes together, finishing with a thick layer on top.

Mocha Layer Cake

186

- Add 2 tablespoons of espresso to the cake batter mix for a mocha style sponge. Optional extra to add 1 tablespoon of camp coffee extract to the ganache topping.

PREPARATION TIME 10 MINUTES

COOKING TIME 30-35 MINUTES

INGREDIENTS

225 g / 8 oz / 1 ½ cups self-raising flour
55 g / 2 oz / ½ cupunsweetened cocoa powder
3 tsp baking powder
225 g / 8 oz / 1 cup caster (superfine) sugar
225 g / 8 oz / 1 cup butter
4 large eggs

FOR THE GANACHE

300 ml / 10 ½ fl. oz / 1 ¼ cups double cream
300 g / 10 ½ oz dark chocolate (minimum 60 % cocoa solids), chopped
75 g / 2 ½ oz / ⅓ cup butter, cubed

187
MAKES 6
Tourteau Cheesecakes

PREPARATION TIME 20 MINUTES

COOKING TIME 50 MINUTES

INGREDIENTS

125 g / 4 ½ oz / ½ cup fresh goats'
cheese
25 g / ¾ oz / 2 tbsp cornflour
75 g / 2 ½ oz / ⅓ cup caster
(superfine) sugar
1 tbsp milk
1 tsp vanilla extract
3 eggs, separated

FOR THE PASTRY

110 g / 4 oz / ½ cup butter, cubed and
chilled
225 g / 8 oz / 1 ½ cups plain (all
purpose) flour

- Preheat the oven to 180°C (160° fan), 355F, gas 4.
- Rub the butter into the flour until the mixture resembles fine breadcrumbs.
- Stir in just enough cold water to bring the pastry together into a pliable dough.
- Roll out the pastry on a floured surface and cut out 6 circles then use them to line 6 Tourteau moulds.
- Beat the goats' cheese with the cornflour, sugar, milk and vanilla extract until smooth then beat in the egg yolks.
- Whisk the egg whites in a clean, grease-free bowl until stiff then fold them into the goat's cheese mixture.
- Spoon the filling into the pastry cases and bake for 50 minutes or until the tops are dark brown and the centres have set.

Vanilla Cheesecakes 188

- Add 1 teaspoon of vanilla extract to the goats cheese filling for extra flavour.

189
SERVES 8
White Chocolate Loaf Cake

PREPARATION TIME 15 MINUTES

COOKING TIME 55 MINUTES

INGREDIENTS

225 g / 8oz / 1 ½ cups self raising
flour
100 g / 3 ½ oz / ½ cup butter, cubed
85 g / 3oz / ⅓ cup caster (superfine)
sugar
150 g / 5 ½ oz white chocolate,
chopped
1 large egg
75 ml / 2 ½ fl. oz / ⅓ cup whole milk

- Preheat the oven to 180°C (160° fan), 355F, gas 4 and line a loaf tin with non-stick baking paper.
- Sieve the flour into a mixing bowl and rub in the butter until it resembles fine breadcrumbs then stir in the sugar and white chocolate.
- Lightly beat the egg with the milk and stir it into the dry ingredients until just combined.
- Scrape the mixture into the loaf tin and bake for 55 minutes or until a skewer inserted in the centre comes out clean.
- Transfer the cake to a wire rack and leave to cool completely.

Chilli Chocolate Loaf Cake 190

- Swap the white chocolate for dark chocolate infused with chilli for a decadent sweet spicy cake.

191

SERVES 10-12 # Chocolate Ganache Gateau

Passion Fruit Ganache Gateau

 192

- When making the ganache substitute 100ml of cream for passion fruit juice for a rich, fruity decadent gateau.

Spiced Orange Ganache Gateau

193

- Add 2 drops of orange blossom water to the ganache and add the zest of half an orange together with 1 tsp of mixed spice for a more festive gateau.

PREPARATION TIME 10 MINUTES

COOKING TIME 45-50 MINUTES

....

INGREDIENTS

110 g / 4 oz / ⅔ cup self-raising flour
28 g / 1 oz / ¼ cup unsweetened cocoa powder
1 tsp baking powder
110 g / 4 oz / ½ cup caster (superfine) sugar
110 g / 4 oz / ½ cup butter
2 large eggs

FOR THE GANACHE

300 ml / 10 ½ fl. oz / 1 ¼ cups double cream
300 g / 10 ½ oz dark chocolate, chopped
75 g / 2 ½ oz / ⅓ cup butter, cubed

FOR THE WHITE CHOCOLATE CURLS

100 g / 3 ½ oz white chocolate

- Preheat the oven to 180°C (160° fan), 355F, gas 4 and grease and line a 20 cm round spring-form cake tin.
- Whisk together all of the cake ingredients with an electric whisk for 4 minutes.
- Scrape the mixture into the tin and bake for 30 - 35 minutes.
- The cake is ready when a toothpick inserted comes out clean.
- Transfer the cake to a wire rack to cool completely before slicing in half horizontally.
- Bring the cream to simmering point then pour it over the chocolate and stir until smooth.
- Blend in the butter with a stick blender.
- Clean the cake tin and line with clingfilm. Put a cake layer in the tin and pour over half of the ganache.
- Top with the second cake layer and pour the rest of the ganache on top. Level the surface and chill for 4 hours.
- Melt the white chocolate in a microwave or bain marie and spread it onto a clean chopping board or marble slab.
- When it has set, but before it becomes brittle, use a wallpaper scraper to make it into curls.

194

SERVES 8-10

Gluten Free Coconut Cake

PREPARATION TIME 5 MINUTES

COOKING TIME 45-55 MINUTES

INGREDIENTS

225 g / 8 oz / 1 cup butter, softened
225 g / 8 oz / 1 cup caster (superfine) sugar
1 vanilla pod, seeds only
4 large eggs, beaten
225 g/ 4 ½ oz / 1 ½ cups rice flour
1 tsp baking powder
100 g / 3 ½ oz / 1 cup desiccated coconut

- Preheat the oven to 180°C (160° fan), 355F, gas 4 and grease and line a 23 cm round cake tin with greaseproof paper.
- Cream the butter, sugarand vanilla seeds together until well whipped then gradually whisk in the eggs, beating well after each addition.
- Fold in the flour and coconut then scrape the mixture into the tin.
- Bake the cake for 45 - 55 minutes or until a skewer inserted in the centre comes out clean.

Gluten Free Almond Cake
 195
- Substitute the dessicated coconut for ground almonds and decorate with flaked (slivered) almonds if desired.

196

MAKES 6

Fig and Almond Tartlets

PREPARATION TIME 45 MINUTES

COOKING TIME 35 MINUTES

INGREDIENTS

150g / 5 ½ oz / 1 ½ cups ground almonds
150g / 5 ½ oz / ⅔ cup butter, softened
150g / 5 ½ oz / ⅔ cup caster (superfine) sugar
2 large eggs
2 tbsp plain (all purpose) flour
3 fresh figs, chopped
2 tbsp flaked (slivered) almonds

FOR THE PASTRY

200g / 7 oz / 1 ⅓ cups plain (all purpose) flour
100g / 3 ½ oz / ½ cup butter, cubed
50g / 1 ¾ oz / ¼ cup caster (superfine) sugar

- Preheat the oven to 200°C (180° fan), 390F, gas 6.
- To make the pastry, rub the butter into the flour until the mixture resembles fine breadcrumbs.
- Stir in the sugar and add enough cold water to bring the pastry together into a pliable dough.
- Chill the dough for 30 minutes then roll out on a floured surface. Use the pastry to line 6 tartlet cases.
- Prick the pastry with a fork, line with greaseproof paper and fill with baking beans or rice.
- Bake for 10 minutes then remove the paper and beans.
- Return to the oven for 8 minutes to crisp.
- Whisk together the almonds, butter, sugar, eggs and flour until smoothly whipped and fold in the figs.
- Spoon the mixture into the pastry cases, sprinkle with flaked (slivered) almonds and bake for 15 minutes or until the frangipane is cooked through.

Pear and Almond Tarts
197
- Substitute the figs for 4 canned pears roughly chopped for a different fruity tasting tart.

198

MAKES 9

Chocolate and Walnut Brownies

- Preheat the oven to 170°C (150° fan), 340F, gas 3 and oil and line a 20 cm x 20 cm square cake tin.
- Melt the chocolate, cocoa and butter together in a saucepan, then leave to cool a little.
- Whisk the sugar and eggs together with an electric whisk for 3 minutes or until very light and creamy.
- Pour in the chocolate mixture and sieve over the flour, then fold everything together with the walnuts until evenly mixed.
- Scrape into the tin and bake for 35 – 40 minutes or until the outside is set, but the centre is still quite soft, as it will continue to cook as it cools.
- Leave the brownie to cool completely before cutting into 9 squares.

PREPARATION TIME 25 MINUTES

COOKING TIME 35-40 MINUTES

INGREDIENTS

110 g / 4 oz milk chocolate, chopped
85 g / 3 oz / ¾ cup unsweetened cocoa powder, sifted
225 g / 8 oz / 1 cup butter
450 g /15 oz / 2 ½ cups light brown sugar
4 large eggs
110 g / 4 oz / ⅔ cup self-raising flour
110 g / 4 oz / ¾ cup walnuts, chopped

Chocolate and Pine Nut Brownies **199**

- For a milder, nutty tasting brownies use chopped toasted pine nuts instead of the walnuts in this recipe.

200

SERVES 8-10

Chocolate and Pecan Bundt Cake

- Preheat the oven to 180°C (160° fan), 355F, gas 4 and butter a bundt tin.
- Cream the butter and sugar together until well whipped then gradually whisk in the eggs, beating well after each addition.
- Fold in the flour, ground pecans and chocolate chunks then scrape the mixture into the tin.
- Bake the cake for 45 minutes or until a skewer inserted in the centre comes out clean.
- Turn the cake out onto a wire rack and leave to cool.
- Melt the chocolate, butter and syrup together over a low heat, stirring regularly, then spoon it over the cake. Sprinkle with chopped pecan nuts.

PREPARATION TIME 5 MINUTES

COOKING TIME 45 MINUTES

INGREDIENTS

225 g / 8 oz / 1 cup butter, softened
225 g / 8 oz / 1 cup caster (superfine) sugar
4 large eggs, beaten
125 g/ 4 ½ oz / ¾ cup self-raising flour
100 g / 3 ½ oz / 1 cup ground pecan nuts
100 g / 3 ½ oz dark chocolate (minimum 60 % cocoa solids), chopped

TO FINISH
100 g / 3 ½ oz dark chocolate (minimum 60 % cocoa solids), chopped
28 g / 1 oz butter
2 tbsp golden syrup
55 g / 2 oz / ½ cup pecan nuts, chopped

Chocolate and Pistachio Bundt Cake **201**

- Instead of pecans use chopped pistachio for a more colourful take on this traditional round cake.

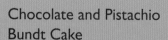

202

SERVES 10-12

Wholemeal Chocolate Cake

Chestnut Chocolate Cake

203

- If you want to try using a different flour to wholemeal try chestnut for a nuttier tasting cake. Decorate with a handful of chopped, candied chestnuts for extra flavour.

Wholemeal Chocolate and Coffee Cake

204

- For lovers of coffee add 2 tablespoons of coffee to the chocolate icing mixture.

PREPARATION TIME 30 MINUTES

COOKING TIME 35-40 MINUTES

INGREDIENTS

150 g / 6 oz / 1 cup stoneground wholemeal flour
1 tsp baking powder
28 g / 1 oz / ¼ cup unsweetened cocoa powder
2 tsp baking powder
175 g / 6 oz / ¾ cup caster (superfine) sugar
175 g / 6 oz / ¾ cup butter
3 large eggs

TO DECORATE

200 ml / 7 fl. oz / ¾ cup double cream
200 g / 7 oz milk chocolate, chopped
50 g / 1 ¾ oz / ¼ cup butter
2 tbsp runny honey

- Preheat the oven to 180°C (160° fan), 355F, gas 4 and grease and line 2 x 20 cm round cake tins.
- Whisk together all of the cake ingredients with an electric whisk for 4 minutes or until well whipped.
- Divide the mixture between the tins and bake for 35 - 40 minutes.
- The cakes are ready when a toothpick inserted in the centre comes out clean.
- Transfer the cakes to a wire rack to cool completely.
- Bring the cream to a simmer then pour it over the chopped chocolate and stir until smooth.
- Blend in the butter and honey with a stick blender.
- When the ganache has cooled to a spreadable consistency, use a third of it to sandwich the cakes together. Spread the rest over the top and sides of the cake with a palette knife.

205 **SERVES 8**

Almond Filo Pie

- Preheat the oven to 180°C (160° fan), 355F, gas 4 and butter a round baking dish.
- Brush 10 sheets of filo pastry with melted butter and use to line the baking dish.
- Put the almonds, sugar and lemon zest in a food processor and pulse until finely chopped.
- Add half of the remaining butter and pulse again.
- Spread a third of the almond mixture across the bottom of the pastry case.
- Top with a third of the remaining pastry sheets, making sure each one is well buttered.
- Continue layering, finishing with a layer of buttered filo, then fold in the edges to neaten.
- Bake the pie in the oven for 35 – 45 minutes or until the pastry is golden and cooked through in the centre.
- Unmould the pie and dust liberally with icing sugar.

PREPARATION TIME 25 MINUTES

COOKING TIME 35-45 MINUTES

INGREDIENTS

450 g / 1 lb filo pastry
200 g / 7 oz / ¾ cup butter, melted
450 g / 1 lb / 3 cups blanched almonds
100 g / 3 ½ oz / ½ cup caster (superfine) sugar
1 lemon, zest finely grated
icing (confectioners) sugar to dust

Hazelnut Filo Pie 206

- If you love nuts swap the almonds for hazelnuts (cob nuts) for extra flavour and texture.

207 **SERVES 8**

Plum and Honey Loaf Cake

- Preheat the oven to 180°C (160° fan), 355F, gas 4 and line a loaf tin with non-stick baking paper.
- Sieve the flour into a mixing bowl and rub in the butter until it resembles fine breadcrumbs then stir in the sugar and plums.
- Lightly beat the egg with the milk and honey then stir it into the dry ingredients until just combined.
- Scrape the mixture into the loaf tin and bake for 55 minutes or until a skewer inserted comes out clean.
- Transfer the cake to a wire rack and leave to cool completely.

PREPARATION TIME 15 MINUTES

COOKING TIME 55 MINUTES

INGREDIENTS

225 g / 8oz / 1 ½ cups self raising flour
100 g / 3 ½ oz / ½ cup butter, cubed
85 g / 3oz / ⅓ cup caster (superfine) sugar
4 plums, stoned and chopped
1 large egg
75 ml / 2 ½ fl. oz / ⅓ cup whole milk
3 tbsp runny honey

Fig and Honey Loaf Cake 208

- Chop three figs and use instead of the plums for extra texture and a richer flavour to this delicious loaf cake.

209

SERVES 10-12 # Almond Cake with Crème Patisserie

PREPARATION TIME 30 MINUTES

COOKING TIME 45-50 MINUTES

....

INGREDIENTS

50 g / 6 oz / ⅓ cup stoneground
wholemeal flour
1 tsp baking powder
28 g / 1 oz cup ground almonds
28 g / 1 oz ¼ cup almonds, chopped
2 tsp baking powder
175 g / 6 oz / ¾ cup caster sugar
175 g / 6 oz / ¾ cup butter
3 large eggs

FOR THE CRÈME PATISSERIE
4 large egg yolks
75 g / 2 ½ oz / ⅓ cup caster sugar
1 tsp vanilla extract
2 tsp cornflour
450 ml / 16 fl. oz / 1 ¾ cups whole milk

TO FINISH
55 g / 2 oz / ⅔ cup flaked (slivered)
almonds, toasted
icing (confectioners) sugar, to dust

• Preheat the oven to 180°C (160° fan), 355F, gas 4
  and grease and line a deep 20 cm round cake tin.
• Whisk together all of the cake ingredients with an
  electric whisk for 4 minutes or until well whipped.
• Scrape the mixture into the tin and bake for 45 - 50
  minutes.
• The cake is ready when a toothpick inserted comes
  out clean.
• Transfer the cake to a wire rack to cool completely.
• To make the crème patisserie, whisk together the egg
  yolks, sugar, vanilla extract and cornflour.
• Heat the milk almost to a simmer then gradually
  whisk it into the egg mixture.
• Scrape the custard back into the saucepan and cook
  over a medium heat until it thickens, stirring constantly.
• Pour it into a bowl and leave to cool to room
  temperature.
• Spoon the crème patisserie into a piping bag fitted
  with a large star nozzle. Pipe a layer on top of the cake
  and a ring of stars round the outside.
• Fill the centre with toasted almonds and give a final
  dusting of icing (confectioners) sugar before serving.

210

SERVES 8 # Apple and Cinnamon Cake

PREPARATION TIME 15 MINUTES

COOKING TIME 55 MINUTES

....

INGREDIENTS

225 g / 8 oz / 1 ½ cups self-raising
flour
1 tsp ground cinnamon
100 g / 3 ½ oz / ½ cup butter, cubed
100 g / 3 ½ oz / ½ cup caster
(superfine) sugar
1 large egg
75 ml / 2 ½ fl. oz / ⅓ cup whole milk
2 apples, peeled and grated

FOR THE TOPPING
100 g / 3 ½ oz / ½ cup cream cheese
4 tbsp golden syrup
1 tsp ground cinnamon

• Preheat the oven to 180°C (160° fan), 355F, gas 4 and
  grease and line a 23 cm round cake tin.
• Sieve the flour and cinnamon into a mixing bowl and
  rub in the butter until it resembles fine breadcrumbs,
  then stir in the sugar.
• Lightly beat the egg with the milk and grated apple and
  stir it into the dry ingredients until just combined.
• Scrape the mixture into the cake tin and bake for 55
  minutes or until a skewer inserted comes out clean.
• Transfer the cake to a wire rack and leave to cool
  completely.
• Spread the top of the cake with cream cheese, swirling
  it with the back of the spoon.
• Heat the golden syrup with the cinnamon until runny
  then spoon it all over the cake to glaze.

211

MAKES 9 # Almond and White Chocolate Blondies

- Preheat the oven to 170°C (150° fan), 340F, gas 3 and oil and line a 20 cm x 20 cm square cake tin.
- Melt the chocolate and butter together in a saucepan, then leave to cool a little.
- Whisk the sugar and eggs together with an electric whisk for 3 minutes or until very light and creamy.
- Pour in the chocolate mixture and sieve over the flour, then fold everything together with the almonds until evenly mixed.
- Scrape into the tin and bake for 35 – 40 minutes or until the outside is set, but the centre is still quite soft, as it will continue to cook as it cools.
- Leave the blondie to cool completely before cutting into 9 squares.

PREPARATION TIME 25 MINUTES

COOKING TIME 15-20 MINUTES

INGREDIENTS

110g / 4 oz white chocolate, chopped
225 g / 8 oz / 1 cup butter
450 g / 15 oz / 2 ½ cups light brown sugar
4 large eggs
110 g / 4 oz / ⅔ cup self-raising flour
110 g / 4 oz / ⅔ cup almonds

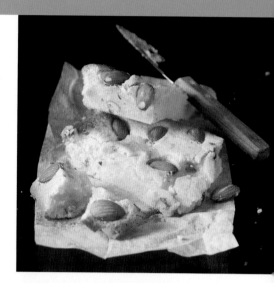

Tropical Sponge Pudding

212

SERVES 8

PREPARATION TIME 20 MINUTES

COOKING TIME 35-45 MINUTES

INGREDIENTS

110 g / 4 oz / ⅔ cup self-raising flour, sifted
55 g / 2 oz / ½ cup desiccated coconut, plus extra for sprinkling

110 g / 4 oz / ½ cup caster (superfine) sugar
110 g / 4 oz / ½ cup butter, softened
2 large eggs
1 tsp vanilla extract
1 can pineapple chunks, drained
1 can pink grapefruit segments, drained

- Preheat the oven to 190°C (170° fan), 375F, gas 5 and butter a small baking dish.
- Combine the flour, coconut, sugar, butter, eggs and vanilla extract in a bowl and whisk together for 2 minutes or until smooth.
- Spoon a third of the cake mixture into the baking dish. Mix the second third of the mixture with the pineapple chunks and spoon it into the baking dish.
- Fold the grapefruit segments into the rest of the cake mixture and spoon it on top then sprinkle with a little extra coconut.
- Bake the cake for 35 – 45 minutes.
- Test with a wooden toothpick, if it comes out clean, the cake is done.
- Serve warm with custard or cream.

Apple, Almond and Sultana Loaf

213

SERVES 8

PREPARATION TIME 10 MINUTES

COOKING TIME 55 MINUTES

INGREDIENTS

300 g / 10 ½ oz / 2 cups self-raising flour
2 tsp baking powder
250 g / 9 oz / 1 ½ cups brown sugar

250 g / 9 oz / 1 ¼ cups butter, softened
5 large eggs
2 eating apples, cored and chopped
75 g / 2 ½ oz / ½ cup almonds
75 g / 2 ½ oz / ⅓ cup sultanas

- Preheat the oven to 170°C (150° fan), gas 3 and line a large loaf tin with non-stick baking paper.
- Sieve the flour and baking powder into a mixing bowl and add the sugar, butter and eggs.
- Beat the mixture with an electric whisk for 4 minutes or until smooth and well whipped.
- Fold in the apple, almonds and sultanas and scrape the mixture into the loaf tin.
- Bake for 55 minutes or until a skewer inserted comes out clean.
- Transfer the cake to a wire rack and leave to cool completely.

214

SERVES 8

Apple Crumble Tart

PREPARATION TIME 50 MINUTES

COOKING TIME 20 MINUTES

....

INGREDIENTS

450 g / 1 lb bramley apples, peeled and chopped
50 g / 1 ¾ oz / ¼ cup caster (superfine) sugar
1 tbsp cornflour

FOR THE PASTRY

200 g / 7 oz / 1 ⅓ cups plain (all purpose) flour
100 g / 3 ½ oz / ½ cup butter, cubed and chilled

FOR THE CRUMBLE

150 g / 5 oz / ⅔ cup butter
100 g / 3 ½ oz / ⅔ cup plain (all purpose) flour
50 g / 1 ¾ oz / ½ cup ground almonds
75 g / 2 ½ oz / ½ cup light brown sugar

- Preheat the oven to 200°C (180° fan), 390F, gas 6.
- First make the pastry. Sieve the flour into a mixing bowl then rub in the butter until the mixture resembles fine breadcrumbs.
- Stir in just enough cold water to bring the pastry together into a pliable dough then chill for 30 minutes.
- Mix the chopped apple with the sugar and cornflour.
- Roll out the pastry on a floured surface and use it to line a 23 cm round pie dish. Spoon in the apples and level the top.
- To make the crumble topping, rub the butter into the flour then stir in the almonds and sugar.
- Take handfuls of the topping and squeeze it into a clump, then crumble it over the apple.
- Bake the tart for 35 – 40 minutes until the crumble is golden brown. Leave to cool for 20 minutes before cutting.

Apple, Pear and Raisin Crumble Tart

215

- Use half apple and half pear for your fruit filling and add 4 tablespoons of raisins to the crumble mixture.

216

MAKES 6

Wholemeal Apple Tartlets

PREPARATION TIME 15 MINUTES

COOKING TIME 25-35 MINUTES

....

INGREDIENTS

110 g / 4 oz / ½ cup butter, cubed and chilled
110 g / 4 oz / ⅔ cup stoneground wholemeal flour
110 g / 4 oz / ⅔ cup plain (all purpose) flour
3 apples, peeled and halved
6 tbsp apricot jam (jelly)

- Preheat the oven to 200°C (180° fan), 390F, gas 6.
- Rub the butter into the flours until the mixture resembles fine breadcrumbs.
- Stir in just enough cold water to bring the pastry together into a pliable dough.
- Roll out the pastry on a floured surface and cut out 6 circles then use them to line 6 tartlet tins.
- Slice each apple half and fan them out inside the pastry cases. Spoon a tablespoon of apricot jam on top of each one.
- Bake for 25 – 35 minutes or until the pastry is crisp and the jam has melted around the apples.

Wholemeal Pineapple Tartlets

 217

- Use one small pineapple peeled, cored and sliced instead of the apples for a tropical tasting tartlet.

MAKES 6

Apple, Walnut and Honey Tartlets

Apple, Honey and Walnut Tartlets

- Maple syrup instead of the honey to glaze these tartlets gives a richer flavour to these delicious treats.

Peach, Pistachio and Lavender Honey Tartlets

- Use 4 peaches instead of apples to fill your tartlets. Use chopped pistachios with lavender honey for a fragrant colourful glaze.

PREPARATION TIME 30 MINUTES

COOKING TIME 20 MINUTES

INGREDIENTS

225 g / 8 oz puff pastry
150g / 5 ½ oz / 1 ½ cups ground walnuts
150g / 5 ½ oz / ⅔ cup butter, softened
150g / 5 ½ oz / ⅔ cup caster (superfine) sugar
2 large eggs
2 tbsp plain (all purpose) flour
4 eating apples, cored and sliced
4 tbsp runny honey
2 tbsp chopped walnuts

- Preheat the oven to 200°C (180° fan), 390F, gas 6.
- Roll out the pastry on a floured surface and use it to line 6 round loose-bottomed tartlet cases.
- Prick the pastry with a fork, line with greaseproof paper and fill with baking beans or rice.
- Bake for 10 minutes then remove the paper and baking beans.
- Whisk together the ground walnuts, butter, sugar, eggs and flour until smoothly whipped and spoon the mixture into the pastry case.
- Arrange the apple slices on top and bake for 20 minutes or until the frangipane is cooked through and the pastry is crisp underneath.
- Heat the honey until very liquid and stir in the walnuts then drizzle it over the hot tarts.
- Serve warm with clotted cream or ice cream.

221

SERVES 12

Apricot Frangipane Tart

PREPARATION TIME 30 MINUTES

COOKING TIME 35 MINUTES

....

INGREDIENTS

450 g / 1 lb puff pastry
225 g / 8 oz / 2 ¼ cups ground almonds
225 g / 8 oz / 1 cup butter, softened
225 g / 8 oz / 1 cup caster (superfine) sugar
3 large eggs
3 tbsp plain (all purpose) flour
12 apricots, stoned and halved

- Preheat the oven to 200°C (180° fan), gas 6.
- Roll out the pastry on a floured surface and use it to line a large rectangular tart case.
- Prick the pastry with a fork, line with greaseproof paper and fill with baking beans or rice.
- Bake for 10 minutes then remove the paper and baking beans.
- Whisk together the almonds, butter, sugar, eggs and flour until smoothly whipped and spoon the mixture into the pastry case.
- Press the apricots into the frangipane, cut side down and bake the tart for 25 minutes or until the frangipane is cooked through and the pastry is crisp underneath.

Pear Frangipane Tart

 222

- Use 6 pears instead of the apricots for a slightly different texture to this delicious tart.

223

SERVES 8

Apricot and Lavender Loaf Cake

PREPARATION TIME I5 MINUTES

COOKING TIME 55 MINUTES

....

INGREDIENTS

225 g / 8 oz / 1 ½ cups self raising flour
100 g / 3 ½ oz / ½ cup butter, cubed
85 g / 3 oz caster / ⅓ cup (superfine) sugar
1 tbsp dried lavender flowers
6 apricots, stoned and quartered
1 large egg
75 ml / 2 ½ fl. oz / ⅓ cup whole milk

- Preheat the oven to 180°C (160° fan), 355F, gas 4 and line a loaf tin with non-stick baking paper.
- Sieve the flour into a mixing bowl and rub in the butter until it resembles fine breadcrumbs then stir in the sugar, apricots and lavender.
- Lightly beat the egg with the milk then stir it into the dry ingredients until just combined.
- Scrape the mixture into the loaf tin and bake for 55 minutes or until a skewer inserted in the centre comes out clean.
- Transfer the cake to a wire rack and leave to cool completely.

Apricot and Green Tea Loaf Cake

224

- Use Matcha green tea powder instead of the lavender for a delicate and Asian twist.

225

SERVES 8

Apricot Lattice Tart

- Preheat the oven to 200°C (180° fan), 390F, gas 6.
- Sieve the flour into a mixing bowl then rub in the butter until the mixture resembles fine breadcrumbs.
- Stir in just enough cold water to bring the pastry together into a pliable dough then chill for 30 minutes.
- Mix the chopped apricots with the sugar.
- Roll out the pastry on a floured surface and use it to line a 23 cm round pie dish. Trim the edges and reserve.
- Spoon in the apricots and level the top.
- Roll out the pastry trimmings then cut them into strips and lay them across the tart in a lattice pattern. Use a beaten egg at the ends to stick them to the pastry case.
- Brush the pastry with beaten egg and sprinkle with caster (superfine) sugar.
- Bake the tart for 35 – 40 minutes or until the pastry underneath has cooked through.

PREPARATION TIME 50 MINUTES

COOKING TIME 35-45 MINUTES

....

INGREDIENTS

450 g / 1 lb apricots, stoned and halved
50 g / 1 ¾ oz / ¼ cup caster (superfine) sugar

FOR THE PASTRY
200 g / 7 oz / ⅓ cup plain (all purpose) flour
100 g / 3 ½ oz / ½ cup butter, cubed and chilled
1 egg, beaten
2 tbsp caster (superfine) sugar

Fig Lattice Tart

226

- Use fresh figs in this tart instead of the apricots for a sweet and delicious take on this beautiful tart.

227

MAKES 36

Chocolate Chip Quinoa Biscuits

- Put the quinoa flakes, oats, flour and baking powder in a food processor and blitz until fine.
- Cream the butter with the sugar then beat in the dry ingredients.
- Fold in the quinoa and chocolate chips then bring the dough together and shape into a log. Chill for 30 minutes.
- Preheat the oven to 180°C (160° fan), 355F, gas 4 and line 2 baking sheets with greaseproof paper.
- Slice the log into 1 cm slices and spread out on the prepared trays.
- Bake for 20 – 25 minutes or until cooked through and golden brown.
- Transfer the biscuits to a wire rack and leave to cool completely.

PREPARATION TIME 40 MINUTES

COOKING TIME 20-25 MINUTES

....

INGREDIENTS

150 g / 5 ½ oz 1 ½ cups quinoa flakes
50 g / 1 ¾ oz / ½ cup porridge oats
125 g / 4 ½ oz / ¾ cup stoneground wholemeal flour
1 tsp baking powder
175 g / 6 oz / ¾ cup butter
150 g / 5 ½ oz / ¾ cup soft brown sugar
2 tbsp raw quinoa
150 g / 5 ½ oz / 1 cup chocolate chips

Chocolate, Raisin and Pinenut Quinoa Biscuits

228

- Use 50g/ 1 oz of chocolate, the same of raisins and pine nuts for a fruit and nut take on this biscuit.

229

SERVES 8

Blackcurrant Tart

Fresh Raspberry and Lemon Curd Tart

230

- Use 4 tablespoons of lemon curd at the base of the tart case and top with fresh raspberries for a sweet tangy tart. Dust with a little icing sugar to finish.

Strawberries and Cream Tart

231

- Use 4 tablespoons of lightly whipped double cream at the base of the tart and top with chopped fresh strawberries.

PREPARATION TIME 40 MINUTES

COOKING TIME 40 MINUTES

INGREDIENTS

400 g / 14 oz / 2 ⅔ cups fresh blackcurrants
200 g / 7 oz / ¾ cup caster (superfine) sugar

FOR THE PASTRY
200 g / 7 oz / ⅓ cup plain (all purpose) flour
100 g / 3 ½ oz / ½ cup butter, cubed
50 g / 1 ¾ oz / ¼ cup caster (superfine) sugar
1 large egg, beaten

- Preheat the oven to 200°C (180° fan), 390F, gas 6.
- To make the pastry, rub the butter into the flour until the mixture resembles fine breadcrumbs.
- Stir in the sugar and add enough cold water to bring the pastry together into a pliable dough.
- Chill for 30 minutes then roll out on a floured surface.
- Use the pastry to line a 24cm round loose-bottomed tart case and trim the edges, leaving a 1cm overhang to allow for shrinkage.
- Prick the pastry all over with a fork, line with clingfilm and fill with baking beans or rice.
- Bake the case for 10 minutes then remove the clingfilm and baking beans.
- Brush the inside with egg and return to the oven for 8 minutes or until golden and crisp.
- Meanwhile, put the blackcurrants in a large saucepan with 100ml water and bring to a simmer.
- Cook for 10 minutes until the skins have softened then add the sugar and stir well to dissolve.
- Boil for 8 minutes then pour the mixture into the pastry case and leave to cool and thicken.

232

MAKES 6

Blueberry Tartlets

- To make the pastry, rub the butter into the flour and add just enough cold water to bind. Chill for 30 minutes.
- Preheat the oven to 200°C (180° fan), 390F, gas 6.
- Roll out the pastry on a floured surface and use it to line 6 tartlet cases, rerolling the trimmings as necessary.
- Prick the pastry with a fork, line with clingfilm and fill with baking beans or rice. Bake for 10 minutes then remove the clingfilm and baking beans.
- Brush the inside of the pastry cases with beaten egg and cook for another 8 minutes to crisp.
- Whisk the custard ingredients together in a jug and ¾ fill the pastry cases.
- Bake the tarts for 15 – 20 minutes or until the custard has set.
- Leave the tartlets to cool completely before topping with the blueberries.

Summer Berry Tartlets

233

- Use a mix of fresh summer berries such as strawberries and raspberries for a bright colourful topping.

PREPARATION TIME 45 MINUTES

COOKING TIME 15-20 MINUTES

INGREDIENTS

200 g / 7 oz blueberries

FOR THE PASTRY
200g / 7 oz plain (all purpose) flour
100g / 3 ½ oz butter, cubed
1 egg, beaten

FOR THE CUSTARD
2 large egg yolks
55 g / 2 oz caster (superfine) sugar
1 tsp vanilla extract
2 tsp cornflour
225 ml / 8 fl. oz / 1 cup whole milk

234

SERVES 10-12

Orange, Almond and Cardamom Sponge

- Preheat the oven to 180°C (160° fan), 355F, gas 4 and grease and line a deep 20 cm round cake tin.
- Whisk together all of the cake ingredients with an electric whisk for 4 minutes or until well whipped.
- Scrape the mixture into the tin and bake for 45 - 50 minutes. The cake is ready when a toothpick inserted in the centre comes out clean.
- Transfer the cake to a wire rack to cool completely before cutting in half horizontally.
- To make the crème patisserie, whisk together the egg yolks, sugar, vanilla extract and cornflour.
- Heat the milk and cardamom almost to a simmer then strain it through a sieve and gradually whisk it into the egg mixture.
- Scrape the custard back into the saucepan and cook over a medium heat until it thickens, stirring constantly.
- Pour it into a bowl and leave to cool to room temperature.
- Beat the crème patisserie until smooth and use it to sandwich the cake back together. Dust with icing (confectioners) sugar before serving.

PREPARATION TIME 30 MINUTES

COOKING TIME 45-50 MINUTES

INGREDIENTS

150 g / 6 oz / 1 cup stoneground wholemeal flour
1 tsp baking powder
28 g / 1 oz / ¼ cup ground almonds
28 g / 1 oz / ¼ cup blanched almonds, finely chopped
2 tsp baking powder
175 g / 6 oz / ¾ cup caster (superfine) sugar
175 g / 6 oz / ¾ cup butter
3 large eggs
1 orange, zest finely grated

FOR THE CRÈME PATISSERIE
4 large egg yolks
75 g / 2 ½ oz / ⅓ cup caster sugar
1 tsp vanilla extract
2 tsp cornflour
450 ml / 16 fl. oz / 1 ¾ cups whole milk
4 cardamom pods, crushed
icing (confectioners) sugar to dust

235

MAKES 12

Chocolate and Cherry Cupcakes

PREPARATION TIME 25 MINUTES

COOKING TIME 15-20 MINUTES

INGREDIENTS

100 g / 3 ½ oz / ⅔ cup self-raising
flour, sifted
28g / 1 oz / ¼ cup unsweetened cocoa
powder, sifted
100 g / 3 ½ oz / ½ cup caster
(superfine) sugar
100 g / 3 ½ oz / ½ cup butter,
softened
3 large eggs
75 g / 2 ½ oz / ⅓ cup glace cherries,
chopped

TO DECORATE

225 ml / 8 fl. oz / 1 cup double cream
2 tbsp icing (confectioners) sugar
½ tsp vanilla extract
12 glace cherries
chocolate shavings

- Preheat the oven to 190⁰C (170⁰ fan) / 375F / gas 5 and line a 12-hole cupcake tin with paper cases.
- Combine the flour, cocoa, sugar, butter and eggs in a bowl and whisk together for 2 minutes or until smooth. Fold in the chopped cherries
- Divide the mixture between the paper cases, then transfer to the oven and bake for 15 – 20 minutes.
- Test with a wooden toothpick, if it comes out clean, the cakes are done.
- Transfer the cakes to a wire rack and leave to cool.
- Whip the cream with the icing (confectioners) sugar and vanilla until thick then spoon it into a piping bag fitted with a large star nozzle.
- Pipe a rosette of cream on top of each cake then top each one with a cherry and a sprinkle of chocolate shavings.

Chocolate and
Cranberry Cupcakes

236

- For a more tart tasting cupcake use chopped dried cranberries and for the cupcake filling and use chopped cranberries to top.

237

MAKES 12

Black Sesame and Orange Cupcakes

PREPARATION TIME 25 MINUTES

COOKING TIME 15-20 MINUTES

INGREDIENTS

100 g / 3 ½ oz / ⅔ cup self-raising
flour, sifted
100 g / 3 ½ oz / ½ cup caster
(superfine) sugar
100 g / 3 ½ oz / cup butter, softened
3 large eggs
1 orange, zest finely grated
2 tbsp black sesame seeds

- Preheat the oven to 190⁰C (170⁰ fan) / 375F / gas 5 and oil 12 silicone cupcake cases.
- Combine the flour, sugar, butter and eggs in a bowl and whisk together for 2 minutes or until smooth. Fold in the orange zest and sesame seeds.
- Divide the mixture between the cupcake cases, then transfer the tin to the oven and bake for 15 – 20 minutes.
- Test with a wooden toothpick, if it comes out clean, the cakes are done.
- Transfer the cakes to a wire rack and leave to cool completely.

Lemon and Poppy Seed Cupcakes

238

- Use the zest of 2 lemons instead of the orange and swap the black sesame for poppy seeds for a more classic take on this cupcake.

MAKES 24

239

Blackberry Mini Muffins

Blackberry and Orange Mini Muffins

240

- By using the zest of one orange and adding it to the cupcake mixture you will have an even more fruity tasting cake.

Lemon and Blueberry Mini Muffins

241

- Use the zest of one lemon and substitute the blackberries for blueberries for a delicious tasting mini muffin.

Chocolate and Blackberry Muffins

242

- Melt a bar of dark chocolate and drizzle over the top before serving.

PREPARATION TIME 25 MINUTES

COOKING TIME 15-20 MINUTES

....

INGREDIENTS

1 large egg
120 ml / 4 fl. oz / ½ cup sunflower oil
120 ml / 4 fl. oz / ½ cup milk
375 g / 12 ½ oz / 2 ½ cups self-raising flour, sifted
1 tsp baking powder
200 g / 7 oz / ¾ cup caster (superfine) sugar
200 g / 7 oz / 1 ⅓ cups blackberries

- Preheat the oven to 180⁰C (160⁰ fan), gas 4 and line a 24-hole mini muffin tin with paper cases.
- Beat the egg in a jug with the oil and milk until well mixed.
- Mix the flour, baking powder and sugar in a bowl.
- Pour in the egg mixture and stir just enough to combine then fold in the blackberries.
- Divide the mixture between the paper cases and bake for 15 – 20 minutes.
- Test with a wooden toothpick, if it comes out clean, the cakes are done.
- Transfer the muffins to a wire rack and leave to cool completely.

243

MAKES 12

Blackberry Tartlets

PREPARATION TIME 15 MINUTES

COOKING TIME 25-35 MINUTES

....

INGREDIENTS

110 g / 4 oz / ½ cup butter, cubed and chilled
225 g / 8 oz / 1 ½ cups plain (all purpose) flour
225g / 8 oz / ⅔ cup bramble jam (jelly)
300 g / 10 ½ oz / 2 cups blackberries

- Preheat the oven to 200⁰C (180⁰ fan), 390F, gas 6.
- Rub the butter into the flours until the mixture resembles fine breadcrumbs.
- Stir in just enough cold water to bring the pastry together into a pliable dough.
- Roll out the pastry on a floured surface and cut out 12 circles then use them to line a 12-hole mini tartlet tray.
- Divide the jam between the cases and bake for 15 – 20 minutes or until the pastry is crisp.
- Leave the tartlets to cool before arranging the blackberries on top.

Loganberry Tartlets 244

- Loganberries make a beautiful alternative to this tart when in season.

245

MAKES 12

Blueberry Financiers

PREPARATION TIME 1 HOUR 30 MINUTES

COOKING TIME 10-15 MINUTES

....

INGREDIENTS

110 g / 4 oz / ½ cup butter
55 g / 2 oz / ⅓ cup plain (all purpose) flour
55 g / 2 oz / ½ cup ground almonds
110 g / 4 oz / 1 cup icing (confectioners) sugar
3 large egg whites
100 g / 3 ½ oz / ⅔ cup blueberries

- Preheat the oven to 170⁰C (150⁰ fan), 325F, gas 3 and oil and flour a 12-hole financier mould.
- Heat the butter until it foams and starts to smell nutty then leave to cool.
- Combine the flour, ground almonds and icing (confectioners) sugar in a bowl and whisk in the eggs whites.
- Pour the cooled butter through a sieve into the bowl and whisk into the mixture until evenly mixed.
- Spoon the mixture into the moulds and sprinkle over the blueberries, then transfer the tin to the oven and bake for 10 – 15 minutes.
- Test with a wooden toothpick, if it comes out clean, the cakes are done.
- Transfer the cakes to a wire rack to cool for 5 minutes before serving.

Raspberry and Vanilla Financiers 246

- Swap the blueberries for raspberries and add _ teaspoon of vanilla to the financier mix.

Blackcurrant Mini Muffins

MAKES 24 · 247

- Preheat the oven to 180°C (160° fan), gas 4 and line a 24-hole mini muffin tin with paper cases.
- Beat the egg in a jug with the oil, milk and cordial until well mixed.
- Mix the flour, baking powder and sugar in a bowl.
- Pour in the egg mixture and stir just enough to combine then fold in the blackcurrants.
- Divide the mixture between the paper cases and bake for 15 – 20 minutes.
- Test with a wooden toothpick, if it comes out clean, the cakes are done.
- Transfer the muffins to a wire rack and leave to cool completely.

PREPARATION TIME 25 MINUTES

COOKING TIME 15-20 MINUTES

INGREDIENTS

1 large egg
120 ml / 4 fl. oz / ½ cup sunflower oil
60 ml / 2 fl. oz / ¼ cup milk
60 ml / 2 fl. oz / ¼ cup blackcurrant cordial
375 g / 12 ½ oz / 2 ½ cups self-raising flour, sifted
1 tsp baking powder
200 g / 7 oz / ¾ cup caster (superfine) sugar
200 g / 7 oz / 1 ⅓ cups blackcurrants

Cherry Mini Muffins
248

- Use pitted and quartered cherries instead of the blackcurrants and use cherry cordial in with the egg and oil mixture.

Blackcurrant Frangipane Tart

SERVES 8 · 249

- Preheat the oven to 200°C (180° fan), gas 6.
- To make the pastry, rub the butter into the flour until the mixture resembles fine breadcrumbs.
- Stir in the sugar and add enough cold water to bring the pastry together into a pliable dough.
- Chill the dough for 30 minutes then roll out on a floured surface. Use the pastry to line a 24cm round cake tin.
- Prick the pastry with a fork, line with greaseproof paper and fill with baking beans or rice.
- Bake for 10 minutes then remove the paper and beans. Return to the oven for 8 minutes to crisp.
- Whisk together the almonds, butter, sugar, eggs and flour until smoothly whipped and fold in the blackcurrants.
- Spoon the mixture into the pastry case and bake the tart for 25 minutes or until cooked through.

PREPARATION TIME 45 MINUTES

COOKING TIME 45 MINUTES

INGREDIENTS

150g / 5 ½ oz / 1 ½ cups ground almonds
150g / 5 ½ oz / ⅔ cup butter, softened
150g / 5 ½ oz / ⅔ cup caster (superfine) sugar
2 large eggs
2 tbsp plain (all purpose) flour
4 tbsp apricot jam
300 g / 10 ½ oz / 2 cups blackcurrants

FOR THE PASTRY

200 g / 7 oz / 1 ⅓ cups plain (all purpose) flour
100 g / 3 ½ oz / ½ cup butter, cubed
50 g / 1 ¾ oz / ¼ cup caster (superfine) sugar

Blueberry Frangipane Tart
250

- Blueberries make a great slightly sweet alternative to the blackcurrants in this delicious tart.

251

SERVES 4

Baked Apple Sponge Pudding

Festive Apple and Mincemeat Sponge Pudding

252

- Use mincemeat instead of plum jam to fill the apples and sprinkle with a little cinnamon before baking.

Baked Pear and Walnut Sponge Pudding

253

- Change the apples for pears and stuff with 4 tablespoons of chopped walnuts bound with a little honey for a nutty taste and texture.

PREPARATION TIME 15 MINUTES

COOKING TIME 30-35 MINUTES

INGREDIENTS

110 g / 4 oz / ⅔ cup self-raising flour, sifted
110 g / 4 oz / ½ cup caster (superfine) sugar
110 g / 4 oz / ½ cup butter, softened
2 large eggs
1 tsp vanilla extract
4 bramley apples, peeled and cored
4 tbsp plum jam

- Preheat the oven to 190°C (170° fan), 375F, gas 5 and butter a small baking dish.
- Combine the flour, sugar, butter, eggs and vanilla extract in a bowl and whisk together for 2 minutes or until smooth.
- Spoon the cake mixture into the baking dish and level the top.
- Stuff the apples with the plum jam and push them into the cake mixture.
- Bake the pudding for 30 – 35 minutes.
- Test with a wooden toothpick, if it comes out clean, the cake is done.
- Serve warm with custard or cream.

254

SERVES 8

Wholemeal Banana Loaf Cake

- Preheat the oven to 170°C (150° fan), gas 3 and line a long thin loaf tin with non-stick baking paper.
- Mash the bananas roughly with a fork then whisk in the sugar, eggs and oil.
- Sieve the flour and baking powder into the bowl and stir just enough to evenly mix all the ingredients together.
- Scrape the mixture into the loaf tin and bake for 55 minutes or until a skewer inserted comes out clean.
- Transfer the cake to a wire rack and leave to cool completely.

PREPARATION TIME 10 MINUTES

COOKING TIME 55 MINUTES

INGREDIENTS

3 very ripe bananas
110 g / 4 oz / ½ cup soft light brown sugar
2 large eggs
120 ml / 4 fl. oz / ½ cup sunflower oil
225 g / 8 oz / 1 ½ cups stoneground wholemeal flour
2 tsp baking powder

Chocolate and Banana Wholemeal Loaf Cake 255

- Add 55g/ 2oz of dark chocolate chips to the cake mixture for an extra decadent taste.

256

SERVES 8-10

Carrot and Walnut Cake

- Preheat the oven to 190°C (170° fan), 375F, gas 5 and line 2 x 20 cm round cake tins with greaseproof paper.
- Whisk the sugar, eggs and oil together until thick.
- Fold in the flour, baking powder and cinnamon, followed by the orange zest, carrots and walnuts.
- Divide the mixture between the tins and bake for 30 - 35 minutes.
- Transfer the cakes to a wire rack and leave to cool.
- To make the icing, beat the cream cheese and butter together with a wooden spoon until light and fluffy then beat in the icing (confectioners) sugar a quarter at a time.
- Add the vanilla extract then use a whisk to whip the mixture until smooth and light.
- Use a third of the icing to sandwich the cakes together and spread the rest over the top and sides.

PREPARATION TIME 25 MINUTES

COOKING TIME 30-35 MINUTES

INGREDIENTS

175 g / 6 oz / 1 cup soft light brown sugar
2 large eggs
150 ml / 5 fl. oz / ⅔ cup sunflower oil
175 g / 6 oz / 1 ¼ cups stoneground wholemeal flour
3 tsp baking powder
2 tsp ground cinnamon
1 orange, zest finely grated
200 g / 7 oz / 1 ⅔ cups carrots, washed and coarsely grated
100 g / 3 ½ oz / ¾ cup walnuts, chopped

FOR THE ICING

225g / 8 oz / 1 cup cream cheese
110 g / 4 oz / ½ cup butter, softened
225 g / 8 oz / 2 ¼ cups icing (confectioners) sugar
1 tsp vanilla extract

Carrot and Hazelnut Cake 257

- For those who can find walnuts a little strong in flavour, the milder nutty flavour of hazelnuts (cob nuts) roughly chopped work well in this recipe.

258

SERVES 8-10

Carrot and Rye Cake

PREPARATION TIME 25 MINUTES

COOKING TIME 30-35 MINUTES

INGREDIENTS

175 g / 6 oz / 1 cup soft light brown sugar
2 large eggs
150 ml / 5 fl. oz / ⅔ cup cup sunflower oil
100 g / 3 ½ oz / ⅔ cup stoneground wholemeal flour
75 g / 2 ½ oz / ½ cup rye flour
3 tsp baking powder
2 tsp ground cinnamon
200 g / 7 oz 1 ⅔ cups carrots, washed and coarsely grated

FOR THE ICING

225g / 8 oz / 1 cup cream cheese
110 g / 4 oz / ½ cup butter, softened
225 g / 8 oz / 2 ¼ cup icing (confectioners) sugar
1 tsp vanilla extract

- Preheat the oven to 190°C (170° fan), 375F, gas 5 and line 2 x 20 cm round cake tins with greaseproof paper.
- Whisk the sugar, eggs and oil together for 3 minutes until thick.
- Fold in the flour, baking powder and cinnamon, followed by the carrots.
- Divide the mixture between the tins and bake for 30 - 35 minutes. Transfer the cakes to a wire rack and leave to cool completely.
- To make the icing, beat the cream cheese and butter together with a wooden spoon until light and fluffy then beat in the icing (confectioners) sugar a quarter at a time.
- Add the vanilla extract then use a whisk to whip the mixture until smooth.
- Use a third of the icing to sandwich the cakes together and spread the rest over the top and sides.

Carrot, Rye and Honey Cake

 259

- Adding 2 tablespoons of honey to the cake batter adds a warm sweet note to this delicious cake.

260

SERVES 8-10

Carrot and Walnut Loaf Cake

PREPARATION TIME 25 MINUTES

COOKING TIME 40-45 MINUTES

INGREDIENTS

175 g / 6 oz / 1 cup soft light brown sugar
2 large eggs
150 ml / 5 fl. oz / ⅔ cup sunflower oil
175 g / 6 oz stoneground wholemeal flour
3 tsp baking powder
2 tsp ground cinnamon
1 orange, zest finely grated
200 g / 7 oz / 1 ⅔ cup carrots, washed and coarsely grated
100 g / 3 ½ oz / ⅔ cup walnuts, chopped

- Preheat the oven to 190°C (170° fan), 375F, gas 5 and line a loaf tin with greaseproof paper.
- Whisk the sugar, eggs and oil together for 3 minutes until thick.
- Fold in the flour, baking powder and cinnamon, followed by the orange zest, carrots and walnuts.
- Scrape the mixture into the tin and bake for 40 - 45 minutes.
- Test with a wooden toothpick, if it comes out clean, the cake is done.
- Transfer the cake to a wire rack and leave to cool completely.

Carrot and Pecan Loaf

261

- For some walnuts can taste quite strong but substituting them here for chopped pecans adds a rich but nutty taste to the cake.

262

SERVES 8

Carrot and Cumin Loaf Cake

Carrot and Cardamom Loaf Cake

 263

- Take 1 tbsp of cardamom and crack, cook with the carrots to infuse their delicate spice into them. The flavour is subtle in the cake giving it a warm delicious taste.

Carrot and Coconut Loaf Cake

 264

- Carrot and coconut work well together in this delicious loaf cake use dessicated coconut instead of the cumin.

PREPARATION TIME 10 MINUTES

COOKING TIME 55 MINUTES

INGREDIENTS

200 g / 7 oz / 1 ⅓ cups carrots, chopped
300 g / 10 ½ oz / 2 cups self-raising flour
2 tsp baking powder
250 g / 9 oz / 1 ¼ cups butter, softened
4 large eggs
2 tsp cumin seeds

- Preheat the oven to 170°C (150° fan), 340F, gas 3 and line a large loaf tin with non-stick baking paper.
- Boil the carrots for 15 minutes then drain and puree in a food processor. Leave to cool
- Sieve the flour and baking powder into a mixing bowl and add the butter, eggs, carrot puree and cumin.
- Beat the mixture with an electric whisk for 4 minutes or until smooth and well whipped.
- Scrape the mixture into the loaf tin and bake for 55 minutes or until a skewer inserted comes out clean.
- Transfer the cake to a wire rack and leave to cool completely before serving.

265

SERVES 8

Red Leicester and Pine Nut Loaf Cake

PREPARATION TIME 10 MINUTES

COOKING TIME 55 MINUTES

....

INGREDIENTS

300 g / 10 ½ oz / 2 cups self-raising flour
2 tsp baking powder
250 g / 9 oz / 1 ¼ cups butter, softened
5 large eggs
4 tbsp pine nuts
200 g / 7 oz / 2 cups Red Leicester cheese, grated

- Preheat the oven to 170°C (150° fan), 340F, gas 3 and line a large loaf tin with non-stick baking paper.
- Sieve the flour and baking powder into a mixing bowl and add the butter and eggs.
- Beat the mixture with an electric whisk for 4 minutes or until smooth and well whipped.
- Fold in the pine nuts and cheese then scrape the mixture into the loaf tin.
- Bake for 55 minutes or until a skewer inserted comes out clean.
- Transfer the cake to a wire rack and leave to cool completely before serving.

Mature Cheddar and Hazelnut Loaf Cake

266

- A good strong cheese combined with the hazelnuts works well in this loaf cake recipe. Be sure to swap the same quantities of each when making this cake.

267

SERVES 8-10

Coffee and Coconut Ring Cake

PREPARATION TIME 25 MINUTES

COOKING TIME 40-45 MINUTES

....

INGREDIENTS

225 g / 8 oz / 1 cup butter, softened
225 g / 8 oz / 1 cup caster (superfine) sugar
1 tbsp instant espresso powder
4 large eggs, beaten
225 g / 4 ½ oz / 1 ½ cups self-raising flour
100 g / 3 ½ oz / 1 cup desiccated coconut

FOR THE TOPPING
1 tsp instant espresso powder
1 tbsp milk
200 ml / 7 fl. oz / ¾ cup condensed milk
3 tbsp desiccated coconut

- Preheat the oven to 180°C (160° fan), 355F, gas 4 and butter a ring mould.
- Cream the butter, sugar and espresso powder together until well whipped then gradually whisk in the eggs, beating well after each addition.
- Fold in the flour and coconut then spoon the mixture into the tin.
- Bake the cake for 40 - 45 minutes or until a skewer inserted in the centre comes out clean.
- Transfer the cake to a wire rack and leave to cool.
- Dissolve the espresso powder in the milk then stir into the condensed milk and spoon it over the cake. Sprinkle the top with desiccated coconut.

Chocolate and Coconut Ring Cake

268

- Use 2 tsp of cocoa powder instead of espresso for topping and swap the half the coconut in the cake mix for dark chocolate chips.

Carrot and Chestnut Marble Loaf Cake

SERVES 8

- Preheat the oven to 170°C (150° fan), 340F, gas 3 and line a large loaf tin with non-stick baking paper.
- Boil the carrots for 15 minutes then drain and puree in a food processor. Leave to cool
- Sieve the flour and baking powder into a mixing bowl and add the butter and eggs.
- Beat the mixture with an electric whisk for 4 minutes or until smooth and well whipped.
- Split the mixture between 2 bowls. Fold the chopped chestnuts into one bowl and spoon it into the tin.
- Fold the carrot puree into the other bowl and spoon it on top of the chestnut mixture then drag a butter knife through the mixture to marble.
- Bake the cake for 55 minutes or until a skewer inserted in the centre comes out clean.
- Transfer the cake to a wire rack and leave to cool.

PREPARATION TIME 10 MINUTES

COOKING TIME 55 MINUTES

INGREDIENTS

200 g / 7 oz / 1 ⅓ cup carrots, chopped
300 g / 10 ½ oz / 2 cups self-raising flour
2 tsp baking powder
250 g / 9 oz / 1 ¼ cups butter, softened
4 large eggs
100 g / 3 ½ oz / ⅔ cup cooked chestnuts, chopped

Parsnip and Chestnut Marble Loaf Cake

270

- For a more savoury note to this cake use parsnips instead of carrots.

Chocolate and Almond Loaf Cake

271

SERVES 8

- Preheat the oven to 180°C (160° fan), 355F, gas 4 and butter a terrine dish.
- Sieve the flour, baking powder and cocoa into a mixing bowl then add the ground almonds, sugar, butter and eggs and whisk with an electric whisk for 4 minutes or until pale and well whipped.
- Fold in the chocolate and almonds and spoon into the terrine, then bake for 45 - 50 minutes.
- The cake is ready when a toothpick inserted in the centre comes out clean.
- Transfer the cake to a wire rack to cool completely.

PREPARATION TIME 10 MINUTES

COOKING TIME 45-50 MINUTES

INGREDIENTS

100 g / 3 ½ oz / ⅔ cup self-raising flour
1 tsp baking powder
2 tbsp cocoa powder
50 g / 1 ¾ oz / ½ cup ground almonds
150 g / 5 ½ oz / ⅔ cup caster (superfine) sugar
150 g / 5 ½ oz / ⅔ cup butter
3 large eggs
100 g / 3 ½ oz dark chocolate (minimum 60 % cocoa solids), chopped
100 g / 3 ½ oz / ⅔ cup blanched almonds

Chocolate and Hazelnut Loaf Cake

272

- Use skinned chopped hazelnuts (cob nuts) instead of almonds for a delicious twist to this classic loaf cake.

273

SERVES 8

Chocolate and Marmalade Swiss Roll

Chocolate and Apricot Swiss Roll

274

- Swap the marmalade for a good quality apricot jam, if you prefer a more fruity swiss roll stir into the jam 4 coarsely chopped dried apricots.

Milk Chocolate and Marmalade Swiss Roll

275

- Use milk chocolate instead of dark for a less bitter more creamy tasting swiss roll.

PREPARATION TIME 45 MINUTES

COOKING TIME 15-20 MINUTES

INGREDIENTS

100 g / 3 ½ oz / ⅔ cup self-raising flour
28 g / 1 oz / ¼ cup unsweetened cocoa powder
1 tsp baking powder
100 g / 3 ½ oz / ½ cup caster (superfine) sugar
100 g / 3 ½ oz / ½ cup butter
2 large eggs

TO DECORATE
200 g / 7 oz / ⅔ cup marmalade
100 g / 3 ½ oz dark chocolate (minimum 60 % cocoa solids)

- Preheat the oven to 180°C (160° fan), 355F, gas 4 and grease and line a Swiss roll tin.
- Put all of the cake ingredients in a large mixing bowl and whisk them together with an electric whisk for 4 minutes or until pale and well whipped.
- Spoon the mixture into the tin and spread into an even layer with a palette knife.
- Bake for 15 - 20 minutes or until springy to the touch.
- Turn the cake out onto a sheet of greaseproof paper and peel off the lining paper. Spread the cake with marmalade and roll up whilst warm, using the greaseproof paper to help you.
- Leave the cake to cool.
- Melt the chocolate in a microwave or bain marie then leave it to cool and thicken a little.
- Drizzle the chocolate all over the cake, spreading it round the sides with a palette knife.

276

MAKES 9

Chocolate and Pecan Brownies

- Preheat the oven to 170°C (150° fan), 340F, gas 3 and oil and line a 20 cm x 20 cm square cake tin.
- Melt the chocolate, cocoa and butter together in a saucepan, then leave to cool a little.
- Whisk the sugar and eggs together with an electric whisk for 3 minutes or until very light and creamy.
- Pour in the chocolate mixture and sieve over the flour, then fold everything together with the pecans until evenly mixed.
- Scrape into the tin and bake for 35 – 40 minutes or until the outside is set, but the centre is still quite soft, as it will continue to cook as it cools.
- Leave the brownie to cool for 10 minutes then cut into squares and serve warm with the ginger ice cream.

PREPARATION TIME 25 MINUTES

COOKING TIME 35-40 MINUTES

INGREDIENTS

110g / 4 oz dark chocolate, chopped
85 g / 3 oz / ¾ cup unsweetened cocoa powder, sifted
225 g / 8 oz / 1 cup butter
450 g / 15 oz / 2 ½ cups light brown sugar
4 large eggs
110 g / 4 oz / ⅔ cup self-raising flour
110 g / 4 oz / ¾ cup pecan nuts, chopped

TO SERVE
ginger ice cream

Chocolate and Walnut Brownies

277

- Walnuts work well in this recipe, swap the same quantity of pecans for these sharper tasting nuts.

278

SERVES 8

Dark and White Chocolate Layer Cake

- Preheat the oven to 180°C (160 fan), gas 4 and grease and line 2 Swiss roll tins.
- Put all of the chocolate cake ingredients in a large mixing bowl and whisk them together with an electric whisk for 4 minutes or until pale and well whipped.
- Spoon the mixture into one of the tins and spread into an even layer with a palette knife.
- Bake for 15 - 20 minutes or until springy to the touch.
- Make the plain cake layer in the same way.
- To make the white chocolate ganache, chop the chocolate and transfer to a mixing bowl.
- Heat the cream until it starts to simmer, then pour over the chopped chocolate and stir until the mixture has cooled and thickened.
- Cut the 2 cakes into thirds and sandwich alternate layers together with the white chocolate ganache.

PREPARATION TIME 45 MINUTES

COOKING TIME 15-20 MINUTES

INGREDIENTS

FOR THE DARK CHOCOLATE
CAKE LAYER
100 g / 3 ½ oz / ⅔ cup self-raising flour
28 g / 1 oz / ¼ cup cocoa powder
1 tsp baking powder
100 g / 3 ½ oz / ½ cup caster (superfine) sugar
100 g / 3 ½ oz / ½ cup butter
2 large eggs

FOR THE PLAIN CAKE LAYER
100 g / 3 ½ oz / ⅔ cup self-raising flour
1 tsp baking powder
100 g / 3 ½ oz / ½ cup caster sugar
100 g / 3 ½ oz / ½ cup butter
2 large eggs

FOR THE WHITE CHOCOLATE
GANACHE
225 g / 8 oz white chocolate
225 ml / 8 fl. oz / 1 cup double cream

Dark and White Chocolate Layer Cake with Rum

279

- Add 1-2 tablespoons of brandy into the white chocolate ganache for a richer tasting cake.

Chocolate-Covered Coconut Loaf Cake

280

SERVES 8-10

PREPARATION TIME 15 MINUTES

COOKING TIME 45-55 MINUTES

INGREDIENTS

225 g / 8 oz / 1 cup butter, softened
225 g / 8 oz / 1 cup caster (superfine) sugar
4 large eggs, beaten
225 g / 4 ½ oz / 1 ½ cups self-raising flour
100 g / 3 ½ oz / 1 cup desiccated coconut
200 g / 7 oz dark chocolate (minimum 60 % cocoa solids)

- Preheat the oven to 180°C (160° fan), 355F, gas 4 and grease and line a loaf tin with greaseproof paper.
- Cream the butter and sugar together until well whipped then gradually whisk in the eggs, beating well after each addition.
- Fold in the flour and coconut then scrape the mixture into the tin.
- Bake the cake for 45 - 55 minutes or until a skewer inserted in the centre comes out clean.
- Transfer the cake to a wire rack and leave to cool completely.
- Melt the chocolate in a microwave or bain marie then pour it over the cake and smooth the sides with a palette knife. Leave to set before serving.

Chocolate and Sponge Biscuit Brownies

281

MAKES 9

PREPARATION TIME 25 MINUTES

COOKING TIME 35-40 MINUTES

INGREDIENTS

110g / 4 oz milk chocolate, chopped
85 g / 3 oz / ¾ cup cocoa powder, sifted
225 g / 8 oz / 1 cup butter
450 g / 15 oz / 2 ½ cups light brown sugar
4 large eggs
110 g / 4 oz / ⅔ cup self-raising flour
8 sponge finger biscuits, broken into pieces

- Preheat the oven to 170°C (150° fan), 340F, gas 3 and oil and line a 20 cm x 20 cm square cake tin.
- Melt the chocolate, cocoa and butter together in a saucepan, then leave to cool a little.
- Whisk the sugar and eggs together with an electric whisk for 3 minutes or until very light and creamy.
- Pour in the chocolate mixture and sieve over the flour, then fold everything together with the sponge finger biscuits until evenly mixed.
- Scrape into the tin and bake for 35 – 40 minutes or until a skewer inserted comes out clean.
- Leave the brownie to cool completely before cutting into 9 squares.

282

SERVES 8

Chocolate and Mandarin Cake

- Preheat the oven to 170°C (150° fan), gas 3 and butter a 23 cm round cake tin.
- Sieve the flour, cocoa and baking powder into a mixing bowl and add sugar, butter and eggs.
- Beat the mixture with an electric whisk for 4 minutes or until smooth and well whipped.
- Arrange the mandarin segments in the bottom of the tin and spoon the cake mixture on top.
- Bake for 35 minutes or until a skewer inserted comes out clean.
- Leave the cake to cool for 20 minutes before turning out onto a serving plate.

PREPARATION TIME 15 MINUTES

COOKING TIME 35 MINUTES

INGREDIENTS

300 g / 10 ½ oz / 2 cups self-raising flour
28 g / 1 oz / ¼ cup unsweetened cocoa powder
2 tsp baking powder
250 g / 9 oz / 1 ¼ cup caster (superfine) sugar
250 g / 9 oz / 1 ¼ cup butter, softened
5 large eggs
1 can mandarin segments in syrup, drained

Chocolate and Apricot Tart

283

SERVES 8-10

PREPARATION TIME 25 MINUTES

COOKING TIME 15-20 MINUTES

INGREDIENTS

250 ml / 9 fl. oz / 1 cup double cream
250 g / 9 oz dark chocolate, chopped
55 g / 2 oz / ¼ cup butter, softened
100 g / 3 ½ oz / ½ cup dried apricots, chopped

FOR THE PASTRY

100 g / 3 ½ oz / ½ cup butter, cubed
200 g / 7 oz / 1 ⅓ cups plain (all purpose) flour
55 g / 2 oz / ¼ cups caster sugar
1 egg, beaten

TO DECORATE

cocoa powder for dusting
2 dried apricots, halved
1 physalis

- Preheat the oven to 200°C (180° fan), 390F, gas 6.
- To make the pastry, rub the butter into the flour and sugar and add the egg with just enough cold water to bind.
- Wrap the dough in clingfilm and chill for 30 minutes then roll out on a floured surface. Use the pastry to line a 23 cm loose-bottomed tart tin and trim the edges.
- Prick the pastry with a fork, line with clingfilm and fill with baking beans or rice. Bake for 10 minutes then remove the clingfilm and baking beans and cook for another 8 minutes to crisp.
- Heat the cream to simmering point then pour it over the chocolate and stir until smooth.
- Add the butter and blend it in with a stick blender. Sprinkle the chopped apricots over the pastry base and pour the ganache on top.
- Leave the ganache to cool for 2 hours. Just before serving, dust the top of the tart with cocoa and arrange the apricots and physalis on top.
- Apply the gold leaf with a dry brush.

Chocolate and Pine Nut Loaf

284

SERVES 8

PREPARATION TIME 10 MINUTES

COOKING TIME 45-50 MINUTES

INGREDIENTS

100 g / 3 ½ oz / ⅔ cup self-raising flour
1 tsp baking powder
2 tbsp cocoa powder
50 g / 1 ¾ oz / ½ cup ground almonds
150 g / 5 ½ oz / ⅔ cup caster (superfine) sugar
150 g / 5 ½ oz / ⅔ cup butter
3 large eggs
100 g / 3 ½ oz / ¾ cup pine nuts

- Preheat the oven to 180°C (160° fan), 355F, gas 4 and line a loaf tin with greaseproof paper.
- Sieve the flour, baking powder and cocoa into a mixing bowl then add the ground almonds, sugar, butter and eggs and whisk with an electric whisk for 4 minutes or until pale and well whipped.
- Fold in the pine nuts and spoon into the tin, then bake for 45 - 50 minutes.
- The cake is ready when a toothpick inserted in the centre comes out clean.
- Transfer the cake to a wire rack and leave to cool completely.

285

MAKES 12

Chocolate, Walnut and Redcurrant Minis

PREPARATION TIME 45 MINUTES

COOKING TIME 15-20 MINUTES

....

INGREDIENTS

100 g / 3 ½ oz / ⅔ cup self-raising flour
28 g / 1 oz / ¼ cup unsweetened cocoa powder
1 tsp baking powder
100 g / 3 ½ oz / ½ cup caster (superfine) sugar
100 g / 3 ½ oz / ½ cup butter
2 large eggs
100 g / 3 ½ oz / ¾ cup walnuts, chopped

TO DECORATE

200 ml / 7 fl. oz / ¾ cup double cream
200 g / 7 oz dark chocolate (minimum 60 % cocoa solids), chopped
200 g / 7 oz / 1 ⅓ cups redcurrants

- Preheat the oven to 180°C (160° fan), 355F, gas 4 and grease and line a Swiss roll tin.
- Put all of the cake ingredients in a large mixing bowl and whisk them together with an electric whisk for 4 minutes or until pale and well whipped.
- Spoon the mixture into the tin and spread into an even layer with a palette knife.
- Bake for 15 - 20 minutes or until springy to the touch.
- Bring the cream to simmering point then pour it over the chocolate. Stir until smooth then pour it over the cake and chill for 2 hours to set.
- Use a cookie cutter to cut out 12 small cakes and decorate the tops with the redcurrants.

Chocolate and Walnut Brownies 286

- Walnuts work well in this recipe, swap the same quantity of pecans for these sharper tasting nuts.

287

MAKES 9

Chocolate and Cashew Nut Brownies

PREPARATION TIME 25 MINUTES

COOKING TIME 35-40 MINUTES

....

INGREDIENTS

110g / 4 oz milk chocolate, chopped
85 g / 3 oz / ¾ cups unsweetened cocoa powder, sifted
225 g / 8 oz / 1 cup butter
450 g / 15 oz / 2 ½ cups light brown sugar
4 large eggs
110 g / 4 oz / ⅔ cup self-raising flour
110 g / 4 oz / ¾ cup cashew nuts, chopped

- Preheat the oven to 170°C (150° fan), 340F, gas 3 and oil and line a 20 cm x 20 cm square cake tin.
- Melt the chocolate, cocoa and butter together in a saucepan, then leave to cool a little.
- Whisk the sugar and eggs together with an electric whisk for 3 minutes or until very light and creamy.
- Pour in the chocolate mixture and sieve over the flour, then fold everything together with the cashew nuts until evenly mixed.
- Scrape into the tin and bake for 35 – 40 minutes or until the outside is set, but the centre is still quite soft, as it will continue to cook as it cools.
- Leave the brownie to cool completely before cutting into 9 squares.

Chocolate and Pine Nut Brownies 288

- You can use most nuts in this recipe, using chopped pine nuts gives this brownie a more subtle tasting flavour.

289

MAKES 12

Chocolate Chip Muffins

Chocolate Chip and Cherry Muffins

290

- Use half chocolate chips half chopped sour cherries for a delicious tasting moist muffin.

Double Chocolate Chip Muffins

291

- Add 2 tablespoons of cocoa into the flour for an added chocolate taste.

PREPARATION TIME 25 MINUTES

COOKING TIME 20-25 MINUTES

INGREDIENTS

1 large egg
120 ml / 4 fl. oz / ½ cup sunflower oil
120 ml / 4 fl. oz / ½ cup milk
375 g / 12 ½ oz / 2 ½ cups self-raising flour, sifted
1 tsp baking powder
200 g / 7 oz / ¾ cup caster (superfine) sugar
150 g / 5 ½ oz / 1 cup chocolate chips

- Preheat the oven to 180°C (160° fan), 355F, gas 4 and line a 12-hole muffin tin with paper cases.
- Beat the egg in a jug with the oil and milk until well mixed.
- Mix the flour, baking powder, sugar and chocolate chips in a bowl.
- Pour in the egg mixture and stir just enough to combine.
- Divide the mixture between the paper cases and bake for 20 – 25 minutes.
- Test with a wooden toothpick, if it comes out clean, the cakes are done.
- Transfer the muffins to a wire rack and leave to cool completely.

SERVES 8

Chocolate Chip Loaf Cake

PREPARATION TIME 15 MINUTES

COOKING TIME 55 MINUTES

INGREDIENTS

225 g / 8oz / 1 ½ cups self raising flour
100 g / 3 ½ oz / ½ cup butter, cubed
85 g / 3oz / ⅓ cup caster (superfine) sugar
150 g / 5 ½ oz / 1 cup chocolate chips
1 large egg
75 ml / 2 ½ fl. oz / ⅓ cup whole milk

- Preheat the oven to 180°C (160° fan), 355F, gas 4 and line a loaf tin with non-stick baking paper.
- Sieve the flour into a mixing bowl and rub in the butter until it resembles fine breadcrumbs then stir in the sugar and chocolate chips.
- Lightly beat the egg with the milk and stir it into the dry ingredients until just combined.
- Scrape the mixture into the loaf tin and bake for 55 minutes or until a skewer inserted in the centre comes out clean.
- Transfer the cake to a wire rack and leave to cool completely.

Double Chocolate Chip Loaf

293

- Vary the chocolate chips by using some white and some dark for a more intense chocolate flavoured loaf.

294

MAKES 12

Chocolate Buttercream Cupcakes

PREPARATION TIME 30 MINUTES

COOKING TIME 15-20 MINUTES

INGREDIENTS

110 g / 4 oz / ⅔ cup self-raising flour, sifted
110 g / 4 oz / ½ cup caster (superfine) sugar
110 g / 4 oz / ½ cup butter, softened
2 large eggs
1 tsp vanilla extract

FOR THE BUTTERCREAM

55 g / 2 oz / ¼ cup butter, softened
225 g / 8 oz / 2 ¼ cups icing (confectioners) sugar
2 tbsp unsweetened cocoa powder
2 tbsp milk

- Preheat the oven to 190°C (170° fan), 375F, gas 5 and line a 12-hole cupcake tin with paper cases.
- Combine the flour, sugar, butter, eggs and vanilla extract in a bowl and whisk for 2 minutes or until smooth.
- Divide the mixture between the paper cases, then transfer the tin to the oven and bake for 15 – 20 minutes.
- Test with a wooden toothpick, if it comes out clean, the cakes are done.
- Transfer the cakes to a wire rack and leave to cool completely.
- To make the icing, beat the butter with a wooden spoon until light and fluffy then beat in the icing (confectioners) sugar and cocoa powder a quarter at a time.
- Add the milk then use a whisk to whip the mixture for 2 minutes or until smooth and light.
- Spoon the icing onto the cakes and swirl with the back of the spoon.

Chocolate and Lime
295
Buttercream Cupcakes

- Add 1 tbsp of lime juice and the zest of half a lime to the chocolate buttercream for a zingy tasting muffin.

296

SERVES 8

Pistachio and Chocolate Chunk Loaf

- Preheat the oven to 180°C (160° fan), 355F, gas 4 and line a loaf tin with non-stick baking paper.
- Sieve the flour into a mixing bowl and rub in the butter until it resembles fine breadcrumbs then stir in the sugar, pistachios and chocolate chunks.
- Lightly beat the egg with the milk and stir it into the dry ingredients until just combined.
- Scrape the mixture into the loaf tin and bake for 55 minutes or until a skewer inserted comes out clean.
- Transfer the cake to a wire rack and leave to cool completely.

PREPARATION TIME 15 MINUTES

COOKING TIME 55 MINUTES

INGREDIENTS

225 g / 8oz / 1 ½ cups self-raising flour
100 g / 3 ½ oz / ½ cup butter, cubed
85 g / 3oz / ⅓ cup caster (superfine) sugar
100 g / 3 ½ oz / ¾ cup pistachio nuts, chopped
200 g / 7 oz milk chocolate, broken into squares
1 large egg
75 ml / 2 ½ fl. oz / ⅓ cup whole milk

Pistachio and White Chocolate Chunk Loaf

297

- For a sweeter tasting loaf cake use chunks of white chocolate which work well with the pistachios.

298

SERVES 8

Chocolate Loaf Cake

- Preheat the oven to 180°C (160° fan), 355F, gas 4 and grease and line a loaf tin with greaseproof paper.
- Cream together the butter and sugar until well whipped then gradually whisk in the eggs, beating well after each addition.
- Sift over the flour and cocoa powder and fold in with the grated chocolate.
- Scrape the mixture into the tin and bake for 45 minutes or until a skewer inserted in the centre comes out clean.
- Turn the loaf out onto a wire rack and leave to cool.

PREPARATION TIME 15 MINUTES

COOKING TIME 45 MINUTES

INGREDIENTS

225 g / 8 oz / 1 cup butter, softened
225 g / 8 oz / 1 cup caster (superfine) sugar
4 large eggs, beaten
225 g / 8 oz / 1 ½ cups self-raising flour
2 tbsp unsweetened cocoa powder
100 g / 3 ½ oz milk chocolate, grated

Chocolate and Espresso Loaf Cake

299

- Before adding the flour to the cake batter mix stir through 2 tablespoons of espresso coffee for a richer flavoured loaf cake.

300

SERVES 8

Chocolate and Walnut Tart

Chocolate and Pistachio Tart

301

- You can swap the walnuts for pistachios in this rich, delicious tasting tart.

Chocolate and Stem Ginger Tart

302

- Use 60g/ 2 oz of finely chopped stem ginger instead of the nuts for a warm tasting, rich tart.

PREPARATION TIME 25 MINUTES

COOKING TIME 15-20 MINUTES

INGREDIENTS

250 ml / 9 fl. oz / 1 cup double cream
250 g / 9 oz dark chocolate
(minimum 60 % cocoa solids),
chopped
55 g / 2 oz / ¼ cup butter, softened
150 g / 5 ½ oz / 1 ¼ cups walnuts,
chopped

FOR THE PASTRY

100 g / 3 ½ oz / ½ cup butter, cubed
200g / 7 oz / 1 ⅓ cups plain (all
purpose) flour
55 g / 2 oz / ¼ cup light brown sugar
1 egg, beaten

- Preheat the oven to 200°C (180° fan), 390F, gas 6.
- To make the pastry, rub the butter into the flour and sugar and add the egg with just enough cold water to bind.
- Wrap the dough in clingfilm and chill for 30 minutes then roll out on a floured surface.
- Use the pastry to line a 23 cm loose-bottomed tart tin and trim the edges.
- Prick the pastry with a fork, line with clingfilm and fill with baking beans or rice.
- Bake for 10 minutes then remove the clingfilm and baking beans and cook for another 8 minutes to crisp.
- Heat the cream to simmering point then pour it over the chocolate and stir until smooth.
- Add the butter and blend it in with a stick blender.
- Scatter the walnuts over the bottom of the pastry case then pour in the ganache and level the top with a palette knife.
- Leave the ganache to cool and set for at least 2 hours before cutting and serving.

303

MAKES 12

Wholemeal Chocolate Muffins

- Preheat the oven to 180°C (160° fan), 355F, gas 4 and line a 12-hole muffin tin with paper cases.
- Beat the egg in a jug with the oil and milk until well mixed.
- Mix the flour, cocoa, baking powder, sugar and chocolate in a bowl.
- Pour in the egg mixture and stir just enough to combine.
- Divide the mixture between the paper cases and bake for 20 – 25 minutes.
- Test with a wooden toothpick, if it comes out clean, the cakes are done.
- Transfer the muffins to a wire rack and leave to cool completely.

PREPARATION TIME 25 MINUTES

COOKING TIME 20-25 MINUTES

INGREDIENTS

1 large egg
120 ml / 4 fl. oz / ½ cup sunflower oil
120 ml / 4 fl. oz / ½ cup milk
200 g / 7 oz / 1 ⅓ cups self-raising flour, sifted
175 g / 6 oz / 1 ¼ cups stoneground wholemeal flour
2 tbsp cocoa powder
2 tsp baking powder
200 g / 7 oz / ¾ cup caster (superfine) sugar
150 g / 5 ½ oz dark chocolate (minimum 60% cocoa solids), grated

Wholemeal, Chestnut and Chocolate Muffins

304

- Swap out half the wholemeal flour and use half chestnut flour for a nuttier tasting chocolate muffin.

305

SERVES 8-10

Chocolate Truffle Loaf Cake

- Preheat the oven to 180°C (160° fan), 355F, gas 4 and grease and line a large loaf tin with greaseproof paper.
- Put all of the ingredients in a bowl and whisk together until smooth.
- Scrape the mixture into the loaf tin and level the top with a palette knife.
- Put the tin in a large roasting tin pour around enough boiling water to come half way up the side of the loaf tin.
- Bake the cake for 40 – 50 minutes or until the centre is only just set.
- Leave to cool completely in the tin then refrigerate for 2 hours before turning out and dusting with cocoa.

PREPARATION TIME 15 MINUTES

COOKING TIME 40-50 MINUTES

INGREDIENTS

600g / 1 lb 5 oz / 2 ¾ cups cream cheese
150 ml / 5 fl. oz / ⅔ cup soured cream
175g / 6 oz / ¾ cup caster (superfine) sugar
2 large eggs
1 egg yolk
2 tbsp plain (all purpose) flour
2 tbsp cocoa powder, plus extra for dusting
200 g / 7 oz dark chocolate (minimum 60 % cocoa solids), melted

Chocolate and Mint Truffle Loaf Cake

306

- Add 2 teaspoons of peppermint essence to the truffle mix for a subtle mint flavour.

Chocolate and Date Squares

PREPARATION TIME 10 MINUTES

COOKING TIME 30-35 MINUTES

INGREDIENTS

150 g / 6 oz / 1 cup self-raising flour
28 g / 1 oz / ¼ cup unsweetened cocoa powder
2 tsp baking powder
175 g / 6 oz / ¾ cup caster (superfine) sugar
175 g / 6 oz / ¾ cup butter
3 eggs
100 g / 3 ½ oz / ½ cup dates, stoned and chopped

- Preheat the oven to 180°C (160° fan), 355F, gas 4 and grease and line a square cake tin.
- Put all of the cake ingredients in a large mixing bowl and whisk them together with an electric whisk for 4 minutes or until pale and well whipped. Fold in the dates.
- Scrape the mixture into the tin and level the top with a spatula.
- Bake for 30 - 35 minutes. The cake is ready when a toothpick inserted in the centre comes out clean.
- Transfer the cake to a wire rack to cool completely before cutting into squares.

Chocolate, Raisin and Sultana Squares

- Instead of the dates use half raisins and half sultanas for a different twist to this chocolate cake.

Raspberry and Coconut Cake

PREPARATION TIME 5 MINUTES

COOKING TIME 45-55 MINUTES

INGREDIENTS

225 g / 8 oz / 1 cup butter, softened
225 g / 8 oz / 1 cup caster (superfine) sugar
4 large eggs, beaten
225 g/ 4 ½ oz / 1 ½ cups self-raising flour
100 g / 3 ½ oz / 1 cup desiccated coconut
150 g / 5 ½ oz / 1 cup raspberries
3 tbsp toasted coconut flakes

- Preheat the oven to 180°C (160° fan), 355F, gas 4 and grease and line a 23 cm round cake tin with greaseproof paper.
- Cream the butter and sugar together until well whipped then gradually whisk in the eggs, beating well after each addition.
- Fold in the flour, desiccated coconut and raspberries then scrape the mixture into the tin. Sprinkle over the coconut flakes.
- Bake the cakefor 45 - 55 minutes or until a skewer inserted in the centre comes out clean.
- Transfer the cake to a wire rack and leave to cool.

Blueberry and Coconut Cake

- Out of season you can use blueberries instead of raspberries which are equally delicious in this coconut cake.

311

SERVES 8

Coconut, Pineapple and Kiwi Loaf Cake

Coconut, Mango and Banana Loaf Cake

312

- Chop two bananas and substitute them for the pineapple in the cake mix. Dice half a mango into 1 cm chunks to decorate.

Coconut, Pineapple and Chocolate Loaf Cake

313

- When decorating the cake gently melt 150 g/ 6 oz of dark chocolate and drizzle over the cake then sprinkle with the dessicated coconut.

PREPARATION TIME 30 MINUTES

COOKING TIME 45-50 MINUTES

....

INGREDIENTS

150 g / 6 oz / 1 cup plain (all purpose) flour
28 g / 1 oz / ¼ cup desiccated coconut
2 tsp baking powder
175 g / 6 oz / ¾ cup caster (superfine) sugar
175 g / 6 oz / ¾ cup butter
3 large eggs

FOR THE CRÈME PATISSERIE
4 large egg yolks
75 g / 2 ½ oz / ⅓ cup caster (superfine) sugar
1 tsp vanilla extract
2 tsp cornflour
450 ml / 16 fl. oz / 1 ¾ cups whole milk
1 can pineapple chunks, drained

TO DECORATE
2 tbsp desiccated coconut, toasted
1 kiwi, sliced

- Preheat the oven to 180°C (160° fan), 355F, gas 4 and grease and line a loaf tin with greaseproof paper.
- Whisk together all of the cake ingredients with an electric whisk for 4 minutes or until well whipped.
- Scrape the mixture into the tin and bake for 45 - 50 minutes.
- The cake is ready when a toothpick inserted comes out clean.
- Transfer the cake to a wire rack to cool completely before cutting in half horizontally.
- To make the crème patisserie, whisk together the egg yolks, sugar, vanilla extract and cornflour.
- Heat the milk almost to a simmer then strain it through a sieve and gradually whisk it into the egg mixture.
- Scrape the custard back into the saucepan and cook over a medium heat until it thickens, stirring constantly.
- Pour it into a bowl and stir in the pineapple then leave it to cool to room temperature.
- Beat the crème patisserie until smooth and use it to sandwich the cake back together.
- Sprinkle the cake with toasted coconut and arrange the kiwi slices on top.

Coffee and Walnut Sponge

314

SERVES 12

PREPARATION TIME 10 MINUTES

COOKING TIME 35-40 MINUTES

INGREDIENTS

200 g / 7 oz / 1 ⅓ cups self-raising flour
200 g / 7 oz / ¾ cup caster (superfine) sugar
200 g / 7 oz / ¾ cup butter
4 eggs
1 tsp baking powder
1 tbsp instant espresso powder
75 g / 2 ½ oz / ⅔ cup walnuts, finely chopped

TO DECORATE

200 g / 7 oz / ¾ cup butter, softened
400 g / 14 oz / 4 cups icing (confectioners) sugar
1 tbsp instant espresso powder
75 g / 2 ½ oz / ⅔ cup walnuts, chopped

- Preheat the oven to 180°C (160° fan), 355F, gas 4 and grease a 2 x 20 cm round loose-bottomed cake tins.
- Put all of the cake ingredients in a large mixing bowl and whisk them together with an electric whisk for 4 minutes or until pale and well whipped.
- Divide the mixture between the 2 tins and bake for 35 – 40 minutes. The cakes are ready when a toothpick inserted in the centre comes out clean.
- Transfer the cakes to a wire rack to cool completely.
- To make the buttercream, whisk the butter with an electric whisk then gradually add the icing (confectioners) sugar and espresso powder. Whisk until smooth.
- Use half of the buttercream to sandwich the 2 cakes together and spread the rest over the top.
- Sprinkle with the chopped walnuts before serving.

Coffee, Chocolate and Walnut Sponge

 315

- When making the buttercream icing add 1 teaspoon of cocoa powder for a subtle chocolate undertone to the cake frostin

Coffee and Chocolate Loaf Cake

316

SERVES 8

PREPARATION TIME 15 MINUTES

COOKING TIME 45 MINUTES

INGREDIENTS

225 g / 8 oz / 1 cup butter, softened
225 g / 8 oz / 1 cup caster (superfine) sugar
4 large eggs, beaten
225 g / 8 oz / 1 ½ cups self-raising flour
2 tbsp unsweetened cocoa powder
1 tbsp instant espresso powder
100 g / 3 ½ oz milk chocolate, grated

FOR THE ICING

200 g / 7 oz / 2 cups icing (confectioners) sugar
1 tbsp instant espresso powder

- Preheat the oven to 180°C (160° fan), 355F, gas 4 and grease and line a loaf tin with greaseproof paper.
- Cream together the butter and sugar until well whipped then gradually whisk in the eggs, beating well after each addition.
- Sift over the flour and cocoa powder and fold in with the espresso powder and grated chocolate.
- Scrape the mixture into the tin and bake for 45 minutes or until a skewer inserted in the centre comes out clean.
- Turn the loaf out onto a wire rack and leave to cool.
- Mix the icing (confectioners) sugar with the espresso powder and stir in enough hot water, drop by drop, to produce a thick, spreadable icing.
- Spoon the icing onto the cake and spread over the top with a palette knife.

Coffee, Chocolate and Coconut Loaf Cake

317

- Add 2 tablespoons of dessicated coconut to the cake batter and sprinkle the same amount on top of the cake after icing.

318

MAKES 6

Coffee Buttercream Tartlets

- Preheat the oven to 200°C (180° fan), 390F, gas 6.
- To make the pastry, rub the butter into the flour until the mixture resembles fine breadcrumbs.
- Stir in the sugar and espresso powder and add enough cold water to bring the pastry together into a dough.
- Chill the dough for 30 minutes then roll out on a floured surface. Use the pastry to line 6 tartlet cases.
- Prick the pastry with a fork, line with clingfilm and fill with baking beans or rice.
- Bake for 10 minutes then remove the clingfilm and baking beans.
- Whisk together the frangipane ingredients until smoothly whipped. Spoon the mixture into the pastry cases and bake for 15 minutes. Leave to cool completely.
- To make the buttercream, whisk the butter with an electric whisk then gradually add the icing (confectioners) sugar and espresso powder. Whisk until smooth then add the milk and whisk for 2 more minutes.
- Pipe the buttercream onto the tartlets and top with chocolate balls and dusted cocoa.

PREPARATION TIME 45 MINUTES

COOKING TIME 25 MINUTES

INGREDIENTS

FOR THE PASTRY

200g / 7 oz / 1 ⅓ cups plain flour
100g / 3 ½ oz / ½ cup butter, cubed
50g / 1 ¾ oz / ¼ cup dark brown sugar
1 tsp instant espresso powder

FOR THE COFFEE FRANGIPANE

150g / 5 ½ oz / 1 ½ cups ground almonds
150g / 5 ½ oz / ⅔ cup butter, softened
150g / 5 ½ oz / ⅔ cup caster sugar
2 large eggs
2 tbsp plain (all purpose) flour
1 tbsp instant espresso powder

FOR THE BUTTERCREAM

200 g / 7 oz / ¾ cup butter, softened
400 g / 14 oz / 4 cups icing sugar
1 tbsp instant espresso powder
2 tbsp milk
2 tbsp chocolate balls
1 tsp cocoa powder

319

MAKES 12

Redcurrant and Candyfloss Cupcakes

- Preheat the oven to 190°C (170° fan) / 375F / gas 5 and oil 12 silicone cupcake cases.
- Combine the flour, sugar, butter and eggsin a bowl and whisk together for 2 minutes or until smooth. Fold in the redcurrants.
- Divide the mixture between the cupcake cases, then transfer to the oven and bake for 15 – 20 minutes.
- Test with a wooden toothpick, if it comes out clean, the cakes are done.
- Transfer the cakes to a wire rack and leave to cool completely.
- Top the cakes with the candyfloss and a sprig of redcurrants and serve immediately. If there is a lot of moisture in the air, the candyfloss will start to dissolve quite quickly.

PREPARATION TIME 25 MINUTES

COOKING TIME 15-20 MINUTES

INGREDIENTS

100 g / 3 ½ oz / ⅔ cup self-raising flour, sifted
100 g / 3 ½ oz / ½ cup caster (superfine) sugar
100 g / 3 ½ oz / ½ cup butter, softened
3 large eggs
100 g / 3 ½ oz / ⅔ cup redcurrants

TO DECORATE

50 g / 1 ¾ oz / 2 ½ cups candyfloss
12 sprigs redcurrants

320

Raspberry and Candyfloss Cupcakes

- Use 100g/ 3 _ oz of raspberries in place of the redcurrants for an extra sweet flavour to these cute cupcakes.

321

SERVES 8

Almond Meringue with Chocolate and Nuts

Fruit and Nut Meringue with Chocolate

 322

- Swap the hazelnuts (cob nuts) for a mix of raisins and sultanas for a tasty fruit and nut taste, combined with the chocolate this meringue is truly delicious.

Almond Meringue with Coffee and Chocolate

 323

- Add 2 tablespoons of espresso to the ganache mixture for a sharper tasting filling.

Almond Meringue with Fruit

 324

- Try changing the nuts for the same quantity of dried fruit instead.

PREPARATION TIME 20 MINUTES

COOKING TIME 15 MINUTES

INGREDIENTS

4 large egg whites
a pinch cream of tartar
200 g / 7 oz / ¾ cup caster (superfine) sugar
200 g / 7 oz / 2 cups ground almonds

FOR THE GANACHE
200 ml / 7 fl. oz / ¾ cup double cream
200 g / 7 oz dark chocolate (minimum 60 % cocoa solids), chopped

FOR THE CARAMELISED NUTS
100 g / 3 ½ oz / ½ cup caster (superfine) sugar
75 g / 2 ½ oz / ⅔ cup pistachio nuts
75 g / 2 ½ oz / ⅔ cup blanched almonds
75 g / 2 ½ oz / ⅔ cup toasted hazelnuts (cob nuts), chopped

- Preheat the oven to 180ºC (160º fan), 355F, gas 4 and line a Swiss roll tin with non-stick baking paper.
- Whisk the egg whites with the cream of tartar until stiff then whisk in the caster (superfine) sugar a tablespoon at a time.
- Fold in the ground almonds then spread the mixture onto the Swiss roll tray in an even layer.
- Bake for 15 minutes then leave to cool completely.
- Bring the cream to simmering point then pour it over the chocolate. Stir until smooth then leave to cool and thicken to a pipable consistency.
- Put the sugar in a heavy-bottomed saucepan and heat gently, without stirring, until it starts to melt round the edges. Continue to cook, swirling the pan occasionally, until the sugar has all dissolved and the caramel is golden.
- Spread the nuts out on a baking tray lined with a non-stick baking mat and drizzle the caramel all over the top. Leave to cool then break it up with your fingers.
- Pipe the ganache on top of the meringue and sprinkle with the caramelised nuts.

325

SERVES 8

Apple Crumble One Crust Pie

- Preheat the oven to 200°C (180° fan), 390F, gas 6.
- First make the pastry. Sieve the flour into a mixing bowl then rub in the butter until the mixture resembles fine breadcrumbs.
- Stir in just enough cold water to bring the pastry together into a pliable dough then chill for 30 minutes.
- Mix the chopped apple with the sugar and cornflour.
- Roll out the pastry on a floured surface into a large circle. Prick it with a fork and transfer to a tray.
- Spoon the apples into a pile in the middle.
- To make the crumble topping, rub the butter into the flour then stir in the almonds and brown sugar.
- Take handfuls of the topping and squeeze it into a clump, then crumble it over the apples.
- Fold up the pastry edges and pinch to secure. Bake the tart for 35 – 40 minutes until golden brown.

PREPARATION TIME 50 MINUTES

COOKING TIME 35-40 MINUTES

INGREDIENTS

450 g / 1 lb bramley apples, peeled and chopped
50 g / 1 ¾ oz / ¼ cup caster (superfine) sugar
1 tbsp cornflour

FOR THE PASTRY
200 g / 7 oz / 1 ⅓ cups plain (all purpose) flour
100 g / 3 ½ oz / ½ cup butter, cubed and chilled

FOR THE CRUMBLE
150g / 5 oz / ⅔ cup butter
100g / 3 ½ oz / ⅔ cup plain (all purpose) flour
50g / 1 ¾ oz / ½ cup ground almonds
75g / 2 ½ oz / ½ cup light brown sugar

Apricot Crumble One Crust Pie   326

- This crumble works well with fresh apricots, instead of the apples. Be sure to halve and stone the apricots before using in the above recipe as you would the apples.

327

MAKES 12

Mini Apricot Loaf Cakes

- Preheat the oven to 190°C (170° fan), 375F, gas 5 and oil a 12-hole silicone mini loaf cake mould.
- Combine the flour, sugar, butter, eggs and vanilla in a bowl and whisk together for 2 minutes or until smooth. Fold in the chopped apricots.
- Divide the mixture between the moulds, then transfer the mould to the oven and bake for 15 – 20 minutes.
- Test with a wooden toothpick, if it comes out clean, the cakes are done.
- Transfer the cakes to a wire rack and leave to cool completely.

PREPARATION TIME 10 MINUTES

COOKING TIME 15-20 MINUTES

INGREDIENTS

110 g / 4 oz / ⅔ cup self-raising flour, sifted
110 g / 4 oz / ½ cup caster (superfine) sugar
110 g / 4 oz / ½ cup butter, softened
2 large eggs
1 tsp vanilla extract
75 g / 2 ½ oz / ⅓ cup dried apricots, chopped

Date Mini Loaf Cakes   328

- For a richer slightly darker looking loaf cake use chopped dates instead of the apricots.

329

MAKES 12

Fig and Honey Muffins

PREPARATION TIME 25 MINUTES

COOKING TIME 20-25 MINUTES

INGREDIENTS

1 large egg
120 ml / 4 fl. oz / ½ cup sunflower oil
120 ml / 4 fl. oz / ½ cup milk
100 g / 3 ½ oz / ⅓ cup runny honey
375 g / 12 ½ oz / 2 ½ cups self-raising flour, sifted
1 tsp baking powder
100 g / 3 ½ oz / ½ cup caster (superfine) sugar
4 fresh figs, chopped

- Preheat the oven to 180°C (160° fan), gas 4 and line a 12-hole muffin tin with greaseproof paper.
- Beat the egg in a jug with the oil, milk and honey until well mixed.
- Mix the flour, baking powder, and sugar in a bowl.
- Pour in the egg mixture and stir just enough to combine then fold in the figs.
- Divide the mixture between the paper cases and bake for 20 – 25 minutes.
- Test with a wooden toothpick, if it comes out clean, the cakes are done.
- Transfer the muffins to a wire rack and leave to cool completely.

Date and Maple Syrup Muffins

 330

- Use 6 chopped figs and maple syrup instead of the honey for a delicious, rich tasting muffin.

331

MAKES 12

Orange Flower Financiers

PREPARATION TIME 30 MINUTES

COOKING TIME 10-15 MINUTES

INGREDIENTS

110 g / 4 oz / ½ cup butter
55 g / 2 oz / ⅓ cup plain (all purpose) flour
55 g / 2 oz / ½ cup ground almonds
110 g / 4 oz / 1 cup icing (confectioners) sugar
3 large egg whites
1 tsp orange flower water

- Preheat the oven to 170°C (150° fan), 325F, gas 3 and oil and flour a 12-hole financier mould.
- Heat the butter until it foams and starts to smell nutty then leave to cool.
- Combine the flour, ground almonds and icing (confectioners) sugar in a bowl and whisk in the eggs whites and orange flower water.
- Pour the cooled butter through a sieve into the bowl and whisk into the mixture until evenly mixed.
- Spoon the mixture into the moulds, then transfer the tin to the oven and bake for 10 – 15 minutes.
- Test with a wooden toothpick, if it comes out clean, the cakes are done.
- Transfer the cakes to a wire rack to cool for 5 minutes before serving.

Rose Water Financiers

 332

- These delicious financiers work well with rose water for a delicate floral taste use 1 teaspoon.

Fig and Raspberry Loaf Cake

Fig and Date Loaf

 334

- For a denser but equally tasty loaf use dates roughly chopped instead of the raspberries.

Fig, Raspberry and Vanilla Loaf

335

- Take 1 vanilla pod, split and scrape the seeds into the batter mix for a fuller tasting loaf cake.

PREPARATION TIME 10 MINUTES

COOKING TIME 55 MINUTES

INGREDIENTS

300 g / 10 ½ oz / 2 cups self-raising flour
2 tsp baking powder
250 g / 9 oz / 1 ¼ cups caster (superfine) sugar
250 g / 9 oz / 1 ¼ cups butter, softened
5 large eggs
75 g / 2 ½ oz / ½ cup raspberries
4 fresh figs, sliced

- Preheat the oven to 170°C (150° fan), 340F, gas 3 and line a loaf tin with greaseproof paper.
- Sieve the flour and baking powder into a mixing bowl and add the sugar, butter and eggs.
- Beat the mixture with an electric whisk for 4 minutes or until smooth and well whipped.
- Fold in the raspberries and figs and scrape the mixture into the loaf tin.
- Bake for 55 minutes or until a skewer inserted comes out clean.
- Transfer the cake to a wire rack and leave to cool completely.

336

SERVES 12

Apricot, Chocolate and Almond Tart

PREPARATION TIME 30 MINUTES

COOKING TIME 35 MINUTES

....

INGREDIENTS

225 g / 8 oz / 2 ¼ cups ground almonds
225 g / 8 oz / 1 cup butter, softened
225 g / 8 oz / 1 cup caster (superfine) sugar
3 large eggs
2 tbsp unsweetened cocoa powder, plus extra for dusting
75 g / 2 ½ oz milk chocolate, grated
3 tbsp plain (all purpose) flour
8 apricots, stoned and halved

FOR THE PASTRY

200 g / 7 oz / 1 ⅓ cups plain (all purpose) flour
100 g / 3 ½ oz / ½ cup butter, cubed and chilled
1 egg, beaten
2 tbsp caster (superfine) sugar

- Sieve the flour into a mixing bowl then rub in the butter until the mixture resembles fine breadcrumbs.
- Stir in just enough cold water to bring the pastry together into a pliable dough then chill for 30 minutes.
- Preheat the oven to 200°C (180° fan), 390F, gas 6.
- Roll out the pastry on a floured surface and use it to line a 23 cm round tart case.
- Prick the pastry with a fork, line with clingfilm and fill with baking beans or rice. Bake for 10 minutes then remove the clingfilm and baking beans.
- Whisk together the almonds, butter, sugar, eggs, cocoa, chocolate and flour until smoothly whipped and spoon the mixture into the pastry case.
- Dust over a little extra cocoa powder then press the apricots into the frangipane.
- Bake the tart for 25 minutes.

Apricot, Chocolate, Almond and Rum Tart

337

- Add 1-2 tablespoons of brandy to the tart filling mix for a warm tasting, extra decadent tasting filling.

338

SERVES 8-10

Peach and Ricotta Pie

PREPARATION TIME 25 MINUTES

COOKING TIME 40-45 MINUTES

....

INGREDIENTS

250 g / 9 oz / 1 ¼ cups butter, cubed
250 g / 9 oz / 1 ⅔ cups plain (all purpose) flour
250 g / 9 oz / 1 ¼ cups caster (superfine) sugar
6 large egg yolks

FOR THE FILLING

450 g / 1 lb / 2 cups ricotta
100 g / 3 ½ oz / 1 cup icing (confectioners) sugar
4 ripe peaches, skinned, stoned and chopped

- Preheat the oven to 180°C (160° fan), gas 4 and butter a 23 cm round spring-form cake tin.
- Rub the butter into the flour with a pinch of salt then stir in the sugar.
- Beat 5 of the egg yolks and stir them into the dry ingredients. Bring the mixture together into a soft dough and divide it in two.
- Press one half into the bottom and up the sides of the cake tin to form an even layer.
- Beat the ricotta with the icing (confectioners) sugar until smooth then fold in the peaches and spoon it into the tin.
- Roll out the other half of the dough between 2 sheets of greaseproof paper then peel away the paper and lay it on top of the ricotta. Press around the edges to seal.
- Brush the top of the pie with the final egg yolk then bake for 40 – 45 minutes.

Apricot and Ricotta Pie

339

- Use 6 Apricots stoned and halved or quartered if desired instead of the peaches for a delicious twist on this ricotta pie.

Banana and Dried Fruit Loaf Cake

340

SERVES 8

- Preheat the oven to 170°C (150° fan), gas 3 and line a long thin loaf tin with non-stick baking paper.
- Mash the bananas roughly with a fork then whisk in the sugar, eggs and oil.
- Sieve the flour and bicarbonate of soda into the bowl and add the dried fruit. Stir just enough to evenly mix all the ingredients together.
- Scrape the mixture into the loaf tin and bake for 55 minutes or until a skewer inserted in the centre comes out clean.
- Transfer the cake to a wire rack and leave to cool completely.

PREPARATION TIME 10 MINUTES

COOKING TIME 55 MINUTES

INGREDIENTS

3 very ripe bananas
110 g / 4 oz / ½ cup soft light brown sugar
2 large eggs
120 ml / 4 fl. oz / ½ cup sunflower oil
225 g / 8 oz / 1 ½ cups plain (all purpose) flour
1 tsp bicarbonate of soda
75 g / 2 ½ oz / ⅓ cup sultanas
75 g / 2 ½ oz / ⅓ cup prunes, stoned and chopped
75 g / 2 ½ oz / ⅓ cup dates, stoned and chopped

Banana and Double Chocolate Loaf Cake

341

- Instead of the dried fruit use 200g/7 oz of mixed chocolate chip chunks for a rich chocolate taste to this delicious loaf cake.

Dundee Loaf Cake

342

SERVES 10

- Mix the dried fruit and cherries together and pour over the whisky. Leave to macerate overnight.
- Preheat the oven to 150°C (130° fan), 300F, gas 2 and grease and line a loaf tin with greaseproof paper.
- Cream the butter, treacle and sugar together until well whipped then gradually whisk in the eggs, beating well after each addition.
- Sift over the flour and spice and fold in with the ground almonds and dried fruit.
- Scrape the mixture into the tin and arrange the cherries, walnuts and Brazil nuts on top
- Bake for 1 hour 45 minutes or until a skewer inserted in the centre comes out clean.
- Turn the loaf out onto a wire rack and leave to cool.
- Heat the apricot jam and whisky together until runny then brush it over the cake to glaze.

PREPARATION TIME OVERNIGHT

COOKING TIME 1 HOUR 45 MINUTES

INGREDIENTS

350 g / 12 oz / 1 ¾ cups mixed dried fruit
55 g / 2 oz / ¼ cup glace cherries, quartered
55 ml / 2 fl. oz / ¼ cup whisky
110 g / 4 oz / ½ cup butter, softened
2 tbsp treacle
110 g / 4 oz / ½ cup dark brown sugar
2 large eggs, beaten
55 g / 2 oz / ⅓ cup self-raising flour
2 tsp mixed spice
1 tbsp ground almonds

TO DECORATE

7 glace cherries
6 walnut halves
3 Brazil nuts
4 tbsp apricot jam
1 tbsp whisky

Spiced Dundee Cake

343

- Add 2 teaspoons of mixed spice to the cake mix for a festive twist to this classic cake.

344

MAKES 1

Sweet Cinnamon Nut Bread

Cinnamon and Chocolate Bread

345

- Instead of the hazelnuts (cob nuts) sprinkle dark chocolate chips onto the bread 10 minutes before the end of the baking time.

Mixed Spice Nut Bread

346

- For a more festive flavour to this delicious bread use mixed spice instead of cinnamon.

PREPARATION TIME 2 HOURS 30 MINUTES

COOKING TIME 25-35 MINUTES

INGREDIENTS

250 g / 9 oz / 1 ¼ cups butter, cubed
200 g / 7 oz / 1 ⅓ cups strong white bread flour
200 g / 7 oz / 1 ⅓ cups stoneground wholemeal flour
2 ½ tsp easy blend dried yeast
4 tbsp caster (superfine) sugar
1 tsp fine sea salt
4 large eggs, plus 3 extra yolks
100 g / 3 ½ oz / ½ cup soft brown sugar
3 tsp ground cinnamon
75 g / 2 ½ oz / ⅔ cup hazelnuts (cob nuts), chopped

- Rub half the butter into the flour then stir in the yeast, sugar and salt. Beat the whole eggs and yolks together and stir into the dry ingredients.

- Knead the very soft dough on a lightly oiled surface with 2 plastic scrapers for 10 minutes or until smooth and elastic.

- Leave the dough to rest in a lightly oiled bowl, covered with oiled clingfilm, for 2 hours or until doubled in size.

- Roll out the dough as big as possible on a floured surface.

- Cream the rest of the butter with the brown sugar and cinnamon and spread ¾ of it over the dough.

- Roll the dough up tightly and transfer to a greased baking tray.

- Cover with oiled clingfilm and leave to prove for 2 hours or until doubled in size.

- Meanwhile, preheat the oven to 220°C (200° fan), 430F, gas 7.

- Brush the top of the loaf with the reserved cinnamon mixture and make a few slashes across with a knife.

- Sprinkle with hazelnuts (cob nuts) and bake for 25 – 35 minutes or until golden brown.

SERVES 8 347

Light Orange and Fruit Cake

- Preheat the oven to 180°C (160° fan), 355F, gas 4 and line a loaf tin with non-stick baking paper.
- Sieve the flour into a mixing bowl and rub in the butter until it resembles fine breadcrumbs then stir in the sugar, sultanas, candied peel, cherries and orange zest.
- Lightly beat the egg with the milk and stir it into the dry ingredients until just combined.
- Scrape the mixture into the loaf tin and bake for 55 minutes or until a skewer inserted in the centre comes out clean.
- Transfer the cake to a wire rack and leave to cool completely.

PREPARATION TIME 15 MINUTES

COOKING TIME 55 MINUTES

INGREDIENTS

225 g / 8 oz / 1 ½ cups self raising flour
100 g / 3 ½ oz / ½ cup butter, cubed
100 g / 3 ½ oz / ½ cup caster (superfine) sugar
100 g / 3 ½ oz / ½ cup sultanas
150 g / 5 ½ oz / ¾ cup candied orange peel, chopped
100 g / 3 ½ oz / ½ cup glace cherries, halved
1 orange zest finely grated
1 large egg
75 ml / 2 ½ fl. oz / ⅓ cup whole milk

Light Orange and Whisky Fruit Cake 348

- After baking the cake drizzle whilst warm 2 tablespoons of whisky on top. Pierce the cake with a skewer to allow the whisky to absorb.

MAKES 12 349

Banana Party Cupcakes

- Preheat the oven to 190°C (170° fan), 375F, gas 5 and line a 12-hole cupcake tin with paper cases.
- Combine the flour, sugar, butter, eggs and banana in a bowl and whisk together for 2 minutes or until smooth.
- Divide the mixture between the paper cases, then transfer the tin to the oven and bake for 15 – 20 minutes.
- Test with a wooden toothpick, if it comes out clean, the cakes are done.
- Transfer the cakes to a wire rack and leave to cool completely.
- To make the icing, mix the icing (confectioners) sugar with the banana syrup and food colouring, adding a few drops of water if the icing is too stiff.
- Spoon the icing over the cakes and sprinkle each one with hundreds and thousands or sugar stars.

PREPARATION TIME 1 HOUR

COOKING TIME 15-20 MINUTES

INGREDIENTS

110 g / 4 oz / ⅔ cup self-raising flour, sifted
110 g / 4 oz / ½ cup caster (superfine) sugar
110 g / 4 oz / ½ cup butter, softened
2 large eggs
1 banana, chopped
225 g / 8 oz / 2 ¼ cups icing (confectioners) sugar
1 tbsp banana flavoured syrup
a few drops yellow food colouring
hundreds and thousands and sugar stars

Banana and Chocolate Cupcakes 350

- Stir through 55g/2 oz of chocolate chips into the cake batter mixture.

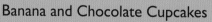

351

SERVES 8

Apple and Rosemary Tarte Tatin

PREPARATION TIME 10 MINUTES

COOKING TIME 20-25 MINUTES

INGREDIENTS

2 tbsp butter
2 tbsp dark brown sugar
6 small apples, peeled, cored and halved
2 tbsp rosemary leaves
250 g / 9 oz all-butter puff pastry
2 tbsp flaked (slivered) almonds

- Preheat the oven to 220°C (200° fan), 430F, gas 7.
- Heat the butter and sugar in an ovenproof frying pan and add the apples and rosemary. Cook over a very low heat for 5 minutes, turning occasionally, until they start to colour and soften.
- Arrange the apples, cut side up and leave to cool a little.
- Roll out the pastry on a floured surface and cut out a circle the same size as the frying pan.
- Lay the pastry over the apples and tuck in the edges, then transfer the pan to the oven and bake for 25 minutes or until the pastry is golden brown and cooked through.
- Using oven gloves, put a large plate on top of the frying pan and turn them both over in one smooth movement to unmold the tart.
- Scatter over the flaked (slivered) almonds and serve immediately.

352

MAKES 12

Vanilla Sponge Rings

PREPARATION TIME 30 MINUTES

COOKING TIME 10-15 MINUTES

INGREDIENTS

110 g / 4 oz butter
55 g / 2 oz / ⅓ cup plain (all purpose) flour
55 g / 2 oz / ½ cup ground almonds
110 g / 4 oz / 1 cup icing (confectioners) sugar
3 large egg whites
1 vanilla pod, seeds only

- Preheat the oven to 170°C (150° fan), 325F, gas 3 and oil and flour 12 mini ring moulds.
- Heat the butter until it foams and starts to smell nutty then leave to cool.
- Combine the flour, ground almonds and icing (confectioners) sugar in a bowl and whisk in the eggs whites and vanilla seeds.
- Pour the cooled butter through a sieve into the bowl and whisk into the mixture until evenly mixed.
- Spoon the mixture into the moulds, then transfer the tin to the oven and bake for 10 – 15 minutes.
- Test with a wooden toothpick, if it comes out clean, the cakes are done.
- Transfer the cakes to a wire rack to cool for 5 minutes before serving.

353

MAKES 12 Chocolate and Walnut Sponge Squares

- Preheat the oven to 180°C (160° fan), 355F, gas 4 and grease and line a 30 cm x 23 cm cake tin.
- Put all of the ingredients except the walnuts in a large mixing bowl and whisk them together with an electric whisk for 4 minutes or until pale and well whipped.
- Scrape the mixture into the tin and level the top with a spatula then sprinkle over the walnuts.
- Bake for 30 - 35 minutes. The cake is ready when a toothpick inserted comes out clean.
- Transfer the cake to a wire rack to cool completely before cutting into 12 squares and dusting with cocoa.

PREPARATION TIME 10 MINUTES

COOKING TIME 30-35 MINUTES

INGREDIENTS

150 g / 6 oz / 1 cup self-raising flour
28 g / 1 oz / ¼ cup unsweetened cocoa powder, plus extra for dusting
2 tsp baking powder
175 g / 6 oz / ¾ cup caster sugar
175 g / 6 oz / ¾ cup butter
3 eggs
100 g / 3 ½ oz / ⅓ cup walnuts, chopped

354

Hazelnut Madeleines

MAKES 12

PREPARATION TIME 1 HOUR 30 MINUTES

COOKING TIME 10-15 MINS

INGREDIENTS

110 g / 4 oz / ½ cup butter
55 g / 2 oz / ⅓ cup plain flour
55 g / 2 oz / ½ cup ground hazelnuts (cob nuts)
110 g / 4 oz / 1 cup icing (confectioners) sugar
3 large egg whites

- Heat the butter until it foams and starts to smell nutty then leave to cool.
- Combine the flour, ground hazelnuts (cob nuts) and icing (confectioners) sugar in a bowl and whisk in the eggs whites.
- Pour the cooled butter through a sieve into the bowl and whisk into the mixture until evenly mixed.
- Leave the cake mixture to rest in the fridge for an hour.
- Preheat the oven to 170°C (150° fan), 325F, gas 3 and oil and flour a 12-hole Madeleine mould.
- Spoon the mixture into the moulds, then transfer the tin to the oven and bake for 10 – 15 minutes.
- Test with a wooden toothpick, if it comes out clean, the cakes are done.
- Transfer the cakes to a wire rack to cool for 5 minutes before serving.

355

Bundt Cake

SERVES 8-10

PREPARATION TIME 5 MINUTES

COOKING TIME 45 MINUTES

INGREDIENTS

225 g / 8 oz / 1 cup butter, softened
225 g / 8 oz / 1 cup caster (superfine) sugar
4 large eggs, beaten
125 g/ 4 ½ oz / ¾ cup self-raising flour

- Preheat the oven to 180°C (160° fan), 355F, gas 4 and butter a bundt tin.
- Cream the butter and sugar together until well whipped then gradually whisk in the eggs, beating well after each addition.
- Fold in the flour then scrape the mixture into the tin.
- Bake the cakefor 45 minutes or until a skewer inserted comes out clean.
- Turn the cake out onto a wire rack and leave to cool.

356

MAKES 6

Cherry Frangipane Cakes

PREPARATION TIME 20 MINUTES

COOKING TIME 20-25 MINUTES

INGREDIENTS

55 g / 2 oz / ⅓ cup self-raising flour, sifted
55 g / 2 oz / ½ cup ground almonds
110 g / 4 oz / ½ cup caster (superfine) sugar
110 g / 4 oz / ½ cup butter, softened
2 large eggs
1 tsp almond essence
350 g / 12 oz / 2 ⅓ cups fresh cherries
2 tbsp icing (confectioners) sugar

- Preheat the oven to 190⁰C (170⁰ fan), 375F, gas 5 and oil a 6-hole silicone tartlet mould or 6 individual tartlet tins.
- Combine the flour, ground almonds, sugar, butter, eggs and almond essence in a bowl and whisk together for 2 minutes or until smooth.
- Divide the mixture between the moulds.
- Stone the cherries with a cherry pitter and press 6 or 7 into the top of each cake.
- Transfer the cakes to the oven and bake for 20 – 25 minutes.
- Test with a wooden toothpick, if it comes out clean, the cakes are done.
- Transfer the cakes to a wire rack to cool.
- Dust the top of the cakes with icing (confectioners) sugar just before serving.

Fig Frangipane Cakes

357

- Use 8 chopped fresh figs in exchange for the fresh cherries for an extra sweet frangipane cake.

358

SERVES 8

Kiwi Loaf Cake

PREPARATION TIME 10 MINUTES

COOKING TIME 55 MINUTES

INGREDIENTS

300 g / 10 ½ oz / 2 cups self-raising flour
2 tsp baking powder
250 g / 9 oz / 1 ¼ cups caster (superfine) sugar
250 g / 9 oz / 1 ¼ cups butter, softened
5 large eggs
4 kiwi fruit, peeled and cubed

- Preheat the oven to 170⁰C (150⁰ fan), 340F, gas 3 and line a large loaf tin with non-stick baking paper.
- Sieve the flour and baking powder into a mixing bowl and add the sugar, butter and eggs.
- Beat the mixture with an electric whisk for 4 minutes or until smooth and well whipped then fold in the kiwi fruit.
- Scrape the mixture into the loaf tin and bake for 55 minutes or until a skewer inserted in the centre comes out clean.
- Transfer the cake to a wire rack and leave to cool completely.

Kiwi and Banana Loaf Cake

359

- Use 2 kiwi fruit and 2 bananas for a tropical tasting loaf cake.

360

MAKES 6

Dried Fig Tartlets

Dried Fig and Lavender Honey Tartlets

361

- After baking drizzle the warm tarts with Lavender honey for an aromatic glossy finish to these delicious tartlets.

Dried Apricot Tartlets

362

- Use dried apricots instead of figs for a delicious twist on these beautiful tartlets.

PREPARATION TIME 45 MINUTES

COOKING TIME 40-50 MINUTES

....

INGREDIENTS

450 g / 1 lb / 2 ¼ cups dried figs, chopped,
plus a few extra for decorating
400 ml / 14 fl. oz / 1 ⅔ cups orange juice

FOR THE PASTRY
200g / 7 oz / 1 ⅓ cups plain (all purpose) flour
100g / 3 ½ oz / ½ cups butter, cubed
50g / 1 ¾ oz / ¼ cup caster (superfine) sugar

- To make the pastry, rub the butter into the flour until the mixture resembles fine breadcrumbs.
- Stir in the sugar and add enough cold water to bring the pastry together into a pliable dough.
- Chill the dough for 30 minutes.
- Meanwhile, put the figs in a saucepan with the orange juice and simmer for 20 – 30 minutes or until the figs are soft and the liquid has reduced to a syrupy consistency.
- Transfer the fig mixture to a food processor and puree.
- Preheat the oven to 200°C (180° fan), 390F, gas 6.
- Roll out the pastry on a floured surface and use it to line 6 tartlet cases.
- Prick the pastry with a fork, line with clingfilm and fill with baking beans or rice.
- Bake for 10 minutes then remove the clingfilm and baking beans.
- Return to the oven for 8 minutes to crisp.
- Spoon the fig puree into the pastry cases and return to the oven for 10 minutes.
- Serve the tarts hot or at room temperature, garnished with slices of dried fig.

363

SERVES 8

Kiwi and Custard Tart

PREPARATION TIME 40 MINUTES

COOKING TIME 25 MINUTES

....

INGREDIENTS

6 kiwi fruit, peeled and sliced

FOR THE PASTRY

200g / 7 oz / 1 ⅓ cups plain (all purpose) flour
100g / 3 ½ oz / ½ cup butter, cubed

FOR THE CUSTARD

4 large egg yolks
75 g / 2 ½ oz / ⅓ cup caster (superfine) sugar
1 tsp vanilla extract
2 tsp cornflour
450 ml / 16 fl. oz / 1 ¾ cups whole milk

- Preheat the oven to 200°C (180° fan), 390F, gas 6.
- Rub the butter into the flour and add just enough cold water to bind.
- Chill for 30 minutes then roll out on a floured surface. Use the pastry to line a 23 cm round loose-bottomed tart tin.
- Prick the pastry with a fork, line with clingfilm and fill with baking beans or rice.
- Bake for 10 minutes then remove the clingfilm and baking beans and cook for another 8 minutes to crisp.
- Reduce the oven temperature to 170°C (150° fan), 340F, gas 3.
- Whisk the custard ingredients together in a saucepan then stir over a low heat for 5 minutes.
- Pour the custard into the pastry case and leave to cool before arranging the kiwi fruit on top.

Mango and Custard Tart 364

- Substitute 6 kiwi fruit for 2 mangos and slice thinly arranging in a fan like shape around the tart.

365

SERVES 8

Lemon and Poppy Seed Loaf Cake

PREPARATION TIME 10 MINUTES

COOKING TIME 35-40 MINUTES

....

INGREDIENTS

150 g / 5 ½ oz / 1 cup self-raising flour
150 g / 5 ½ oz / ⅔ cup caster (superfine) sugar
150 g / 5 ½ oz / ⅔ cup butter
3 eggs
1 tsp baking powder
1 tbsp lemon zest
2 tbsp lemon juice
2 tbsp poppy seeds

TO DECORATE

candied lemon peel, thinly sliced

- Preheat the oven to 180°C (160° fan), 355F, gas 4 and grease and line a small loaf tin.
- Put all of the cake ingredients in a large mixing bowl and whisk them together with an electric whisk for 4 minutes or until pale and well whipped.
- Scrape the mixture into the tin and level the top with a spatula.
- Bake for 35 - 40 minutes. The cake is ready when a toothpick inserted in the centre comes out clean.
- Transfer the cake to a wire rack to cool completely before garnishing with the candied lemon peel.

St Clements and Poppy Seed Loaf 366

- Mix one tablespoon of orange with the lemon juice and add one tablespoon of orange zest to the recipe. Use candied orange and lemon peel to decorate for a less acidic tasting topping.

367

MAKES 12

Candied Lemon Sponge Squares

- Blanch the lemon slices in boiling water for 5 minutes then drain well.
- Put the sugar in a saucepan with 200 ml water and stir over a low heat until dissolved. Bring to the boil and simmer then add the lemon slices and simmer for 10 minutes.
- Remove from the pan with a slotted spoon and leave to drip dry on a wire rack.
- Preheat the oven to 180°C (160° fan), 355F, gas 4 and grease and line a 30 cm x 23 cm cake tin.
- Put all of the cake ingredients in a large mixing bowl and whisk them together with an electric whisk for 4 minutes or until pale and well whipped.
- Scrape the mixture into the tin and level the top with a spatula then arrange 9 of the lemon slices on top.
- Bake for 30 - 35 minutes. The cake is ready when a toothpick inserted comes out clean.

Candied Orange Sponge Squares
368

- For a slight twist on this delicious cake use orange slices instead of lemon.

PREPARATION TIME 30 MINUTES

COOKING TIME 40-45 MINUTES

INGREDIENTS

175 g / 6 oz / 1 ¼ cups self-raising flour
2 tsp baking powder
175 g / 6 oz / ¾ cups caster (superfine) sugar
175 g / 6 oz / ¾ cups butter
3 eggs
1 lemon, juice and zest

FOR THE CANDIED
LEMON SLICES
2 lemons, thinly sliced
400 g / 14 oz / 1 ¾ cups caster (superfine) sugar

369

SERVES 10

Iced Lemon Loaf Cake

- Preheat the oven to 180°C (160° fan), 355F, gas 4 and grease and line a small loaf tin.
- Put all of the cake ingredients in a large mixing bowl and whisk them together with an electric whisk for 4 minutes or until pale and well whipped.
- Scrape the mixture into the tin and level the top with a spatula.
- Bake for 35 - 40 minutes. The cake is ready when a toothpick inserted in the centre comes out clean.
- Transfer the cake to a wire rack to cool completely.
- Sieve the icing (confectioners) sugar and stir in just enough lemon juice to produce a pourable icing.
- Pour the icing all over the cake and allow it to drip down the sides. Garnish with twisted lemon slices.

Iced Lemon and
Lavender Loaf Cake
370

- Add two tablespoons of edible lavender flowers to the cake batter mix and sprinkle some extra onto the icing for decoration.

PREPARATION TIME 20 MINUTES

COOKING TIME 35-40 MINUTES

INGREDIENTS

150 g / 5 ½ oz / 1 cup self-raising flour
150 g / 5 ½ oz / ⅔ cup caster (superfine) sugar
150 g / 5 ½ oz / ⅔ cup butter
3 eggs
1 tsp baking powder
1 tbsp lemon zest
2 tbsp lemon juice

TO DECORATE
200 g / 7 oz / 2 cups icing (confectioners) sugar
1 – 2 tbsp lemon juice
lemon sliced

371

SERVES 8

Lemon Meringue Pie

Lemon and Lime Meringue Pie

372

- Use the juice and zest of 2 lemons and 2 limes and incorporate into the recipe as above for an extra sharp taste to this classic meringue pie.

Lemon and Coconut Meringue Pie

373

- Into the meringue mixture, stir through 3 tablespoons of dessicated coconut and follow recipe as above. Sprinkle a little more on top after baking.

PREPARATION TIME 55 MINUTES

COOKING TIME 25-30 MINUTES

INGREDIENTS

2 tsp cornflour
4 lemons, zest and juice
4 large eggs, beaten
225 g / 8 oz / 1 cup butter
175 g / 6 oz / ¾ cups caster (superfine) sugar

FOR THE PASTRY
100 g / 3 ½ oz / ½ cups butter, cubed
200 g / 7 oz / 1 ⅓ cups plain (all purpose) flour

FOR THE MERINGUE
4 large egg whites
110g / 4 oz / ½ cups caster (superfine) sugar

- Preheat the oven to 200°C (180° fan), 390F, gas 6.
- Rub the butter into the flour and add just enough cold water to bind.
- Chill for 30 minutes then roll out on a floured surface.
- Use the pastry to line a 24 cm loose-bottomed tart tin and prick it with a fork.
- Line the pastry with clingfilm and fill with baking beans or rice then bake for 10 minutes.
- Remove the clingfilm and beans and cook for another 8 minutes to crisp.
- Meanwhile, dissolve the cornflour in the lemon juice and put it in a saucepan with the rest of the ingredients.
- Stir constantly over a medium heat to melt the butter and dissolve the sugar. Bring to a gentle simmer then pour it into the pastry case.
- Whisk the egg whites until stiff, then gradually add the sugar and whisk until the mixture is thick and shiny.
- Spoon the meringue on top of the lemon curd, making peaks with the spoon.
- Bake for 10 minutes or until golden brown.

SERVES 8

Lemon and Almond Treacle Tart

- Preheat the oven to 200°C (180° fan), 390F, gas 6.
- First make the pastry. Sieve the flour into a mixing bowl then rub in the butter until the mixture resembles fine breadcrumbs.
- Stir in just enough cold water to bring the pastry together into a pliable dough then chill for 30 minutes.
- Heat the golden syrup with the lemon zest and juice until runny then stir in the breadcrumbs and almonds.
- Roll out the pastry on a floured surface and use it to line a 23 cm round pie dish.
- Spoon the filling into the pastry case and level the top.
- Bake for 25 – 30 minutes or until the pastry is cooked through underneath.

PREPARATION TIME 50 MINUTES

COOKING TIME 35-40 MINUTES

INGREDIENTS

350 g / 12 ½ oz / 1 cup golden syrup
2 lemons, zest and juice
100 g / 3 ½ oz / 1 ⅓ cups white breadcrumbs
75 g / 2 ½ oz / ¾ cups ground almonds

FOR THE PASTRY
200 g / 7 oz / 1 ⅓ cups plain (all purpose) flour
100 g / 3 ½ oz / ½ cup butter, cubed and chilled

Orange and Almond Treacle Tart
375

- Add the zest and juice of 1 large navel orange to the treacle tart filling for a sweeter taste.

376
MAKES 6

Orange Custard Tartlets

- To make the pastry, rub the butter into the flour and add just enough cold water to bind.
- Chill for 30 minutes.
- Preheat the oven to 200°C (180° fan), 390F, gas 6.
- Roll out the pastry on a floured surface and use it to line 6 tartlet cases, rerolling the trimmings as necessary.
- Prick the pastry with a fork, line with clingfilm and fill with baking beans or rice.
- Bake for 10 minutes then remove the clingfilm and baking beans.
- Whisk the custard ingredients together in a jug and ¾ fill the pastry cases.
- Bake the tarts for 15 – 20 minutes or until the custard has set and the pastry is crisp.

PREPARATION TIME 45 MINUTES

COOKING TIME 25-30 MINUTES

INGREDIENTS

FOR THE PASTRY
200g / 7 oz / 1 ⅓ cups plain (all purpose) flour
100g / 3 ½ oz / ½ cup butter, cubed

FOR THE CUSTARD
2 large egg yolks
55 g / 2 oz / ¼ cup caster (superfine) sugar
2 tsp cornflour
125 ml / 4 ½ fl. oz / ½ cup whole milk
100 ml / 3 ½ fl. oz / ½ cup fresh orange juice, sieved
1 tbsp orange zest, finely grated

Orange and Cinnamon Custard Tartlets

377

- Add _ a teaspoon of ground cinnamon to the custard mix for a warm winter spiced tartlet.

378

SERVES 8

Candied Lemon and Ginger Loaf Cake

PREPARATION TIME 30 MINUTES

COOKING TIME 50-55 MINUTES

....

INGREDIENTS

175 g / 6 oz / 1 ¼ cup self-raising
flour
2 tsp baking powder
175 g / 6 oz / ¾ cup caster (superfine)
sugar
175 g / 6 oz / ¾ cup butter
3 eggs
1 lemon, juice and zest
100 g / 3 ½ oz / ½ cup crystallised
ginger, finely chopped

FOR THE CANDIED LEMONS

3 lemons, quartered and thinly sliced
400 g / 14 oz / 1 ¾ cup caster
(superfine) sugar

- Blanch the lemon slices in boiling water for 5 minutes
  then drain well. Put the sugar in a saucepan with
  200 ml water and stir over a low heat until dissolved.
- Bring to the boil and simmer for 5 minutes then add
  the lemon slices and simmer for 10 minutes.
- Remove from the pan with a slotted spoon and leave to
  drip dry on a wire rack.
- Preheat the oven to 180⁰C (160⁰ fan), 355F, gas 4 and
  grease and line a loaf tin.
- Put all of the cake ingredients in a large mixing bowl
  and whisk them together with an electric whisk for
  4 minutes or until pale and well whipped. Fold in the
  candied lemon pieces.
- Scrape the mixture into the tin and level the top with
  a spatula then bake for 30 - 35 minutes.
- Transfer the cake to a wire rack to cool completely.

Candied Orange and Ginger Loaf Cake

379

- Use the zest and juice of one orange in place of the
  lemon in the cake mix. For the candied orange use
  2 oranges cut into six and thinly sliced.

380

SERVES 8

Wholemeal Raisin Loaf Cake

PREPARATION TIME 10 MINUTES

COOKING TIME 35-40 MINUTES

....

INGREDIENTS

100 g / 3 ½ oz / ⅔ cup stoneground
wholemeal flour
50 g / 1 ¾ oz / ⅓ cup self-raising
flour
150 g / 5 ½ oz / ⅔ cup caster
(superfine) sugar
150 g / 5 ½ oz / ⅔ cup butter
3 eggs
2 tsp baking powder
150 g / 5 ½ oz / ¾ cup raisins

- Preheat the oven to 180⁰C (160⁰ fan), 355F, gas 4 and
  grease and line a small loaf tin.
- Put all of the cake ingredients in a large mixing bowl
  and whisk them together with an electric whisk for
  4 minutes or until pale and well whipped.
- Scrape the mixture into the tin and level the top with
  a spatula.
- Bake for 35 - 40 minutes. The cake is ready when a
  toothpick inserted comes out clean.
- Transfer the cake to a wire rack to cool completely.

Wholemeal Date Loaf Cake

381

- Use finely chopped dates instead of
  the raisins for a denser, richer cake.

382

SERVES 12

Chocolate Coated Sponge Cake

White Chocolate Coated Sponge Cake

383

- Using white chocolate instead of the dark and milk will give a sweeter taste to this delicious cake.

Chocolate and Coconut Coated Sponge Cake

384

- Follow the recipe above but sprinkle a few tablespoons of dessicated coconut onto the chocolate before it sets.

PREPARATION TIME 10 MINUTES

COOKING TIME 45-50 MINUTES

INGREDIENTS

150 g / 5 ½ oz / 1 cup self-raising flour
150 g / 5 ½ oz / ⅔ cup caster (superfine) sugar
150 g / 5 ½ oz / ⅔ cup butter
3 eggs
1 tsp baking powder
1 tsp vanilla extract

TO DECORATE

100 g / 3 ½ oz dark chocolate
40 g / 1 ½ oz / ¼ cup butter
25 g / ¾ oz milk chocolate, coarsely grated

- Preheat the oven to 180°C (160° fan), 355F, gas 4 and grease and line a deep 20 cm round loose-bottomed cake tin.
- Put all of the cake ingredients in a large mixing bowl and whisk them together with an electric whisk for 4 minutes or until pale and well whipped.
- Scrape the mixture into the tin and level the top with a spatula.
- Bake for 45 - 50 minutes. The cake is ready when a toothpick inserted in the centre comes out clean.
- Transfer the cake to a wire rack to cool completely.
- To make the chocolate glaze, melt the chocolate in a microwave or bain marie then stir in the butter.
- Spoon the glaze over the cake and leave to set for 30 minutes.
- Sprinkle over the grated chocolate.

385

SERVES 8

Banana and Hazelnut Loaf Cake

PREPARATION TIME 10 MINUTES

COOKING TIME 55 MINUTES

....

INGREDIENTS

3 very ripe bananas
110 g / 4 oz / ½ cup soft light brown sugar
2 large eggs
120 ml / 4 fl. oz / ½ cup sunflower oil
125 g / 4 ½ oz / ¾ cup plain (all purpose) flour
2 tsp baking powder
100 g / 3 ½ oz / 1 cup ground hazelnuts
(cob nuts)

- Preheat the oven to 170°C (150° fan), gas 3 and line a long thin loaf tin with non-stick baking paper.
- Mash the bananas roughly with a fork then whisk in the sugar, eggs and oil.
- Sieve the flour and bicarbonate of soda into the bowl and add the ground hazelnuts (cob nuts). Stir just enough to evenly mix all the ingredients together.
- Scrape the mixture into the loaf tin and bake for 55 minutes or until a skewer inserted in the centre comes out clean.
- Transfer the cake to a wire rack and leave to cool completely.

Banana and Pinenut Loaf Cake

386

- Substitute 100g/ 3 _ oz of chopped toasted pine nuts to give a mild nutty taste to this loaf cake.

387

SERVES 8

Lime, Chilli and Mango Tart

PREPARATION TIME 40 MINUTES

COOKING TIME 40-50 MINUTES

....

INGREDIENTS

3 mangos, peeled, stoned and sliced
1 lime, zest finely pared
½ tsp Cayenne pepper

FOR THE PASTRY
100 g / 3 ½ oz / ½ cup butter, cubed
200 g / 7 oz / 1 ⅓ cup plain (all purpose) flour

FOR THE CUSTARD
4 large egg yolks
75 g / 2 ½ oz / ⅓ cup caster (superfine) sugar
2 tsp cornflour
350 ml / 12 ½ fl. oz / 1 ½ cups whole milk
100 ml / 3 ½ fl. oz / ½ cup fresh lime juice
1 mild red chilli, finely chopped

- Preheat the oven to 200°C (180° fan), 390F, gas 6.
- Rub the butter into the flour and add just enough cold water to bind.
- Chill for 30 minutes then roll out on a floured surface. Use the pastry to line a 23 cm round loose-bottomed tart tin.
- Prick the pastry with a fork, line with clingfilm and fill with baking beans or rice.
- Bake for 10 minutes then remove the clingfilm and baking beans and cook for another 8 minutes to crisp.
- Reduce the oven temperature to 170°C (150° fan), 340F, gas 3.
- Whisk the custard ingredients together in a saucepan then stir over a low heat for 5 minutes.
- Pour the custard into the pastry case and leave to cool before arranging the mango slices on top and sprinkling with lime zest and cayenne pepper.

Lime, Chilli and Pineapple Tart

388

- Using 1 small pineapple instead of the mango makes a delicious sharp, sweet tang to this tropical tart.

389

SERVES 10

Mango and Vanilla Loaf Cake

- Preheat the oven to 180°C (160° fan), 355F, gas 4 and grease and line a loaf tin.
- Cut the vanilla pod in half lengthways and scrape out the seeds.
- Reserve the pod and put the seeds in a mixing bowl with the flour, sugar, butter, eggs and baking powder and whisk for 4 minutes or until pale and well whipped.
- Fold in the mango then scrape the mixture into the tin and lay the vanilla pod halves on top.
- Bake for 35 - 40 minutes. The cake is ready when a toothpick inserted in the centre comes out clean.
- Transfer the cake to a wire rack to cool completely.

PREPARATION TIME 20 MINUTES

COOKING TIME 35-40 MINUTES

INGREDIENTS

1 vanilla pod
150 g / 5 ½ oz / 1 cup self-raising flour
150 g / 5 ½ oz / ⅔ cup caster (superfine) sugar
150 g / 5 ½ oz / ⅔ cup butter
3 eggs
1 tsp baking powder
2 mangos, peeled, stoned and chopped

Pineapple and Vanilla Loaf Cake

390

- Use 1 small pineapple instead of the mango in this delicious loaf cake.

391

SERVES 8

Spicy Wholemeal Loaf Cake

- Preheat the oven to 180°C (160° fan), 355F, gas 4 and grease and line a small loaf tin.
- Put all of the cake ingredients in a large mixing bowl and whisk them together with an electric whisk for 4 minutes or until pale and well whipped.
- Scrape the mixture into the tin and level the top with a spatula.
- Bake for 35 - 40 minutes. The cake is ready when a toothpick inserted in the centre comes out clean.
- Transfer the cake to a wire rack to cool completely.

PREPARATION TIME 10 MINUTES

COOKING TIME 35-40 MINUTES

INGREDIENTS

100 g / 3 ½ oz / ⅔ cup stoneground wholemeal flour
50 g / 1 ¾ oz / ⅓ cup self-raising flour
2 tsp baking powder
150 g / 5 ½ oz / ⅔ cup caster (superfine) sugar
150 g / 5 ½ oz / ⅔ cup butter
3 eggs
1 tsp ground cinnamon
1 tsp ground ginger
½ tsp freshly grated nutmeg

Spicy Wholemeal and Banana Loaf Cake

392

- Add one mashed very ripe banana for a rich slightly moister loaf cake.

Pear and Marmalade Frangipane Tart

393

SERVES 8

Pear and Apricot Frangipane Tart

394

- Use apricot jam instead of marmalade for a sweeter less acidic frangipane tart.

Peach and Marmalade Frangipane Tart

395

- Use 5 tinned peaches instead of the pears for an extra sweet delicious frangipane tart.

PREPARATION TIME 45 MINUTES

COOKING TIME 40-50 MINUTES

INGREDIENTS

150g / 5 ½ oz / 1 ½ cup ground almonds
150g / 5 ½ oz / ⅔ cup butter, softened
150g / 5 ½ oz / ⅔ cup caster (superfine) sugar
2 large eggs
2 tbsp plain (all purpose) flour
5 pears, peeled, cored and halved
4 tbsp marmalade
2 tbsp flaked (slivered) almonds

FOR THE PASTRY

200g / 7 oz / 1 ⅓ cup plain (all purpose) flour
100g / 3 ½ oz / ½ cup butter, cubed
50g / 1 ¾ oz / ¼ cup caster (superfine) sugar

- Preheat the oven to 200°C (180° fan), 390F, gas 6.
- To make the pastry, rub the butter into the flour until the mixture resembles fine breadcrumbs.
- Stir in the sugar and add enough cold water to bring the pastry together into a pliable dough.
- Chill the dough for 30 minutes then roll out on a floured surface. Use the pastry to line a 24 cm round pie tin.
- Prick the pastry with a fork, line with clingfilm and fill with baking beans or rice.
- Bake for 10 minutes then remove the clingfilm and baking beans.
- Return to the oven for 8 minutes to crisp.
- Whisk together the almonds, butter, sugar, eggs and flour until smoothly whipped and spoon the mixture into the pastry case.
- Arrange the pear halves on top of the frangipane and bake the tart for 25 minutes or until the frangipane is cooked through.
- Heat the marmalade until runny and brush it over the pears then sprinkle with flaked (slivered) almonds.

396

MAKES 18

Vanilla and Chocolate Whoopee Pies

- Preheat the oven to 190°C (170° fan), 375F, gas 5 and line 2 large baking trays with non-stick baking mats.
- Combine the flour, baking powder, sugar, butter, eggs and vanilla extract in a bowl and whisk together for 2 minutes or until smooth.
- Separate it into 2 bowls and stir the cocoa powder into one of them.
- Spoon the plain mixture down one side of a piping bag fitted with a large plain nozzle and spoon the chocolate mixture down the other side.
- Pipe 18 walnut-sized domes onto each tray.
- Transfer the trays to the oven and bake for 10 – 15 minutes. The cakes will be ready when springy to the touch.
- Leave the cakes to cool on the tray then lift them off with a palette knife. Sandwich the cakes together in pairs with chocolate spread.

PREPARATION TIME 20 MINUTES

COOKING TIME 10-15 MINUTES

INGREDIENTS

110 g / 4 oz / ⅔ cup self-raising flour, sifted
2 tsp baking powder
110 g / 4 oz / ½ cup caster (superfine) sugar
110 g / 4 oz / ½ cup butter, softened
2 large eggs
1 tsp vanilla extract
2 tbsp unsweetened cocoa powder

TO DECORATE
½ jar chocolate spread

Orange and Chocolate Whoopee Pies

397

- Substitute the vanilla essence with ½ tsp orange essence for a fruity whoopee pie.

398

SERVES 8

Almond Torte

- Preheat the oven to 180°C (160° fan), 355F, gas 4 and line a loose-bottomed round cake tin.
- Whisk the egg yolks, caster (superfine) sugar and butter together for 4 minutes or until pale and thick, then fold in the ground almonds.
- Whip the egg whites to stiff peaks in a very clean bowl, then fold it into the cake mixture in two stages.
- Scrape the mixture into the tin, being careful to retain as many air bubbles as possible, and bake for 25 – 30 minutes or until a skewer inserted comes out clean.
- Leave to cool in the tin for 10 minutes before transferring to a wire rack to cool completely.
- Dust with icing (confectioners) sugar before serving.

PREPARATION TIME 15 MINUTES

COOKING TIME 25-30 MINUTES

INGREDIENTS

2 large eggs, separated
150 g / 5 ½ oz / ⅔ cup caster (superfine) sugar
150 g / 5 ½ oz ⅔ cup butter, melted
200 g / 7 oz / 2 cups ground almonds
icing (confectioners) sugar to dust

Almond Torte with White Chocolate

399

- When cooled, before dusting with icing surgar, drizzle with a small bar of melted white chooclate for a richer treat.

400

MAKES 24

Rose Petal Mini Muffins

PREPARATION TIME 25 MINUTES

COOKING TIME 15-20 MINUTES

INGREDIENTS

1 large egg
120 ml / 4 fl. oz / ½ cup sunflower oil
120 ml / 4 fl. oz / ½ cup milk
1 tbsp rose water
375 g / 12 ½ oz / 2 ½ cups self-raising flour, sifted
1 tsp baking powder
200 g / 7 oz / ¾ cup caster (superfine) sugar
55 g / 2 oz / ½ cup ground almonds
2 tbsp crystallised rose petals
icing (confectioners) sugar to dust

TO DECORATE

225 g / 8 oz / 2 ¼ cups icing (confectioners) sugar
2 – 4 tsp rose water
crystallised rose petals

- Preheat the oven to 180°C (160° fan), 350F, gas 4 and oil a 24-hole silicone mini muffin mould.
- Beat the egg in a jug with the oil, milk and rose water until well mixed.
- Mix the flour, baking powder, sugar, ground almonds and rose petals in a bowl, then pour in the egg mixture and stir just enough to combine.
- Divide the mixture between the moulds and bake in the oven for 15 – 20 minutes. Test with a wooden toothpick, if it comes out clean, the cakes are done.
- Transfer the cakes to a wire rack and leave to cool before dusting with icing (confectioners) sugar.
- To decorate, sieve the icing (confectioners) sugar into a bowl and add just enough rose water to make a thick icing.
- Spoon the icing over the cakes and decorate with crystallised rose petals.

Violet Mini Muffins

401

- Swap the rose petals for crystallised violet petals for a more flowery taste.

402

MAKES 6

Peach, Amoretti and Mascarpone Tartlets

PREPARATION TIME 45 MINUTES

COOKING TIME 18 MINUTES

INGREDIENTS

450 g / 1 lb / 2 cups mascarpone
100 g / 3 ½ oz / 2 cups icing (confectioners) sugar
2 tbsp amoretto liqueur
4 peaches, peeled, stoned and thinly sliced
3 tbsp soft brown sugar
75 g / 2 ½ oz / ½ cup amoretti biscuits, crushed

FOR THE PASTRY

200g / 7 oz / 1 ⅓ cups plain (all purpose) flour
100g / 3 ½ oz / ½ cup butter, cubed
1 egg, beaten

- Preheat the oven to 200°C (180° fan), 390F, gas 6.
- To make the pastry, rub the butter into the flour and add just enough cold water to bind.
- Chill for 30 minutes then roll out on a floured surface. Use the pastry to line 6 tartlet cases.
- Prick the pastry with a fork, line with clingfilm and fill with baking beans or rice. Bake for 10 minutes then remove the clingfilm and baking beans.
- Brush the inside of the pastry cases with beaten egg and cook for another 8 minutes to crisp.
- Whisk the mascarpone with the icing (confectioners) sugar and amoretto liqueur until smooth. Spoon in the filling into the cooled cases.
- Arrange the peach slices on top and sprinkle with brown sugar then caramelise the tops with a blow torch or under a hot grill.
- Sprinkle over the crushed amoretti before serving.

Peach, Ginger and Mascarpone Tartlets

403

- Substitute the amoretti biscuits for giner snap biscuits for a more spicy kick.

404

MAKES 6

Cherry and Marzipan Tartlets

Strawberry and Marzipan Tartlets

405

- Substitute the cherries and cherry jam with firm strawberries and strawberry jam for a delicious fruity alternative.

Grape and Marzipan Tartlets

406

- Swap the cherries and jam with sweet red grapes and grape jelly for a less tart taste.

PREPARATION TIME 1 HOUR

COOKING TIME 30 MINUTES

INGREDIENTS

400 g / 14 oz / 2 ⅔ cups cherries, stoned and halved
100 g / 3 ½ oz / ⅓ cup cherry jam
300 g / 10 ½ oz golden marzipan

FOR THE PASTRY

100 g / 3 ½ oz / ½ cup butter, cubed
200 g / 7 oz / 1 ⅓ cups plain (all purpose) flour
55 g / 2 oz / ¼ cup caster (superfine) sugar
1 egg, beaten

TO DECORATE

6 whole cherries with stalks, pitted
100 g / 3 ½ oz / golden marzipan
icing (confectioners) sugar to dust

- Preheat the oven to 200°C (180° fan), 390F, gas 6.
- To make the pastry, rub the butter into the flour and sugar then add the egg with just enough cold water to bind.
- Wrap the dough in clingfilm and chill for 30 minutes then roll out on a floured surface.
- Use the pastry to line 6 tartlet tins and trim the edges.
- Prick the pastry with a fork, line with clingfilm and fill with baking beans or rice.
- Bake for 10 minutes then remove the clingfilm and baking beans and cook for another 8 minutes to crisp.
- Mix the halved cherries with the cherry jam and spoon the mixture into the tartlet cases.
- Roll out the marzipan and cut out 6 circles to make the pie lids, pinching around the top to seal.
- Return the tarts to the oven for 10 minutes or until the tops are golden brown.
- To decorate the tartlets, wrap each whole cherry in a layer of marzipan. Dust the tartlets with icing (confectioners) sugar then position a marzipan cherry on top.

407

MAKES 24

Chocolate and Orange Mini Muffins

PREPARATION TIME 25 MINUTES

COOKING TIME 15-20 MINUTES

INGREDIENTS

1 large egg
120 ml / 4 fl. oz / ½ cup sunflower oil
120 ml / 4 fl. oz / ½ cup milk
1 orange, juice and zest
375 g / 12 ½ oz / 2 ½ cups self-raising
flour, sifted
1 tsp baking powder
2 tbsp cocoa powder
75 g / 2 ½ oz / ½ cup chocolate chips
75 g / 2 ½ oz / ½ cup candied orange
peel, chopped
200 g / 7 oz / ¾ cup caster (superfine)
sugar

- Preheat the oven to 180°C (160° fan), gas 4 and line a 24-hole mini muffin tin with paper cases.
- Beat the egg in a jug with the oil, milk and orange juice and zest until well mixed.
- Mix the flour, baking powder, cocoa, chocolate chips, candied peel and sugar in a bowl.
- Pour in the egg mixture and stir just enough to combine.
- Divide the mixture between the paper cases and bake for 15 – 20 minutes.
- Test with a wooden toothpick, if it comes out clean, the cakes are done.
- Transfer the muffins to a wire rack and leave to cool completely.

Spiced Chocolate Orange Mini Muffins

408

- Add 1 tsp of ground cinnamon and pinch of ground nutmeg to the mixture for a spiced alternative.

409

SERVES 8-10

Mirabelle Plum Cake

PREPARATION TIME 5 MINUTES

COOKING TIME 45-55 MINUTES

INGREDIENTS

225 g / 8 oz / 1 cup butter, softened
225 g / 8 oz / 1 cup caster (superfine)
sugar
5 large eggs, beaten
225 g / 4 ½ oz / 1 ½ cups self-raising
flour
350 g / 12 ½ oz / 2 ⅓ cups mirabelles,
stoned

- Preheat the oven to 180°C (160° fan), 355F, gas 4 and grease and line a 23 cm round cake tin with greaseproof paper.
- Cream the butter and sugar together until well whipped then gradually whisk in the eggs, beating well after each addition.
- Fold in the flour then scrape the mixture into the tin and scatter over the mirabelles.
- Bake the cake for 45 - 55 minutes or until a skewer inserted in the centre comes out clean.
- Transfer the cake to a wire rack and leave to cool.

Damson Plum Cakes

410

- Swap the Mirabelle plums for Damson plums for a darker, more intense fruity cake.

411

SERVES 6

Chocolate, Orange and Almond Torte

- Preheat the oven to 180°C (160° fan), 355F, gas 4 and line a round spring-form cake tin.
- Whisk the egg yolks and sugar together for 4 minutes.
- Melt the butter, cocoa and chocolate together then fold into the egg yolk mixture with the ground almonds.
- Whip the egg whites to stiff peaks in a very clean bowl and fold them into the cake mixture.
- Scrape the mixture into the tin, being careful to retain as many air bubbles as possible, and bake for 25 – 30 minutes or until the centre is just set.
- Transfer to a wire rack to cool. Heat the sugar in a small saucepan until it has all dissolved and turned a light caramel colour.
- Use a fork to dip the almonds and orange zest in the caramel and leave them to set on a non-stick baking mat.
- Cut the torte into wedges and decorate with the caramel almonds and orange zest.

Chocolate, Orange and Hazelnut Torte

412

- Change the ground almonds for ground hazelnuts (cob nuts) for a more nutty flavour.

PREPARATION TIME 15 MINUTES

COOKING TIME 25-30 MINUTES

....

INGREDIENTS

2 large eggs, separated
150 g / 5 ½ oz / ⅔ cup caster (superfine) sugar
75 g / 2 ½ oz / ⅓ cup butter
2 tbsp unsweetened cocoa powder
100 g / 3 ½ oz dark chocolate (minimum 60% cocoa solids), chopped
150 g / 5 ½ oz / 1 ½ cups ground almonds
1 orange, zest finely grated

TO DECORATE
100 g / 3 ½ oz / ½ cup caster (superfine) sugar
6 almonds
1 orange, zest finely pared

413

SERVES 12

Gluten-Free Sponge Cake

- Preheat the oven to 180°C (160° fan), 355F, gas 4 and grease and line a 20 cm round loose-bottomed cake tin.
- Put all of the cake ingredients in a large mixing bowl and whisk them together with an electric whisk for 4 minutes or until pale and well whipped.
- Scrape the mixture into the tin and level the top with a spatula.
- Bake for 45 - 50 minutes. The cake is ready when a toothpick inserted in the centre comes out clean.
- Transfer the cake to a wire rack to cool completely.

PREPARATION TIME 10 MINUTES

COOKING TIME 45-50 MINUTES

....

INGREDIENTS

50 g / 1 ¾ oz / ⅓ cup rice flour
50 g / 1 ¾ oz / ⅓ cup potato flour
50 g / 1 ¾ oz / ⅓ cup tapioca flour
150 g / 5 ½ oz / ⅔ cup caster (superfine) sugar
150 g / 5 ½ oz / ⅔ cup butter
3 eggs
2 tsp baking powder
1 tsp vanilla extract

Gluten Free Orange Sponge Cake

 414

- Swap the vanilla extract with a ½ a teaspoon of orange essence and add 1 tbsp finely grated orange zest for a citrus flavour.

415

SERVES 8

Wholemeal Muesli Loaf Cake

Cranberry Muesli Loaf Cake

 416

- Mix 2 tbsp of dried cranberries into the mixture for a more fruity loaf.

Cinnamon Muesli Loaf Cake

 417

- Add 1 tbsp ground cinnamon to the mixture for a slightly spicy finish.

Muesli and Chocolate Chip Loaf

 418

- Add a tbsp of chocolate chips to the mixture and combine well.

PREPARATION TIME 10 MINUTES

COOKING TIME 35-40 MINUTES

....

INGREDIENTS

100 g / 3 ½ oz / ⅔ cup stoneground wholemeal flour
50 g / 1 ¾ oz / ⅓ cup self-raising flour
150 g / 5 ½ oz / ⅔ cup caster (superfine) sugar
150 g / 5 ½ oz / ⅔ cup butter
3 eggs
2 tsp baking powder
150 g / 5 ½ oz / 1 ½ cup nutty muesli

- Preheat the oven to 180°C (160° fan), 355F, gas 4 and grease and line a small loaf tin.
- Put all of the cake ingredients in a large mixing bowl and whisk them together with an electric whisk for 4 minutes or until pale and well whipped.
- Scrape the mixture into the tin and level the top with a spatula.
- Bake for 35 - 40 minutes. The cake is ready when a toothpick inserted in the centre comes out clean.
- Transfer the cake to a wire rack to cool completely.

419

SERVES 4

Hazelnut Choux Bun Ring

- Preheat the oven to 200°C (180° fan), 400F, gas 6.
- Oil and line a large baking tray with greaseproof paper, then spray it with water.
- Bring the butter and 150 ml cold water to the boil then beat in the flour off the heat.
- Continue to beat until you have a smooth ball of pastry that leaves the sides of the saucepan clean. Stir in the beaten egg a little at a time to make a glossy paste.
- Spoon the pastry into a piping bag fitted with a large plain nozzle and pipe 8 buns in a ring on the tray.
- Bake for 20 minutes, increasing the heat to 220°C (200° fan), 425F, gas 7 halfway through.
- Transfer the ring to a wire rack, cut in half horizontally and leave to cool completely.
- Whip the cream with the icing (confectioners) sugar and vanilla until thick, then fold in the ground hazelnuts (cob nuts).
- Spoon the hazelnut cream into a piping bag fitted with a large plain nozzle and fill the bottom halves of the buns.
- Replace the tops and dust with icing (confectioners) sugar.

PREPARATION TIME 45 MINUTES

COOKING TIME 20 MINUTES

INGREDIENTS

55 g / 2 oz / ¼ cup butter, cubed
70 g / 2 ½ oz / ½ cup strong white bread flour, sieved
2 large eggs, beaten
icing (confectioners) sugar to dust

FOR THE FILLING
225 ml / 8 fl. oz / ¾ cup double cream
2 tbsp icing (confectioners) sugar
½ tsp vanilla extract
55 g / 2 oz / ½ cup ground hazelnuts (cob nuts)

420

SERVES 8

Paris Brest Gateau

- Preheat the oven to 200°C (180° fan), 400F, gas 6.
- Oil and line a large baking tray with greaseproof paper, then spray it with water.
- Bring the butter and 150 ml cold water to the boil then beat in the flour off the heat.
- Continue to beat until you have a smooth ball of pastry that leaves the sides of the saucepan clean. Stir in the beaten egg a little at a time to make a glossy paste.
- Spoon the pastry into a piping bag fitted with a large star nozzle and pipe the choux into a large ring on the baking tray.
- Sprinkle with almonds and bake for 20 minutes, increasing the heat to 220°C (200° fan), 425F, gas 7 halfway through.
- Transfer the ring to a wire rack, cut in half horizontally and leave to cool completely.
- Whip the cream with the hazelnut syrup until thick then spoon into a piping bag fitted with a large star nozzle.
- Fill the bottom half of the ring with cream then replace the top and dust with icing (confectioners) sugar.

PREPARATION TIME 45 MINUTES

COOKING TIME 20 MINUTES

INGREDIENTS

55 g / 2 oz / ¼ cup butter, cubed
70 g / 2 ½ oz / ½ cup strong white bread flour, sieved
2 large eggs, beaten
50 g / 2 ½ oz / ⅔ cup flaked (slivered) almonds
icing (confectioners) sugar to dust

FOR THE FILLING
225 ml / 8 fl. oz / ¾ cup double cream
4 tbsp hazelnut (cob nut) syrup

MAKES 12

Peach Cupcakes

PREPARATION TIME I HOUR

COOKING TIME 15-20 MINUTES

....

INGREDIENTS

1 can peach slices, drained, syrup reserved
110 g / 4 oz / ⅔ cup self-raising flour, sifted
110 g / 4 oz / ½ cup caster (superfine) sugar
110 g / 4 oz / ½ cup butter, softened
2 large eggs
300 ml / 10 ½ fl. oz / 1 ¼ cups double cream

- Preheat the oven to 190⁰C (170⁰ fan), 375F, gas 5 and line a 12-hole cupcake tin with paper cases.
- Reserve 12 of the peach slices and finely chop the rest. Combine the flour, sugar, butter, eggs and chopped peaches in a bowl and whisk together for 2 minutes or until smooth.
- Divide the mixture between the paper cases, then transfer the tin to the oven and bake for 15 – 20 minutes.
- Test with a wooden toothpick, if it comes out clean, the cakes are done.
- Transfer the cakes to a wire rack and leave to cool completely.
- Whip the cream until thick then fill a piping bag fitted with a large star nozzle and pipe a rosette on top of each cake.
- Lay a slice of peach next to the cream and drizzle a little of the reserved peach syrup on top.

MAKES 18

Peanut Butter Whoopee Pies

PREPARATION TIME 20 MINUTES

COOKING TIME 10-15 MINUTES

....

INGREDIENTS

110 g / 4 oz / ⅔ cup self-raising flour, sifted
2 tsp baking powder
110 g / 4 oz / ½ cup caster (superfine) sugar
110 g / 4 oz / ½ cup butter, softened
2 large eggs
75 g / 2 ½ oz / ⅔ cup peanuts, chopped

TO DECORATE
½ jar smooth peanut butter

- Preheat the oven to 190⁰C (170⁰ fan), 375F, gas 5 and line 2 large baking trays with non-stick baking mats.
- Combine the flour, baking powder, sugar, butter, eggs and chopped peanuts in a bowl and whisk together for 2 minutes or until smooth.
- Spoon the mixture into a piping bag fitted with a large plain nozzle and pipe 18 walnut-sized domes onto each tray.
- Transfer the trays to the oven and bake for 10 – 15 minutes. The mixture should spread a little whilst cooking and the cakes will be ready when springy to the touch.
- Leave the cakes to cool on the tray then lift them off with a palette knife.
- Sandwich the cakes together in pairs with the peanut butter.

Chocolate and Peanut Butter Whoopee Pies

423

- Add a layer of chocolate spread on top of the peanut butter for a sweeter taste.

424

MAKES 12

Peanut Muffins

- Preheat the oven to 180°C (160° fan), 355F, gas 4 and line a 12-hole muffin tin with paper cases.
- Beat the egg in a jug with the oil and milk until well mixed.
- Mix the flour, baking powder, sugar and peanuts in a bowl.
- Pour in the egg mixture and stir just enough to combine.
- Divide the mixture between the paper cases and bake for 20 – 25 minutes.
- Test with a wooden toothpick, if it comes out clean, the cakes are done.
- Transfer the muffins to a wire rack and leave to cool completely.

PREPARATION TIME 25 MINUTES

COOKING TIME 20-25 MINUTES

INGREDIENTS

1 large egg
120 ml / 4 fl. oz / ½ cup sunflower oil
120 ml / 4 fl. oz / ½ cup milk
375 g / 12 ½ oz / 2 ½ cups self-raising flour, sifted
1 tsp baking powder
200 g / 7 oz / ¾ cup caster (superfine) sugar
150 g / 5 ½ oz / 1 cup peanuts

Pear, Cardamom and Honey Tarts

425

MAKES 6

PREPARATION TIME 45 MINUTES

COOKING TIME 30 MINUTES

INGREDIENTS

200 ml / 7 fl. oz / ⅔ cup runny honey
6 cardamom pods, bruised
4 ripe pears, 2 chopped and 2 sliced

FOR THE PASTRY

200g / 7 oz plain / 1 ⅓ cups (all purpose) flour
100g / 3 ½ oz / ½ cup butter, cubed
50g / 1 ¾ oz / ¼ cup caster (superfine) sugar

- To make the pastry, rub the butter into the flour until the mixture resembles fine breadcrumbs. Stir in the sugar and add enough cold water to bring the pastry together into a pliable dough.
- Chill the dough for 30 minutes.
- Put the honey and cardamom in a small saucepan and bring to a simmer, then turn off the heat and leave to infuse for 30 minutes.
- Preheat the oven to 200°C (180° fan), 390F, gas 6.
- Roll out the pastry and use it to line 6 tartlet cases.
- Prick the pastry with a fork, line with clingfilm and fill with baking beans or rice.
- Bake for 10 minutes then remove the clingfilm and baking beans.
- Return to the oven for 8 minutes to crisp.
- Arrange the pears in the pastry case and spoon over the cardamom honey.
- Bake for 10 minutes.

Gateau Breton with Pears

426

SERVES 8

PREPARATION TIME 15 MINUTES

COOKING TIME 40-45 MINUTES

INGREDIENTS

250 g / 9 oz / 1 ¼ cup butter, cubed
250 g / 9 oz / ⅔ cup plain (all purpose) flour
250 g / 9 oz / 1 ¼ cup caster (superfine) sugar
6 large egg yolks
2 pears, peeled, cored and sliced

- Preheat the oven to 180°C (160° fan), 355F, gas 4 and butter a 23 cm round tart tin.
- Rub the butter into the flour then stir in the sugar.
- Beat 5 of the egg yolks and stir them into the dry ingredients.
- Bring the mixture together into a soft dough and divide it in two.
- Press one half into the bottom of the tart tin to form an even layer.
- Arrange the pears on top, leaving a clear border round the outside.
- Roll out the other half of the dough between 2 sheets of greaseproof paper then peel away the paper and lay it on top of the pears.
- Brush the top of the gateau with the final egg yolk then score a pattern on top.
- Bake the gateau for 40 – 45 minutes or until golden brown.
- Cool completely before unmolding and cutting into slices.

427

MAKES 9

Pecan Pie Brownies

PREPARATION TIME 25 MINUTES

COOKING TIME 35-40 MINUTES

INGREDIENTS

110g / 4 oz dark chocolate (minimum 60 % cocoa solids), chopped
85 g / 3 oz / ¾ cup unsweetened cocoa powder, sifted
225 g / 8 oz / 1 cup butter
450 g /15 oz / 2 ½ cups light brown sugar
4 large eggs
110 g / 4 oz / ⅔ cup self-raising flour
110 g / 4 oz pecan pie, crumbled
18 pecan halves

- Preheat the oven to 170°C (150° fan), 340F, gas 3 and oil and line a 20 cm x 20 cm square cake tin.
- Melt the chocolate, cocoa and butter together in a saucepan, then leave to cool a little.
- Whisk the sugar and eggs together with an electric whisk for 3 minutes or until very light and creamy.
- Pour in the chocolate mixture and sieve over the flour, then fold everything together with the pecan pie pieces until evenly mixed.
- Scrape into the tin and top with the pecan halves.
- Bake for 35 – 40 minutes or until the outside is set, but the centre is still quite soft, as it will continue to cook as it cools.
- Leave the brownie to cool completely on a wire rack before cutting into squares.

Maple Pecan Pie Brownies

 428

- Add 2 tbsp of real maple syrup to the mixture for a richer flavour.

429

MAKES 24

Pecan Mini Muffins

PREPARATION TIME 25 MINUTES

COOKING TIME 15-20 MINUTES

INGREDIENTS

1 large egg
120 ml / 4 fl. oz / ½ cup sunflower oil
120 ml / 4 fl. oz / ½ cup milk
1 tsp vanilla extract
375 g / 12 ½ oz / 2 ½ cups self-raising flour, sifted
1 tsp baking powder
200 g / 7 oz / 1 ¼ cups soft brown sugar
55 g / 2 oz / ½ cup ground almonds
75 g / 2 ½ oz / ⅔ cup pecan nuts, chopped

- Preheat the oven to 180°C (160° fan), 350F, gas 4 and oil a 24-hole silicone mini muffin mould.
- Beat the egg in a jug with the oil, milk and vanilla extract until well mixed.
- Mix the flour, baking powder, sugar, ground almonds and pecan nuts in a bowl, then pour in the egg mixture and stir just enough to combine.
- Divide the mixture between the moulds and bake in the oven for 15 – 20 minutes.
- Test with a wooden toothpick, if it comes out clean, the cakes are done.
- Transfer the cakes to a wire rack and leave to cool completely.

Almond Pecan Mini Muffins

 430

- Swap the vanilla extract for almond essence for an alternative taste combination.

431

SERVES 8

Sugared Almond Loaf Cake

Lemon Sugared Almond Loaf Cake

432

- Add the juice and grated zest of half a lemon for a zesty citrus alternative.

Blueberry Sugared Almond Loaf Cake

433

- Add a handful of dried blueberries to the mixture for a more fruity loaf.

PREPARATION TIME 10 MINUTES

COOKING TIME 35-40 MINUTES

INGREDIENTS

150 g / 5 ½ oz / 1 cup self-raising flour
150 g / 5 ½ oz / ⅔ cup caster (superfine) sugar
150 g / 5 ½ oz / ⅔ cup butter
3 eggs
1 tsp baking powder
100 g / 3 ½ oz / ⅔ cup sugared almonds

- Preheat the oven to 180°C (160° fan), 355F, gas 4 and grease and line a small loaf tin.
- Put all of the cake ingredients except the sugared almonds in a large mixing bowl and whisk them together with an electric whisk for 4 minutes or until pale and well whipped.
- Fold in the sugared almonds then scrape the mixture into the tin and level the top with a spatula.
- Bake for 35 - 40 minutes. The cake is ready when a toothpick inserted in the centre comes out clean.
- Transfer the cake to a wire rack to cool completely before slicing.

434

MAKES 12

Plain Muffins

PREPARATION TIME 10 MINUTES

COOKING TIME 20-25 MINUTES

....

INGREDIENTS

1 large egg
120 ml / 4 fl. oz / ½ cup sunflower oil
120 ml / 4 fl. oz / ½ cup milk
375 g / 12 ½ oz / 2 ½ cups self-raising
flour, sifted
1 tsp baking powder
200 g / 7 oz / ¾ cup caster (superfine)
sugar

- Preheat the oven to 180°C (160° fan), 355F, gas 4 and oil 12 silicone muffin cases.
- Beat the egg in a jug with the oil and milk until well mixed.
- Mix the flour, baking powder and sugar in a bowl.
- Pour in the egg mixture and stir just enough to combine.
- Divide the mixture between the cases and bake for 20 – 25 minutes.
- Test with a wooden toothpick, if it comes out clean, the cakes are done.
- Transfer the muffins to a wire rack and leave to cool completely.

Chocolate Blueberry Muffins

435

- Add 3 tablespoons of blueberries and 3 tablespoons of white chocolate chips to the mixture for a touch of luxury.

436

SERVES 6-8

Plum Pie

PREPARATION TIME 15 MINUTES

COOKING TIME 35-40 MINUTES

....

INGREDIENTS

450 g / 1 lb all-butter puff pastry
450 g / 1 lb plums, stoned and
chopped
3 tbsp caster (superfine) sugar
2 tsp cornflour
1 egg, beaten

- Preheat the oven to 200°C (180° fan), 390F, gas 6.
- Roll out half the pastry on a floured surface and use it to line a pie dish.
- Toss the plums with the sugar and cornflower and pack them into the pastry case.
- Roll out the other half of the pastry. Brush the rim of the bottom crust with beaten egg then lay the pie lid on top and crimp around the edges to seal.
- Trim away any excess pastry and use the scraps to decorate the top.
- Brush the top of the pie with beaten egg and bake for 35 – 40 minutes or until the pastry is golden brown and cooked through underneath.

Spiced Plum Pie

437

- Add a teaspoon of ground cinnamon, a ¼ teaspoon of ground nutmeg and a teaspoon of grated orange peel to the filling for a more spicy finish.

438

MAKES 12

Poppy Seed and Apricot Jam Muffins

- Preheat the oven to 180°C (160° fan), 355F, gas 4 and oil 12 silicone muffin cases.
- Beat the egg in a jug with the oil and milk.
- Mix the flour, baking powder and sugar in a bowl.
- Pour in the egg mixture and stir just enough to combine.
- Divide half the mixture between the cases and top each one with a big spoonful of apricot jam.
- Spoon the rest of the muffin mixture on top then sprinkle with poppy seeds.
- Transfer the muffins to the oven and bake for 20 – 25 minutes.
- Test with a wooden toothpick, if it comes out clean, the cakes are done.
- Transfer the muffins to a wire rack and leave to cool completely.

PREPARATION TIME 10 MINUTES

COOKING TIME 20-25 MINUTES

INGREDIENTS

1 large egg
120 ml / 4 fl. oz / ½ cup sunflower oil
120 ml / 4 fl. oz / ½ cup milk
375 g / 12 ½ oz / 2 ½ cups self-raising flour, sifted
1 tsp baking powder
200 g / 7 oz / ¾ cup caster (superfine) sugar
200 g / 7 oz / ⅔ cup apricot jam
2 tbsp poppy seeds

Poppy Seed and Raspberry Jam Muffins

 439

- Swap the apricot jam for raspberry jam for a different fruity flavour.

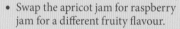

440

MAKES 12

Chocolate and Cream Sponge Squares

- Preheat the oven to 180°C (160 fan), gas 4 and grease and line a 30 cm x 23 cm cake tin.
- Put all of the cake ingredients in a large mixing bowl and whisk them together with an electric whisk for 4 minutes or until pale and well whipped.
- Scrape the mixture into the tin and level the top with a spatula.
- Bake for 30 - 35 minutes. The cake is ready when a toothpick inserted in the centre comes out clean.
- Transfer the cake to a wire rack to cool completely.
- Cut the cake horizontally into 3 layers.
- Whip the cream until thick then use it to sandwich the cake back together.
- Use a very sharp knife to cut the cake into 12 squares then dust the top with cocoa powder.

PREPARATION TIME 10 MINUTES

COOKING TIME 45-50 MINUTES

INGREDIENTS

150 g / 6 oz / 1 cup self-raising flour
28 g / 1 oz / ¼ cup unsweetened cocoa powder
2 tsp baking powder
175 g / 6 oz / ¾ cup caster (superfine) sugar
175 g / 6 oz / ¾ cup butter
3 large eggs

TO DECORATE
600 ml / 2 pints / 2 ½ cups double cream
2 tbsp unsweetened cocoa powder

Chocolate, Raspberry and Cream Sponge Squares

 441

- Sandwich halved raspberries between the layers amongst the cream for a more decadent treat.

442

SERVES 12

Chestnut Sponge with Chocolate Drizzle

Marron Glace Sponge with Chocolate Drizzle

443

- Add 6-8 chopped marron glace (candied chestnuts) to the mixture for a more nutty texture.

Chestnut Sponge with Chocolate Orange Drizzle

444

- Add a few drops of orange essence to the chocolate drizzle mixture for a citrus finish.

PREPARATION TIME 10 MINUTES

COOKING TIME 45-50 MINUTES

INGREDIENTS

75 g / 2 ½ oz / ½ cup self-raising flour
75 g / 2 ½ oz / ½ cup chestnut flour
150 g / 5 ½ oz / ⅔ cup caster (superfine) sugar
150 g / 5 ½ oz / ⅔ cup butter
3 eggs
2 tsp baking powder
1 tsp vanilla extract

TO DECORATE

55 g / 2 oz dark chocolate
25 g / 1 oz butter

- Preheat the oven to 180°C (160° fan), 355F, gas 4 and grease and line a deep 20 cm round loose-bottomed cake tin.
- Put all of the cake ingredients in a large mixing bowl and whisk them together with an electric whisk for 4 minutes or until pale and well whipped.
- Scrape the mixture into the tin and level the top with a spatula.
- Bake for 45 - 50 minutes. The cake is ready when a toothpick inserted in the centre comes out clean.
- Transfer the cake to a wire rack to cool completely.
- To make the chocolate drizzle, melt the chocolate in a microwave or bain marie then stir in the butter.
- Drizzle it over the top of the cake with a spoon before serving.

445

SERVES 8

Rhubarb Tart

- Preheat the oven to 200⁰C (180⁰ fan), 390F, gas 6.
- Rub the butter into the flour and add just enough cold water to bind.
- Chill for 30 minutes then roll out on a floured surface. Use the pastry to line a 23 cm round tart tin.
- Prick the pastry with a fork, line with clingfilm and fill with baking beans or rice.
- Bake for 10 minutes then remove the clingfilm and baking beans.
- Sprinkle the pastry case with ground almonds then arrange the rhubarb pieces on top and scatter over the sugar.
- Bake the tart for 20 - 25 minutes or until the rhubarb is tender and starting to brown on top.

PREPARATION TIME 40 MINUTES

COOKING TIME 30-35 MINUTES

INGREDIENTS

50 g / 1 ¾ oz / ½ cup ground almonds
3 sticks rhubarb, chopped
4 tbsp Demerara sugar

FOR THE PASTRY
200g / 7 oz / 1 ⅓ cups plain (all purpose) flour
100g / 3 ½ oz / ½ cup butter, cubed

Rhubarb Tart with Coconut

446

- Sprinkle 2-3 tablespoons of desiccated coconut before baking for an alternative tropical hint.

447

SERVES 6-8

Yellow Plum Tart

- Preheat the oven to 200⁰C (180⁰ fan), 390F, gas 6.
- Roll out half the pastry on a floured surface and use it to line a pie dish.
- Sprinkle the bottom with ground almonds then arrange the plums on top and sprinkle with sugar.
- Bake the tart for 35 – 40 minutes or until the plums are tender and the pastry has cooked through underneath.

PREPARATION TIME 15 MINUTES

COOKING TIME 35-40 MINUTES

INGREDIENTS

225 g / 8 oz all-butter puff pastry
50 g / 1 ¾ oz / ½ cup ground almonds
450 g / 1 lb yellow plums, halved and stoned
3 tbsp Demerara sugar

Yellow and Black Plum Tart

448

- Swap half the yellow plums for black plums for a more colourful tart.

449

MAKES 12 # Lemon Drizzle Cupcakes

PREPARATION TIME 10 MINUTES

COOKING TIME 15-20 MINUTES

INGREDIENTS

110 g / 4 oz / ⅔ cup self-raising flour, sifted
110 g / 4 oz / ½ cup caster (superfine) sugar
110 g / 4 oz / ½ cup butter, softened
2 large eggs
1 lemon, zest finely grated

FOR THE SOAKING SYRUP

2 lemons, juice and zest finely grated
4 tbsp caster (superfine) sugar
2 tbsp lemon curd

- Preheat the oven to 190°C (170° fan), 375F, gas 5 and oil a 12-hole silicone cupcake mould.
- Combine the flour, sugar, butter, eggs and lemon zest in a bowl and whisk together for 2 minutes or until smooth.
- Divide the mixture between the paper cases, then transfer the tin to the oven and bake for 15 – 20 minutes.
- Meanwhile, put the lemon juice, zest and sugar in a small saucepan and heat until the sugar dissolves. Stir in the lemon curd.
- When the cakes come out of the oven, spoon the syrup over the top and allow it to soak in as the cakes cool.

Clementine Drizzle Cupcakes

 450

- Swap the lemon zest and juice for clementine zest and juice for a different citrus finish.

 451

MAKES 12 # Rice, Nut and Honey Biscuits

PREPARATION TIME 15 MINUTES

COOKING TIME 15-20 MINUTES

INGREDIENTS

125 g / 4 ½ oz / ⅓ cup runny honey
75 g / 2 ½ oz / ⅓ cup butter, cubed
100 g / 3 ½ oz / 1 ⅓ cups puffed rice
100 g / 3 ½ oz / ⅔ cup blanched almonds
100 g / 3 ½ oz / ⅔ cup cashew nuts
25 g / 1 oz glace cherries, finely chopped
25 g / 1 oz dried apricots, finely chopped

- Preheat the oven to 180°C (160° fan), 355F, gas 4 and line 2 baking trays with a non-stick baking mats.
- Put the honey and butter in a small saucepan and heat together until bubbling.
- Mix the rice, nuts and dried fruit together then stir in the honey mixture.
- Make six piles of the mixture on each baking tray and flatten them with the back of a spoon.
- Bake for 15 – 20 minutes or until the biscuits are a golden caramel colour.
- Leave the biscuits to cool and harden on the tray then lift off with a palette knife and store between sheets of greaseproof paper.

Chocolate, Rice, Nut and Honey Biscuits

 452

- After they've cooled dip ½ of each biscuit in melted chocolate and allow to set for a more luxurious treat.

453

MAKES 12

Honey and Orange Sponge Squares

Honey and Lemon Sponge Squares

454

- Swap the orange juice and zest for lemon juice and zest for a sharper tasting treat.

Chocolate Chip, Orange and Honey Squares

455

- Mix a large handful of chocolate chips into the mixture for a naughty, tempting variation.

PREPARATION TIME 10 MINUTES

COOKING TIME 30-35 MINUTES

INGREDIENTS

175 g / 6 oz / 1 ¼ cups self-raising flour
2 tsp baking powder
175 g / 6 oz / ¾ cup caster (superfine) sugar
175 g / 6 oz / ¾ cup butter
3 eggs
3 tbsp orange juice

TO DECORATE

3 oranges, zest finely pared
225 g / 8 oz / ⅔ cup runny honey

- Preheat the oven to 180°C (160° fan), 355F, gas 4 and grease and line a 30 cm x 23 cm cake tin.
- Put all of the cake ingredients in a large mixing bowl and whisk them together with an electric whisk for 4 minutes or until pale and well whipped.
- Scrape the mixture into the tin and level the top with a spatula.
- Bake for 30 - 35 minutes. The cake is ready when a toothpick inserted in the centre comes out clean.
- Meanwhile, put the orange zest and honey in a small saucepan and bring to a gentle simmer. Cook for 3 minutes then spoon the mixture all over the cake when it comes out of the oven.
- Leave the cake to soak up the honey as it cools in the tin.

456

MAKES 12

Pumpkin Muffins

PREPARATION TIME 15 MINUTES

COOKING TIME 20-25 MINUTES

································

INGREDIENTS

1 large egg
120 ml / 4 fl. oz / ½ cup sunflower oil
120 ml / 4 fl. oz / ½ cup milk
150 g / 4 ½ oz / 1 ¼ cups pumpkin, finely grated
375 g / 12 ½ oz / 2 ½ cups self-raising flour, sifted
1 tsp baking powder
200 g / 7 oz / ¾ cup caster (superfine) sugar

TO DECORATE
4 tbsp cream cheese
2 tbsp icing (confectioners) sugar
3 tbsp pumpkin seeds

- Preheat the oven to 180°C (160° fan), 355F, gas 4 and line a 12-hole muffin tin with paper cases.
- Beat the egg in a jug with the oil, milk and grated pumpkin until well mixed.
- Mix the flour, baking powder and sugar in a bowl.
- Pour in the egg mixture and stir just enough to combine.
- Divide the mixture between the cases and bake for 20 – 25 minutes.
- Test with a wooden toothpick, if it comes out clean, the cakes are done.
- Transfer the muffins to a wire rack and leave to cool completely.
- Whip the cream cheese with the icing (confectioners) sugar and spread it on top of the cakes with a palette knife.
- Sprinkle over the pumpkin seeds.

Pumpkin and Date Muffins

457

- Add a small handful of chopped dates to the mixture for a fruity, chewy texture.

458

MAKES 12

Pumpkin and Orange Cupcakes

PREPARATION TIME 10 MINUTES

COOKING TIME 15-20 MINUTES

································

INGREDIENTS

100 g / 3 ½ oz / ⅔ cup self-raising flour, sifted
100 g / 3 ½ oz / ½ cup caster (superfine) sugar
100 g / 3 ½ oz / ½ cup butter, softened
3 large eggs
1 orange, zest finely grated
100 g / 3 ½ oz / ¾ cup pumpkin, finely grated
½ tsp nutmeg, freshly grated

- Preheat the oven to 190°C (170° fan) / 375F / gas 5 and line a 12-hole cupcake tin with paper cases.
- Combine the flour, sugar, butter and eggs in a bowl and whisk together for 2 minutes or until smooth. Fold in the orange zest and grated pumpkin.
- Divide the mixture between the cupcake cases and sprinkle with nutmeg, then transfer the tin to the oven and bake for 15 – 20 minutes.
- Test with a wooden toothpick, if it comes out clean, the cakes are done.
- Transfer the cakes to a wire rack and leave to cool completely.

White Chocolate, Pumpkin and Orange Cupcakes

459

- Add a handful of white chocolate chips to the mixture for a more decadent treat.

460

SERVES 8

Damson Tart

- Preheat the oven to 200°C (180° fan), 390F, gas 6.
- Rub the butter into the flour and add just enough cold water to bind.
- Chill for 30 minutes then roll out on a floured surface. Use the pastry to line a 23 cm round tart tin.
- Prick the pastry with a fork, line with clingfilm and fill with baking beans or rice.
- Bake for 10 minutes then remove the clingfilm and baking beans.
- Sprinkle the pastry case with ground almonds then arrange the damson quarters on top and scatter over the sugar.
- Bake the tart for 20 - 25 minutes or until the damsons are tender and the pastry has cooked through underneath.

PREPARATION TIME 40 MINUTES

COOKING TIME 30-40 MINUTES

INGREDIENTS

50 g / 1 ¾ oz / ½ cup ground almonds
450 g / 1 lb damsons, stoned and quartered
4 tbsp granulated sugar

FOR THE PASTRY
200g / 7 oz / 1 ⅓ cup plain (all purpose) flour
100g / 3 ½ oz / ½ cup butter, cubed

Damson and Apple Tart

461

- Swap half the weight of damsons for firm apple slices for a varied fruity flavour.

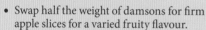

462

SERVES 8

Wholemeal Raisin Loaf Cake

- Preheat the oven to 180°C (160° fan), 355F, gas 4 and grease and line a small loaf tin.
- Put all of the cake ingredients in a large mixing bowl and whisk them together with an electric whisk for 4 minutes or until pale and well whipped.
- Scrape the mixture into the tin and level the top with a spatula.
- Bake for 35 - 40 minutes. The cake is ready when a toothpick inserted in the centre comes out clean.
- Transfer the cake to a wire rack to cool completely.

PREPARATION TIME 10 MINUTES

COOKING TIME 35-40 MINUTES

INGREDIENTS

100 g / 3 ½ oz / ⅔ cup stoneground wholemeal flour
50 g / 1 ¾ oz / ⅓ cup self-raising flour
2 tsp baking powder
150 g / 5 ½ oz / ⅔ cup caster (superfine) sugar
150 g / 5 ½ oz / ⅔ cup butter
3 large eggs
150 g / 5 ½ oz / ¾ cup raisins

Wholemeal Cranberry Loaf Cake

463

- Substitute the raisins with dried cranberries for a sweeter fruity favour.

464

SERVES 8

Wholemeal Raspberry Custard Tart

Wholemeal Cherry Custard Tart

465

- Swap the raspberries for the same weight in drained tinned cherries for a varied fruity taste.

Wholemeal Strawberry Custard Tart

466

- Swap the raspberries for the same weight of chopped strawberries for a sweeter flavour.

PREPARATION TIME 40 MINUTES

COOKING TIME 40-50 MINUTES

INGREDIENTS

200 g / 7 oz / 1 ⅓ cups raspberries

FOR THE PASTRY
100 g / 3 ½ oz / ½ cup butter, cubed
200 g / 7 oz / 1 ⅓ cups stoneground wholemeal flour

FOR THE CUSTARD
4 large egg yolks
75 g / 2 ½ oz / ⅓ cup caster (superfine) sugar
1 tsp vanilla extract
2 tsp cornflour
450 ml / 16 fl. oz / 1 ¾ cups whole milk

- Preheat the oven to 200°C (180° fan), 390F, gas 6.
- Rub the butter into the flour and add just enough cold water to bind.
- Chill for 30 minutes then roll out on a floured surface. Use the pastry to line a 23 cm round tart tin.
- Prick the pastry with a fork, line with clingfilm and fill with baking beans or rice.
- Bake for 10 minutes then remove the clingfilm and baking beans and cook for another 8 minutes to crisp.
- Reduce the oven temperature to 170°C (150° fan), 340F, gas 3.
- Whisk together the custard ingredients and pour into the pastry case. Arrange the raspberries on top.
- Bake the tart for 25 – 35 minutes or until the custard is just set in the centre.

467

SERVES 8

Cranberry and Orange Loaf Cake

- Preheat the oven to 180°C (160° fan), 355F, gas 4 and line a loaf tin with non-stick baking paper.
- Sieve the flour into a mixing bowl and rub in the butter until it resembles fine breadcrumbs then stir in the sugar, cranberries and orange zest.
- Lightly beat the egg with the orange juice and stir it into the dry ingredients until just combined.
- Scrape the mixture into the loaf tin and bake for 55 minutes or until a skewer inserted in the centre comes out clean.
- Transfer the cake to a wire rack and leave to cool completely before dusting with icing (confectioners) sugar.

PREPARATION TIME 15 MINUTES

COOKING TIME 55 MINUTES

INGREDIENTS

225 g / 8oz / 1 ½ cups self raising flour
100 g / 3 ½ oz / ½ cup butter, cubed
85 g / 3oz / ⅓ cup caster (superfine) sugar
150 g / 5 ½ oz dried cranberries
2 oranges, juice and zest finely grated
1 large egg
icing (confectioners) sugar to dust

Blueberry and Orange Loaf Cake   **468**

- Substitute the cranberries with dried blueberries for a a delicious fruity change.

469

MAKES 4

Raspberry Charlottes

- Preheat the oven to 190°C (170° fan), 375F, gas 5 and grease and line 2 large baking trays.
- Put the egg yolks in a bowl with half of the caster (superfine) sugar and the vanilla extract. Whisk with an electric whisk for 4 minutes or until very thick and pale.
- Whisk the egg whites with the cream of tartar until they reach soft peak stage, then gradually whisk in the remaining sugar.
- Sieve the flour over the egg yolk mixture and scrape in the egg whites, then carefully fold it all together.
- Spoon the mixture into a piping bag fitted with a large plain nozzle. Pipe 2 rows of 14 adjoining biscuits on each tray and sprinkle with granulated sugar.
- Bake the biscuits for 10 – 15 minutes.
- While the biscuits are still hot, lift them off the baking tray and curve each line round inside a ramekin dish. Leave to cool and harden.
- Unmould the charlottes and fill the centres with raspberries.
- Melt the raspberry jam in the microwave then spoon it over the top.

PREPARATION TIME 20 MINUTES

COOKING TIME 10-15 MINUTES

INGREDIENTS

4 large eggs, separated
125 g / 4 ½ oz / ½ cup caster (superfine) sugar
1 tsp vanilla extract
a pinch cream of tartar
115 g / 4 oz / ⅔ cup plain (all purpose) flour
2 tbsp granulated sugar
200 g / 7 oz / 1 ⅓ cup raspberries
4 tbsp seedless raspberry jam (jelly)

470

SERVES 8

Raspberry Swiss Roll

PREPARATION TIME 30 MINUTES

COOKING TIME 15-20 MINUTES

INGREDIENTS

100 g / 3 ½ oz / ⅔ cup self-raising flour
1 tsp baking powder
100 g / 3 ½ oz / ½ cup caster (superfine) sugar
100 g / 3 ½ oz / ½ cup butter
2 large eggs
1 tsp vanilla extract

TO DECORATE

200 g / 7 oz / ⅔ cup raspberry jam (jelly)
pink sugar sprinkles

- Preheat the oven to 180°C (160° fan), 355F, gas 4 and grease and line a Swiss roll tin.
- Put all of the cake ingredients in a large mixing bowl and whisk them together with an electric whisk for 4 minutes or until pale and well whipped.
- Spoon the mixture into the tin and spread into an even layer with a palette knife.
- Bake for 15 - 20 minutes or until the cake is springy to the touch.
- Turn the cake out onto a sheet of greaseproof paper and peel off the lining paper. Spread the cake with raspberry jam then roll up whilst warm, using the greaseproof paper to help you.
- Leave the cake to cool then sprinkle with the pink sugar sprinkles before slicing.

Blackcurrant Swiss Roll

471

- Change the raspberry jam for blackcurrant jam for a sharper flavour.

472

MAKES 12

Rose Water Cupcakes

PREPARATION TIME 20 MINUTES

COOKING TIME 15-20 MINUTES

INGREDIENTS

110 g / 4 oz / ⅔ cup self-raising flour, sifted
110 g / 4 oz / ½ cup caster (superfine) sugar
110 g / 4 oz / ½ cup butter, softened
2 large eggs
1 tbsp rose water
55 g / 2 oz / ¼ cup butter, softened
225 g / 8 oz / 2 ¼ cups icing (confectioners) sugar
1 tbsp rose syrup
purple sugar sprinkles
12 pink sweets

- Preheat the oven to 190°C (170° fan), 375F, gas 5 and line a 12-hole cupcake tin with paper cases.
- Combine the flour, sugar, butter, eggs and rose water in a bowl and whisk together for 2 minutes or until smooth.
- Divide the mixture between the paper cases, then transfer the tin to the oven and bake for 15 – 20 minutes.
- Test with a wooden toothpick, if it comes out clean, the cakes are done. Transfer the cakes to a wire rack and leave to cool completely.
- To make the icing, beat the butter with a wooden spoon until light and fluffy then beat in the icing (confectioners) sugar.
- Add the rose syrup then use a whisk to whip the mixture for 2 minutes or until smooth and light.
- Spoon the icing onto the cakes and decorate with the sugar sprinkles and top each cake with a pink sweet.

Orange Blossom Cupcakes

473

- Swap the rose water and the rose syrup for orange blossom water and orange syrup to give a different fragrant taste.

474

SERVES 8

Almond and Amoretti Cake

Pistachio and Amoretti Cake

475

- Change the blacnhed almonds for chopped blanched pistachio nuts for a varied nutty flavour.

Kaluha and Amoretti Cake

476

- As the cake cools, drizzle the top with Kaluha to add a moist texture and tempting liquour kick.

Peanut, Walnut and Amoretti Cake

477

- Swap the almonds for pecans and walnuts.

PREPARATION TIME 15 MINUTES

COOKING TIME 55 MINUTES

INGREDIENTS

225 g / 8 oz / 1 ½ cups self raising flour
100 g / 3 ½ oz / ½ cup butter, cubed
100 g / 3 ½ oz / ½ cup caster (superfine) sugar
150 g / 5 ½ oz / 1 ¼ cups blanched almonds, chopped
100 g / 3 ½ oz / 1 ⅓ cups flaked (slivered) almonds
75 g / 2 ½ oz / ½ cup amoretti biscuits, crumbled
1 large egg
75 ml / 2 ½ fl. oz / ⅓ cup whole milk

- Preheat the oven to 180°C (160° fan), 355F, gas 4 and line a 23 cm round cake tin with non-stick baking paper.
- Sieve the flour into a mixing bowl and rub in the butter until it resembles fine breadcrumbs then stir in the sugar. Mix together the chopped and flaked (slivered) almonds and the amoretti biscuits and add ¾ of it to the bowl.
- Lightly beat the egg with the milk and stir it into the dry ingredients until just combined.
- Scrape the mixture into the tin and bake for 55 minutes or until a skewer inserted in the centre comes out clean.
- Transfer the cake to a wire rack and leave to cool completely before topping with the reserved almond mix.

478

SERVES 8

Rum and Golden Sultana Loaf Cake

PREPARATION TIME 15 MINUTES

COOKING TIME 55 MINUTES

INGREDIENTS

225 g / 8oz / 1 ½ cups self raising flour
100 g / 3 ½ oz / ½ cup butter, cubed
85 g / 3oz / ⅓ cup caster (superfine) sugar
150 g / 5 ½ oz / ¾ cup golden sultanas
25 ml / 1 fl. oz rum
50 ml / 1 ¾ fl. oz / ¼ cup milk
1 large egg

- Preheat the oven to 180°C (160° fan), 355F, gas 4 and line a loaf tin with non-stick baking paper.
- Sieve the flour into a mixing bowl and rub in the butter until it resembles fine breadcrumbs then stir in the sugar and golden sultanas.
- Lightly beat the egg with the rum and milk then stir it into the dry ingredients until just combined.
- Scrape the mixture into the loaf tin and bake for 55 minutes or until a skewer inserted comes out clean.
- Transfer the cake to a wire rack and leave to cool completely before slicing.

Rum and Raisin Loaf Cake

479

- Substitute the sultanas for raisans for a darker fruitier taste.

480

SERVES 8

Tea and Almond Cake

PREPARATION TIME 15 MINUTES

COOKING TIME 55 MINUTES

INGREDIENTS

225 g / 8 oz / 1 ½ cups self raising flour
100 g / 3 ½ oz / ½ cup butter, cubed
100 g / 3 ½ oz / ½ cup caster (superfine) sugar
150 g / 5 ½ oz / 2 cups slivered (flaked) almonds
3 tbsp loose leaf tea
1 large egg
75 ml / 2 ½ fl. oz / ⅓ cup strongly brewed tea, cold

- Preheat the oven to 180°C (160° fan), 355F, gas 4 and line a 23 cm round cake tin with non-stick baking paper.
- Sieve the flour into a mixing bowl and rub in the butter until it resembles fine breadcrumbs then stir in all but 2 tablespoons of the sugar. Mix the slivered almonds and tea leaves with the rest of the sugar and add half of it to the bowl.
- Lightly beat the egg with the tea and stir it into the dry ingredients until just combined.
- Scrape the mixture into the tin and scatter the rest of the almond mixture on top.
- Bake for 55 minutes or until a skewer inserted in the centre comes out clean.
- Transfer the cake to a wire rack and leave to cool completely.

Tea and Hazelnut Cake

481

- Change the slivered almonds for chopped hazelnuts (cob nuts) to change the nutty flavour.

482
SERVES 8 Savoie Cake

- Preheat the oven to 180°C (160° fan), 355F, gas 4 and butter a bundt tin.
- Whisk the egg yolks and caster (superfine) sugar together for 4 minutes or until pale and thick, then fold in the flour.
- Whip the egg whites to stiff peaks in a very clean bowl, then fold them into the cake mixture in two stages.
- Scrape the mixture into the tin, being careful to retain as many air bubbles as possible, and bake for 25 – 30 minutes or until a skewer inserted in the centre comes out clean.
- Leave to cool in the tin for 10 minutes before transferring to a wire rack to cool completely.
- Dust with icing (confectioners) sugar before serving.

PREPARATION TIME 15 MINUTES

COOKING TIME 25-30 MINUTES

INGREDIENTS

4 large eggs, separated
175 g / 6 oz / ¾ cup caster (superfine) sugar
100 g / 3 ½ oz / ⅔ cup self raising flour
icing (confectioners) sugar to dust

Chocolate Savoie Cake 483

- After the cake has cooled spread some melted white, dark or milk chocolate across the top for a decadent finish.

484
SERVES 10-12 Chocolate and Raspberry Sponge Cake

- Preheat the oven to 180°C (160° fan), 355F, gas 4 and grease and line a deep 23 cm round cake tin.
- Whisk together the flour, cocoa, baking powder, sugar, butter and eggs with an electric whisk for 4 minutes or until well whipped.
- Scrape the mixture into the tin and bake for 45 - 50 minutes.
- Meanwhile, put the jam and liqueur in a small saucepan and heat until bubbling, stirring to dissolve the jam.
- When the cake is ready, prick the surface all over with a skewer and spoon over the raspberry mixture.
- Leave to cool completely in the tin before unmoulding and sprinkling with white chocolate curls.

PREPARATION TIME 10 MINUTES

COOKING TIME 45-50 MINUTES

INGREDIENTS

225 g / 8 oz / 1 ½ cups self-raising flour
55 g / 2 oz / ½ cup unsweetened cocoa powder
3 tsp baking powder
225 g / 8 oz / 1 cup caster (superfine) sugar
225 g / 8 oz / 1 cup butter
4 large eggs
200 g / 7 oz / ⅔ cup seedless raspberry jam (jelly)
100 ml / 3 ½ fl. oz / ½ cup raspberry liqueur
white chocolate curls

Chocolate and Cherry Sponge Cake 485

- Exchange the raspberry jam and liqueur with cherry jam and liquer for a richer flavour.

486

MAKES 12

Orange and Cardamom Rolls

Raisin, Orange and Cardamom Rolls

487

- Before rolling the pastry up, sprinkle over a handful of juicy rasins for a richer fruity taste.

Lemon and Cardamom Rolls

488

- Swap the orange zest for lemon zest for a sharper citrus flavour.

PREPARATION TIME 2 HOURS 30 MINUTES

COOKING TIME 10-12 MINUTES

INGREDIENTS

400 g / 14 oz / 2 ⅔ cups strong white bread flour
½ tsp easy blend dried yeast
4 tbsp caster (superfine) sugar
1 tsp fine sea salt
1 tbsp olive oil
75 g / 2 ½ oz / ½ cup dark brown sugar
25 g / ¾ oz butter, softened
1 orange, zest finely grated
1 tsp ground cardamom
1 egg, beaten
3 tbsp sugar nibs

- Mix together the flour, yeast, caster (superfine) sugar and salt. Stir the oil into 280 ml of warm water then stir the liquid into the dry ingredients.
- Knead the mixture on a lightly oiled surface for 10 minutes or until the dough is smooth and elastic.
- Leave the dough to rest, covered with oiled clingfilm, for 1 – 2 hours or until doubled in size.
- Roll out the dough into a large rectangle.
- Cream the brown sugar and butter together and stir in the orange zest and cardamom.
- Spread the mixture over the surface of the dough and roll it up tightly.
- Cut the roll into 12 slices and spread them out on a greased baking tray.
- Cover the rolls with oiled clingfilm and leave to prove for 1 hour or until doubled in size.
- Preheat the oven to 220°C (200° fan), 430F, gas 7.
- Brush the rolls with beaten egg and sprinkle with sugar nibs.
- Bake the rolls for 10 - 12 minutes or until they are cooked through and golden brown.

489

SERVES 12 Gluten-Free Orange Sponge Cake

- Preheat the oven to 180°C (160° fan), 355F, gas 4 and grease and line a 20 cm round loose-bottomed cake tin.
- Put all of the cake ingredients in a large mixing bowl and whisk them together with an electric whisk for 4 minutes or until pale and well whipped.
- Scrape the mixture into the tin and level the top with a spatula.
- Bake for 45 - 50 minutes. The cake is ready when a toothpick inserted in the centre comes out clean.
- Transfer the cake to a wire rack to cool completely.

PREPARATION TIME 10 MINUTES

COOKING TIME 45-50 MINUTES

INGREDIENTS

50 g / 1 ¾ oz / ⅓ cup rice flour
50 g / 1 ¾ oz / ⅓ cup potato flour
50 g / 1 ¾ oz / ⅓ cup tapioca flour
150 g / 5 ½ oz / ⅔ cup caster (superfine) sugar
150 g / 5 ½ oz / ⅔ cup butter
3 large eggs
2 tsp baking powder
1 orange, juice and zest finely grated

Gluten Free Sultana and Orange Cake

490

- Add a handful of sultanas to the mixture to get a more fruity texture.

491

MAKES 12 Ginger Muffins

- Preheat the oven to 180°C (160° fan), 355F, gas 4 and oil a 12-hole silicone oval muffin mould.
- Beat the egg in a jug with the oil, milk and stem ginger until well mixed.
- Mix the flour, baking powder, ground ginger and sugar in a bowl.
- Pour in the egg mixture and stir just enough to combine.
- Divide the mixture between the moulds and bake for 20 – 25 minutes.
- Test with a wooden toothpick, if it comes out clean, the cakes are done.
- Transfer the muffins to a wire rack and leave to cool completely.

PREPARATION TIME 15 MINUTES

COOKING TIME 20-25 MINUTES

INGREDIENTS

1 large egg
120 ml / 4 fl. oz / ½ cup sunflower oil
120 ml / 4 fl. oz / ½ cup milk
4 pieces stem ginger in syrup, chopped
375 g / 12 ½ oz / 2 cups self-raising flour, sifted
1 tsp baking powder
1 tsp ground ginger
200 g / 7 oz / ¾ cup caster (superfine) sugar

Ginger Blueberry Muffins

492

- Mix in a handful of blueberries before cooking to give the muffins a more fruity taste.

MAKES 12

Custard and Frangipane Cakes

PREPARATION TIME 20 MINUTES

COOKING TIME 15-20 MINUTES

INGREDIENTS

55 g / 2 oz / ⅓ cup self-raising flour, sifted
55 g / 2 oz / ½ cup ground almonds
110 g / 4 oz ½ cup caster (superfine) sugar
110 g / 4 oz / ½ cup butter, softened
2 large eggs
1 tsp almond essence

FOR THE CUSTARD

2 large egg yolks
55 g / 2 oz / ¼ cup caster (superfine) sugar
2 tbsp plain (all purpose) flour
2 tbsp cornflour
1 tsp vanilla extract
240 ml / 8 fl. oz / 1 cup milk

- Preheat the oven to 190°C (170° fan), 375F, gas 5 and line a 12-hole cupcake tin with paper cases.
- Combine the flour, ground almonds, sugar, butter, eggs and almond essence in a bowl and whisk together for 2 minutes or until smooth.
- Divide the mixture between the cases.
- To make the custard, stir the egg yolks, sugar, flours and vanilla extract together in a saucepan, then gradually add the milk.
- Heat the mixture until it starts to boil, stirring all the time, then take off the heat and beat vigorously to remove any lumps.
- Spoon the custard into a piping bag and pipe a design on top of the cakes then transfer the tin to the oven and bake for 15 – 20 minutes.
- Test with a wooden toothpick, if it comes out clean, the cakes are done.
- Transfer the cakes to a wire rack to cool.

SERVES 8

Black Cherry and Maple Syrup Cake

PREPARATION TIME 15 MINUTES

COOKING TIME 55 MINUTES

INGREDIENTS

225 g / 8 oz / 1 ½ cups self raising flour
100 g / 3 ½ oz / ½ cup butter, cubed
100 g / 3 ½ oz / ½ cup caster (superfine) sugar
150 g / 5 ½ oz / 1 cup black cherries in syrup, drained
1 large egg
75 ml / 2 ½ fl. oz / ⅓ cup whole milk
200 ml / 7 fl. oz / ⅔ cup maple syrup

- Preheat the oven to 180°C (160° fan), 355F, gas 4 and line a 23 cm round cake tin with non-stick baking paper.
- Sieve the flour into a mixing bowl and rub in the butter until it resembles fine breadcrumbs then stir in the sugar and cherries.
- Lightly beat the egg with the milk and stir it into the dry ingredients until just combined.
- Scrape the mixture into the tin and bake for 55 minutes, or until a skewer inserted in the centre comes out clean.
- Transfer the cake to a wire rack and pour over the maple syrup.

SERVES 8

Chocolate Torte

- Preheat the oven to 170°C (150° fan), 340F, gas 3 and oil and line a 23 cm round cake tin.
- Melt the chocolate, cocoa and butter together in a saucepan, then leave to cool a little.
- Whisk the sugar and eggs together with an electric whisk for 3 minutes or until very light and creamy.
- Pour in the chocolate mixture and ground almonds, then fold everything together until evenly mixed.
- Scrape into the tin and bake for 35 – 40 minutes or until the outside is set, but the centre is still quite soft, as it will continue to cook as it cools.
- Leave the torte to cool completely in its tin then unmould and dust with cocoa powder.

PREPARATION TIME 25 MINUTES

COOKING TIME 35-40 MINUTES

INGREDIENTS

110g / 4 oz dark chocolate (minimum 60 % cocoa solids), chopped
85 g / 3 oz / ¾ cup unsweetened cocoa powder, plus extra for dusting
225 g / 8 oz / 1 cup butter
450 g /15 oz / 2 ½ cups light brown sugar
4 large eggs
110 g / 4 oz / 1 cup ground almonds

Banana and Peel Loaf

496

SERVES 8

PREPARATION TIME 10 MINUTES

COOKING TIME 55 MINUTES

INGREDIENTS

3 very ripe bananas
110 g / 4 oz dark / ½ cup brown sugar
2 large eggs
120 ml / 4 fl. oz / ½ cup sunflower oil

225 g / 8 oz / 1 ½ cups plain (all purpose) flour
1 tsp bicarbonate of soda
75 g / 2 ½ oz / ⅓ cup mixed candied peel, chopped

- Preheat the oven to 170°C (150° fan), 340F, gas 3 and line a loaf tin with non-stick baking paper.
- Mash the bananas roughly with a fork then whisk in the sugar, eggs and oil.
- Sieve the flour and bicarbonate of soda into the bowl and add the candied peel. Stir just enough to evenly mix all the ingredients together.
- Scrape the mixture into the loaf tin and bake for 55 minutes or until a skewer inserted in the centre comes out clean.
- Transfer the cake to a wire rack and leave to cool completely.

Mixed Spice Muffins

497

MAKES 12

PREPARATION TIME 25 MINUTES

COOKING TIME 20-25 MINUTES

INGREDIENTS

1 large egg
120 ml / 4 fl. oz / ½ cup sunflower oil
120 ml / 4 fl. oz / ½ cup milk
375 g / 12 ½ oz / 2 ½ cups self-raising flour, sifted
1 tsp baking powder
2 tsp mixed spice
200 g / 7 oz / ¾ cup caster (superfine) sugar

- Preheat the oven to 180°C (160° fan), 355F, gas 4 and line a 12-hole muffin tin with paper cases.
- Beat the egg in a jug with the oil and milk until well mixed.
- Mix the flour, baking powder, mixed spice and sugar in a bowl.
- Pour in the egg mixture and stir just enough to combine.
- Divide the mixture between the cases and bake for 20 – 25 minutes.
- Test with a wooden toothpick, if it comes out clean, the cakes are done.
- Transfer the muffins to a wire rack and leave to cool completely.

Stollen

498

MAKES 1 LOAF

PREPARATION TIME 2 HOURS
30 MINUTES

COOKING TIME 35-40 MINUTES

INGREDIENTS

55 g / 2 oz / ¼ cup butter, cubed
400 g / 14 oz / 2 ⅔ cups strong white
bread flour, plus extra for dusting
½ tsp easy blend dried yeast
4 tbsp caster (superfine) sugar
1 tsp fine sea salt
2 tsp mixed spice
100 g / 3 ½ oz / ½ cup mixed dried
fruit
1 egg, beaten
300 g / 10 ½ oz marzipan
icing (confectioners) sugar to dust

- Rub the butter into the bread flour and stir in the yeast, sugar, salt and spice. Stir the dried fruit and egg into 250 ml of warm water and stir into the dry ingredients.
- Knead the mixture on a lightly oiled surface for 10 minutes or until the dough is smooth and elastic.
- Leave the dough to rest, covered with a lightly oiled bowl, for 1 – 2 hours or until doubled in size.
- Dust the work surface with icing (confectioners) sugar and press the dough out into a rectangle.
- Shape the marzipan into a long sausage and roll it up inside the dough.
- Transfer the stollen to a greased baking tray and leave to prove, covered, for 45 minutes.
- Preheat the oven to 220°C (200° fan), 430F, gas 7.
- Bake for 35 – 40 minutes then dust liberally with icing (confectioners) sugar.

White Chocolate Coated Stollen
499

- When the stollen has cooled drizzle melted white chocolate all over the surface instead of icing (confectioners) sugar for a more decadent finish.

Sugar Crust Sponge Cake

500

SERVES 8

PREPARATION TIME 15 MINUTES

COOKING TIME 55 MINUTES

INGREDIENTS

225 g / 8 oz / 1 ½ cups self raising
flour
100 g / 3 ½ oz / ½ cup butter, cubed
150 g / 5 ½ oz / ⅔ cup caster
(superfine) sugar
1 large egg
75 ml / 2 ½ fl. oz / ⅓ cup whole milk

- Preheat the oven to 180°C (160° fan), 355F, gas 4 and line a 23 cm round cake tin with non-stick baking paper.
- Sieve the flour into a mixing bowl and rub in the butter until it resembles fine breadcrumbs then stir in ⅔ of the sugar.
- Lightly beat the egg with the milk and stir it into the dry ingredients until just combined.
- Scrape the mixture into the tin and sprinkle over the rest of the sugar then bake for 55 minutes, or until a skewer inserted comes out clean.
- Transfer the cake to a wire rack and leave to cool.

Sugar Crust Chocolate Chip Sponge Cake
501

- Add a handful of dark chocolate chips to the mixture for a more luxurious tasting cake.

502

SERVES 8

Toffee Cake

Toffee Apple Cake

 503

- Mix in a finely choppped peel and cored apple before cooking as a delciious fruity variation.

Spiced Toffee Cake

 504

- Add a teaspoon of ground cinnamon, a ¼ teaspoon of ground nutmeg to the mixture for a more spicy finish.

PREPARATION TIME 15 MINUTES

COOKING TIME 55 MINUTES

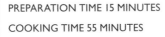

INGREDIENTS

225 g / 8 oz / 1 ½ cups self raising flour
100 g / 3 ½ oz / ½ cup butter, cubed
100 g / 3 ½ oz / ½ cup light brown sugar
150 g / 5 ½ oz chewy toffee, chopped
1 large egg
75 ml / 2 ½ fl. oz / ⅓ cup whole milk

- Preheat the oven to 180°C (160° fan), 355F, gas 4 and line a 23 cm round cake tin with non-stick baking paper.
- Sieve the flour into a mixing bowl and rub in the butter until it resembles fine breadcrumbs then stir in the sugar and toffee.
- Lightly beat the egg with the milk and stir it into the dry ingredients until just combined.
- Scrape the mixture into the tin and bake for 55 minutes, or until a skewer inserted in the centre comes out clean.
- Transfer the cake to a wire rack and leave to cool.

505

MAKES 1

Sugar and Mascarpone Pizza

PREPARATION TIME 2 HOURS 30 MINUTES

COOKING TIME 15-20 MINUTES

INGREDIENTS

200 g / 7 oz / 1 ⅓ cups strong white bread flour, plus extra for dusting
½ tsp easy blend dried yeast
1 tbsp caster (superfine) sugar
½ tsp fine sea salt
1 tbsp sunflower oil

FOR THE TOPPING

200 g / 7 oz / ¾ cup mascarpone
75 g / 2 ½ oz / ⅓ cup granulated sugar

- Mix together the flour, yeast, sugar and salt. Stir the oil into 280 ml of warm water then stir it into the dry ingredients.
- Knead the mixture on a lightly oiled surface with your hands for 10 minutes or until smooth and elastic.
- Leave the dough to rest in a lightly oiled bowl, covered with oiled clingfilm, for 1 – 2 hours or until doubled in size.
- Preheat the oven to 220°C (200° fan), 430F, gas 7.
- Press the dough out into an even round on an oiled baking tray.
- Spread over the mascarpone and sprinkle with granulated sugar then bake for 15 – 20 minutes or until golden on top and cooked through underneath.

Cinnamon and Mascarpone Pizza 506

- Mix a teaspoon of ground cinnamon into the mascarpone and sugar before topping the pizza for a smooth and spicy taste.

507

MAKES 1

Sugar and Butter Pizza

PREPARATION TIME 2 HOURS 30 MINUTES

COOKING TIME 15-20 MINUTES

INGREDIENTS

200 g / 7 oz / 1 ⅓ cups strong white bread flour, plus extra for dusting
½ tsp easy blend dried yeast
1 tbsp caster (superfine) sugar
½ tsp fine sea salt
1 tbsp sunflower oil

FOR THE TOPPING

100 g / 3 ½ oz / ½ cup butter
100 g / 3 ½ oz / ½ cup light brown sugar

- Mix together the flour, yeast, sugar and salt. Stir the oil into 280 ml of warm water then stir it into the dry ingredients.
- Knead the mixture on a lightly oiled surface with your hands for 10 minutes or until smooth and elastic.
- Leave the dough to rest in a lightly oiled bowl, covered with oiled clingfilm, for 1 – 2 hours or until doubled in size.
- Preheat the oven to 220°C (200° fan), 430F, gas 7.
- Press the dough out into an even round on an oiled baking tray and pinch round the edge to form a rim.
- Cream the butter and brown sugar together then spread it over the bread.
- Bake the pizza for 15 – 20 minutes or until golden on top and cooked through underneath.

Maple Pecan Pizza 508

- Add 2-3 tablespoons of maple syrup, and a handful of chopped pecans to the topping mixture for a delicious alternative.

MAKES 12

Fatless Sponge Cakes

- Preheat the oven to 180°C (160° fan), 355F, gas 4 and oil 12 shallow Yorkshire pudding moulds.
- Whisk the egg yolks and caster (superfine) sugar together for 4 minutes or until pale and thick, then fold in the flour.
- Whip the egg whites to stiff peaks in a very clean bowl, then fold them into the cake mixture in two stages.
- Spoon the mixture into the tins, being careful to retain as many air bubbles as possible, and bake for 10 – 15 minutes or until a skewer inserted in the centre comes out clean.
- Leave to cool in the tin for 10 minutes before transferring to a wire rack to cool completely.

PREPARATION TIME 15 MINUTES

COOKING TIME 10-15 MINUTES

INGREDIENTS

4 large eggs, separated
175 g / 6 oz / ¾ cup caster (superfine) sugar
100 g / 3 ½ oz / ⅔ cup self raising flour
icing (confectioners) sugar to dust

Fatless Cranberry Sponge Cakes 510

- Sprinkle a few dried cranberries onto the tops of each mould before cooking for a sweeter fruitier flavour.

MAKES 12

Summer Berry Cupcakes

- Preheat the oven to 190°C (170° fan), 375F, gas 5 and line a 12-hole cupcake tin with paper cases.
- Combine the flour, sugar, butter, eggs and vanilla extract in a bowl and whisk together for 2 minutes or until smooth. Fold in the raspberries and blueberries.
- Divide the mixture between the paper cases, then bake for 15 – 20 minutes.
- Test with a wooden toothpick, if it comes out clean, the cakes are done. Transfer the cakes to a wire rack and leave to cool completely.
- To make the icing, beat the butter with a wooden spoon until light and fluffy then beat in the icing (confectioners) sugar.
- Add the milk then use a whisk to whip the mixture for 2 minutes or until smooth and light.
- Spoon the icing onto the cakes and top with the berries and a sprinkle of icing (confectioners) sugar.

PREPARATION TIME I HOUR

COOKING TIME 15-20 MINUTES

INGREDIENTS

110 g / 4 oz / ⅔ cup self-raising flour, sifted
110 g / 4 oz / ½ cup caster (superfine) sugar
110 g / 4 oz / ½ cup butter, softened
2 large eggs
1 tsp vanilla extract
75 g / 2 ½ oz / ½ cup raspberries
75 g / 2 ½ oz / ½ cup blueberries

TO DECORATE

55 g / 2 oz / ¼ cup butter, softened
225 g / 8 oz / 2 ¼ cup icing (confectioners) sugar, plus extra to dust
1 tbsp milk
12 raspberries
75 g / 2 ½ oz / ½ cup blueberries

Chocolate Berry Cupcakes 512

- Sprinkle a handful of white chocolate chips into the mixture before cooking for a richer taste.

513

SERVES 8-10

Carrot Layer Cake

PREPARATION TIME 25 MINUTES

COOKING TIME 30-35 MINUTES

INGREDIENTS

175 g / 6 oz / 1 cup light brown sugar
2 large eggs
150 ml / 5 fl. oz / ⅔ cup sunflower oil
175 g / 6 oz / 1 ¼ cup stoneground wholemeal flour
3 tsp baking powder
2 tsp ground cinnamon
½ tsp nutmeg freshly grated
1 orange, zest finely grated
200 g / 7 oz / 1 ⅔ cup carrots, washed and coarsely grated

FOR THE SOAKING SYRUP

1 orange, juiced
2 tbsp light brown sugar

FOR THE ICING

225g / 8 oz / 1 cup cream cheese
110 g / 4 oz / ½ cup butter, softened
225 g / 8 oz / 2 ¼ cups icing (confectioners) sugar
1 tsp vanilla extract

- Preheat the oven to 190°C (170° fan), 375F, gas 5 and line 2 x 20 cm round cake tins with greaseproof paper.
- Whisk the sugar, eggs and oil together for 3 minutes until thick.
- Fold in the flour, baking powder and spices, followed by the orange zest and carrots.
- Divide the mixture between the tins and bake for 30 - 35 minutes.
- Test with a wooden toothpick, if it comes out clean, the cakes are done. Transfer the cakes to a wire rack and leave to cool completely.
- To make the icing, beat the cream cheese and butter together with a wooden spoon until light and fluffy then beat in the icing (confectioners) sugar a quarter at a time.
- Add the vanilla extract then use a whisk to whip the mixture for 2 minutes or until smooth and light.
- Use half of the icing to sandwich the cakes together and spread the rest over the top of the cake with a palette knife. Grate over a little nutmeg to finish.

514

SERVES 12

Toffee Sponge Cake

PREPARATION TIME 20 MINUTES

COOKING TIME 45-50 MINUTES

INGREDIENTS

150 g / 5 ½ oz / 1 cup self-raising flour
150 g / 5 ½ oz / ¾ cup muscovado sugar
150 g / 5 ½ oz / ⅔ cup butter
3 large eggs
1 tsp baking powder
1 tsp vanilla extract

FOR THE TOFFEE SAUCE

100 g / 3 ½ oz / ½ cup butter
100 g / 3 ½ oz / ½ cup muscovado sugar
100 g / 3 ½ oz / ⅓ cup golden syrup

- Preheat the oven to 180°C (160° fan), 355F, gas 4 and grease and line a deep 20 cm round loose-bottomed cake tin.
- Put all of the cake ingredients in a large mixing bowl and whisk them together with an electric whisk for 4 minutes or until pale and well whipped.
- Scrape the mixture into the tin and level the top with a spatula.
- Bake for 45 - 50 minutes. The cake is ready when a toothpick inserted in the centre comes out clean.
- Meanwhile, put the toffee sauce ingredients in a small saucepan and stir over a low heat until the butter melts and the sugar dissolves.
- Bring the toffee sauce to the boil then take it off the heat.
- When the cake comes out of the oven, prick the top with a skewer and spoon over half of the toffee sauce.
- Allow the cake to cool for at least 15 minutes then cut into wedges and serve the rest of the sauce alongside.

Raspberry Upside-Down Cake

515

SERVES 8

- Preheat the oven to 170°C (150° fan), gas 3 and butter a 23 cm round cake tin.
- Sieve the flour and baking powder into a mixing bowl and add sugar, butter and eggs.
- Beat the mixture with an electric whisk for 4 minutes or until smooth and well whipped.
- Spread the jam over the base of the cake tin and arrange the raspberries on top.
- Spoon in the cake mixture and bake for 35 minutes or until a skewer inserted in the centre comes out clean.
- Leave the cake to cool for 20 minutes before turning out onto a serving plate.

PREPARATION TIME 15 MINUTES

COOKING TIME 35 MINUTES

INGREDIENTS

300 g / 10 ½ oz / 2 cups self-raising flour
2 tsp baking powder
250 g / 9 oz / 1 ¼ cups caster (superfine) sugar
250 g / 9 oz / 1 ¼ cups butter, softened
5 large eggs
4 tbsp raspberry jam
200 g / 7 oz raspberries

Vanilla and Honey Loaf Cake

516

SERVES 8

PREPARATION TIME 10 MINUTES

COOKING TIME 35-40 MINUTES

INGREDIENTS

150 g / 5 ½ oz / 1 cup self-raising flour
150 g / 5 ½ oz / ⅔ cup caster (superfine) sugar

150 g / 5 ½ oz / ⅔ cup butter
3 eggs
1 tsp baking powder
2 tsp vanilla extract
200 g / 7 oz / ⅔ cup runny honey

- Preheat the oven to 180°C (160° fan), 355F, gas 4 and grease and line a small loaf tin.
- Put all of the cake ingredients except the honey in a large mixing bowl and whisk them together with an electric whisk for 4 minutes or until pale and well whipped.
- Scrape the mixture into the tin and level the top with a spatula.
- Bake for 35 - 40 minutes. The cake is ready when a toothpick inserted comes out clean.
- While the cake is cooking, put the honey in a small saucepan and heat until very liquid.
- When the cake is ready, prick all over the surface with a skewer and spoon over the hot honey.
- Leave the cake to cool completely in the tin.

Cinnamon and Lime Whoopees

517

MAKES 18

PREPARATION TIME 20 MINUTES

COOKING TIME 10-15 MINUTES

INGREDIENTS

110 g / 4 oz / ⅔ cup self-raising flour, sifted
2 tsp baking powder
110 g / 4 oz / ½ cup caster sugar

110 g / 4 oz / ½ cup butter, softened
2 large eggs
1 tsp ground cinnamon

TO DECORATE
½ jar lime curd
a few drops of green food dye

- Preheat the oven to 190°C (170° fan), 375F, gas 5 and line 2 large baking trays with non-stick baking mats.
- Combine the flour, baking powder, sugar, butter, eggs and cinnamon in a bowl and whisk together for 2 minutes or until smooth.
- Spoon the mixture into a piping bag fitted with a large plain nozzle and pipe 18 walnut-sized domes onto each tray.
- Transfer the trays to the oven and bake for 10 – 15 minutes. The mixture should spread a little whilst cooking and the cakes will be ready when springy to the touch.
- Leave the cakes to cool on the tray then lift them off with a palette knife.
- Mix the lime curd with the food colouring until evenly coloured then sandwich the cakes together in pairs.

518

SERVES 8

Glace Fruit Cake

Frosted Fruit Cake

519

- Swap out the glace fruits for the same weight of mixed sultanas, raisins and candied peel for a richer flavour.

Hazelnut Frosted Fruit Cake

520

- Swap the flaked (slivered) almonds for chopped hazelnuts (cob nuts) for a more nutty finish.

PREPARATION TIME 15 MINUTES

COOKING TIME 55 MINUTES

INGREDIENTS

225 g / 8 oz / 1 ½ cups self raising flour
100 g / 3 ½ oz / ½ cup butter, cubed
100 g / 3 ½ oz / ½ cup caster (superfine) sugar
75 g / 2 ½ oz / ⅓ cup glace cherries, chopped
75 g / 2 ½ oz / ⅓ cup glace angelica, chopped
75 g / 2 ½ oz / ⅓ cup glace pineapple, chopped
1 large egg
75 ml / 2 ½ fl. oz / ⅓ cup whole milk

FOR THE TOPPING
200 g / 7 oz / 2 cups icing (confectioners) sugar
50 g / 1 ¾ oz / ⅔ cup flaked (slivered) almonds, toasted

- Preheat the oven to 180°C (160° fan), 355F, gas 4 and line a 23 cm round cake tin with non-stick baking paper.
- Sieve the flour into a mixing bowl and rub in the butter until it resembles fine breadcrumbs then stir in the sugar and glace fruit.
- Lightly beat the egg with the milk and stir it into the dry ingredients until just combined.
- Scrape the mixture into the tin and bake for 55 minutes or until a skewer inserted in the centre comes out clean.
- Transfer the cake to a wire rack and leave to cool completely.
- Mix the icing (confectioners) sugar with enough cold water, drop by drop, to make a thick icing.
- Spoon the icing over the cake and sprinkle with the toasted almonds.

521
SERVES 8

Almond, Walnut and Cranberry Loaf

- Preheat the oven to 180°C (160° fan), 355F, gas 4 and line a loaf tin with non-stick baking paper.
- Sieve the flour into a mixing bowl and rub in the butter until it resembles fine breadcrumbs then stir in the sugar, cranberries and nuts.
- Lightly beat the egg with the milk and stir it into the dry ingredients until just combined.
- Scrape the mixture into the loaf tin and bake for 55 minutes or until a skewer inserted in the centre comes out clean.
- Transfer the cake to a wire rack and leave to cool completely before slicing.

PREPARATION TIME 15 MINUTES

COOKING TIME 55 MINUTES

INGREDIENTS

225 g / 8oz / 1 ½ cups self raising flour
100 g / 3 ½ oz / ½ cup butter, cubed
85 g / 3oz / cup muscovado sugar
75 g / 2 ½ oz / ⅓ cup dried cranberries
75 g / 2 ½ oz / ⅔ cup walnuts, chopped
75 g / 2 ½ oz / ½ cup almonds
1 large egg
75 ml / 2 ½ fl. oz / ⅓ cup whole milk

Almond, Pecan and Cranberry Loaf

522

- Change the walnuts for chopped pecan nuts for a richer, sweeter flavour.

523
MAKES 8

Chocolate, Walnut and Toffee Brownies

- Preheat the oven to 170°C (150° fan), 340F, gas 3 and oil and butter 8 ramekins.
- Melt the chocolate, cocoa and butter together in a saucepan, then leave to cool a little.
- Whisk the sugar and eggs together with an electric whisk for 3 minutes or until very light and creamy.
- Pour in the chocolate mixture and sieve over the flour, then fold everything together with the walnuts and toffee pieces until evenly mixed.
- Divide between the ramekins and bake for 20 – 25 minutes or until the outsides are set, but the centres are still quite soft.
- Leave to cool and firm up for 10 minutes before serving warm with ice cream.

PREPARATION TIME 15 MINUTES

COOKING TIME 20-25 MINUTES

INGREDIENTS

110g / 4 oz dark chocolate (minimum 60 % cocoa solids), chopped
85 g / 3 oz / ¾ cup unsweetened cocoa powder, sifted
225 g / 8 oz / 1 cup butter
450 g /15 oz / 2 ½ cups light brown sugar
4 large eggs
110 g / 4 oz / ⅔ cup self-raising flour
75 g / 2 ½ oz / ⅔ cup walnuts, chopped
75 g / 2 ½ oz chewy toffee, chopped

Chocolate, Hazelnut and Toffee Brownies

524

- Swap the walnuts for chopped hazelnuts (cob nuts) for a different nutty variation.

BREADS AND BISCUITS

525

MAKES 16

Lemon and Almond Shortbread Biscuits

PREPARATION TIME 20 MINUTES

COOKING TIME 15-20 MINUTES

INGREDIENTS

175 g / 6 oz / 1 cup plain (all purpose) flour
55 g / 2 oz / ½ cup ground almonds
75 g / 2 ½ oz / ⅓ cup caster (superfine) sugar
150 g / 5 oz / ⅔ cup butter, cubed
1 lemon, zest finely grated
50 g / 1 ¾ oz / ¼ cup granulated sugar

- Preheat the oven to 180°C (160° fan), gas 4 and line a baking tray with greaseproof paper.
- Mix together the flour, ground almonds and caster (superfine) sugar in a bowl, then rub in the butter and lemon zest.
- Knead gently until the mixture forms a smooth dough then form into cylinder 6 cm in diameter and roll in granulated sugar.
- Slice the roll into 1 cm thick slices and spread them out on the baking tray.
- Bake the biscuits for 15-20 minutes, turning the tray round halfway through.
- Transfer the biscuits to a wire rack and leave to cool.

St.Clement's Almond Shortbread Biscuits

526

- Mix together the flour, ground almonds and caster (superfine) sugar in a bowl, then rub in the butter, lemon zest and the zest of an orange.

527

MAKES 12

Almond Rock Cookies

PREPARATION TIME 30 MINUTES

COOKING TIME 15 MINUTES

INGREDIENTS

100 g / 3 ½ oz / ½ cup butter
200 g / 7 oz / 1 1/3 cups self-raising flour
100 g / 3 ½ oz / ½ cup caster sugar
100 g / 3 ½ oz / ⅔ cup blanched almonds
1 large egg
2 tbsp whole milk
icing (confectioners) sugar to dust

- Preheat the oven to 200°C (180° fan), gas 6 and grease a large baking tray.
- Rub the butter into the flour until the mixture resembles fine breadcrumbs then stir in the sugar and almonds.
- Beat the egg with the milk and stir it into the dry ingredients to make a sticky dough.
- Use a dessert spoon to portion the mixture onto the baking tray, flattening the cookies a bit with the back of the spoon but leaving the surface quite rough.
- Bake the cookies for 15 minutes then transfer them to a wire rack and leave to cool.
- Dust the cookies with icing (confectioners) sugar before serving.

Almond and Cherry Rock Cookies

528

- Add 100 g / 3 ½ oz of glacé cherries at the same time as the almonds.

529

MAKES 6

Almond Tuile Millefeuille

Pistachio Tuile Millefeuille

530

- Replace the flaked (slivered) almonds with the same weight of crushed pistachios for a different nutty flavour.

Almond and Mandarin Tuile Millefeuille

531

- Replace the grapefruit garnish with segments of mandarin for a sweeter taste.

PREPARATION TIME 45 MINUTES

COOKING TIME 8-10 MINUTES

INGREDIENTS

110 g / 4 oz / ⅔ cup plain (all purpose) flour
110 g / 4 oz / ½ cup caster (superfine) sugar
2 large egg whites
110 g / 4 oz / ½ cup butter, melted
55 g / 2 oz / ⅔ cup flaked almonds

TO DECORATE

2 grapefruits
225 ml / 8 fl. oz / ¾ cup double cream
1 lemon, zest finely pared

- Beat together the flour, sugar and egg whites until smooth, then beat in the melted butter.
- Refrigerate for 30 minutes.
- Preheat the oven to 180°C (160° fan) / 350F / gas 4 and oil 2 large baking trays.
- Spoon teaspoonfuls of the mixture onto the first baking tray and spread out with the back of the spoon to make 8 cm circles.
- Sprinkle with flaked (slivered) almonds and bake for 8 – 10 minutes then repeat with the second tray. You need to make 18 biscuits in total.
- Leave the biscuits to cool and crisp up on the tray then transfer to a wire rack.
- Cut the top and bottom off the grapefruits then cut away the peel. Cut out each segment then discard the skin.
- Whip the cream until thick.
- To assemble the millefeuilles, start with a tuile and top it with 2 grapefruit segments. Add a spoonful of cream and a sprinkle of lemon zest then top with another tuile. Repeat again to create a stack of 3 biscuits.

Secret-Centre Apple Loaf Cake

532

SERVES 8

PREPARATION TIME 15 MINUTES

COOKING TIME 55 MINUTES

INGREDIENTS

300 g / 10 ½ oz / 2 cups self-raising flour
2 tsp baking powder
250 g / 9 oz / 1 ¼ cup caster (superfine) sugar
250 g / 9 oz / 1 ¼ cup butter, softened
5 large eggs
1 eating apple, cored and finely chopped
1 tsp mixed spice
4 tbsp sultanas
1 lemon, zest finely grated
2 tbsp granulated sugar

- Preheat the oven to 170ºC (150º fan), gas 3 and line a large loaf tin with non-stick baking paper.
- Sieve the flour and baking powder into a mixing bowl and add the sugar, butter and eggs.
- Beat the mixture with an electric whisk for 4 minutes or until smooth and well whipped.
- Mix the chopped apple with the mixed spice, sultanas and lemon zest.
- Spoon half of the cake mixture into the lined tin then spoon the apple mixture on top, leaving a border round the outside.
- Spoon the rest of the cake mixture on top and level the surface then sprinkle with granulated sugar.
- Bake the cake for 55 minutes or until a skewer inserted comes out clean. Transfer the cake to a wire rack and leave to cool completely before slicing.

Secret-Centre Berry Loaf Cake

533

- Replace the eating apple with 200 g frozen mixed berries that have been thawed.

534

Crusty Farmhouse Rolls

MAKES 12

PREPARATION TIME 2 HOURS 30 MINUTES

COOKING TIME 15-20 MINUTES

INGREDIENTS

350 g / 12 ½ oz/ 2 ⅓ cups strong white bread flour, plus extra for dusting
50 g / 1 ¾ oz / ⅓ cup stoneground wholemeal flour
½ tsp easy blend dried yeast
1 tbsp caster (superfine) sugar
1 tsp fine sea salt
1 tbsp olive oil

- Mix together the flours, yeast, sugar and salt. Stir in the oil and 280 ml of warm water.
- Knead the mixture on a lightly oiled surface with your hands for 10 minutes or until smooth and elastic.
- Leave the dough to rest in an oiled bowl, covered with oiled clingfilm, for 2 hours. Knead it for 2 more minutes then split into 12 even pieces and shape into rolls.
- Transfer the rolls to a greased baking tray and cover with oiled clingfilm. Leave to prove for 1 hour.
- Meanwhile, preheat the oven to 220ºC (200º fan), gas 7.
- Dust the rolls with flour and slash the tops with a knife.
- Transfer the tray to the top shelf of the oven then quickly throw a small cupful of water onto the oven floor and close the door.
- Bake for 15 – 20 minutes or until the rolls sound hollow when you tap them underneath.
- Transfer to a wire rack and leave to cool.

Olive Farmhouse Rolls

535

- Add 55 g / 2 oz finely chopped black olives when the dough is kneaded the second time for a more savoury taste.

536 MAKES 12

Viennese Whirls

- Preheat the oven to 170°C (150° fan), gas 3 and line 2 baking trays with non-stick baking paper.
- Cream the butter, sugar and vanilla extract together with an electric whisk then stir in the flour.
- Spoon the mixture into a piping bag fitted with a large star nozzle and pipe 12 rosettes onto each tray. Bake the biscuits for 15 – 20 minutes.
- Transfer the biscuits to a wire rack and leave to cool before dusting with icing (confectioners) sugar.
- To make the buttercream, beat the butter with a wooden spoon until light and fluffy then beat in the icing sugar.
- Use a whisk to incorporate the milk, then whisk for 2 minutes or until smooth and well whipped.
- Spoon the buttercream into a piping bag and pipe a swirl onto the flat side of 12 biscuits.
- Top each one with a spoonful of jam and sandwich together with the remaining biscuits.

Chocolate Viennese Whirls 537

- Replace 30 g / 1 oz of the self-raising flour with 55 g / 2 oz good-quality cocoa powder for a more decadent flavour. Add the cocoa powder at the same time as the rest of the self-raising flour.

PREPARATION TIME 10 MINUTES

COOKING TIME 15-20 MINUTES

INGREDIENTS

175 g / 6 oz / ¾ cup butter, softened
50 g / 1 ¾ oz / ¼ cup caster (superfine) sugar
½ tsp vanilla extract
175 g / 6 oz / 1 ¼ cup self-raising flour
2 tbsp icing (confectioners) sugar

FOR THE FILLING
100 g / 3 ½ oz / ½ cup butter, softened
200 g / 7oz / 2 cups icing (confectioners) sugar
½ jar strawberry jam

538 MAKES 36

Chocolate Chip and Hazelnut Cookies

- Preheat the oven to 170°C (150° fan), gas 3 and line 2 baking sheets with greaseproof paper.
- Cream together the two sugars, butter and vanilla extract until pale and well whipped then beat in the egg and yolk, followed by the flour, chocolate and hazelnuts.
- Drop tablespoons of the mixture onto the prepared trays, leaving plenty of room to spread.
- Bake the cookies in batches for 12 - 15 minutes or until the edges are starting to brown, but the centres are still chewy.
- Transfer to a wire rack and leave to cool.

PREPARATION TIME 10 MINUTES

COOKING TIME 12-15 MINUTES

INGREDIENTS

175 g / 6 oz / ¾ cup butter, melted
225 g / 8 oz / 1 ⅓ cups dark brown sugar
100 g / 3 ½ oz / ½ cup caster (superfine) sugar
2 tsp vanilla extract
1 egg, plus 1 egg yolk
250 g / 9 oz / 1 ⅔ cups self-raising flour
175 g / 6 oz / 1 ¼ cups chocolate chips
175 g / 6 oz / 1 ½ cups hazelnuts (cob nuts), chopped

White and Dark Chocolate Chip Cookies 539

- Replace the hazelnuts with with the same weight of finely chopped white chocolate and add to the dough at the same time as the chocolate chips.

540

MAKES 36

Double Chocolate and Pistachio Cookies

Chocolate and Pistachio Cookies

541

- Replace the cocoa powder with the same weight of self-raising flour for a less chocolatey flavour.

Chocolate and Raspberry Cookies

542

- Replace the pistachios with the 110 g / 4 oz chopped, dried raspberries for a fruiter flavour.

PREPARATION TIME 10 MINUTES

COOKING TIME 12-15 MINUTES

INGREDIENTS

175 g / 6 oz / ¾ cup butter, melted
225 g / 8 oz / 1 ⅓ cup dark brown sugar
100 g / 3 ½ oz / ½ cup caster (superfine) sugar
2 tsp vanilla extract
1 egg, plus 1 egg yolk
250 g / 9 oz / 1 ⅔ cup self-raising flour
2 tbsp unsweetened cocoa powder
175 g / 6 oz / 1 ¼ cups chocolate chips
175 g / 6 oz / 1 ½ cups pistachio nuts, chopped

- Preheat the oven to 170°C (150° fan), gas 3 and line 2 baking sheets with greaseproof paper.
- Cream together the two sugars, butter and vanilla extract until pale and well whipped then beat in the egg and yolk, followed by the flour, cocoa, chocolate and pistachio nuts.
- Drop tablespoons of the mixture onto the prepared trays, leaving plenty of room to spread.
- Bake the cookiesin batches for 12 - 15 minutes or until the edges are starting to brown, but the centres are still chewy.
- Transfer to a wire rack and leave to cool.

543

MAKES 16 # Cocoa Shortbread Biscuits

- Preheat the oven to 180°C (160° fan), 355F, gas 4 and line a baking tray with greaseproof paper.
- Mix together the flour, cocoa and caster (superfine) sugar in a bowl, then rub in the butter.
- Knead gently until the mixture forms a smooth dough then form into a cylinder 6 cm in diameter and roll in granulated sugar.
- Slice the roll into 1 cm thick slices and spread them out on the baking tray.
- Bake the biscuits for 15-20 minutes, turning the tray round halfway through.
- Transfer the biscuits to a wire rack and leave to cool.

PREPARATION TIME 20 MINUTES

COOKING TIME 15-20 MINUTES

INGREDIENTS

230 g / 8 oz / 1 ½ cups plain (all purpose) flour
2 tbsp cocoa powder
75 g / 2 ½ oz / ⅓ cup caster (superfine) sugar
150 g / 5 oz / ⅔ cup butter, cubed
50 g / 1 ¾ oz / cup granulated sugar

Cocoa and Orange Shortbread Biscuits

544

- Add 1 tbsp orange flour water at the same time as rubbing the butter into the flour mixture.

545

MAKES 12 # Chocolate Madeleines

- Heat the butter until it foams and starts to smell nutty, then leave to cool.
- Combine the flour, cocoa, ground almonds and icing (confectioners) sugar in a bowl and whisk in the eggs whites.
- Pour the cooled butter through a sieve into the bowl and whisk into the mixture until evenly mixed.
- Leave the cake mixture to rest in the fridge for 1 hour.
- Preheat the oven to 170°C (150° fan), 325F, gas 3 and oil and flour a 12-hole Madeleine mould.
- Spoon the mixture into the moulds, then transfer the tin to the oven and bake for 10 – 15 minutes.
- Test with a wooden toothpick, if it comes out clean, the cakes are done.
- Transfer the cakes to a wire rack to cool for 5 minutes before serving.

PREPARATION TIME 1 HOUR 30 MINUTES

COOKING TIME 10-15 MINUTES

INGREDIENTS

110 g / 4 oz / ½ cup butter
55 g / 2 oz / ⅓ cup plain (all purpose) flour
28g / 1 oz / ¼ cup unsweetened cocoa powder
55 g / 2 oz / ½ cup ground almonds
110 g / 4 oz / 1 cup icing (confectioners) sugar
3 large egg whites

Almond Madeleines

546

- Replace the cocoa powder with and additional 30 g / 1 oz of ground almonds for a more traditional flavour.

547

MAKES 18

Vanilla and Chocolate Whoopee Pies

PREPARATION TIME 20 MINUTES

COOKING TIME 10-15 MINUTES

INGREDIENTS

110 g / 4 oz / ⅔ cup self-raising flour, sifted
2 tsp baking powder
110 g / 4 oz / ½ cup caster (superfine) sugar
110 g / 4 oz / ½ cup butter, softened
2 large eggs
1 tsp vanilla extract

TO DECORATE

½ jar chocolate spread
cocoa powder for dusting

- Preheat the oven to 190°C (170° fan), 375F, gas 5 and line 2 large baking trays with non-stick baking mats.
- Combine the flour, baking powder, sugar, butter, eggs and vanilla extract in a bowl and whisk together for 2 minutes or until smooth.
- Spoon the mixture into a piping bag fitted with a large plain nozzle and pipe 18 walnut-sized domes onto each tray.
- Transfer the trays to the oven and bake for 10 – 15 minutes. The mixture should spread a little whilst cooking and the cakes will be ready when springy to the touch.
- Leave the cakes to cool on the tray then lift them off with a palette knife.
- Sandwich the cakes together in pairs with the chocolate spread and sprinkle with cocoa before serving.

Vanilla and Nutella Whoopie Pies **548**

- Replace the chocolate spread for Nutella or any chocolate and hazelnut spread for a nuttier flavour.

549

MAKES 6

Chocolate Tuile and Pear Millefeuille

PREPARATION TIME 45 MINUTES

COOKING TIME 8-10 MINUTES

INGREDIENTS

110 g / 4 oz / ⅔ cup plain (all purpose) flour
1 tbsp unsweetened cocoa powder
110 g / 4 oz / ½ cup caster (superfine) sugar
2 large egg whites
110 g / 4 oz / ½ cup butter, melted

TO DECORATE

55 g / 2 oz dark chocolate (minimum 60 % cocoa solids)
4 ripe pears, peeled and chopped
cocoa powder to dust

- Beat together the flour, cocoa, sugar and egg whites until smooth, then beat in the melted butter.
- Refrigerate for 30 minutes.
- Preheat the oven to 180°C (160° fan), 350F, gas 4 and oil 2 large baking trays.
- Spoon teaspoonfuls of the mixture onto the first baking tray and spread out with the back of the spoon to make 8 cm circles.
- Bake the tuiles for 8 – 10 minutes then repeat with the second tray. You need to make 18 biscuits in total.
- Leave the biscuits to cool and crisp up on the tray then transfer to a wire rack.
- Melt the chocolate in a microwave or bain marie then dip the top of each biscuit to coat. Leave to set for 1 hour.
- Sandwich the tuiles together with the chopped pears and sprinkle with cocoa powder.

Chocolate Tuile and Mango Millefeuille **550**

- Use 2 diced mangoes instead of the pears as a filling for an exotic tasting millefeuille.

551

MAKES 6

Coconut Tuile and Pineapple Millefeuille

- Beat together the flour, sugar and egg whites until smooth, then beat in the melted butter.
- Refrigerate for 30 minutes.
- Preheat the oven to 180°C (160° fan), 350F, gas 4 and oil 2 large baking trays.
- Spoon teaspoonfuls of the mixture onto the first baking tray and spread out with the back of the spoon to make 8 cm circles.
- Bake for 8 – 10 minutes then repeat with the second tray. You need to make 18 biscuits in total.
- Leave the biscuits to cool and crisp up on the tray then transfer to a wire rack.
- Reserve a few tablespoons of the syrup and drain the rest then finely chop the pineapple chunks.
- Layer the tuiles with the pineapple, drizzling over a little syrup and sprinkle the final tuile with desiccated coconut.

PREPARATION TIME 45 MINUTES

COOKING TIME 8-10 MINUTES

INGREDIENTS

110 g / 4 oz / ⅔ cup plain (all purpose) flour
110 g / 4 oz / ½ cup caster (superfine) sugar
2 large egg whites
110 g / 4 oz / ½ cup butter, melted

TO DECORATE

1 tin pineapple chunks in syrup
3 tbsp desiccated coconut

Coconut Tuile, Chocolate and Pineapple Millefeuille

552

- Replace the desiccated coconut with drizzles of chocolate sauce instead for a more decadent flavour.

553

MAKES 16

Wholemeal Hazelnut Shortbread

- Preheat the oven to 180°C (160° fan), 355F, gas 4 and line a baking tray with greaseproof paper.
- Mix together the flours, ground hazelnuts and caster (superfine) sugar in a bowl, then rub in the butter.
- Knead gently until the mixture forms a smooth dough then roll it out to a thickness of 5 mm.
- Use a round cookie cutter to cut out the biscuits and spread them out on the baking tray.
- You can score a design in the top with a cocktail stick at this stage if you like.
- Bake the biscuits for 15 - 20 minutes, turning the tray round halfway through.
- Transfer the biscuits to a wire rack and leave to cool.

PREPARATION TIME 20 MINUTES

COOKING TIME 15-20 MINUTES

INGREDIENTS

100 g / 3 ½ oz / ⅔ cup stoneground wholemeal flour
100 g / 3 ½ oz / ⅔ cup plain (all purpose) flour
30 g / 1 oz / ⅓ cup ground hazelnuts (cob nuts)
75 g / 2 ½ oz / ⅓ cup caster (superfine) sugar
150 g / 5 oz / ⅔ cup butter, cubed

Traditional Hazelnut Shortbread

554

- Replace the wholemeal flour with 50 g / 2 oz of both plain (all purpose) flour and cornflour for a more traditional tasting shortbread.

555

MAKES 45-50 # Sponge Finger Biscuits

PREPARATION TIME 20 MINUTES

COOKING TIME 10-15 MINUTES

INGREDIENTS

4 large eggs
125 g / 4 ½ oz / ½ cup caster (superfine) sugar
1 tsp vanilla extract
a pinch cream of tartar
115 g / 4 oz / ¾ cup plain (all purpose) flour

- Preheat the oven to 190°C (170° fan), 375F, gas 5 and grease and line 2 large trays with greaseproof paper.
- Separate the eggs and put the yolks in a bowl with half of the sugar and the vanilla extract. Whisk with an electric whisk for 4 minutes or until thick and pale.
- Whisk the egg whites with the cream of tartar, making sure the whisk and bowl are completely clean.
- When the egg white reaches the soft peak stage, gradually whisk in the remaining sugar.
- Sieve the flour over the yolk mixture and scrape in the egg whites, then fold it all together with a metal spoon.
- Spoon the mixture into a piping bag fitted with a large plain nozzle. Pipe 10 cm lines onto the baking trays, leaving room for the biscuits to spread.
- Bake the biscuits for 10 – 15 minutes.
- Transfer to a wire rack and leave to cool completely.

Amaretto Sponge Finger Biscuits   556

- Replace the vanilla extract with 30 ml / 1 fl. oz amaretto, whisking it into the egg yolks at the same time as you would add the vanilla extract.

557

MAKES 36 # Iced Heart Biscuits

PREPARATION TIME 1 HOUR
15 MINUTES

COOKING TIME 25-30 MINUTES

INGREDIENTS

100 g / 3 ½ oz / ½ cup caster (superfine) sugar
100 g / 3 ½ oz / ½ cup butter, softenedsugar
1 tsp vanilla extract
1 large egg, beaten
300 g / 10 ½ oz / 2 cups plain (all purpose) flour

TO DECORATE

150 g / 5 ½ oz royal icing powder
pink food dye

- Cream together the sugar, butter and vanilla extract until pale and well whipped then beat in the egg, followed by the flour.
- Bring the mixture together into a ball with your hands then wrap in clingfilm and refrigerate for 45 minutes.
- Preheat the oven to 190°C (170° fan), 375F, gas 5 and line 2 baking sheets with greaseproof paper.
- Roll out the dough on a lightly floured surface to 5mm thick. Use a heart-shaped cutter to cut out the biscuits.
- Transfer the biscuits to the prepared trays in batches and bake for 8 – 10 minutes.
- Transfer the biscuits to a wire rack and leave to cool.
- Whisk the royal icing powder with a few drops of pink food dye and 25 ml water for 5 minutes.
- Spoon it into a piping bag and pipe your designs onto the biscuits.

Sugar Heart Biscuits   558

- Instead of icing the biscuits, sprinkle over 50 g / 2 oz caster (superfine) sugar as soon as they leave the oven. Let them cool on wire racks before serving.

559

MAKES 36

Ginger Snap Biscuits

Lemon Snap Biscuits

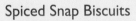 560

- Replace the ground ginger with 2 tsp lemon extract for a tart, citrus taste to these biscuits.

Spiced Snap Biscuits

561

- Replace the ground ginger with 1 ½ tsp ground mixed allspice for a Christmassy flavour.

PREPARATION TIME 10 MINUTES

COOKING TIME 12-15 MINUTES

INGREDIENTS

75 g / 2 ½ oz / ⅓ cup butter, softened
100 g / 3 ½ oz / ⅓ cup golden syrup
225 g / 8 oz / 1 ½ cups self-raising flour
100 g / 3 ½ oz / ½ cup caster (superfine) sugar
1 tsp ground ginger
1 large egg, beaten

- Preheat the oven to 180°C (160° fan), 355F, gas 4 and line 2 baking sheets with greaseproof paper.
- Melt the butter and golden syrup together in a saucepan.
- Mix the flour, sugar and ground ginger together then stir in the melted butter mixture and the beaten egg.
- Use a teaspoon to portion the mixture onto the baking trays, leaving plenty of room for the biscuits to spread.
- Bake in batches for 12 – 15 minutes or until golden brown.
- Transfer the biscuits to a wire rack and leave to cool and harden.

562

MAKES 1 LOAF Hot Cross Bun Loaf

PREPARATION TIME 2 HOURS
30 MINUTES

COOKING TIME 35-40 MINUTES

INGREDIENTS

55 g / 2 oz / ¼ cup butter, cubed
400 g / 14 oz / 2 ⅔ cups strong white
bread flour, plus extra for dusting
½ tsp easy blend dried yeast
4 tbsp caster (superfine) sugar
1 tsp fine sea salt
2 tsp mixed spice
100 g / 3 ½ oz / ½ cup mixed dried
fruit
4 tbsp plain (all purpose) flour
1 egg, beaten

- Rub the butter into the bread flour and stir in the yeast, sugar, salt and spice. Stir the dried fruit into 280 ml of warm water and stir into the dry ingredients.
- Knead the mixture on a lightly oiled surface for 10 minutes or until the dough is smooth and elastic.
- Leave the dough to rest, covered with a lightly oiled bowl, for 1 – 2 hours or until doubled in size.
- Roll the dough into a fat sausage. Turn it 90⁰ and roll it tightly the other way then tuck the ends under and transfer to the tin. Leave to prove for 45 minutes.
- Preheat the oven to 220⁰C (200⁰ fan), 430F, gas 7.
- Mix the plain (all purpose) flour with just enough water to make a thick paste and spoon it into a piping bag. Brush the loaf with egg and pipe the flour mixture on top into crosses.
- Bake for 35 – 40 minutes or until the underneath sounds hollow when tapped.

Raisin and Apple Loaf

563

- Replace the mixed dried fruit with 75 g / 3 oz raisins and 2 small diced eating apples that have been peeled and cored.

564

MAKES 36 Nutmeg Star Biscuits

PREPARATION TIME 1 HOUR
15 MINUTES

COOKING TIME 8-10 MINUTES

INGREDIENTS

100 g / 3 ½ oz / ½ cup caster
(superfine) sugar
100 g / 3 ½ oz / ½ cup butter,
softenedsugar
½ tsp nutmeg, freshly grated
1 large egg, beaten
300 g / 10 ½ oz / 2 cups plain (all
purpose) flour
icing (confectioners) sugar to dust

- Cream together the sugar, butter and grated nutmeg until pale and well whipped then beat in the egg, followed by the flour.
- Bring the mixture together into a ball with your hands then wrap in clingfilm and refrigerate for 45 minutes.
- Preheat the oven to 190⁰C (170⁰ fan), 375F, gas 5 and line 2 baking sheets with greaseproof paper.
- Roll out the dough on a lightly floured surface to 5mm thick. Use a star-shaped cutter to cut out the biscuits, rerolling the trimmings as necessary.
- Transfer the biscuits to the prepared trays in batches and bake for 8 – 10 minutes or until cooked through and golden brown.
- Transfer the biscuits to a wire rack and leave to cool completely before dusting with icing (confectioners) sugar.

Cinnamon Sugar Star Biscuits

565

- Instead of using icing sugar to decorate combine ½ tsp ground cinnamon with 50g of sugar in a food processor. Pulse and sprinkle over the biscuits.

566

MAKES 36

Cheese Wafer Biscuits

- Preheat the oven to 180°C (160° fan), 355F, gas 4 and line 2 baking sheets with greaseproof paper.
- Melt the butter with the cayenne pepper in a saucepan.
- Stir in the cheese and flour, beating rapidly to form a paste.
- Use a teaspoon to portion the mixture onto the baking trays and spread the biscuits out thinly with the back of the spoon.
- Bake in batches for 8 – 10 minutes.
- Leave the biscuits to harden on the tray for a few minutes then transfer them to a wire rack to cool.

PREPARATION TIME 10 MINUTES

COOKING TIME 8-10 MINUTES

INGREDIENTS

225 g / 8 oz / 1 cup butter
½ tsp cayenne pepper
175 g / 6 oz / 1 ¾ cups Red Leicester cheese, grated
300 g / 10 ½ oz / 2 cups plain (all purpose) flour

Cheese and Black Pepper Wafer Biscuits

567

- Combine 2 tsp of freshly ground black pepper with the grated cheese before stirring into the butter for a more piquant flavour.

568

SERVES 8

Black Cherry Crumble Cake

- Preheat the oven to 180°C (160° fan), 355F, gas 4 and line a loaf tin with non-stick baking paper.
- Sieve the flour into a mixing bowl and rub in the butter until it resembles fine breadcrumbs then stir in the sugar and cherries.
- Lightly beat the egg with the milk and stir it into the dry ingredients until just combined.
- Scrape the mixture into the loaf tin and level the surface.
- To make the crumble layer, rub the butter into the flour and stir in the ground almonds and brown sugar.
- Take a handful of the topping and squeeze it into a clump, then crumble it over the cake mixture. Repeat with the rest of the mixture then bake the cake for 55 minutes or until a skewer inserted comes out clean.
- Transfer the cake to a wire rack and leave to cool.

PREPARATION TIME 15 MINUTES

COOKING TIME 55 MINUTES

INGREDIENTS

225 g / 8 oz / 1 ½ cups self-raising flour
100 g / 3 ½ oz / ½ cup butter, cubed
100 g / 3 ½ oz / ½ cup caster (superfine) sugar
150 g / 5 ½ oz / 1 cup black cherries, pitted
1 large egg
75 ml / 2 ½ fl. oz / ⅓ cup whole milk

FOR THE CRUMBLE

75 g / 2 ½ oz / ⅓ cup butter
50 g / 1 ¾ oz / ⅓ cup plain (all purpose) flour
25 g / 1 oz / ¼ cup ground almonds
40 g / 1 ½ oz / ¼ cup light brown sugar

Black Cherry and Almond Crumble Cake

569

- Add an additional 75 g / 3 oz ground almonds to the crumble mixture for a nuttier flavour.

570

MAKES 2

White Cob Loaf

Sun-dried Tomato Cob Loaf

571

- Add 2 tbsp drained and finely chopped sun-dried tomatoes to the dough when you knead it the first time for a Mediterranean look and flavour.

Raisin Cob Loaf

572

- Add 50 g / 2 oz raisins to the dough when you knead it the first time for a fruity tasting loaf.

PREPARATION TIME 2 HOURS 30 MINUTES

COOKING TIME 35-40 MINUTES

INGREDIENTS

400 g / 14 oz / 2 ⅔ cups strong white bread flour, plus extra for dusting
½ tsp easy blend dried yeast
1 tbsp caster (superfine) sugar
1 tsp fine sea salt
1 tbsp olive oil

- Mix together the flour, yeast, sugar and salt. Stir the oil into 280 ml of warm water then stir it into the dry ingredients.
- Knead the mixture on a lightly oiled surface with your hands for 10 minutes or until smooth and elastic.
- Leave the dough to rest in a lightly oiled bowl, covered with oiled clingfilm, for 1 – 2 hours or until doubled in size.
- Knead it for 2 more minutes then split it into 2 even pieces and shape into 2 round loaves
- Transfer the cobs to a greased baking tray and cover with oiled clingfilm. Leave to prove for 1 hour or until doubled in size.
- Meanwhile, preheat the oven to 220⁰C (200⁰ fan), gas 7.
- Dust the cobs with flour and slash a cross in the tops with a knife.
- Transfer the tray to the top shelf of the oven then quickly throw a small cupful of water onto the oven floor and close the door.
- Bake for 35 - 40 minutes or until the loaves sound hollow when you tap them underneath.
- Transfer to a wire rack and leave to cool.

573

MAKES 6

Olive and Pepper Millefeuille

- Preheat the oven to 220°C (200° fan), 430F, gas 7.
- Roll out the pastry on a floured surface and press the olive slices into the surface.
- Cut the pastry into 18 rectangles and transfer them to 2 baking trays
- Bake in the oven for 15 - 20 minutes or until the top is golden brown and the bottom is cooked through.
- Layer the pastries with the roasted peppers and serve warm.

PREPARATION TIME 10 MINUTES

COOKING TIME 15-20 MINUTES

INGREDIENTS

225 g / 8 oz all-butter puff pastry
200 g / 7 oz / 1 ⅓ cups black olives, pitted and sliced
1 jar sliced roasted peppers in oil, drained

Two Olive Millefeuille

574

- Replace the pepper with 150 g / 5 oz pitted and sliced green olives for a savoury bite.

575

MAKES 36

Buckwheat Crackers

- Preheat the oven to 190°C (170° fan), 375F, gas 5 and line 2 baking sheets with greaseproof paper.
- Rub the butter into the wholemeal flour then stir in the rest of the ingredients.
- Add enough water to bind it together into a pastry-like dough and roll out on a floured surface.
- Cut the dough into square biscuits with a sharp knife, rerolling the trimmings as necessary.
- Transfer the biscuits to the prepared trays in batches and bake for 8 – 10 minutes or until cooked through and golden brown.
- Transfer the biscuits to a wire rack and leave to cool completely.

PREPARATION TIME 15 MINUTES

COOKING TIME 8-10 MINUTES

INGREDIENTS

110 g / 4 oz butter
225 g / 8 oz / 1 ½ cups stoneground wholemeal flour
225 g / 8 oz / 1 ½ cups buckwheat flour
1 tsp salt
1 tsp baking powder
110 g / 4 oz / ⅔ cup whole raw buckwheat

Buckwheat Crackers with Cream Cheese

576

- Once the crackers have cooled, garnish them with teaspoon of cream cheese for a rich, creamy snack.

577

MAKES 16

Parmesan and Olive Shortbread Biscuits

PREPARATION TIME 20 MINUTES

COOKING TIME 15-20 MINUTES

....

INGREDIENTS

150 g / 5 oz / ⅔ cup butter, cubed
230 g / 8 oz / 1 ½ cup plain (all purpose) flour
50 g / 1 ¾ oz / ½ cup Parmesan, grated
50 g / 1 ¾ oz / ⅓ cup black olives, pitted and finely chopped
sea salt flakes for sprinkling

• Preheat the oven to 180°C (160° fan), 355F, gas 4 and line a baking tray with greaseproof paper.
• Rub the butter into the flour and stir in the Parmesan and olives.
• Knead gently until the mixture forms a smooth dough then form into a cylinder 6 cm in diameter.
• Slice the roll into 1 cm thick slices and spread them out on the baking tray.
• Bake the biscuits for 15 - 20 minutes, turning the tray round halfway through.
• Sprinkle the biscuits with sea salt flakes then transfer to a wire rack and leave to cool.

Three Cheese Shortbread Biscuits

578

• Remove the olive from the recipe and replace with 30 g of both grated Gruyere and grated Cheddar for a pronounced cheese flavour to these biscuits.

579

MAKES 16

Pistachio Palmiers

PREPARATION TIME 10 MINUTES

COOKING TIME 15-20 MINUTES

....

INGREDIENTS

250 g / 9 oz all-butter puff pastry
100 g / 3 ½ oz / ⅔ cup pistachio nuts, chopped
2 tbsp light brown sugar
¼ tsp ground cardamom
1 egg, beaten

• Preheat the oven to 220°C (200° fan), 430F, gas 7 and line a baking tray with non-stick baking paper.
• Roll out the pastry on a floured surface into a large rectangle.
• Mix the chopped pistachios with the sugar and cardamom.
• Brush the surface of the pastry with egg and scatter over the nut mixture.
• Starting at one long edge, roll the pastry up into a tight sausage, stopping when you get to the centre.
• Roll up the other side of the pastry to meet the first in the middle then use a sharp knife to cut the roll into 1 cm thick slices and spread them out on the baking tray.
• Bake in the oven for 15 – 20 minutes or until golden brown and cooked through.
• Serve warm.

Hazelnut Palmiers

580

• Replace the pistachios in the recipe with the same weight of finely chopped hazelnuts for an alternative nut flavour.

581

MAKES 36 Candied Pumpkin and Choc-chip Cookies

- To make the candied pumpkin, put the sugar in a saucepan with 200 ml water and stir over a low heat.
- Bring the sugar syrup to the boil then add the cubed pumpkin and simmer for 10 minutes.
- Remove from the pan with a slotted spoon and leave to drip dry on a wire rack.
- Preheat the oven to 170°C (150° fan), gas 3 and line 2 baking sheets with greaseproof paper.
- Cream together the two sugars, butter and vanilla extract until pale and well whipped then beat in the egg and yolk, followed by the flour, chocolate and pumpkin.
- Drop tablespoons of the mixture onto the prepared trays, leaving plenty of room to spread.
- Bake the cookies in batches for 12 – 15 minutes.
- Transfer to a wire rack and leave to cool.

PREPARATION TIME 25 MINUTES

COOKING TIME 12-15 MINUTES

INGREDIENTS

175 g / 6 oz / ¾ cup butter, melted
225 g / 8 oz / 1 ⅓ cup dark brown sugar
100 g / 3 ½ oz / ½ cup caster (superfine) sugar
2 tsp vanilla extract
1 egg, plus 1 egg yolk
250 g / 9 oz / 1 ⅔ cup self-raising flour
175 g / 6 oz / 1 ¼ cup chocolate chips

FOR THE CANDIED PUMPKIN

400 g / 14 oz / 1 ¾ cup caster (superfine) sugar
200 g / 7 oz pumpkin or butternut squash, diced

Candied Pumpkin and Cherry Cookies

582

- Instead of using chocolate chips, use 150 g / 5 oz chopped glacé cherries for a more colourful cookie.

583

MAKES 36 Quinoa Biscuits

- Put the quinoa flakes, oats, flour and baking powder in a food processor and blitz until fine.
- Cream the butter with the sugar then beat in the dry ingredients.
- Bring the dough together and shape into a log then chill for 30 minutes.
- Preheat the oven to 180°C (160° fan), 355F, gas 4 and line 2 baking sheets with greaseproof paper.
- Slice the log into 1 cm slices and roll in the raw quinoa to coat.
- Transfer the biscuits to the prepared trays and bake for 20 – 25 minutes or until cooked through and golden brown.
- Transfer the biscuits to a wire rack and leave to cool completely.

PREPARATION TIME 40 MINUTES

COOKING TIME 20-25 MINUTES

INGREDIENTS

150 g / 5 ½ oz / 1 ½ cup quinoa flakes
50 g / 1 ¾ oz / ½ cup porridge oats
125 g / 4 ½ oz / ¾ cup stoneground wholemeal flour
1 tsp baking powder
175 g / 6 oz / ¾ cup butter
150 g / 5 ½ oz / ¾ cup soft brown sugar
110 g / 4 oz / ½ cup raw quinoa

Semolina Biscuits

584

- Roll the biscuit dough in 200 g / 7 oz semolina before baking them for a finer crunch to these biscuits.

585

MAKES 2

Wholemeal Cob Loaf

PREPARATION TIME 2 HOURS
30 MINUTES

COOKING TIME 35-40 MINUTES

INGREDIENTS

300 g / 10 ½ oz / 2 cup stoneground
wholemeal flour
100 g / 3 ½ oz / ⅔ cup strong white
bread flour, plus extra for dusting
½ tsp easy blend dried yeast
2 tbsp caster (superfine) sugar
1 tsp fine sea salt
1 tbsp olive oil

- Mix together the flours, yeast, sugar and salt. Stir the oil and 280 ml of warm water into the dry ingredients.
- Knead the mixture on an oiled surface for 10 minutes.
- Leave the dough to rest in a lightly oiled bowl, covered with oiled clingfilm, for 1 – 2 hours.
- Knead it for 2 more minutes then split it into 2 even pieces and shape into 2 round loaves.
- Transfer the cobs to a greased baking tray and cover with oiled clingfilm. Leave to prove for 1 hour.
- Meanwhile, preheat the oven to 220°C(200° fan), gas 7.
- Dust with flour and slash across the tops with a knife.
- Transfer the tray to the top shelf of the oven then quickly throw a small cupful of water onto the oven floor and close the door.
- Bake for 35 - 40 minutes or until the loaves sound hollow when you tap them underneath.

Herbed Cob Loaf
586

- Add 1 tsp of dried rosemary, oregano and basil to the flour before mixing into a dough for an aromatic, savoury dough.

587

MAKES 4

Wholemeal Sesame Baguettes

PREPARATION TIME 2 HOURS
30 MINUTES

COOKING TIME 25-30 MINUTES

INGREDIENTS

300 g / 10 ½ oz / 2 cup stoneground
wholemeal flour
100 g / 3 ½ oz / ½ cup strong white
bread flour, plus extra for dusting
½ tsp easy blend dried yeast
2 tbsp caster (superfine) sugar
1 tsp fine sea salt
1 tbsp sesame oil
1 egg, beaten
3 tbsp sesame seeds

- Mix together the flours, yeast, sugar and salt. Stir the oil and 280 ml of warm water into the dry ingredients.
- Knead the mixture on a lightly oiled surface with your hands for 10 minutes or until smooth and elastic.
- Leave the dough to rest in an oiled bowl, covered with oiled film, for 2 hours. Knead it for 2 more minutes then split it into 4 even pieces and shape into baguettes.
- Transfer the baguettes to a greased baking tray and cover with oiled clingfilm. Leave to prove for 1 hour.
- Preheat the oven to 220°C (200° fan), 430F, gas 7.
- Brush the baguettes with beaten egg and sprinkle with sesame seeds then slash across the tops with a knife.
- Transfer the tray to the top shelf of the oven then quickly throw a small cupful of water onto the oven floor and close the door.
- Bake for 25 - 30 minutes or until the loaves sound hollow when you tap them underneath.

Poppy Seed Baguettes
588

- Use 4 tbsp of black poppy seeds to garnish the loaves instead of the sesame seeds for a stark colour contrast.

589

MAKES 36

Chocolate Sprinkle Star Biscuits

Honey Star Biscuits

590

- Add 2 tbsp runny honey to the dough mixture before mixing. These biscuits can be garnished with grated chocolate if desired.

Multicoloured Sprinkle Star Biscuits

591

- Replace the grated chocolate garnish with multicoloured sugar sprinkles, sprinkling them over the cookies as soon as they leave the oven.

PREPARATION TIME I HOUR

COOKING TIME 8-10 MINUTES

....

INGREDIENTS

100 g / 3 ½ oz / ½ cup caster (superfine) sugar
100 g / 3 ½ oz / ½ cup butter, softenedsugar
1 large egg, beaten
300 g / 10 ½ oz / 2 cup plain (all purpose) flour

TO FINISH

1 egg, beaten
4 tbsp caster (superfine) sugar
30 g / 1 oz grated dark chocolate

- Cream together the sugar and butter until pale and well whipped then beat in the egg, followed by the flour.
- Bring the mixture together into a ball with your hands then wrap in clingfilm and refrigerate for 45 minutes.
- Preheat the oven to 190°C (170° fan), 375F, gas 5 and line 2 baking sheets with greaseproof paper.
- Roll out the dough on a lightly floured surface to 5mm thick. Use a star-shaped cutter to cut out the biscuits, rerolling the trimmings as necessary.
- Transfer the biscuits to the prepared trays, brush with beaten egg and sprinkle with caster (superfine) sugar.
- Bake for 8 – 10 minutes or until cooked through and golden brown.
- Transfer the biscuits to a wire rack and leave to cool completely before sprinkling with grated chocolate.

592

MAKES 36

Flower Biscuits

PREPARATION TIME 1 HOUR

COOKING TIME 8-10 MINUTES

....

INGREDIENTS

100 g / 3 ½ oz / ½ cup caster
(superfine) sugar
100 g / 3 ½ oz / ½ cup butter,
softenedsugar
1 tsp orange flower water
1 large egg, beaten
300 g / 10 ½ oz / 2 cup plain (all
purpose) flour

- Cream together the sugar, butter and orange flower
  water until pale and well whipped then beat in the egg,
  followed by the flour.
- Bring the mixture together into a ball then wrap in
  clingfilm and refrigerate for 45 minutes.
- Preheat the oven to 190°C (170° fan), 375F, gas 5 and
  line 2 baking sheets with greaseproof paper.
- Roll out the dough on a lightly floured surface to 5 mm
  thick. Use a flower-shaped cutter to cut out the biscuits,
  rerolling the trimmings as necessary.
- Transfer the biscuits to the prepared trays and bake
  for 8 – 10 minutes or until cooked through and golden
  brown.
- Transfer the biscuits to a wire rack and leave to cool
  completely.

Iced Flower Biscuits

593

- Use a icing decoration pen to decorate
  the biscuits once they have cooled for
  a colourful appearance.

594

MAKES 36

Lebkuchen Stars

PREPARATION TIME 25 MINUTES

COOKING TIME 15-20 MINUTES

....

INGREDIENTS

4 large eggs
200 g / 7 oz / ¾ cup caster (superfine)
sugar
1 tsp vanilla extract
250 g / 9 oz / 1 ⅔ cup plain (all
purpose) flour, plus extra for dusting
1 tsp baking powder
200 g / 7 oz / 2 cup ground almonds
100 g / 3 ½ oz / ½ cup mixed peel,
finely chopped
1 tbsp unsweetened cocoa powder
1 tsp mixed spice
1 tsp ground ginger

FOR THE ICING
150 g / 5 ½ oz / 1 ½ cup royal icing
powder

- Preheat the oven to 190°C (170° fan), 375F, gas 5 and
  line 2 baking sheets with greaseproof paper.
- Beat the eggs with the sugar and vanilla extract until
  pale and creamy then fold in the rest of the ingredients
  to form a soft dough.
- Roll the dough out on a lightly floured surface to 5 mm
  thick and use a star-shaped cutter to cut out the biscuits.
- Transfer the biscuits to the prepared trays and bake for
  15 – 20 minutes or until crisp and brown.
- Transfer the biscuits to a wire rack and leave to cool
  completely.
- Whisk the royal icing powder with 25 ml water using an
  electric whisk for 5 minutes.
- Use a palette knife or piping bag to apply the icing to the
  top of the biscuits and leave to set for at least 1 hour.

Soft Lebkuchen Stars

595

- Reduce the cooking time by
  5 minutes for a softer biscuit.

596

MAKES 36 # Garibaldi Stars

- Cream together the sugar, butter and vanilla extract until pale and well whipped then beat in the egg, followed by the flour and currants.
- Bring the mixture together into a ball then wrap in clingfilm and refrigerate for 45 minutes.
- Preheat the oven to 190°C (170° fan), 375F, gas 5 and line 2 baking sheets with greaseproof paper.
- Roll out the dough on a lightly floured surface to 5 mm thick. Use a star-shaped cutter to cut out the biscuits, rerolling the trimmings as necessary.
- Transfer the biscuits to the prepared trays in batches and bake for 8 – 10 minutes or until cooked through.
- Transfer the biscuits to a wire rack and leave to cool.
- Whisk the royal icing powder with 25 ml water using an electric whisk for 5 minutes.
- Pipe your designs onto the biscuits.

PREPARATION TIME 1 HOUR 15 MINUTES

COOKING TIME 8-10 MINUTES

....

INGREDIENTS

100 g / 3 ½ oz / ½ cup caster (superfine) sugar
100 g / 3 ½ oz / ½ cup butter, softenedsugar
1 tsp vanilla extract
1 large egg, beaten
300 g / 10 ½ oz / 2 cup plain (all purpose) flour
150 g / 5 ½ oz / 1 cup currants

TO DECORATE
150 g / 5 ½ oz / 1 ½ cup royal icing powder

Mixed Fruit Garibaldi Stars   **597**

- Add 30 g / 1 oz mixed dried peel to the dough before rolling and cutting for a more pronounced fruity taste.

598

MAKES 36 # Hazelnut and Rosewater Cookies

- Preheat the oven to 170°C (150° fan), 340F, gas 3 and line 2 baking sheets with greaseproof paper.
- Cream together the two sugars, butter and rosewater until pale and well whipped then beat in the egg and yolk, followed by the flour and ground hazelnuts.
- Drop tablespoons of the mixture onto the prepared trays, leaving plenty of room to spread.
- Bake the cookies in batches for 12 – 15 minutes or until the edges are starting to brown, but the centres are still chewy.
- Transfer to a wire rack and leave to cool before sprinkling with crystallised flowers.

PREPARATION TIME 10 MINUTES

COOKING TIME 12-15 MINUTES

....

INGREDIENTS

175 g / 6 oz / ¾ cup butter, melted
225 g / 8 oz / 1 ⅓ cup dark brown sugar
100 g / 3 ½ oz / ½ cup caster (superfine) sugar
2 tsp rosewater
1 egg, plus 1 egg yolk
200 g / 7 oz / 1 ⅓ cup self-raising flour
55 g / 2 oz / ½ cup ground hazelnuts (cob nuts)
crystallised violets and rose petals

Hazelnut and Orange   **599**
Flower Water Cookies

- Replace the rosewater with the same amount of orange flower water for a fragrant, citrus-like flavour.

600

MAKES 36

Fondant Flower Biscuits

Fondant Animal Biscuits   601

- Use animal-shaped cutters for the fondant to create fun animal biscuits for kids.

Ginger Flower Biscuits   602

- Add 1 heaped teaspoon of ground ginger to the butter and golden syrup when you melt them together for a spicy, warming flavour.

PREPARATION TIME 10 MINUTES

COOKING TIME 12-15 MINUTES

INGREDIENTS

75 g / 2 ½ oz / ⅓ cup butter, softened
100 g / 3 ½ oz / ⅓ cup golden syrup
225 g / 8 oz / 1 ½ cups self-raising flour
100 g / 3 ½ oz / ½ cup caster (superfine) sugar
1 large egg, beaten

FOR THE FLOWERS
200 g / 7 oz ready to roll fondant icing
a few drops of food dye

- Preheat the oven to 180°C (160° fan), 355F, gas 4 and line 2 baking sheets with greaseproof paper.
- Melt the butter and golden syrup together in a saucepan.
- Mix the flour and sugar together then stir in the melted butter mixture and the beaten egg.
- Use a teaspoon to portion the mixture onto the baking trays, leaving plenty of room for the biscuits to spread.
- Bake in batches for 12 – 15 minutes or until golden brown.
- Transfer the biscuits to a wire rack and leave to cool and harden.
- Take a small ball of icing and knead it with your chosen food dye.
- Roll it out between 2 sheets of greaseproof paper and use a flower-shaped cutter to cut out the flowers. Repeat with the rest of the icing, using a variety of different colours.
- Wet the back of the flowers with a little water and stick them onto the biscuits. Use a contrasting coloured icing for the centres.

603

MAKES 24 # Almond Biscotti

- Preheat the oven to 180°C (160° fan), 355F, gas 4 and line 2 baking sheets with greaseproof paper.
- Beat the eggs and butter together then add the flour, caster (superfine) sugar and almonds.
- Bring the mixture together into a soft dough and shape into 2 long rolls.
- Transfer the rolls to one of the prepared trays and flatten slightly.
- Bake for 20 minutes or until golden then leave to cool for 15 minutes.
- Cut the rolls across into 1 cm thick pieces and spread them out on the baking trays.
- Bake the biscuits for 15 minutes or until golden and crisp.
- Transfer the biscuits to a wire rack and leave to cool completely.

PREPARATION TIME 25 MINUTES

COOKING TIME 35 MINUTES

INGREDIENTS

2 large eggs
55 g / 2 oz / ¼ cup butter, melted
225 g / 8 oz / 1 ½ cups self-raising flour
100 g / 3 ½ oz / ½ cup caster (superfine) sugar
100 g / 3 ½ oz / ⅔ cup blanched almonds

Lemon and Thyme Biscotti

604

- Replace the almonds in the recipe with the finely grated zest of 2 lemons and 1 tbsp finely chopped thyme leaves for a citrus and herb twist to these biscotti.

605

MAKES 24 # Almond and Cranberry Biscotti

- Preheat the oven to 180°C (160° fan), 355F, gas 4 and line 2 baking sheets with greaseproof paper.
- Beat the eggs and butter together then add the flour, caster (superfine) sugar, almonds and cranberries.
- Bring the mixture together into a soft dough and shape into 2 long rolls.
- Transfer the rolls to one of the prepared trays and flatten slightly.
- Bake for 20 minutes or until golden then leave to cool for 15 minutes.
- Cut the rolls across into 1 cm thick sliced and spread them out on the baking trays.
- Bake the biscuits for 15 minutes or until golden and crisp.
- Transfer the biscuits to a wire rack and leave to cool completely.

PREPARATION TIME 20 MINUTES

COOKING TIME 35 MINUTES

INGREDIENTS

2 large eggs
55 g / 2 oz / ¼ cup butter, melted
225 g / 8 oz / 1 ½ cups self-raising flour
100 g / 3 ½ oz / ½ cup caster (superfine) sugar
100 g / 3 ½ oz / ⅔ cup blanched almonds
100 g / 3 ½ oz / / ⅔ cup dried cranberries

Almond and Sultana Biscotti

606

- Replace the cranberries with the same weight of sultanas; golden sultanas can be used for a brighter flavour.

607

MAKES 12

Almond and Parmesan Tuiles

PREPARATION TIME 5 MINUTES

COOKING TIME 8-10 MINUTES

INGREDIENTS

200 g / 7 oz / 3 cup Parmesan, grated
100 g / 3 ½ oz / ¾ cup blanched
almonds, chopped

- Preheat the oven to 200°C (180° fan), 390F, gas 6.
- Mix the Parmesan with the almonds and space out tablespoons of the mixture on a large baking tray.
- Bake them in the oven for 5 – 10 minutes or until lacy and golden brown.
- Leave the tuiles to set on the tray for 30 seconds then use a palette knife to lift them off.
- Drape them over a rolling pin and leave to cool and harden.

Parmesan Tuiles

 608

- Remove the almonds from the recipe for a nut-free tuile.

609

MAKES 18

Almond Tuiles

PREPARATION TIME 45 MINUTES

COOKING TIME 8-10 MINUTES

INGREDIENTS

110 g / 4 oz / ⅔ cup plain (all
purpose) flour
110 g / 4 oz caster / ½ cup (superfine)
sugar
2 large egg whites
110 g / 4 oz / ½ cup butter, melted
55 g / 2 oz / ⅔ cup flaked (slivered)
almonds

- Beat together the flour, sugar and egg whites until smooth, then beat in the melted butter.
- Refrigerate for 30 minutes.
- Preheat the oven to 180°C (160° fan), 350F, gas 4 and oil 2 large baking trays.
- Spoon teaspoonfuls of the mixture onto the baking trays and spread out with the back of the spoon to make 10 cm circles.
- Sprinkle with flaked (slivered) almonds and bake for 8 – 10 minutes. Lift the biscuits off the trays with a palette knife and drape over a rolling pin while still soft. Leave to cool and harden.

Pistachio Tuiles

610

- Instead of using flaked (slivered) almonds, use 55 g / 2 oz lightly crushed pistachios for green tint to these tuiles.

611

MAKES 36

Oat and Raisin Cookies

- Preheat the oven to 170°C (150° fan), gas 3 and line 2 baking sheets with greaseproof paper.
- Cream together the two sugars, butter and vanilla extract until pale and well whipped then beat in the egg and yolk, followed by the flour, oats and raisins.
- Drop tablespoons of the mixture onto the prepared trays, leaving plenty of room to spread.
- Bake the cookies in batches for 12 – 15 minutes or until the edges are starting to brown, but the centres are still chewy.
- Transfer to a wire rack and leave to cool.

PREPARATION TIME 10 MINUTES

COOKING TIME 12-15 MINUTES

....

INGREDIENTS

175 g / 6 oz / ¾ cup butter, melted
225 g / 8 oz / 1 ⅓ cup dark brown sugar
100 g / 3 ½ oz / ½ cup caster (superfine) sugar
2 tsp vanilla extract
1 egg, plus 1 egg yolk
250 g / 9 oz / 1 ⅔ cups self-raising flour
100 g / 3 ½ oz / 1 cup oats
100 g / 3 ½ oz / ½ cup raisins

Oat and Chocolate Cookies

612

- Replace the raisins with 100 g / 3 ½ oz milk chocolate chips for a chocolatey twist to these cookies.

613

MAKES 36

Apricot Jam Biscuits

- Cream together the sugar, butter and vanilla extract until pale and well whipped then stir in the flour and ground almonds.
- Bring the mixture together into a ball with your hands then wrap in clingfilm and refrigerate for 45 minutes.
- Preheat the oven to 140°C (120° fan), 280F, gas 1 and line 2 baking sheets with greaseproof paper.
- Roll out the dough on a lightly floured surface to 5 mm thick. Use a fluted pastry cutter to cut out 72 biscuits.
- Use a small flower-shaped cutter to cut 2 holes out of 36 of the biscuits and prick them with a fork.
- Transfer the biscuits to the prepared trays in batches and bake for 25 – 30 minutes.
- Transfer the biscuits to a wire rack and leave to cool.
- Put a teaspoon of jam on the underside of the plain biscuits and top with a holey biscuit. Dust liberally with icing sugar.

PREPARATION TIME 1 HOUR
15 MINUTES

COOKING TIME 25-30 MINUTES

....

INGREDIENTS

150 g / 5 ½ oz / ⅔ cup caster (superfine) sugar
350 g / 12 oz / 1 ½ cup butter, softened
1 tsp vanilla extract
300 g / 10 ½ oz / 2 cup plain (all purpose) flour
150 g / 5 ½ oz / 1 ½ cup ground almonds
200 g / 7 oz / ⅔ cup apricot jam (jelly)
icing (confectioners) sugar to dust

Raspberry Jam Biscuits

614

- Use raspberry jam instead of apricot jam for a vibrant colour and flavour.

615

MAKES 1 LOAF # Beer and Mustard Seed Bread

PREPARATION TIME 2 HOURS
30 MINUTES

COOKING TIME 35-40 MINUTES

INGREDIENTS

200 g / 7 oz / 1 ⅓ cup strong white
bread flour, plus extra for dusting
200 g / 7 oz / 1 ⅓ cup stoneground
wholemeal flour
½ tsp easy blend dried yeast
1 tbsp caster (superfine) sugar
1 tsp fine sea salt
1 tbsp mustard seeds
280 ml / 10 fl. oz / 1 ¼ cups real ale
1 tbsp mustard oil

- Mix together the flour, yeast, sugar, salt and seeds. Stir in the oil and beer. Knead the mixture on an oiled surface. Leave to rest in an oiled bowl for 2 hours.
- Roll the dough with your hands into a fat sausage, then turn it 90⁰ and roll it tightly the other way. Tuck the ends under and transfer the dough to the tin, keeping the seam underneath.
- Cover the tin loosely with oiled clingfilm and leave to prove somewhere warm for 45 minutes.
- Preheat the oven to 220⁰C (200⁰ fan), 430F, gas 7.
- Transfer the tin to the top shelf of the oven then quickly throw a small cupful of water onto the floor of the oven and close the door.
- Bake for 35 – 40 minutes or until the loaf sounds hollow when you tap it underneath. Transfer the bread to a wire rack and leave to cool completely before slicing.

Stout and Mustard Seed Bread   616

- Replace the real ale with the same volume of stout for a richer, maltier flavour.

617

MAKES 36 # Nutmeg Biscuits

PREPARATION TIME 10 MINUTES

COOKING TIME 12-15 MINUTES

INGREDIENTS

75 g / 2 ½ oz / ⅓ cup butter, softened
100 g / 3 ½ oz / ⅓ cup golden syrup
225 g / 8 oz / 1 ½ cups self-raising
flour
100 g / 3 ½ oz / ½ cup caster
(superfine) sugar
1 tsp nutmeg, freshly grated
1 large egg, beaten

- Preheat the oven to 180⁰C (160⁰ fan), 355F, gas 4 and line 2 baking sheets with greaseproof paper.
- Melt the butter and golden syrup together in a saucepan.
- Mix the flour, sugar and nutmeg together then stir in the melted butter mixture and the beaten egg.
- Use a teaspoon to portion the mixture onto the baking trays, leaving plenty of room for the biscuits to spread.
- Bake in batches for 12 – 15 minutes or until golden brown.
- Transfer the biscuits to a wire rack and leave to cool and crisp.

Cinnamon and Cocoa Biscuits   618

- Add 30 g / 1 oz of cocoa powder to the flour as well as 1 tsp of ground cinnamon instead of the nutmeg for a chocolatey twist to these biscuits.

619

MAKES 36

Muesli Cookies

Chocolate Chip Muesli Cookies

620

- Add 110 g / 4 oz chocolate chips to the mixture at the same time as the flour and muesli for a more luxurious cookie.

Bran and Muesli Cookies

621

- Replace 110 g / 4 oz of the muesli with 110 g / 4 oz lightly crushed bran flakes for a different texture to these cookies.

PREPARATION TIME 10 MINUTES

COOKING TIME 12-15 MINUTES

INGREDIENTS

175 g / 6 oz / ¾ cup butter, melted
225 g / 8 oz / 1 ⅓ cup dark brown sugar
100 g / 3 ½ oz / ½ cup caster (superfine) sugar
2 tsp vanilla extract
1 egg, plus 1 egg yolk
250 g / 9 oz / 1 ⅔ cup self-raising flour
225 g / 8 oz / 2 ¼ cup nutty muesli

- Preheat the oven to 170°C (150° fan), gas 3 and line 2 baking sheets with greaseproof paper.
- Cream together the two sugars, butter and vanilla extract until pale and well whipped then beat in the egg and yolk, followed by the flour and muesli.
- Drop tablespoons of the mixture onto the prepared trays, leaving plenty of room to spread.
- Bake the cookiesin batches for 12 – 15minutes or until the edges are starting to brown, but the centres are still chewy.
- Transfer to a wire rack and leave to cool.

622

MAKES 1 LOAF Wholemeal Olive Bread

PREPARATION TIME 2 HOURS
30 MINUTES

COOKING TIME 35-40 MINUTES

INGREDIENTS

200 g / 7 oz / ⅓ cup strong white
bread flour, plus extra for dusting
200 g / 7 oz / 1 ⅓ cup stoneground
wholemeal flour
½ tsp easy blend dried yeast
1 tbsp caster (superfine) sugar
1 tsp fine sea salt
100 g / 3 ½ oz / ⅔ cup mixed olives,
pitted and sliced
1 tbsp olive oil

- Mix together the flour, yeast, sugar, salt and olives.
- Stir in the oil, 280 ml warm water and dry ingredients.
- Knead the mixture on an oiled surface for 10 minutes.
- Leave the dough to rest in an oiled bowl for 1 – 2 hours.
- Roll the dough with your hands into a fat sausage, then turn it 90° and roll it tightly the other way. Tuck the ends under and transfer the dough to the tin, keeping the seam underneath.
- Cover the tin loosely with oiled clingfilm and leave to prove somewhere warm for 45 minutes.
- Preheat the oven to 220°C (200° fan), 430F, gas 7.
- Transfer the tin to the top shelf of the oven then throw a small cupful of water onto the floor of the oven.
- Bake for 35 – 40 minutes or until the loaf sounds hollow when you tap it underneath. Transfer the bread to a wire rack and leave to cool completely before slicing.

Wholemeal Olive and Nut Bread 623

- Add 110 g / 4 oz of chopped nuts of your choice to the dough when you knead it for a different texture to this bread.

624

MAKES 1 LOAF Black Olive and Feta Bread

PREPARATION TIME 2 HOURS
30 MINUTES

COOKING TIME 35-40 MINUTES

INGREDIENTS

300 g / 10 ½ oz / 2 cup strong white
bread flour, plus extra for dusting
100 g / 3 ½ oz / ⅔ cup stoneground
wholemeal flour
½ tsp easy blend dried yeast
1 tbsp caster (superfine) sugar
1 tsp fine sea salt
100 g / 3 ½ oz / ½ cup feta, cubed
100 g / 3 ½ oz / ⅔ cup black olives,
pitted and sliced

- Mix together the flours, yeast, sugar and salt. Stir the feta, olives and 280 ml of warm water.
- Knead the mixture on a lightly oiled surface for 10 minutes or until the dough is smooth and elastic.
- Leave the dough to rest in a lightly oiled bowl, covered with oiled clingfilm, for 1 – 2 hours.
- Knead the dough for 2 more minutes then roll it into a fat sausage. Turn it 90° and roll it tightly the other way then tuck the ends under and transfer the dough to the tin, keeping the seam underneath.
- Cover the tin with oiled clingfilm and leave to prove for 45 minutes.
- Preheat the oven to 220°C (200° fan), 430F, gas 7.
- Transfer the tin to the top shelf of the oven, then quickly throw a small cupful of water onto the floor of the oven.
- Bake for 35 – 40 minutes. Leave to cool completely on a wire rack before slicing.

Black Olive, Oregano 625
and Feta Bread

- Add 2 tsp dried oregano to the flour before mixing the dough for an added Mediterranean flavour.

626

MAKES 2

Granary Bread

- Mix together the flours, yeast, sugar and salt. Stir in the oil and 280 ml of warm water.
- Knead the mixture on a lightly oiled surface with your hands for 10 minutes or until smooth and elastic.
- Leave the dough to rest in a lightly oiled bowl, covered with oiled clingfilm, for 1 – 2 hours.
- Knead it for 2 more minutes then split it into 2 even pieces and shape into 2 loaves
- Transfer the loaves to a greased baking tray and cover with oiled clingfilm. Leave to prove for 1 hour.
- Meanwhile, preheat the oven to 220°C(200° fan), gas 7.
- Dust with flour and slash across the tops with a knife.
- Transfer the tray to the top shelf of the oven then quickly throw a small cupful of water onto the oven floor.
- Bake for 35 - 40 minutes. Transfer to a wire rack and leave to cool.

PREPARATION TIME 2 HOURS 30 MINUTES

COOKING TIME 35-40 MINUTES

INGREDIENTS

300 g / 10 ½ oz / 2 cup malted granary flour
100 g / 3 ½ oz / ⅔ cup strong white bread flour, plus extra for dusting
½ tsp easy blend dried yeast
2 tbsp caster (superfine) sugar
1 tsp fine sea salt
1 tbsp olive oil

Seeded Granary Bread

627

- Add 55 g / 2 oz sesame seeds and 55 g / 2 oz sunflower seeds to the dough when you knead it for a crunchier texture.

628

MAKES 12

Salt Crust Rolls

- Mix together the flours, yeast, sugar and salt. Stir in the oil and 280 ml of warm water.
- Knead the mixture on a lightly oiled surface with your hands for 10 minutes or until smooth and elastic.
- Leave the dough to rest in a lightly oiled bowl, covered with oiled clingfilm, for 1 – 2 hours.
- Knead it for 2 more minutes then split it into 12 even pieces and shape into rolls
- Transfer the rolls to a greased baking tray and cover with oiled clingfilm. Leave to prove for 1 hour.
- Meanwhile, preheat the oven to 220°C (200° fan), gas 7.
- Stir 2 tablespoons of warm water into the salt to dissolve.
- Brush the salt water over the rolls then transfer the tray to the top shelf of the oven. Bake for 15 – 20 minutes.
- Transfer to a wire rack and leave to cool.

PREPARATION TIME 2 HOURS 30 MINUTES

COOKING TIME 15-20 MINUTES

INGREDIENTS

350 g / 12 ½ oz / 2 ⅓ cup strong white bread flour,
plus extra for dusting
50 g / 1 ¾ oz / ⅓ cup stoneground wholemeal flour
½ tsp easy blend dried yeast
1 tbsp caster (superfine) sugar
1 tsp fine sea salt
1 tbsp olive oil

TO GLAZE
2 tsp fine sea salt

Salt and Pepper Rolls

629

- Add 1 tsp ground black pepper to the glaze before brushing them on the rolls for a peppery bite to these rolls.

630

MAKES 36

Wholemeal Oat Cookies

Wholemeal Oat and Raisin Cookies

631

- Add 55 g / 2 oz of raisins to the cookie dough before mixing for a chewy, fruity cookies.

Wholemeal Treacle Cookies

632

- Replace 55 g / 2 oz of the dark brown sugar with the same amount of black treacle for a darker appearance and a deeper flavour.

PREPARATION TIME 10 MINUTES

COOKING TIME 12-15 MINUTES

INGREDIENTS

175 g / 6 oz / ¾ cup butter, melted
225 g / 8 oz / 1 ⅓ cup dark brown sugar
100 g / 3 ½ oz / ½ cup caster (superfine) sugar
2 tsp vanilla extract
1 egg, plus 1 egg yolk
125 g / 4 ½ oz / ¾ cup self-raising flour
125 g / 4 ½ oz / ¾ cup stoneground wholemeal flour
125 g / 4 ½ oz / 1 ¼ cup oats

- Preheat the oven to 170°C (150° fan), gas 3 and line 2 baking sheets with greaseproof paper.
- Cream together the two sugars, butter and vanilla extract until pale and well whipped then beat in the egg and yolk, followed by the flours and oats.
- Drop tablespoons of the mixture onto the prepared trays, leaving plenty of room to spread.
- Bake the cookies in batches for 12 – 15 minutes or until the edges are starting to brown, but the centres are still chewy.
- Transfer to a wire rack and leave to cool.

633

MAKES 12 # Parmesan Rolls

- In a large bowl, mix together the flour, yeast, sugar and salt. Stir in the oil, Parmesan and 280 ml of warm water.
- Knead the mixture on a lightly oiled surface with your hands for 10 minutes or until smooth and elastic.
- Leave the dough to rest in a lightly oiled bowl, covered with oiled clingfilm, for 1 – 2 hours.
- Knead it for 2 more minutes then split it into 12 even pieces and shape into rolls
- Transfer the rolls to a greased baking tray and cover with oiled clingfilm. Leave to prove for 1 hour.
- Preheat the oven to 220°C (200° fan), 430F, gas 7.
- Cut a cross in the top of each roll and transfer the tray to the top shelf of the oven.
- Bake for 15 – 20 minutes or until the rolls sound hollow when you tap them underneath.
- Transfer to a wire rack and leave to cool.

PREPARATION TIME 2 HOURS 30 MINUTES

COOKING TIME 15-20 MINUTES

INGREDIENTS

400 g / 14 oz / 2 ⅔ cup strong white bread flour
½ tsp easy blend dried yeast
1 tbsp caster (superfine) sugar
1 tsp fine sea salt
1 tbsp olive oil
100 g / 3 ½ oz / 1 cup Parmesan, finely grated

Parmesan and Rosemary Rolls   634

- Add 1 tsp dried rosemary to the dough before kneading for a different appearance and flavour to these rolls.

635

MAKES 12 # Breton Biscuits

- Preheat the oven to 180°C (160° fan), gas 4 and line a baking tray with greaseproof paper.
- Rub the butter into the flour with a pinch of salt then stir in the sugar.
- Beat 5 of the egg yolks and stir them into the dry ingredients.
- Bring the mixture together into a soft dough and roll it out between 2 sheets of greaseproof paper until 2 cm thick.
- Use a cookie cutter to cut out 12 biscuits and transfer them to a baking tray.
- Bake the biscuits for 20 – 25 minutes or until golden brown.
- Transfer the biscuits to a wire rack and leave to cool.

PREPARATION TIME 15 MINUTES

COOKING TIME 20-25 MINUTES

INGREDIENTS

250 g / 9 oz / 1 ¼ cup butter, cubed
250 g / 9 oz / 1 ⅔ cup plain (all purpose) flour
250 g / 9 oz / 1 ¼ cup caster (superfine) sugar
6 large egg yolks

Iced Breton Biscuits   636

- Make up an icing using 200 g / 7 oz icing (confectioners) sugar mixing with enough hot water to make a smooth icing. Let it cool and thicken a little before spreading on the cooled biscuits.

637

MAKES 9

Millionaire's Shortbread

PREPARATION TIME 20 MINUTES

COOKING TIME 15-20 MINUTES

INGREDIENTS

230 g / 8 oz / 1 ½ cups plain (all purpose) flour
2 tbsp cocoa powder
75 g / 2 ½ oz / ⅓ cup caster (superfine) sugar
150 g / 5 oz / ⅔ cup butter, cubed
50 g / 1 ¾ oz / ¼ cup granulated sugar

FOR THE TOPPING

1 can condensed milk
200 g / 7 oz milk chocolate

- Make the caramel layer in advance. Put the unopened can of condensed milk in a saucepan of water and simmer for 3 hours, adding more water as necessary to ensure it doesn't boil dry. Leave the can to cool.
- Preheat the oven to 180⁰C (160⁰ fan), 355F, gas 4 and line a 20 cm square cake tin with greaseproof paper.
- Mix together the flour, cocoa and caster (superfine) sugar in a bowl, then rub in the butter. Knead gently until the mixture forms a smooth dough then press it into the bottom of the tin in an even layer.
- Bake the shortbread for 15-20 minutes, turning the tray round halfway through. Leave to cool.
- Open the can of condensed milk and beat until smooth. Spread it over the shortbread and chill for 1 hour.
- Melt the chocolate in a microwave or bain marie and spread it over the caramel.
- Chill in the fridge for 30 minutes.

Millionaire's Salted Shortbread

638

- Garnish the tops of the shortbread with a pinch of flaked sea salt before serving for a savoury twist.

639

MAKES 36

Chocolate and Coffee Cookies

PREPARATION TIME 10 MINUTES

COOKING TIME 12-15 MINUTES

INGREDIENTS

175 g / 6 oz / ¾ cup butter, melted
225 g / 8 oz / 1 ⅓ cup dark brown sugar
100 g / 3 ½ oz / ½ cup caster (superfine) sugar
2 tsp instant espresso powder
1 egg, plus 1 egg yolk
250 g / 9 oz / 1 ⅔ cup self-raising flour
175 g / 6 oz dark chocolate, grated

- Preheat the oven to 170⁰C (150⁰ fan), gas 3 and line 2 baking sheets with greaseproof paper.
- Cream together the two sugars, butter and espresso powder until pale and well whipped then beat in the egg and yolk, followed by the flour and chocolate.
- Drop tablespoons of the mixture onto the prepared trays, leaving plenty of room to spread.
- Bake the cookies in batches for 12 – 15 minutes or until the edges are starting to brown, but the centres are still chewy.
- Transfer to a wire rack and leave to cool.

White Mocha Cookies

640

- Replace the grated dark chocolate with grated white chocolate for a sweeter flavour.

641

MAKES 36 Chocolate and Pink Peppercorn Cookies

- Preheat the oven to 170°C (150° fan), gas 3 and line 2 baking sheets with greaseproof paper.
- Cream together the two sugars, butter and vanilla extract until pale and well whipped then beat in the egg and yolk, followed by the flour, cocoa and peppercorns.
- Drop tablespoons of the mixture onto the prepared trays, leaving plenty of room to spread.
- Bake the cookies in batches for 12 - 15minutes or until the edges are starting to brown, but the centres are still chewy.
- Transfer to a wire rack and leave to cool.

PREPARATION TIME 10 MINUTES

COOKING TIME 25-30 MINUTES

INGREDIENTS

175 g / 6 oz / ¾ cup butter, melted
225 g / 8 oz / 1 ⅓ cup dark brown sugar
100 g / 3 ½ oz / ½ cup caster (superfine) sugar
2 tsp vanilla extract
1 egg, plus 1 egg yolk
250 g / 9 oz / 1 ⅔ cup self-raising flour
3 tbsp unsweetened cocoa powder
2 tsp pink peppercorns, crushed

Chocolate and Ginger Cookies 642

- Replace the crushed pink peppercorn garnish with 55 g / 2 oz chopped candied ginger for an alternative exotic flavour.

643

MAKES 36 Chocolate Sandwich Biscuits

- Cream together the sugar, butter and vanilla extract then stir in the flour, cocoa and ground almonds.
- Bring the mixture together into a ball with your hands then wrap in clingfilm and refrigerate for 45 minutes.
- Preheat the oven to 140°C (120° fan), 280F, gas 1 and line 2 baking sheets with greaseproof paper.
- Roll out the dough on a lightly floured surface to 5 mm thick. Use a fluted pastry cutter to cut out 72 biscuits.
- Transfer the biscuits to the prepared trays in batches and bake for 25 – 30 minutes. Transfer the biscuits to a wire rack and leave to cool.
- To make the buttercream, beat the butter with a wooden spoon until light and fluffy then beat in the icing sugar.
- Use a whisk to incorporate the milk, then whisk for 2 minutes or until smooth and well whipped.
- Sandwich the biscuits together with the buttercream.

PREPARATION TIME 1 HOUR
15 MINUTES

COOKING TIME 25-30 MINUTES

INGREDIENTS

150 g / 5 ½ oz / ⅔ cup caster (superfine) sugar
350 g / 12 oz / 1 ½ cup butter, softened
1 tsp vanilla extract
300 g / 10 ½ oz / 2 cup plain (all purpose) flour
2 tbsp unsweetened cocoa powder
150 g / 5 ½ oz / 1 ½ cup ground almonds

FOR THE BUTTERCREAM
110 g / 4 oz / ½ cup butter, softened
225 g / 8 oz / 2 ¼ cup icing (confectioners) sugar
2 tbsp milk

Vanilla Sandwich Biscuits 644

- Remove the cocoa powder and replace with 1 tbsp of plain (all purpose) flour and additional 1 tsp of vanilla extract for a more traditional flavour.

645

MAKES 1 LOAF # Wholemeal Chocolate Bread

PREPARATION TIME 2 HOURS
30 MINUTES

COOKING TIME 35 MINUTES

....

INGREDIENTS

200 g / 7 oz / 1 ⅓ cup stoneground
wholemeal flour
200 g / 7 oz / 1 ⅓ cup strong white
bread flour, plus extra for dusting
½ tsp easy blend dried yeast
4 tbsp brown sugar
2 tbsp cocoa powder
1 tsp fine sea salt
1 tbsp sunflower oil
100 g / 3 ½ oz dark chocolate
(minimum 60 % cocoa solids), grated

- In a large bowl, mix together the flour, yeast, sugar, cocoa and salt. Stir the oil and grated chocolate into 280 ml warm water.
- Stir the liquid into the dry ingredients then knead the mixture on a lightly oiled surface with your hands for 10 minutes or until the dough is smooth and elastic.
- Leave the dough to rest in a lightly oiled bowl, covered with oiled clingfilm, for 1 – 2 hours or until doubled in size.
- Punch the dough with your fist to knock out the air then knead it for 2 more minutes. Flatten the dough with your hands then roll it up tightly and tuck under the ends.
- Transfer the loaf to a greased loaf tin and cover again with oiled clingfilm. Leave to prove for 1 hour or until doubled in size.
- Meanwhile, preheat the oven to 220°C (200° fan), 430F, gas 7.
- When the dough has risen, transfer the tin to the top shelf of the oven then quickly throw a small cupful of water onto the floor of the oven and close the door.
- Bake for 35 – 40 minutes or until the loaf sounds hollow when you tap it underneath. Transfer the bread to a wire rack and leave to cool completely before slicing.

646

MAKES 36 # Double Chocolate Cookies

PREPARATION TIME 10 MINUTES

COOKING TIME 12-15 MINUTES

....

INGREDIENTS

175 g / 6 oz / ¾ cup butter, melted
225 g / 8 oz / 1 ⅓ cup dark brown
sugar
100 g / 3 ½ oz / ½ cup caster
(superfine) sugar
2 tsp vanilla extract
1 egg, plus 1 egg yolk
250 g / 9 oz / 1 ⅔ cup self-raising
flour
2 tbsp unsweetened cocoa powder
175 g / 6 oz / 1 ¼ cup chocolate chips

- Preheat the oven to 170°C (150° fan), 340F, gas 3 and line 2 baking sheets with greaseproof paper.
- Cream together the two sugars, butter and vanilla extract until pale and well whipped then beat in the egg and yolk, followed by the flour, cocoa and chocolate chips.
- Drop tablespoons of the mixture onto the prepared trays, leaving plenty of room to spread.
- Bake the cookies in batches for 12 – 15 minutes or until the edges are starting to brown, but the centres are still chewy.
- Transfer to a wire rack and leave to cool.

Double Chocolate and Currant Cookies

- Preheat the oven to 170°C (150° fan), 340F, gas 3 and line 2 baking sheets with greaseproof paper.
- Cream together the two sugars, butter and vanilla extract until pale and well whipped then beat in the egg and yolk, followed by the flour, cocoa, chocolate and currants.
- Drop tablespoons of the mixture onto the prepared trays, leaving plenty of room to spread.
- Bake the cookies in batches for 12 – 15 minutes or until the edges are starting to brown, but the centres are still chewy.
- Transfer to a wire rack and leave to cool.

PREPARATION TIME 10 MINUTES

COOKING TIME 12-15 MINUTES

INGREDIENTS

175 g / 6 oz / ¾ cup butter, melted
225 g / 8 oz / 1 ⅓ cup dark brown sugar
100 g / 3 ½ oz / ½ cup caster (superfine) sugar
2 tsp vanilla extract
1 egg, plus 1 egg yolk
250 g / 9 oz / 1 ⅔ cup self-raising flour
2 tbsp unsweetened cocoa powder
175 g / 6 oz / 1 ¼ cup chocolate chips
175 g / 6 oz / 1 ¼ cup currants

Chocolate and Cinnamon Cookies

PREPARATION TIME 10 MINUTES

COOKING TIME 12-15 MINUTES

INGREDIENTS

175 g / 6 oz / ¾ cup butter, melted
225 g / 8 oz / 1 ⅓ cup dark brown sugar
100 g / 3 ½ oz / ½ cup caster (superfine) sugar
2 tsp vanilla extract
1 egg, plus 1 egg yolk
250 g / 9 oz / 1 ⅔ cups self-raising flour
2 tbsp unsweetened cocoa powder
1 tsp ground cinnamon
175 g / 6 oz / 1 ¼ cups chocolate chips

- Preheat the oven to 170°C (150° fan), 340F, gas 3 and line 2 baking sheets with greaseproof paper.
- Cream together the two sugars, butter and vanilla extract until pale and well whipped then beat in the egg and yolk, followed by the flour, cocoa, cinnamon and chocolate chips.
- Drop tablespoons of the mixture onto the prepared trays, leaving plenty of room to spread.
- Bake the cookies in batches for 12 – 15 minutes or until the edges are starting to brown, but the centres are still chewy.
- Transfer to a wire rack and leave to cool.

Bullseye Biscuits

PREPARATION TIME 10 MINUTES

COOKING TIME 12-15 MINUTES

INGREDIENTS

75 g / 2 ½ oz / ⅓ cup butter, softened
100 g / 3 ½ oz / ⅓ cup golden syrup
225 g / 8 oz / 1 ½ cups self-raising flour
100 g / 3 ½ oz / ½ cup caster (superfine) sugar
1 large egg, beaten
2 tbsp unsweetened cocoa powder
24 glace cherries

- Preheat the oven to 180°C (160° fan), 355F, gas 4 and line 2 baking sheets with greaseproof paper.
- Melt the butter and golden syrup together in a saucepan.
- Mix the flour and sugar together then stir in the melted butter mixture and the beaten egg.
- Spoon two thirds of the mixture into a separate bowl and stir in the cocoa powder.
- Use a teaspoon to portion the cocoa mixture onto the baking trays, leaving plenty of room for the biscuits to spread. Top with a teaspoon of the plain mixture, then half a teaspoon of the cocoa mixture. Press a cherry into the centre of each one.
- Bake the biscuits in batches for 12 – 15 minutes or until they have spread and set.
- Transfer the biscuits to a wire rack and leave to cool and harden.

650

MAKES 45-50 # Coconut Sponge Biscuits

PREPARATION TIME 10 MINUTES

COOKING TIME 10-15 MINUTES

INGREDIENTS

4 large eggs
125 g / 4 ½ oz / ½ cup caster (superfine) sugar
1 tsp vanilla extract
a pinch cream of tartar
115 g / 4 oz / ⅔ cup plain (all purpose) flour
2 tbsp desiccated coconut

- Preheat the oven to 190°C (170° fan), 375F, gas 5 and grease and line 2 large trays with greaseproof paper.
- Separate the eggs and put the yolks in a bowl with half of the sugar and the vanilla extract. Whisk for 4 minutes or until very thick and pale.
- Whisk the egg whites with the cream of tartar, making sure the whisk and bowl are completely clean and grease-free.
- When the egg white reaches the soft peak stage, gradually whisk in the remaining sugar.
- Sieve the flour over the egg yolk mixture and scrape in the egg whites, then carefully fold it all together with the coconut, retaining as much air as possible.
- Spoon teaspoons of the mixture onto the baking tray, spreading it out into rounds with the back of the spoon.
- Bake the biscuits for 10 – 15 minutes or until firm to the touch.

Coconut and Cherry Sponge Biscuits
651

- : Add 55 g / 2 oz finely chopped glace cherries to the mixture before baking for a colourful biscuit.

652

MAKES 16 # Coconut Shortbread Biscuits

PREPARATION TIME 20 MINUTES

COOKING TIME 12-15 MINUTES

INGREDIENTS

150 g / 5 ½ oz / 1 cup plain (all purpose) flour
55 g / 2 oz / ½ cup desiccated coconut
75g / 2 ½ oz / ⅓ cup caster (superfine) sugar
150g / 5 oz / ⅔ cup butter, cubed

- Preheat the oven to 180°C (160° fan), 355F, gas 4 and line a baking tray with greaseproof paper.
- Mix together the flour, coconut and caster (superfine) sugar in a bowl, then rub in the butter.
- Knead gently until the mixture forms a smooth dough then roll out on a lightly floured surface to 5 mm thick.
- Use a fluted cookie cutter to cut out the biscuits and spread them out on the baking tray.
- Bake the biscuits for 12 - 15 minutes, turning the tray round halfway through.
- Transfer the biscuits to a wire rack and leave to cool.

Coconut and Honey Shortbread Biscuits
653

- Drizzle the biscuits with a little runny honey before serving for a sticky and sweet biscuit.

654

MAKES 36

Coconut and Pine Nut Cookies

Coconut and Almond Cookies

655

- Stud each cookie with 1 tbsp chopped almonds before baking for an alternative nut flavour.

Coconut, Pine Nut and Chocolate Chip Cookies

656

- Add 1 tbs of chocolate chips to the mixture.

PREPARATION TIME 10 MINUTES

COOKING TIME 12-15 MINUTES

INGREDIENTS

175 g / 6 oz / ¾ cup butter, melted
225 g / 8 oz / 1 ⅓ cup light brown sugar
100 g / 3 ½ oz / ½ cup caster (superfine) sugar
2 tsp vanilla extract
1 egg, plus 1 egg yolk
250 g / 9 oz / 1 ⅔ cups self-raising flour
100 g / 3 ½ oz / 1 cup desiccated coconut
100 g / 3 ½ oz / ¾ cup pine nuts

- Preheat the oven to 170°C (150° fan), 340F, gas 3 and line 2 baking sheets with greaseproof paper.
- Cream together the two sugars, butter and vanilla extract until pale and well whipped then beat in the egg and yolk, followed by the flour and coconut.
- Drop tablespoons of the mixture onto the prepared trays, leaving plenty of room to spread, and sprinkle with pine nuts.
- Bake the cookies in batches for 12 – 15 minutes or until the edges are starting to brown, but the centres are still chewy.
- Transfer to a wire rack and leave to cool.

657
MAKES 20

Rose and Almond Shortbread Biscuits

PREPARATION TIME 20 MINUTES

COOKING TIME 15-20 MINUTES

INGREDIENTS

175 g / 6 oz / 1 ¼ cup plain (all purpose) flour
55 g / 2 oz / ½ cup ground almonds
75 g / 2 ½ oz / ⅓ cup caster (superfine) sugar
150 g / 5 oz / ⅔ cup butter, cubed
1 tsp rose water
2 tbsp dried rose petals, shredded

- Preheat the oven to 180°C (160° fan), 355F, gas 4 and line a baking tray with greaseproof paper.
- Mix together the flour, ground almonds and caster (superfine) sugar in a bowl, then rub in the butter, rose water and rose petals.
- Knead gently until the mixture forms a smooth dough.
- Divide the dough into 20 balls and flatten slightly onto the baking tray.
- Bake the biscuits for 15-20 minutes, turning the tray round halfway through.
- Transfer the biscuits to a wire rack and leave to cool.

Orange and Almond Shortbread Biscuits

 658

- Replace the rosewater with the same amount of orange flower water for a citrus flavour and fragrance to these biscuits.

659
MAKES 36

Chocolate and Walnut Cookies

PREPARATION TIME 10 MINUTES

COOKING TIME 12-15 MINUTES

INGREDIENTS

175 g / 6 oz / ¾ cup butter, melted
225 g / 8 oz /1 ⅓ cup light brown sugar
100 g / 3 ½ oz / ½ cup caster (superfine) sugar
2 tsp vanilla extract
1 egg, plus 1 egg yolk
250 g / 9 oz / 1 ⅔ cups self-raising flour
100 g / 3 ½ oz / ¾ cup walnuts, chopped
100 g / 3 ½ oz milk chocolate, finely chopped

- Preheat the oven to 170°C (150° fan), 340F, gas 3 and line 2 baking sheets with greaseproof paper.
- Cream together the two sugars, butter and vanilla extract until pale and well whipped then beat in the egg and yolk, followed by the flour, walnuts and chocolate.
- Drop tablespoons of the mixture onto the prepared trays, leaving plenty of room to spread.
- Bake the cookies in batches for 12 – 15 minutes or until the edges are starting to brown, but the centres are still chewy.
- Transfer to a wire rack and leave to cool.

White Chocolate and Pecan Cookies

660

- Replace the milk chocolate with 125 g chopped white chocolate and replace the walnuts with the same weight of chopped pecans.

661

MAKES 1 LOAF Sundried Tomato and Granary Bread

- Mix together the flours, yeast, sugar and salt. Stir in the tomato puree, tomatoes and their oil into 280 ml of warm water.
- Knead on a lightly oiled surface for 10 minutes.
- Leave the dough to rest, covered with oiled clingfilm, for 1 – 2 hours or until doubled in size.
- Knead again then shape it into a round loaf.
- Transfer the loaf to a greased baking tray and cover again with oiled clingfilm. Leave to prove for 1 hour.
- Preheat the oven to 220°C (200° fan), gas 7.
- When the dough has risen, slash a star in the top.
- Transfer the tray to the top shelf of the oven then quickly throw a small cupful of water onto the floor of the oven and close the door.
- Bake for 35 – 40 minutes. Transfer the bread to a wire rack and leave to cool.

PREPARATION TIME 2 HOURS 30 MINUTES

COOKING TIME 35-40 MINUTES

INGREDIENTS

200 g / 7 oz / 1 ⅓ cup strong white bread flour, plus extra for dusting
200 g / 7 oz / 1 ⅓ cup malted granary flour
½ tsp easy blend dried yeast
1 tbsp caster (superfine) sugar
1 tsp fine sea salt
2 tbsp tomato puree
100 g / 3 ½ oz / ½ cup sundried tomatoes
in oil, drained
1 tbsp oil from the sundried tomatoes

Sundried Tomato and Courgette Bread

662

- Replace the granary flour with the same amount of strong white bread flour and add 1 diced courgette to the dough before kneading it.

663

MAKES 36 Walnut Cookies

- Preheat the oven to 170°C (150° fan), 340F, gas 3 and line 2 baking sheets with greaseproof paper.
- Cream together the two sugars, butter and almond extract until pale and well whipped then beat in the egg and yolk, followed by the flour and walnuts.
- Drop tablespoons of the mixture onto the prepared trays, leaving plenty of room to spread.
- Bake the cookies in batches for 12 – 15 minutes or until the edges are starting to brown, but the centres are still chewy.
- Transfer to a wire rack and leave to cool.

PREPARATION TIME 10 MINUTES

COOKING TIME 12-15 MINUTES

INGREDIENTS

175 g / 6 oz / ¾ cup butter, melted
225 g / 8 oz / 1 ⅓ cup light brown sugar
100 g / 3 ½ oz / ½ cup caster (superfine) sugar
2 tsp almond extract
1 egg, plus 1 egg yolk
250 g / 9 oz / 1 ⅔ cups self-raising flour
100 g / 3 ½ oz / ¾ cupwalnuts, chopped

Maple and Walnut Cookies

664

- Add 55 ml / 2 oz maple syrup to the cookie dough instead of the vanilla extract for a distinctly autumnal flavour to these cookies.

665

MAKES 36

Chocolate Caramel Cookies

Salted Caramel Cookies | 666

- Replace the chocolate caramel bars with 75ml / 3 fl. oz dulce de leche and 1 tbsp sea salt flakes when you prepare the cookie dough, for a sweet/savoury contrast.

Chocolate, Caramel and Nut Cookies | 667

- Replace the chocolate caramel bars with the same weight of chopped caramel and nut chocolate bars for a nutty crunch.

PREPARATION TIME 10 MINUTES

COOKING TIME 12-15 MINUTES

INGREDIENTS

175 g / 6 oz / ¾ cup butter, melted
225 g / 8 oz / 1 ⅓ cup light brown sugar
100 g / 3 ½ oz / ½ cup caster (superfine) sugar
2 tsp vanilla extract
1 egg, plus 1 egg yolk
250 g / 9 oz / 1 ⅔ cups self-raising flour
150 g / 5 ½ oz chocolate caramel bars, chopped

- Preheat the oven to 170°C (150° fan), 340F, gas 3 and line 2 baking sheets with greaseproof paper.
- Cream together the two sugars, butter and vanilla extract until pale and well whipped then beat in the egg and yolk, followed by the flour and chopped chocolate caramel bars.
- Drop tablespoons of the mixture onto the prepared trays, leaving plenty of room to spread.
- Bake the cookies in batches for 12 – 15 minutes or until the edges are starting to brown, but the centres are still chewy.
- Transfer to a wire rack and leave to cool.

668

MAKES 36

Marmalade Heart Biscuits

- Cream together the sugar, butter and vanilla extract until pale then stir in the flour and ground almonds.
- Bring the mixture together into a ball with your hands then wrap in clingfilm and refrigerate for 45 minutes.
- Preheat the oven to 140°C (120° fan), 280F, gas 1 and line 2 baking sheets with greaseproof paper.
- Roll out the dough on a lightly floured surface to 5 mm thick. Use a heart-shaped cutter to cut out 72 biscuits.
- Use a small cutter to cut a hole out of 36 of the biscuits.
- Transfer the biscuits to the prepared trays in batches and bake for 25 – 30 minutes or until cooked through and only just golden.
- Transfer the biscuits to a wire rack and leave to cool.
- Put a teaspoon of marmalade on the underside of the plain biscuits and top with the biscuits with the hole cut out. Dust liberally with icing sugar.

PREPARATION TIME I HOUR 15 MINUTES

COOKING TIME 25-30 MINUTES

INGREDIENTS

150 g / 5 ½ oz / ⅔ cup caster (superfine) sugar
350 g / 12 oz / 1 ½ cup butter, softened
1 tsp vanilla extract
300 g / 10 ½ oz / 2 cup plain (all purpose) flour
150 g / 5 ½ oz / 1 ½ cup ground almonds
200 g / 7 oz / ⅔ cup marmalade icing (confectioners) sugar to dust

Apricot Jam Heart Biscuits

669

- Replace the marmalade with the same weight of apricot jam for an alternative fruit flavour.

670

MAKES 25

Parmesan and Herb Shortbread Biscuits

- Preheat the oven to 180°C (160° fan), 355F, gas 4 and line a baking tray with greaseproof paper.
- Rub the butter into the flour and stir in the Parmesan and herbs.
- Knead gently until the mixture forms a smooth dough then roll out on a lightly floured surface to 1 cm thick.
- Use a knife to cut the sheet into small squares and transfer them to the baking tray.
- Bake the biscuits for 12 - 15 minutes, turning the tray round halfway through.
- Transfer the biscuits to a wire rack and leave to cool.

PREPARATION TIME 20 MINUTES

COOKING TIME 15-20 MINUTES

INGREDIENTS

150g / 5 oz / ⅔ cup butter, cubed
230g / 8 oz / 1 ½ cup plain (all purpose) flour
50 g / 1 ¾ oz / ½ cup Parmesan, grated
2 tbsp dried herbs de Provence

Gruyere Shortbread Biscuits

 671

- Replace the Parmesan with the same weight of Gruyere and omit the herbs for a more distinct cheese flavour to these biscuits.

672

MAKES 1

Crusty Baton

PREPARATION TIME 2 HOURS
30 MINUTES

COOKING TIME 25-30 MINUTES

INGREDIENTS

400 g / 14 oz / 2 ⅔ cups strong white
bread flour, plus extra for dusting
½ tsp easy blend dried yeast
1 tbsp caster (superfine) sugar
1 tsp fine sea salt
1 tbsp olive oil

- Mix together the flour, yeast, sugar and salt. Stir in
  the oil and 280 ml of warm water.
- Knead the mixture on a lightly oiled surface for
  10 minutes or until smooth and elastic.
- Leave the dough to rest, covered with oiled clingfilm,
  for 1 – 2 hours or until doubled in size.
- Knead the dough then roll up tightly into a baton.
- Transfer the loaf to a greased baking tray and cover
  with oiled clingfilm. Leave to prove for 1 hour.
- Preheat the oven to 220°C (200° fan), 430F, gas 7.
- Dust the loaf with flour and slash the top with a knife.
- Transfer the tray to the top shelf of the oven then
  quickly throw a small cupful of water onto the oven
  floor and close the door.
- Bake for 25 – 30 minutes. Transfer to a wire rack and
  leave to cool.

Crusty Wholemeal Baton 673

- Replace 200 g / 7 oz of the bread
  flour with 200 g / 7 oz of wholemeal
  flour for a healthier bread.

674

MAKES 24

Gazelle Horn Biscuits

PREPARATION TIME 55 MINUTES

COOKING TIME 15 MINUTES

INGREDIENTS

300 g / 10 ½ oz / 3 cups ground
almonds
100 g / 3 ½ oz / 1 cup icing
(confectioners) sugar, plus extra to
dust
1 tbsp orange flower water
½ tsp ground cinnamon
a few drops almond extract
1 large egg white, beaten
30 g / 1 oz butter, melted
50 g / 1 ¾ oz / ½ cup blanched
almonds, chopped

FOR THE PASTRY
1 egg yolk
2 tbsp orange flower water
30 g / 1 oz butter, melted
300 g / 10 ½ oz / 2 cup plain (all
purpose) flour

- Beat the egg with the orange flower water, butter and
  125 ml of cold water.
- Stir the mixture into the flour and bring it together
  into a pliable dough. Knead for 5 minutes then
  refrigerate for 30 minutes.
- Preheat the oven to 180°C (160° fan), 355F, gas 4 and
  grease and line a large baking tray.
- Mix the ground almonds with the icing sugar, orange
  flower water, cinnamon and almond essence.
- Mix the egg white into the almond mixture with the
  melted butter to form a stiff paste. Roll out the pastry on
  a lightly floured surface and cut into 24 rectangles.
- Shape a tablespoon of the almond paste into a log and
  lay it along one long edge of a pastry rectangle. Roll it up
  and pinch the ends to seal then curl it into a crescent.
- Repeat with the rest of the mixture and bake for 15
  minutes. Dust liberally with icing sugar.

Chocolate Gazelle Horn Biscuit 675

- Replace 55 g / 2 oz of the ground
  almonds with 75 g / 3 oz cocoa powder
  for a darker, richer tasting biscuit.

676

MAKES 12

Wholemeal Baton

Wholemeal Raisin Baton 677

- Add 75 g / 3 oz raisins to the dough before kneading for an interesting fruity taste.

Pine Nut Wholemeal Baton 678

- Add 75 g / 3 oz pine nut to the dough before kneading for a different texture and flavour to this baton.

PREPARATION TIME 2 HOURS 30 MINUTES

COOKING TIME 25-30 MINUTES

INGREDIENTS

400 g / 14 oz / 2 ⅔ cup stoneground wholemeal flour
1 tsp easy blend dried yeast
2 tbsp caster (superfine) sugar
1 tsp fine sea salt
1 tbsp olive oil

- Mix together the flour, yeast, sugar and salt. Stir the oil into 280 ml of warm water then stir it into the dry ingredients.
- Knead the mixture on a lightly oiled surface for 10 minutes or until smooth and elastic.
- Leave the dough to rest, covered with oiled clingfilm, for 1 – 2 hours or until doubled in size.
- Knead the dough for 2 more minutes then roll it up tightly into a baton.
- Transfer the loaf to a greased baking tray and cover with oiled clingfilm. Leave to prove for 1 hour or until doubled in size.
- Meanwhile, preheat the oven to 220°C (200° fan), 430F, gas 7.
- Slash the top of the loaf lengthways with a knife.
- Transfer the tray to the top shelf of the oven then quickly throw a small cupful of water onto the oven floor and close the door.
- Bake for 25 – 30 minutes or until the loaf sounds hollow when you tap it underneath.
- Transfer to a wire rack and leave to cool.

679

MAKES 1

Stuffed Ring Loaf

PREPARATION TIME 2 HOURS
30 MINUTES

COOKING TIME 25-30 MINUTES

INGREDIENTS

400 g / 14 oz / 2 ⅔ cups strong white
bread flour, plus extra for dusting
½ tsp easy blend dried yeast
1 tbsp caster (superfine) sugar
1 tsp fine sea salt
1 tbsp olive oil

FOR THE STUFFING

100 g / 3 ½ oz chorizo, chopped
75 g / 2 ½ oz / ⅓ cup sundried
tomatoes in oil, drained and chopped
100 g / 3 ½ oz mozzarella, cubed
1 tbsp basil leaves, chopped

- Mix together the flour, yeast, sugar and salt. Stir in the oil and 280 ml of warm water.
- Knead the mixture on a lightly oiled surface for 10 minutes or until smooth and elastic.
- Leave the dough to rest, covered with oiled clingfilm, for 1 – 2 hours or until doubled in size.
- Combine the stuffing ingredients.
- Roll the dough out into a rectangle. Put the stuffing ingredients in a line down the middle then fold in the sides and pinch to seal.
- Curl the dough round into a ring with the seam on top and transfer to a greased baking tray. Cover with oiled clingfilm and leave to prove for 1 hour.
- Preheat the oven to 220°C (200° fan), 430F, gas 7.
- Bake for 25 – 30 minutes or until the loaf sounds hollow when you tap it underneath.

Spinach Stuffed Ring Loaf   680

- Replace the chorizo in the recipe for 200 g / 7 oz wilted spinach for a vegetarian take on this loaf.

681

MAKES 18

Black Sesame Tuiles

PREPARATION TIME 45 MINUTES

COOKING TIME 8-10 MINUTES

INGREDIENTS

110 g / 4 oz / ⅔ cup plain (all
purpose) flour
110 g / 4 oz caster / ½ cup (superfine)
sugar
2 large egg whites
110 g / 4 oz / ½ cup butter, melted
2 tbsp black sesame seeds

- Beat together the flour, sugar and egg whites until smooth, then beat in the melted butter and sesame seeds.
- Refrigerate for 30 minutes.
- Preheat the oven to 180°C (160° fan), 350F, gas 4 and oil 2 large baking trays.
- Spoon teaspoonfuls of the mixture onto the baking trays and spread out with the back of the spoon to make 10 cm circles.
- Bake the tuiles for 8 – 10 minutes then lift them off the trays with a palette knife and drape over a rolling pin while still soft. Leave to cool and harden.

Black Sesame and Orange Tuiles   682

- Add 1 tsp of orange flower water and the grated zest of ½ orange to the tuile mixture for an added citrus tang.

MAKES 20 — Chocolate Spring Rolls

683

- Preheat the oven to 180°C (160° fan), 355F, gas 4 and grease a large baking tray.
- Cut the pile of filo sheets in half then take one halved sheet and brush it with melted butter.
- Arrange a tablespoon of chopped chocolate along one side and roll it up, tucking in the sides as you go.
- Transfer the roll to the baking tray and repeat with the rest of the filo and chocolate.
- Brush the spring rolls with beaten egg and bake for 12 – 15 minutes or until the filo is crisp and golden brown.
- Serve warm.

PREPARATION TIME 25 MINUTES

COOKING TIME 12-15 MINUTES

INGREDIENTS

225 g / 8 oz filo pastry
100 g / 3 ½ oz / ½ cup butter, melted
200 g / 7 oz dark chocolate
(minimum 60 % cocoa solids), finely chopped
1 egg, beaten

White Chocolate and Cranberry Spring Rolls

684

- Replace the chocolate for the filling with 150 g chopped white chocolate and 55 g dried cranberries. Combine the two before filling the spring rolls.

MAKES 36 — Cinnamon Snap Biscuits

685

- Preheat the oven to 180°C (160° fan), 355F, gas 4 and line 2 baking sheets with greaseproof paper.
- Melt the butter and golden syrup together in a saucepan.
- Mix the flour, sugar and cinnamon together then stir in the melted butter mixture and the beaten egg.
- Use a teaspoon to portion the mixture onto the baking trays, leaving plenty of room for the biscuits to spread.
- Bake in batches for 12 – 15 minutes or until golden brown.
- Transfer the biscuits to a wire rack and leave to cool and harden.

PREPARATION TIME 10 MINUTES

COOKING TIME 12-15 MINUTES

INGREDIENTS

75 g / 2 ½ oz / ⅓ cup butter, softened
100 g / 3 ½ oz / ⅓ cup golden syrup
225 g / 8 oz / 1 ½ cups self-raising flour
100 g / 3 ½ oz / ½ cup caster (superfine) sugar
1 tsp ground cinnamon
1 large egg, beaten

Spiced Snap Biscuits

686

- Instead of using just cinnamon, use 1 tsp ground mixed allspice for a more varied flavour.

687

MAKES 24

Date Filled Shortbread

Cranberry Filled Shortbread

688

- Soak 250 g / 9 oz of dried cranberries in enough hot water to cover them for an hour. Drain, puree and use to stuff the shortbread.

Caramel Filled Shortbread

689

- Use 200 g / 7 oz dulce de leche as the filled instead of the dates for an even sweeter shortbread.

PREPARATION TIME 20 MINUTES

COOKING TIME 12-15 MINUTES

INGREDIENTS

200 g / 7 oz / 1 cup dates, pitted and chopped
150 g / 5 ½ oz / 1 cup plain (all purpose) flour
75g / 2 ½ oz / ⅓ cup caster (superfine) sugar
150g / 5 oz / ⅔ cup butter, cubed

- Cover the dates with boiling water and leave to soak for 1 hour. Drain well then puree in a food processor.
- Preheat the oven to 180°C (160° fan), 355F, gas 4 and line a baking tray with greaseproof paper.
- Mix the flour and caster (superfine) sugar in a bowl, then rub in the butter.
- Knead gently until the mixture forms a smooth dough then roll out on a lightly floured surface to 5 mm thick and cut the sheet in half.
- Spread the date puree over one half of the shortbread and lay the other sheet on top.
- Cut the shortbread into 24 squares and transfer to the baking tray.
- Bake the biscuits for 12 - 15 minutes, turning them over half way through.
- Transfer the biscuits to a wire rack and leave to cool.

690

MAKES 1 LOAF Curry and Pistachio Bread

- Mix together the flours, yeast, sugar, salt, curry powder and pistachios. Stir in oil and 280 ml of warm water.
- Knead the mixture on a lightly oiled surface for 10 minutes or until the dough is smooth and elastic.
- Leave the dough to rest in a lightly oiled bowl, covered with oiled clingfilm, for 1 – 2 hours.
- Knead the dough for 2 more minutes then roll it into a fat sausage. Turn it 90° and roll it tightly the other way then tuck the ends under and transfer the dough to the tin, keeping the seam underneath.
- Cover the tin with oiled clingfilm and leave to prove for 45 minutes.
- Preheat the oven to 220°C (200° fan), 430F, gas 7.
- Bake for 35 – 40 minutes or until the underneath sounds hollow when tapped.
- Leave to cool completely on a wire rack.

PREPARATION TIME 2 HOURS 30 MINUTES

COOKING TIME 35-40 MINUTES

INGREDIENTS

300 g / 10 ½ oz / 2 cups strong white bread flour, plus extra for dusting
100 g / 3 ½ oz / ⅔ cup stoneground wholemeal flour
½ tsp easy blend dried yeast
1 tbsp caster (superfine) sugar
1 tsp fine sea salt
2 tbsp mild curry powder
75 g / 2 ½ oz / ½ cup pistachio nuts
2 tbsp olive oil

Indian Mixed Seed Bread

691

- Use 75 g / 3 oz of any combination of seeds instead of the pistachios for a nut-free bread.

692

MAKES 24 Fruit and Nut Cookies

- Preheat the oven to 180°C (160° fan), 355F, gas 4 and line a baking tray with greaseproof paper.
- Rub the butter into the flour with a pinch of salt then stir in the sugar.
- Beat the egg yolks and stir them into the dry ingredients with the dried fruit and nuts.
- Bring the mixture together into a soft dough and space tablespoons of the mixture out on the baking tray.
- Bake the biscuits for 20 – 25 minutes or until golden brown.
- Transfer the biscuits to a wire rack and leave to cool.

PREPARATION TIME 15 MINUTES

COOKING TIME 20-25 MINUTES

INGREDIENTS

125 g / 4 ½ oz / ½ cup butter, cubed
125 g / 4 ½ oz / ¾ cup plain (all purpose) flour
125 g / 4 ½ oz / ½ cup caster (superfine) sugar
3 large egg yolks
75 g / 2 ½ oz / 1 cup flaked (slivered) almonds
75 g / 2 ½ oz / ½ cup pistachios, chopped
75 g / 2 ½ oz / ⅓ cup dried apricots, chopped
75 g / 2 ½ oz / ⅓ cup sultanas

Chewy Fruit Cookies

693

- Instead of using nuts, replace the flaked (slivered) almonds and pistachios with the same weight of raisins and chopped glacé cherries for chewy, colourful cookies.

694

MAKES 1 LOAF # Wholemeal Sundried Tomato Bread

PREPARATION TIME 2 HOURS 30 MINUTES

COOKING TIME 35-40 MINUTES

INGREDIENTS

200 g / 7 oz / 1 ⅓ cup strong white bread flour, plus extra for dusting
200 g / 7 oz / 1 ⅓ cup stoneground wholemeal flour
½ tsp easy blend dried yeast
1 tbsp caster (superfine) sugar
1 tsp fine sea salt
150 g 5 ½ oz / ¾ cup sundried tomatoes
in oil, drained
1 tbsp olive oil

- Mix together the flours, yeast, sugar, salt and tomatoes.
- Stir in the oil and 280 ml warm water. Knead the mixture on a lightly oiled surface for 10 minutes or until smooth and elastic.
- Leave the dough to rest in an oiled bowl for 1 – 2 hours.
- Roll the dough with your hands into a fat sausage, then turn it 90⁰ and roll it tightly the other way. Tuck the ends under and transfer the dough to the tin, keeping the seam underneath.
- Cover the tin loosely with oiled clingfilm and leave to prove somewhere warm for 45 minutes.
- Preheat the oven to 220⁰C (200⁰ fan), 430F, gas 7.
- Transfer the tin to the top shelf of the oven then quickly throw a small cupful of water onto the floor of the oven and close the door.
- Bake for 35 – 40 minutes or until the loaf sounds hollow when you tap it underneath.

Sundried Tomato and Basil Bread 695

- Use and additional 200 g / 7 oz of strong plain bread flour instead of the wholemeal flour and use 1 tbsp dried basil mixed into the dough for an added Mediterranean flavour.

696

MAKES 1 # 50-50 Baton

PREPARATION TIME 2 HOURS 30 MINUTES

COOKING TIME 25-30 MINUTES

INGREDIENTS

200 g / 7 oz / 1 ⅓ cup strong white bread flour, plus extra for dusting
200 g / 7 oz / 1 ⅓ cup stoneground wholemeal flour
½ tsp easy blend dried yeast
1 tbsp caster (superfine) sugar
1 tsp fine sea salt
1 tbsp olive oil

- Mix together the flours, yeast, sugar and salt. Stir in the oil and 280 ml of warm water.
- Knead the mixture on a lightly oiled surface for 10 minutes or until smooth and elastic.
- Leave the dough to rest, covered with oiled clingfilm, for 1 – 2 hours or until doubled in size.
- Knead the dough for 2 more minutes then roll it up tightly into a baton.
- Transfer the loaf to a greased baking tray and cover with oiled clingfilm. Leave to prove for 1 hour or until doubled in size.
- Preheat the oven to 220⁰C (200⁰ fan), 430F, gas 7.
- Dust the loaf with flour and slash the top with a knife.
- Bake for 25 – 30 minutes or until the loaf sounds hollow when you tap it underneath.
- Transfer to a wire rack and leave to cool.

50-50 Cheese Baton 697

- Incorporate 110 g / 4 oz grated Cheddar into the dough before kneading for cheesy take on this bread.

698

MAKES 1

Tuscan Saltless Bread

Tuscan Herb Bread 699

- Mix together 1 tsp of dried basil, oregano and rosemary and fold into the dough for an added Italian flavour.

Tuscan Pepper Bread 700

- Grind 1 tbsp black peppercorns in a pestle and mortar before adding to the dough and kneading for a peppery bite to the bread.

PREPARATION TIME 2 HOURS 30 MINUTES

COOKING TIME 35-40 MINUTES

INGREDIENTS

400 g / 14 oz / 2 ⅔ cups strong white bread flour, plus extra for dusting
½ tsp easy blend dried yeast
2 tbsp olive oil

- Mix together the flour and yeast. Stir the oil into 280 ml of warm water then stir it into the dry ingredients.
- Knead the mixture on a lightly oiled surface with your hands for 10 minutes or until smooth and elastic.
- Leave the dough to rest in a lightly oiled bowl, covered with oiled clingfilm, for 1 – 2 hours or until doubled in size.
- Knead it for 2 more minutes, then shape into a round loaf.
- Transfer the loaf to a greased baking tray and cover with oiled clingfilm. Leave to prove for 1 hour or until doubled in size.
- Meanwhile, preheat the oven to 220°C (200° fan), 430F, gas 7.
- Dust the loaf with flour and slash the top with a knife.
- Transfer the tray to the top shelf of the oven then quickly throw a small cupful of water onto the oven floor and close the door.
- Bake for 35 - 40 minutes or until the loaf sounds hollow when you tap it underneath.
- Transfer to a wire rack and leave to cool.

701
MAKES 1 LOAF Fig and Walnut Bread

PREPARATION TIME 2 HOURS
30 MINUTES

COOKING TIME 35-40 MINUTES

INGREDIENTS

400 g / 14 oz / 2 ⅔ cups strong white
bread flour, plus extra for dusting
½ tsp easy blend dried yeast
1 tbsp caster (superfine) sugar
1 tsp fine sea salt
100 g / 3 ½ oz / ½ cup dried figs,
chopped
100 g / 3 ½ oz / ⅔ cup walnut halves

- Mix together the flour, yeast, sugar and salt. Stir in the figs, walnuts and 280 ml of warm water.
- Knead the mixture on a lightly oiled surface with your hands for 10 minutes or until the dough is elastic.
- Leave the dough to rest in a lightly oiled bowl, covered with oiled clingfilm, for 1 – 2 hours.
- Punch the dough with your fist to knock out the air then knead it for 2 more minutes. Cup your hands around the dough and move it in a circular motion whilst pressing down to form a tight round loaf.
- Transfer the dough to a greased round cake tin and cover with oiled clingfilm. Leave to prove for 1 hour or until doubled in size then slash a cross in the top.
- Preheat the oven to 220°C (200° fan), 430F, gas 7.
- Bake for 35 – 40 minutes or until the loaf sounds hollow when you tapped. Transfer the bread to a wire rack and leave to cool completely before slicing.

Apricot and Walnut Bread 702

- Replace the figs in the recipe with 100 g / 3 ½ oz chopped dried apricots instead for a different flavour and texture.

703
MAKES 40 Coffee Sponge Finger Biscuits

PREPARATION TIME 20 MINUTES

COOKING TIME 10-15 MINUTES

INGREDIENTS

4 large eggs
125 g / 4 ½ oz / ½ cup caster
(superfine) sugar
1 tsp instant espresso powder
a pinch cream of tartar
115 g / 4 oz / ⅔ cup plain (all
purpose) flour

- Preheat the oven to 190°C (170° fan), 375F, gas 5 and grease and line 2 large trays with greaseproof paper.
- Separate the eggs and put the yolks in a bowl with half of the sugar and the espresso powder. Whisk with an electric whisk for 4 minutes or until very thick and pale.
- Whisk the egg whites with the cream of tartar, making sure the whisk and bowl are completely clean.
- When the egg white reaches the soft peak stage, gradually whisk in the remaining sugar.
- Sieve the flour over the egg yolk mixture and scrape in the egg whites, then carefully fold it all together with a large metal spoon, retaining as much air as possible.
- Spoon the mixture into a piping bag.
- Pipe 10 cm lines onto the baking trays, leaving room for the biscuits to spread.
- Bake the biscuits for 10 – 15 minutes.
- Transfer to a wire rack and leave to cool completely.

Chocolate Sponge Finger Biscuits 704

- Replace the instant espresso powder in the recipe with 1 tbsp good-quality cocoa powder for a chocolatey take on these biscuits.

705

MAKES 40

Langues Du Chat Biscuits

- Preheat the oven to 190°C (170° fan), 375F, gas 5 and grease and line 2 large trays with greaseproof paper.
- Separate the eggs and put the yolks in a bowl with half of the sugar and the vanilla extract. Whisk with an electric whisk for 4 minutes or until very thick and pale.
- Whisk the egg whites with the cream of tartar, making sure the whisk and bowl are completely clean.
- When the egg white reaches the soft peak stage, gradually whisk in the remaining sugar.
- Sieve the flour over the egg yolk mixture and scrape in the egg whites, then carefully fold it all together with a large metal spoon, retaining as much air as possible.
- Spoon tablespoons of the mixture onto the tray and spread out with the spoon into tongue shapes.
- Bake the biscuits for 10 – 15 minutes.
- Transfer to a wire rack and leave to cool completely.

PREPARATION TIME 20 MINUTES

COOKING TIME 10-15 MINUTES

INGREDIENTS

4 large eggs
125 g / 4 ½ oz / ½ cup caster (superfine) sugar
1 tsp vanilla extract
a pinch cream of tartar
115 g / 4 oz / ⅔ cup plain (all purpose) flour

Amaretto Cat's Tongue Biscuits 706

- Replace the vanilla extract with 1 tbsp of Amaretto for a more complex flavour.

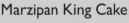 **707**

SERVES 12

Galette Du Roi

- Preheat the oven to 200°C (180° fan), 390F, gas 6 and grease and line a baking tray with greaseproof paper.
- Roll out half the pastry on a floured surface into a large circle and transfer it to the baking sheet.
- Whisk together the almonds, butter, sugar, eggs and flour until smooth then spoon the mixture on top of the pastry, leaving a clear border round the edge.
- Brush the border with a little water. Roll out the other half of the pastry and lay it over the almond paste, pressing around the outside to seal.
- Trim away the excess pastry and score a pattern in the top with a knife.
- Brush the pastry with egg yolk and bake for 35 minutes.
- Traditionally a dried bean or porcelain figurine is hidden inside the galette before baking. The person that finds it in their slice becomes king for the day.

PREPARATION TIME 30 MINUTES

COOKING TIME 35 MINUTES

INGREDIENTS

450 g / 1 lb puff pastry
150 g / 5 ½ oz / 1 ½ cup ground almonds
150 g / 5 ½ oz / ⅔ cup butter, softened
150 g / 5 ½ oz / ⅔ cup caster (superfine) sugar
2 large eggs
2 tbsp plain (all purpose) flour
1 egg yolk

Marzipan King Cake 708

- Divide 200 g / 7 oz of softened natural marzipan into small balls and use them to garnish the top of the cake for an additional almond flavour.

709

MAKES 1 LOAF # Gouda and Cumin Bread

Gruyere and Coriander Bread

710

- Use 100 g / 3 ½ of grated Gruyere instead of Gouda and replace the cumin seeds with 1 tbsp lightly crushed coriander seeds.

Paprika Cheese Bread

711

- Omit the cumin seeds and use 1 tbsp ground paprika incorporated into the dough for a spiced, colourful bread.

PREPARATION TIME 2 HOURS 30 MINUTES

COOKING TIME 35-40 MINUTES

INGREDIENTS

400 g / 14 oz / 2 ⅔ cup strong white bread flour
½ tsp easy blend dried yeast
1 tbsp caster (superfine) sugar
1 tsp fine sea salt
100 g / 3 ½ oz / 1 cup Gouda, grated
1 tbsp cumin seeds, plus extra for sprinkling

- Mix together the flour, yeast, sugar and salt. Stir the gouda into 280 ml of warm water and stir into the dry ingredients.
- Knead the mixture on a lightly oiled surface for 10 minutes or until the dough is smooth and elastic.
- Leave the dough to rest in a lightly oiled bowl, covered with oiled clingfilm, for 1 – 2 hours or until doubled in size.
- Knead the dough for 2 more minutes then roll it into a fat sausage and put it into an empty tin can, lined with greaseproof paper.
- Cover the tin with oiled clingfilm and leave to prove for 45 minutes.
- Preheat the oven to 220°C (200° fan), 430F, gas 7.
- Transfer the tin to the top shelf of the oven, then quickly throw a small cupful of water onto the floor of the oven and close the door.
- Bake for 35 – 40 minutes or until the underneath sounds hollow when tapped.
- Leave to cool completely on a wire rack before slicing.

712

MAKES 16 Ginger Shortbread Biscuits

- Preheat the oven to 180°C (160° fan), 355F, gas 4 and line a baking tray with greaseproof paper.
- Mix together the flour, ginger and caster (superfine) sugar in a bowl, then rub in the butter.
- Knead gently until the mixture forms a smooth dough then roll out to 1 cm thick and cut into triangles.
- Spread the shortbread out on the baking tray and bake for 15-20 minutes, turning the tray round halfway through.
- Transfer the biscuits to a wire rack and leave to cool.

PREPARATION TIME 20 MINUTES

COOKING TIME 15-20 MINUTES

INGREDIENTS

230 g / 8 oz / 1 ½ cups plain (all purpose) flour
2 tsp ground ginger
75 g / 2 ½ oz / ⅓ cup caster (superfine) sugar
150 g / 5 oz / ⅔ cup butter, cubed

Ginger Orange Shortbread Biscuits

713

- Add the finely grated zest of 1 orange to the shortbread mixture before spreading and baking.

714

SERVES 10 Ginger Loaf Cake

- Preheat the oven to 180°C (160° fan), 355F, gas 4and grease and line a loaf tin.
- Sieve the flour, bicarbonate of soda and ginger into a bowl.
- Put the golden syrup, butter and brown sugar in a small saucepan and boil gently for 2 minutes, stirring to dissolve the sugar.
- Add the butter and sugar mixture to the flour with the eggs and milk and fold it all together until smooth.
- Scrape the mixture into the prepared tin and bake for 35 - 40 minutes. The cake is ready when a toothpick inserted in the centre comes out clean.
- Transfer the cake to a wire rack to cool completely.

PREPARATION TIME 15 MINUTES

COOKING TIME 35-40 MINUTES

INGREDIENTS

250 g / 9 oz / 1 ⅔ cups self-raising flour
1 tsp bicarbonate of soda
2 tsp ground ginger
200 g / 8 ½ oz / ⅔ cup golden syrup
125 g / 4 ½ oz / ½ cup butter
125 g / 4 ½ oz / ¾ cup dark brown sugar
2 large eggs, beaten
240 ml / 8 fl. oz / 1 cup milk

Ginger and Treacle Loaf Cake

715

- Replace the Golden Syrup in the recipe with 200 g / 7 oz black treacle, for a deeper, richer flavour and appearance.

716

MAKES 36

Wholemeal Lebkuchen

PREPARATION TIME 25 MINUTES

COOKING TIME 15-20 MINUTES

INGREDIENTS

4 large eggs
200 g / 7 oz / ¾ cup caster (superfine) sugar
1 tsp vanilla extract
150 g / 5 ½ oz / 1 cup plain (all purpose) flour, plus extra for dusting
100 g / 3 ½ oz / ⅔ cup stoneground wholemeal flour
1 tsp baking powder
200 g / 7 oz / 2 cup ground almonds
100 g / 3 ½ oz / ½ cup mixed peel, finely chopped
1 tbsp unsweetened cocoa powder
1 tsp mixed spice
1 tsp ground ginger

FOR THE ICING

150 g / 5 ½ oz / 1 ½ cup royal icing powder

- Preheat the oven to 190°C (170° fan), 375F, gas 5 and line 2 baking sheets with greaseproof paper.
- Beat the eggs with the sugar and vanilla extract until pale and creamy then fold in the rest of the ingredients to form a soft dough.
- Roll the dough out on a lightly floured surface to 5 mm thick and use a variety of cookie cutters to cut out the biscuits.
- Transfer the biscuits to the prepared trays and bake for 15 – 20 minutes or until crisp and brown.
- Transfer the biscuits to a wire rack and leave to cool completely.
- Whisk the royal icing powder with 25 ml water using an electric whisk for 5 minutes.
- Use a palette knife or piping bag to apply the icing to the top of the biscuits and leave to set for at least 1 hour.

717

SERVES 10

Wholemeal Ginger and Orange Loaf

PREPARATION TIME 15 MINUTES

COOKING TIME 35-40 MINUTES

INGREDIENTS

250 g / 9 oz / 1 ⅔ cup stoneground wholemeal flour
2 tsp baking powder
2 tsp ground ginger
200 g / 8 ½ oz / ⅔ cup golden syrup
125 g / 4 ½ oz / ½ cup butter
100 g / 3 ½ oz / ½ cup candied orange peel, chopped
125 g / 4 ½ oz / ¾ cup dark brown sugar
2 large eggs, beaten
240 ml / 8 fl. oz / 1 cup milk

- Preheat the oven to 180°C (160° fan), 355F, gas 4 and grease and line a loaf tin.
- Mix the flour, baking powder and ginger in a bowl.
- Put the golden syrup, butter , candied peel and brown sugar in a small saucepan and boil gently for 2 minutes, stirring to dissolve the sugar.
- Add the butter and sugar mixture to the flour with the eggs and milk and fold it all together until smooth.
- Scrape the mixture into the prepared tin and bake for 35 - 40 minutes. The cake is ready when a toothpick inserted in the centre comes out clean.
- Transfer the cake to a wire rack to cool completely.

718

MAKES 1 Granary Nut Bread

- Mix together the flours, nuts, yeast, sugar and salt. Stir in the oil and 280 ml of warm water.
- Knead the mixture on a lightly oiled surface for 10 minutes or until smooth and elastic.
- Leave the dough to rest, covered with oiled clingfilm, for 1 – 2 hours or until doubled in size.
- Knead for 2 more minutes then roll the dough into a fat sausage. Roll it up the other way and drop it into a loaf tin with the seam underneath.
- Cover the tin with oiled clingfilm and leave to prove for 1 hour or until doubled in size.
- Preheat the oven to 220°C (200° fan), 430F, gas 7.
- Dust the loaf with flour and slash the top with a knife.
- Bake for 35 - 40 minutes or until the loaf sounds hollow when you tap it underneath.
- Transfer to a wire rack and leave to cool.

PREPARATION TIME 2 HOURS
30 MINUTES

COOKING TIME 35-40 MINUTES

INGREDIENTS

300 g / 10 ½ oz / 2 cup malted granary flour
100 g / 3 ½ oz / ⅔ cup strong white bread flour, plus extra for dusting
75 g / 2 ½ oz / ⅔ cup hazelnuts (cob nuts), chopped
75 g / 2 ½ oz / ⅔ cup walnuts, chopped
½ tsp easy blend dried yeast
2 tbsp caster (superfine) sugar
1 tsp fine sea salt
1 tbsp olive oil

Hazelnut Shortbread

719

MAKES 16

PREPARATION TIME 20 MINUTES

COOKING TIME 15-20 MINUTES

INGREDIENTS

230 g / 8 oz / 1 ½ cup plain (all purpose) flour
2 tbsp ground hazelnuts (cob nuts)
75 g / 2 ½ oz / ⅓ cup caster (superfine) sugar
150 g / 5 oz / ⅔ cup butter, cubed

- Preheat the oven to 180°C (160° fan), 355F, gas 4 and line a baking tray with greaseproof paper.
- Mix together the flour, ground hazelnuts and caster (superfine) sugar in a bowl, then rub in the butter.
- Knead gently until the mixture forms a smooth dough then form into a cylinder 6 cm in diameter.
- Slice the roll into 1 cm thick slices and spread them out on the baking tray.
- Bake the biscuits for 15-20 minutes, turning the tray round halfway through.
- Transfer the biscuits to a wire rack and leave to cool.

Basil and Parmesan Tuiles

720

MAKES 15

PREPARATION TIME 5 MINUTES

COOKING TIME 5-10 MINUTES

INGREDIENTS

200 g / 7 oz / 2 cup Parmesan, grated
1 tbsp plain (all purpose) flour
2 tbsp basil leaves, finely chopped

- Preheat the oven to 200°C (180° fan), 390F, gas 6.
- Mix the Parmesan with the flour and basil then space out tablespoons of the mixture on a large baking tray.
- Bake them in the oven for 5 – 10 minutes or until lacy and golden brown.
- Leave the tuiles to set on the tray for 30 seconds then use a palette knife to lift them off.
- Leave to cool and harden on a wire rack.

721

MAKES 24

Almond Snaps

PREPARATION TIME 15 MINUTES

COOKING TIME 15-20 MINUTES

....

INGREDIENTS

2 large egg whites
175 g / 6 oz / 1 ¾ cup ground
almonds
100 g / 3 ½ oz / 1 cup icing
(confectioners) sugar
75 g / 2 ½ oz / ⅓ cup caster
(superfine) sugar
1 tbsp amaretto liqueur

- Preheat the oven to 170°C (150° fan), 325F, gas 3 and oil a large baking tray.
- Whisk the egg whites to stiff peaks in a very clean bowl then carefully fold in the rest of the ingredients.
- Spoon the mixture into a piping bag fitted with a large plain nozzle and pipe 8 cm circles onto the baking tray.
- Bake for 15 – 20 minutes or until golden brown and crisp.
- Transfer to a wire rack to cool.

Almond Kirsch Snaps

722

- Replace the Amaretto in the recipe with the same amount of Kirsch for a fruity kick to these snaps.

723

SERVES 6

Sesame and Poppy Seed Focaccia

PREPARATION TIME 2 HOURS
30 MINUTES

COOKING TIME 25-35 MINUTES

....

INGREDIENTS

300 g / 10 ½ oz / 2 cups strong white
bread flour
½ tsp easy blend dried yeast
1 tsp fine sea salt
2 tbsp olive oil

TO FINISH

50 ml / 1 ¾ fl. oz / ¼ cup olive oil
50 ml / 1 ¾ fl. oz / ¼ cup warm water
½ tsp fine sea salt
1 tbsp sesame seeds
1 tbsp poppy seeds

- Mix together the flour, yeast and salt. Stir in the oil and 280 ml of warm water.
- Knead the mixture on a lightly oiled surface for 10 minutes or until smooth and elastic.
- Leave the dough to rest, covered with oiled clingfilm, for 1 – 2 hours or until doubled in size.
- Oil a rectangular cake tin then stretch out the dough to cover the base.
- Cover the focaccia with oiled clingfilm and leave to prove for 1 hour or until doubled in size.
- Preheat the oven to 220°C (200° fan), 430F, gas 7.
- Put the oil, water and salt in a jar and shake well.
- Pour it all over the dough then sprinkle with the seeds.
- Bake for 25 - 35 minutes or until the top is golden and the base is cooked through.
- Leave to cool on a wire rack before cutting into squares.

Sesame and Onion Seed Focaccia

724

- Replace the poppy seeds in the recipe with black onion seeds (nigella seeds) for a different flavour and appearance.

725

MAKES 18

Double Chocolate Ice Cream Cookies

Chocolate Chip Ice Cream Cookies

726

- Remove the cocoa powder from the cookie recipe and increase the the amount of chocolate chips used by 30 g / 1 oz.

Triple Chocolate Ice Cream Cookies

727

- Replace 100 g / 3 ½ oz of the chocolate chips with 100 g / 3 ½ oz of finely chopped white chocolate for an added chocolate hit.

PREPARATION TIME 20 MINUTES

COOKING TIME 12-15 MINUTES

INGREDIENTS

175 g / 6 oz / ¾ cup butter, melted
225 g / 8 oz / 1 ⅓ cup dark brown sugar
100 g / 3 ½ oz / ½ cup caster (superfine) sugar
2 tsp vanilla extract
1 egg, plus 1 egg yolk
250 g / 9 oz / 1 ⅔ cups self-raising flour
2 tbsp unsweetened cocoa powder
175 g / 6 oz / 1 ¼ cups chocolate chips

TO SERVE

1 litre / 1 pt 15 fl. oz / 4 cup strawberry ice cream log

- Leave the ice cream out of the freezer for 15 minutes to soften then scoop it onto a large sheet of clingfilm.
- Form it into a log shape and roll it in the clingfilm then freeze for 1 hour or until firm.
- Preheat the oven to 170ºC (150º fan), 340F, gas 3 and line 2 baking sheets with greaseproof paper.
- Cream together the two sugars, butter and vanilla extract until pale and well whipped then beat in the egg and yolk, followed by the flour, cocoa and chocolate chips.
- Drop tablespoons of the mixture onto the prepared trays, leaving plenty of room to spread.
- Bake the cookies in batches for 12 – 15 minutes or until the edges are starting to brown, but the centres are still chewy.
- Transfer to a wire rack and leave to cool completely.
- When you're ready to serve, cut the ice cream log into 18 slices and sandwich each one between two cookies.

728

MAKES 36

Sandwich Biscuits

PREPARATION TIME 1 HOUR
15 MINUTES

COOKING TIME 25-30 MINUTES

....

INGREDIENTS

150 g / 5 ½ oz / ⅔ cup caster
(superfine) sugar
350 g / 12 oz / 1 ½ cup butter,
softened
1 tsp vanilla extract
300 g / 10 ½ oz / 2 cup plain (all
purpose) flour
150 g / 5 ½ oz / 1 ½ cup ground
almonds

TO FILL
strawberry jam (jelly)
marmalade
coconut spread

- Cream together the sugar, butter and vanilla extract
  until pale then stir in the flour and ground almonds.
- Bring the mixture together into a ball with your hands
  then wrap in clingfilm and refrigerate for 45 minutes.
- Preheat the oven to 140⁰C (120⁰ fan), 280F, gas 1 and
  line 2 baking sheets with greaseproof paper.
- Roll out the dough on a lightly floured surface to 5 mm
  thick. Use a fluted pastry cutter to cut out 72 biscuits.
- Use small cutters to cut the centre out of 36 of the biscuits.
- Transfer the biscuits to the prepared trays in batches
  and bake for 25 – 30 minutes.
- Transfer the biscuits to a wire rack and leave to cool.
- Put a teaspoon of jam, marmalade or coconut spread on
  the underside of the plain rounds and sandwich each
  one with a cut-out biscuit. Dust liberally with icing
  (confectioners) sugar.

Coconut Sandwich Biscuits

729

- Instead of using strawberry jam and
  marmalade to fill the biscuits, use only coconut
  spread and sprinkle with desiccated coconut
  before sandwiching them for a tropical taste.

730

MAKES 1

Spelt Bread

PREPARATION TIME 2 HOURS
30 MINUTES

COOKING TIME 35-40 MINUTES

....

INGREDIENTS

200 g / 7 oz / 1 ⅓ cup strong white
bread flour, plus extra for dusting
200 g / 7 oz / 1 ⅓ cup spelt flour
½ tsp easy blend dried yeast
1 tbsp caster (superfine) sugar
1 tsp fine sea salt
1 tbsp olive oil

- Mix together the flours, yeast, sugar and salt. Stir in the
  oil and 280 ml of warm water.
- Knead on a lightly oiled surface for 10 minutes or until
  the dough is elastic.
- Leave the dough to rest, covered with oiled clingfilm,
  for 1 – 2 hours or until doubled in size.
- Knead the dough for 2 more minutes, then shape it into
  a round loaf.
- Transfer the loaf to a greased baking tray and cover
  again with oiled clingfilm. Leave to prove for 1 hour
  or until doubled in size.
- Preheat the oven to 220⁰C (200⁰ fan), 430F, gas 7.
- When the dough has risen, score the top with a knife
  and dust with flour.
- Bake for 35 – 40 minutes . Transfer the bread to a wire
  rack and leave to cool.

Spelt Granary Bread

731

- Replace half of the strong white bread flour
  100 g / 3 ½ oz of malted granary flour if
  you'd like a maltier tasting bread.

732

MAKES 12 # Lemon Cakes

- Preheat the oven to 190°C (170° fan), 375F, gas 5 and line a 12-hole cupcake tin with paper cases.
- Combine the flour, sugar, butter, eggs and lemon zest in a bowl and whisk together for 2 minutes or until smooth.
- Divide the mixture between the paper cases, then transfer the tin to the oven and bake for 15 – 20 minutes.
- Test with a wooden toothpick, if it comes out clean, the cakes are done.
- Transfer the cakes to a wire rack and leave to cool completely.

PREPARATION TIME 1 HOUR

COOKING TIME 15-20 MINUTES

INGREDIENTS

110 g / 4 oz / ⅔ cup self-raising flour, sifted
110 g / 4 oz caster / ½ cup (superfine) sugar
110 g / 4 oz / ½ cup butter, softened
2 large eggs
1 lemon, zest finely grated

Lemon and Thyme Cupcakes

733

- Add 1 tsp dried thyme to the batter before mixing for a fragrant savoury twist on these cupcakes.

734

MAKES 1 # Kamut Bread

- Mix together the flours, yeast, sugar and salt. Stir in the oil and 280 ml of warm water.
- Knead on a lightly oiled surface for 10 minutes.
- Leave the dough to rest, covered with oiled clingfilm, for 1 – 2 hours or until doubled in size.
- Knead the dough for 2 more minutes, then shape it into a round loaf.
- Transfer the loaf to a greased baking tray and cover again with oiled clingfilm. Leave to prove for 1 hour or until doubled in size.
- Preheat the oven to 220°C (200° fan), 430F, gas 7.
- When the dough has risen, score the top with a knife and dust with flour.
- Bake for 35 – 40 minutes or until the loaf sounds hollow when tapped. Transfer the bread to a wire rack and leave to cool.

PREPARATION TIME 2 HOURS 30 MINUTES

COOKING TIME 35-40 MINUTES

INGREDIENTS

200 g / 7 oz / 1 ⅓ cup strong white bread flour, plus extra for dusting
200 g / 7 oz / 1 ⅓ cup kamut flour
½ tsp easy blend dried yeast
1 tbsp caster (superfine) sugar
1 tsp fine sea salt
1 tbsp olive oil

Raisin Kamut Bread

735

- Knead 100 g / 3 ½ oz of raisins into the dough before proving, shaping and baking.

736

MAKES 1

Basil and Pine Nut Bread

Basil and Sundried Tomato Bread

737

- Instead of using pine nuts, make a nut-free version using 100 g / 3 ½ oz of chopped sundried tomatoes in the stuffing.

Basil, Pine Nut and Feta Bread

738

- Replace the Parmesan in the stuffing with 100 g / 3 ½ oz finely chopped feta cheese for a salty kick and different colour contrast.

PREPARATION TIME 2 HOURS 30 MINUTES

COOKING TIME 25-30 MINUTES

INGREDIENTS

400 g / 14 oz / 2 ⅔ cups strong white bread flour, plus extra for dusting
½ tsp easy blend dried yeast
1 tbsp caster (superfine) sugar
1 tsp fine sea salt
1 tbsp olive oil

FOR THE STUFFING
a large bunch basil, chopped
100 g / 3 ½ oz / ¾ cup pine nuts
75 g / 2 ½ oz / ¾ cup Parmesan, grated
4 tbsp olive oil

- Mix together the flour, yeast, sugar and salt. Stir the oil into 280 ml of warm water then stir it into the dry ingredients.
- Knead the mixture on a lightly oiled surface for 10 minutes or until smooth and elastic.
- Leave the dough to rest, covered with oiled clingfilm, for 1 – 2 hours or until doubled in size.
- Combine the stuffing ingredients.
- Roll the dough out into a rectangle and spread over the stuffing.
- Roll the bread up tightly and transfer the roll to a greased baking tray. Cover with oiled clingfilm and leave to prove for 1 hour or until doubled in size.
- Meanwhile, preheat the oven to 220⁰C (200⁰ fan), 430F, gas 7.
- Transfer the tray to the top shelf of the oven then quickly throw a small cupful of water onto the oven floor and close the door.
- Bake for 25 – 30 minutes or until the loaf sounds hollow when you tap it underneath.

739
MAKES 1

Rye Bread

- Mix together the flours, yeast, sugar and salt. Stir the oil into 280 ml of warm water.
- Stir the liquid into the dry ingredients then knead on a lightly oiled surface for 10 minutes.
- Leave the dough to rest, covered with oiled clingfilm, for 1 – 2 hours or until doubled in size.
- Knead the dough for 2 more minutes, then shape it into an oval loaf.
- Transfer the loaf to a greased baking tray and cover again with oiled clingfilm. Leave to prove for 1 hour or until doubled in size.
- Preheat the oven to 220°C (200° fan), 430F, gas 7.
- When the dough has risen, score the top with a knife and dust with flour.
- Bake for 35 – 40 minutes. Transfer the bread to a wire rack and leave to cool.

PREPARATION TIME 2 HOURS 30 MINUTES

COOKING TIME 35-40 MINUTES

INGREDIENTS

200 g / 7 oz / 1 ⅓ cup strong white bread flour, plus extra for dusting
200 g / 7 oz / 1 ⅓ cup rye flour
½ tsp easy blend dried yeast
1 tbsp caster (superfine) sugar
1 tsp fine sea salt
1 tbsp olive oil

Rye and Stout Bread

740

- Replace 75 ml / 3 fl. oz of the warm water for 75 ml / 3 fl. oz of warmed stout. The resulting bread will be darker and richer in flavour.

741
MAKES 1

Wheat and Barley Bread

- Mix together the flours, yeast, sugar and salt. Stir the oil into280 ml of warm water.
- Stir the liquid into the dry ingredients then knead on a lightly oiled surface for 10 minutes.
- Leave the dough to rest, covered with oiled clingfilm, for 1 – 2 hours or until doubled in size.
- Knead dough for 2 minutes, then shape into a long loaf.
- Transfer the loaf to a greased baking tray and cover again with oiled clingfilm. Leave to prove for 1 hour or until doubled in size.
- Preheat the oven to 220°C (200° fan), 430F, gas 7.
- When the dough has risen,score the top with a knife and dust with flour.
- Bake for 35 – 40 minutes or until the loaf sounds hollow when tapped. Transfer the bread to a wire rack and leave to cool.

PREPARATION TIME 2 HOURS 30 MINUTES

COOKING TIME 35-40 MINUTES

INGREDIENTS

200 g / 7 oz / 1 ⅓ cup strong white bread flour, plus extra for dusting
200 g / 7 oz / 1 ⅓ cupbarley flour
½ tsp easy blend dried yeast
1 tbsp caster (superfine) sugar
1 tsp fine sea salt
1 tbsp olive oil

Malted Barley Bread

742

- Replace 150 g / 5 oz of the strong white bread flour with 150 g / 5 oz of malted granary flour.

743

MAKES 1

Treacle Bread

PREPARATION TIME 2 HOURS
30 MINUTES

COOKING TIME 35-40 MINUTES

INGREDIENTS

400 g / 14 oz / 2 ⅔ cups strong white
bread flour, plus extra for dusting
½ tsp easy blend dried yeast
3 tbsp treacle
1 tsp fine sea salt
1 tbsp olive oil

- Mix together the flours, yeast, treacle and salt. Stir the oil into 280 ml of warm water.
- Stir the liquid into the dry ingredients then knead on a lightly oiled surface for 10 minutes.
- Leave the dough to rest, covered with oiled clingfilm, for 1 – 2 hours or until doubled in size. Knead the dough for 2 minutes, then shape it into a round loaf.
- Transfer the loaf to a greased baking tray and cover again with oiled clingfilm. Leave to prove for 1 hour or until doubled in size.
- Preheat the oven to 220°C (200° fan), 430F, gas 7.
- When the dough has risen, score the top with a knife and dust with flour.
- Bake for 35 – 40 minutes or until the loaf sounds hollow when tapped. Transfer the bread to a wire rack and leave to cool.

Golden Syrup Bread
744

- Replace the treacle with the same amount of Golden Syrup for a sweeter, milder tasting bread.

745

MAKES 1

Chocolate Chip Baton

PREPARATION TIME 2 HOURS
30 MINUTES

COOKING TIME 25-30 MINUTES

INGREDIENTS

400 g / 14 oz / 2 ⅔ cups strong white
bread flour, plus extra for dusting
½ tsp easy blend dried yeast
1 tbsp caster (superfine) sugar
1 tsp fine sea salt
1 tbsp sunflower oil
200 g / 7 oz / 1 ⅓ cup chocolate chips

- Mix together the flour, yeast, sugar and salt. Stir in the oil and 280 ml of warm water.
- Knead the mixture on a lightly oiled surface for 10 minutes or until smooth and elastic.
- Leave the dough to rest, covered with oiled clingfilm, for 1 – 2 hours or until doubled in size.
- Sprinkle over the chocolate chips and knead for 2 more minutes then roll it up tightly into a baton.
- Transfer the loaf to a greased baking tray and cover with oiled clingfilm. Leave to prove for 1 hour.
- Preheat the oven to 220°C (200° fan), 430F, gas 7.
- Slash the top diagonally with a knife and transfer the tray to the top shelf of the oven, then throw a small cupful of water onto the oven floor and close the door.
- Bake for 25 – 30 minutes or until the loaf sounds hollow when you tap it underneath.

Fruit Baton
746

- Replace the chocolate chips with 150 g / 5 oz mixed candied peel for a fruity, colourful version of this baton

747

MAKES 12

Crusty Finger Rolls

Wholemeal Finger Rolls

748

- Replace 300 g / 10 ½ oz of
  the strong white bread flour
  for wholemeal flour before
  kneading the dough.

Crusty Parmesan Finger Rolls

749

- Incorporate 75 g / 3 oz of
  grated Parmesan into the
  dough before kneading for
  a cheesy take on these rolls.

PREPARATION TIME 2 HOURS
30 MINUTES

COOKING TIME 15-20 MINUTES

INGREDIENTS

400 g / 14 oz / 2 ⅔ cups strong white
bread flour, plus extra for dusting
½ tsp easy blend dried yeast
1 tbsp caster (superfine) sugar
1 tsp fine sea salt
1 tbsp olive oil

- Mix together the flour, yeast, sugar and salt. Stir the
  oil into 280 ml of warm water then stir it into the dry
  ingredients.
- Knead the mixture on a lightly oiled surface with your
  hands for 10 minutes or until smooth and elastic.
- Leave the dough to rest in a lightly oiled bowl, covered
  with oiled clingfilm, for 1 – 2 hours or until doubled
  in size.
- Knead it for 2 more minutes then split it into 12 even
  pieces and shape into finger rolls.
- Transfer the rolls to a greased baking tray and cover
  with oiled clingfilm. Leave to prove for 1 hour or until
  doubled in size.
- Meanwhile, preheat the oven to 220°C(200° fan), gas 7.
- Dust the rolls with flour and slash along the tops with
  a knife.
- Transfer the tray to the top shelf of the oven then
  quickly throw a small cupful of water onto the oven
  floor and close the door.
- Bake for 15 – 20 minutes or until the rolls sound
  hollow when you tap them underneath.
- Transfer to a wire rack and leave to cool.

750

MAKES 16

Poppy Seed Shortbread Biscuits

PREPARATION TIME 20 MINUTES

COOKING TIME 15-20 MINUTES

INGREDIENTS

230 g / 8 oz / 1 ½ cup plain (all purpose) flour
75 g / 2 ½ oz / ⅓ cup caster (superfine) sugar
150 g / 5 oz / ⅔ cup butter, cubed
2 tbsp poppy seeds

- Preheat the oven to 180°C (160° fan), 355F, gas 4 and line a baking tray with greaseproof paper.
- Mix together the flour and caster (superfine) sugar in a bowl, then rub in the butter.
- Knead gently until the mixture forms a smooth dough then roll it into a log, 7 cm in diameter.
- Cut the log into 1 cm slices and spread the shortbread out on the baking tray.
- Sprinkle the biscuits with poppy seeds then bake the biscuits for 15 - 20 minutes, turning the tray round halfway through.
- Transfer the biscuits to a wire rack and leave to cool.

Parmesan Shortbread Biscuits 751

- Omit the poppy seeds and add 55 g / 2 oz finely grated Parmesan to the shortbread dough as well as an additional 30 g / 1 oz butter for a richer flavour.

752

MAKES 16

Chebbakia Biscuits

PREPARATION TIME 20 MINUTES

COOKING TIME 4-5 MINUTES

INGREDIENTS

225 g / 8 oz / 1 ½ cup plain (all purpose) flour
½ tsp baking powder
60 g / 2 oz / ½ cup fine semolina
¼ tsp fine sea salt
2 tsp ground cinnamon
½ tsp ground star anise
2 tbsp butter, melted
75 ml / 2 ½ fl. oz / ⅓ cup olive oil
1 egg yolk
2 litres / 3 ½ pints / 8 cups sunflower oil for deep frying
450 g / 1 lb / 1 ¼ cup runny honey
125 g / 4 ½ oz / 1 ¼ cup sesame seeds

- Mix together the flour, baking powder, semolina, salt and spices. Whisk together the butter, olive oil and egg yolk and stir it into the dry ingredients. Add just enough water to bring the mixture together into a pliable dough and knead until smooth.
- Roll out the dough on a lightly floured surface and cut into 8 cm squares.
- To make the classic shape, make 5 long slits across each square, then push the outside through the middle to make a knotted shape.
- Heat the sunflower oil in a deep fat fryer to a temperature of 180°C.
- Lower the dough knots in the fryer basket in batches and cook for 4 – 5 minutes or until crisp.
- Remove any excess oil, then drop them into the honey.
- Leave to drain and cool on a wire rack. Sprinkle with sesame seeds.

Banana Chebbakia Biscuits 753

- Add 1 mashed banana to the chebbakia dough, incorporating it fully before shaping and frying for a fruity twist to the classic recipe.

754

MAKES 36

Sunflower Seed and Choc-Chip Cookies

- Preheat the oven to 170°C (150° fan), 340F, gas 3 and line 2 baking sheets with greaseproof paper.
- Cream together the two sugars, butter and vanilla extract until pale and well whipped then beat in the egg and yolk, followed by the flour and chocolate chips.
- Drop tablespoons of the mixture onto the prepared trays, leaving plenty of room to spread, and sprinkle with sunflower seeds.
- Bake the cookies in batches for 12 – 15 minutes or until the edges are starting to brown, but the centres are still chewy.
- Transfer to a wire rack and leave to cool.

PREPARATION TIME 10 MINUTES

COOKING TIME 12-15 MINUTES

INGREDIENTS

175 g / 6 oz / ¾ cup butter, melted
225 g / 8 oz / 1 ⅓ cup light brown sugar
100 g / 3 ½ oz / ½ cup caster (superfine) sugar
2 tsp vanilla extract
1 egg, plus 1 egg yolk
250 g / 9 oz / 1 ½ cups self-raising flour
100 g / 3 ½ oz / ⅔ cup chocolate chips
100 g / 3 ½ oz / ⅔ cup sunflower seeds

Pumpkin and Chocolate Chip Cookies

755

- Omit the sunflower seeds and 30 g of butter from the cookie dough and replace with 55 g / 2 oz canned pumpkin for an autumnal flavour.

756

MAKES 12

Mini Muesli Loaf Cakes

- Preheat the oven to 190°C (170° fan), 375F, gas 5 and oil a 12-hole silicone mini loaf cake mould.
- Combine the flour, sugar, butter, eggs and half of the muesli in a bowl and whisk together for 2 minutes or until smooth.
- Divide the mixture between the moulds and sprinkle over the rest of the muesli.
- Transfer the mould to the oven and bake for 15 – 20 minutes.
- Test with a wooden toothpick, if it comes out clean, the cakes are done.
- Transfer the cakes to a wire rack and leave to cool completely.

PREPARATION TIME 10 MINUTES

COOKING TIME 15-20 MINUTES

INGREDIENTS

110 g / 4 oz / ⅔ cup self-raising flour, sifted
110 g / 4 oz caster / ½ cup (superfine) sugar
110 g / 4 oz / ½ cup butter, softened
2 large eggs
100 g / 3 ½ oz / 1 cup muesli

Wholemeal Muesli Loaf Cakes

757

- Substitute the self-raising flour for 110 g / 4 oz wholemeal flour plus 1 tsp baking powder for a healthier loaf cake.

MAKES 1 LOAF Garlic Mushroom Bread

Parsley Mushroom Bread

759

- Replace the garlic in the mushrooms with 55 g / 2 oz finely chopped Italian (curly) parsley for an added parsley flavour and appearance boost.

Garlic and Mushroom Cheese Bread

760

- Add 55 g / 2 oz grated hard cheese of choice to the dough and incorporate before shaping and baking.

PREPARATION TIME 2 HOURS 30 MINUTES

COOKING TIME 35-40 MINUTES

INGREDIENTS

200 g / 7 oz / 1 ⅓ cups strong white bread flour
200 g / 7 oz / 1 ⅓ cups rye flour
1 tsp easy blend dried yeast
1 tbsp caster (superfine) sugar
1 tsp fine sea salt
1 tbsp olive oil

FOR THE MUSHROOMS
50 g / 1 ¾ oz / ¼ cup butter
300 g / 10 ½ oz chestnut mushrooms, sliced
2 cloves of garlic, crushed
50 g / 1 ¾ oz flat leaf parsley, chopped

- Mix together the flours, yeast, sugar and salt. Stir the oil into 280 ml of warm water and mix with the dry ingredients.
- Knead the dough on a lightly oiled surface for 10 minutes or until smooth and elastic.
- Leave the dough to rest, covered with oiled clingfilm, for 1 – 2 hours or until doubled in size.
- Melt the butter in a sauté pan and add the mushrooms and plenty of salt and pepper. Cook for 10 minutes or until any liquid that comes out has evaporated. Add the garlic and parsley and cook for 2 minutes. Leave to cool.
- Knead the mushrooms into the dough and shape into a square loaf.
- Transfer it to a greased baking tray, cover with oiled clingfilm and prove until doubled in size.
- Preheat the oven to 220⁰C (200⁰ fan), 430F, gas 7.
- Transfer the tray to the top shelf of the oven then quickly throw a small cupful of water onto the floor of the oven and close the door.
- Bake for 35 – 40 minutes or until the loaf sounds hollow when tapped. Transfer the bread to a wire rack and leave to cool.

761

MAKES 36

Chocolate Chip Cookies

- Preheat the oven to 170°C (150° fan), 340F, gas 3 and line 2 baking sheets with greaseproof paper.
- Cream together the two sugars, butter and vanilla extract until pale and well whipped then beat in the egg and yolk, followed by the flour and chocolate chips.
- Drop tablespoons of the mixture onto the prepared trays, leaving plenty of room to spread.
- Bake the cookies in batches for 12 – 15 minutes or until the edges are starting to brown, but the centres are still chewy.
- Transfer to a wire rack and leave to cool.

PREPARATION TIME 10 MINUTES

COOKING TIME 12-15 MINUTES

INGREDIENTS

175 g / 6 oz / ¾ cup butter, melted
225 g / 8 oz / 1 ⅓ cups light brown sugar
100 g / 3 ½ oz / ½ cup caster (superfine) sugar
2 tsp vanilla extract
1 egg, plus 1 egg yolk
250 g / 9 oz / 1 ⅔ cups self-raising flour
100 g / 3 ½ oz / ⅔ cup chocolate chips

Chocolate Chip and Cherry Cookies

762

- Add 55 g / 2 oz chopped glacé cherries to the cookies before they are baked for an added hit of colour and fruit flavour.

763

MAKES 36

Wholemeal Chocolate and Nut Cookies

- Preheat the oven to 170°C (150° fan), 340F, gas 3 and line 2 baking sheets with greaseproof paper.
- Cream together the two sugars, butter and vanilla extract until pale and well whipped then beat in the egg and yolk, followed by the flours, cocoa and nuts.
- Drop tablespoons of the mixture onto the prepared trays, leaving plenty of room to spread.
- Bake the cookies in batches for 12 – 15 minutes or until the edges are starting to crisp, but the centres are still chewy.
- Transfer to a wire rack and leave to cool.

PREPARATION TIME 10 MINUTES

COOKING TIME 12-15 MINUTES

INGREDIENTS

175 g / 6 oz / ¾ cup butter, melted
225 g / 8 oz / 1 ⅓ cup dark brown sugar
100 g / 3 ½ oz / ½ cup caster (superfine) sugar
2 tsp vanilla extract
1 egg, plus 1 egg yolk
125 g / 4 ½ oz / ¾ cup self-raising flour
125 g / 4 ½ oz / ¾ cup stoneground wholemeal flour
2 tbsp unsweetened cocoa powder
125 g / 4 ½ oz / 1 cup mixed nuts, chopped

Chocolate and Nut Cookies

 764

- Replace the stoneground wholemeal flour with an additional 125 g / 4 ½ oz self-raising flour for a more traditional cookie.

765

MAKES 36

Date and Oat Cookies

PREPARATION TIME 10 MINUTES

COOKING TIME 12-15 MINUTES

....

INGREDIENTS

175 g / 6 oz / ¾ cup butter, melted
225 g / 8 oz / 1 ⅓ cup dark brown
sugar
100 g / 3 ½ oz / ½ cup caster
(superfine) sugar
2 tsp vanilla extract
1 egg, plus 1 egg yolk
250 g / 9 oz / 1 ⅔ cups self-raising
flour
100 g / 3 ½ oz / 1 cup porridge oats
100 g / 3 ½ oz / ½ cup dates, stoned
and finely chopped

- Preheat the oven to 170⁰C (150⁰ fan), 340F, gas 3 and line 2 baking sheets with greaseproof paper.
- Cream together the two sugars, butter and vanilla extract until pale and well whipped then beat in the egg and yolk, followed by the flour,oats and dates.
- Drop tablespoons of the mixture onto the prepared trays, leaving plenty of room to spread.
- Bake the cookies in batches for 12 – 15 minutes or until the edges are starting to brown, but the centres are still chewy.
- Transfer to a wire rack and leave to cool.

Vanilla Oat Cookies

766

- Remove the dates from the recipe and add an additional 1 tsp of vanilla extract for an added vanilla flavour flavour.

767

MAKES 36

Cinnamon Oat Cookies

PREPARATION TIME 10 MINUTES

COOKING TIME 12-15 MINUTES

....

INGREDIENTS

225 g / 8 oz / 1 ⅓ cup dark brown
sugar
100 g / 3 ½ oz / ½ cup caster
(superfine) sugar
175 g / 6 oz / ¾ cup butter, melted
2 tsp vanilla extract
1 egg, plus 1 egg yolk
250 g / 9 oz / 1 ⅔ cups self-raising
flour
2 tsp ground cinnamon
100 g / 3 ½ oz / 1 cup oats

- Preheat the oven to 170⁰C (150⁰ fan), 340F, gas 3 and line 2 baking sheets with greaseproof paper.
- Cream together the two sugars, butter and vanilla extract until pale and well whipped then beat in the egg and yolk, followed by the flour, cinnamon and oats.
- Drop tablespoons of the mixture onto the prepared trays, leaving plenty of room to spread.
- Bake the cookies in batches for 12 – 15 minutes or until the edges are starting to brown, but the centres are still chewy.
- Transfer to a wire rack and leave to cool.

Cinnamon and Pumpkin Seed Cookies

768

- Stud each of the cookies with ½ tsp pumpkin seeds before baking for a crunchy, nutty addition to these cookies.

769

MAKES 1 LOAF Walnut Bread

770

Walnut and Pumpkin Bread

- Add 55 g / 2 oz canned pumpkin as well as an additional 30 g / 1 oz wholemeal flour to the dough and incorporate well before kneading.

771

Walnut and Raisin Bread

- Add 100 g / 3 ½ oz raisins to the dough, incorporating them well before kneading.

PREPARATION TIME 2 HOURS
30 MINUTES

COOKING TIME 35-40 MINUTES

INGREDIENTS

200 g / 7 oz / 1 ⅓ cup strong white bread flour, plus extra for dusting
200 g / 7 oz / 1 ⅓ cup stoneground wholemeal flour
½ tsp easy blend dried yeast
1 tbsp caster (superfine) sugar
1 tsp fine sea salt
100 g / 3 ½ oz / ¾ cup walnuts, chopped
1 tbsp walnut oil

- Mix together the flours, yeast, sugar, salt and walnuts. Stir the oil into 280 ml of warm water.
- Stir the liquid into the dry ingredients then knead on a lightly oiled surface for 10 minutes or until the dough is smooth and elastic.
- Leave the dough to rest, covered with oiled clingfilm, for 1 – 2 hours or until doubled in size.
- Knead the dough for 2 more minutes, then shape it into a long loaf.
- Transfer the loaf to a greased baking tray and cover again with oiled clingfilm. Leave to prove for 1 hour or until doubled in size.
- Meanwhile, preheat the oven to 220°C (200° fan), 430F, gas 7.
- When the dough has risen, slash the top with a knife.
- Transfer the tray to the top shelf of the oven then quickly throw a small cupful of water onto the floor of the oven and close the door.
- Bake for 35 – 40 minutes or until the loaf sounds hollow when tapped. Transfer the bread to a wire rack and leave to cool.

772

MAKES 24

Mixed Nut Cookies

PREPARATION TIME 15 MINUTES

COOKING TIME 20-25 MINUTES

....

INGREDIENTS

125 g / 4 ½ oz / ½ cup butter, cubed
125 g / 4 ½ oz / ¾ cup plain (all purpose) flour
125 g / 4 ½ oz / ½ cup caster (superfine) sugar
3 large egg yolks
75 g / 2 ½ oz / 1 cup flaked (slivered) almonds
75 g / 2 ½ oz / ⅔ cup almonds, chopped
75 g / 2 ½ oz / ⅔ cup walnuts, chopped
75 g / 2 ½ oz / ⅔ cup hazelnuts (cob nuts), chopped

- Preheat the oven to 180°C (160° fan), 355F, gas 4 and line a baking tray with greaseproof paper.
- Rub the butter into the flour with a pinch of salt then stir in the sugar.
- Beat the egg yolks and stir them into the dry ingredients with the nuts.
- Bring the mixture together into a soft dough and space tablespoons of the mixture out on the baking tray.
- Bake the biscuits for 20 – 25 minutes or until golden brown.
- Transfer the biscuits to a wire rack and leave to cool.

Mixed Nut and Caramel Cookies **773**

- Add 55 g / 2 oz of dulce de leche and an additional 30 g / 1 oz of plain (all purpose) flour to the cookie dough before shaping and baking for an added sweet flavour.

774

MAKES 36

Treacle and Oat Cookies

PREPARATION TIME 10 MINUTES

COOKING TIME 12-15 MINUTES

....

INGREDIENTS

225 g / 8 oz / 1 ⅓ cup dark brown sugar
75 g / 2 ½ oz caster (superfine) sugar
175 g / 6 oz / ¾ cup butter, melted
2 tbsp treacle
1 egg, plus 1 egg yolk
250 g / 9 oz / 1 ⅔ cups self-raising flour
100 g / 3 ½ oz / 1 cup porridge oats

- Preheat the oven to 170°C (150° fan), 340F, gas 3 and line 2 baking sheets with greaseproof paper.
- Cream together the two sugars, butter and treacle until pale and well whipped then beat in the egg and yolk, followed by the flour and oats.
- Drop tablespoons of the mixture onto the prepared trays, leaving plenty of room to spread.
- Bake the cookies in batches for 12 – 15 minutes or until the edges are starting to brown, but the centres are still chewy.
- Transfer to a wire rack and leave to cool.

Golden Syrup and Oat Cookies **775**

- Replace the treacle with the same amount of Golden Syrup for a lighter cookie in taste and appearance.

776

MAKES 24 Sesame and Tapenade Shortbread

- Preheat the oven to 180°C (160° fan), 355F, gas 4 and line a baking tray with greaseproof paper.
- Rub the butter into the flour and stir in the tapenade.
- Knead gently until the mixture forms a smooth dough then roll out on a lightly floured surface to 1 cm thick.
- Use a round cookie cutter to cut out the biscuits and transfer them to the baking tray.
- Sprinkle with sesame seeds then bake for 12 - 15 minutes, turning the tray round halfway through.
- Transfer the biscuits to a wire rack and leave to cool.

PREPARATION TIME 20 MINUTES

COOKING TIME 12-15 MINUTES

INGREDIENTS

150g / 5 oz / ⅔ cup butter, cubed
230g / 8 oz / 1 ½ cup plain (all purpose) flour
50 g / 1 ¾ oz / ¼ cup black olive tapenade
2 tbsp sesame seeds

Poppy and Tapenade Shortbread   777

- Replace the sesame seeds with mixed poppy seeds for a different looking shortbread.

778

MAKES 1 LOAF Onion Bread

- Fry the onions in the oil for 15 minutes or until starting to caramelise. Leave to cool.
- Mix together the flours, yeast, sugar and salt. Stir the onions and onion seeds into 280 ml of warm water and stir into the dry ingredients.
- Knead the mixture on a lightly oiled surface for 10 minutes or until the dough is smooth and elastic.
- Leave the dough to rest in a lightly oiled bowl, covered with oiled clingfilm, for 1 – 2 hours.
- Roll the dough into a fat sausage. Turn it 90° and roll it tightly the other way then tuck the ends under and transfer the dough to a lined loaf tin, keeping the seam underneath.
- Cover the tin with oiled clingfilm and leave for 1 hour.
- Preheat the oven to 220°C (200° fan), 430F, gas 7.
- Bake the loaf for 35 – 40 minutes or until the underneath sounds hollow when tapped.

PREPARATION TIME 2 HOURS
30 MINUTES

COOKING TIME 35-40 MINUTES

INGREDIENTS

2 large onions, peeled, quartered and sliced
3 tbsp olive oil
300 g / 10 ½ oz / 2 cup strong white bread flour, plus extra for dusting
100 g / 3 ½ oz / ⅔ cup stoneground wholemeal flour
½ tsp easy blend dried yeast
1 tbsp caster (superfine) sugar
1 tsp fine sea salt
2 tbsp black onion seeds

Onion Cheddar Bread   779

- Incorporate 100 g / 3 ½ oz grated Cheddar into the dough before kneading for an additional cheese flavour.

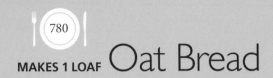

780
MAKES 1 LOAF Oat Bread

Granary Oat Bread
781

- Replace half of the strong white bread flour with 200 g / 7 oz malted granary flour for an additional flavour and a different flavour.

Oat and Ale Bread
782

- Replace 110 ml / 4 fl. oz of the water with warmed real ale for a different, unusual twist on this traditional bread recipe.

PREPARATION TIME 2 HOURS 30 MINUTES

COOKING TIME 35-40 MINUTES

INGREDIENTS

400 g / 14 oz / 2 ⅔ cups strong white bread flour, plus extra for dusting
½ tsp easy blend dried yeast
1 tbsp caster (superfine) sugar
1 tsp fine sea salt
150 g / 5 ½ oz / 1 ½ cup rolled porridge oats
1 tbsp sunflower oil

- Mix together the flour, yeast, sugar, salt and oats. Stir the oil into 280 ml of warm water and stir it into the bowl.
- Knead on a lightly oiled surface for 10 minutes or until the dough is smooth and elastic.
- Leave the dough to rest, covered with oiled clingfilm, for 1 – 2 hours or until doubled in size.
- Knead the dough for 2 more minutes, then roll it up into a fat sausage. Turn the roll 90° and roll it up the other way then tick the ends under and drop it into a lined loaf tin, seam side down.
- Cover with oiled clingfilm and leave to prove for 1 hour or until doubled in size.
- Meanwhile, preheat the oven to 220°C (200° fan), 430F, gas 7.
- Transfer the tray to the top shelf of the oven then quickly throw a small cupful of water onto the floor of the oven and close the door.
- Bake for 35 – 40 minutes or until the loaf sounds hollow when tapped. Transfer the bread to a wire rack and leave to cool.

783

MAKES 18 Orange Tuiles

- Beat together the flour, sugar and egg whites until smooth, then beat in the melted butter and orange zest.
- Refrigerate for 30 minutes.
- Preheat the oven to 180°C (160° fan), 350F, gas 4 and oil 2 large baking trays.
- Spoon teaspoonfuls of the mixture onto the baking trays and spread out with the back of the spoon to make 10 cm circles.
- Bake for 8 – 10 minutes. Lift the biscuits off the trays with a palette knife and drape over a rolling pin while still soft. Leave to cool and harden.

PREPARATION TIME 45 MINUTES

COOKING TIME 8-10 MINUTES

INGREDIENTS

110 g / 4 oz / ⅔ cup plain (all purpose) flour
110 g / 4 oz caster / ½ cup (superfine) sugar
2 large egg whites
110 g / 4 oz / ½ cup butter, melted
2 tbsp orange zest , finely grated

Orange and Lime Tuiles

784

- Replace 1 tbsp of the grated orange zest with 1 tbsp grated lime zest for an additional flavour and colour to these tuiles.

785

MAKES 1 LOAF Oat and Seed Bread

- Mix together the flours, yeast, sugar and salt. Mix together the oats and seeds and add half of the mix to the bowl. Stir the oil into 280 ml of warm water and stir it into the bowl.
- Knead on a lightly oiled surface for 10 minutes or until the dough is smooth and elastic.
- Leave the dough to rest, covered with oiled clingfilm, for 1 – 2 hours or until doubled in size.
- Knead the dough again then shape it into a loaf.
- Transfer the loaf to a greased baking tray and cover again with oiled clingfilm. Leave to prove for 1 hour.
- Preheat the oven to 220°C (200° fan), gas 7.
- When the dough has risen, slash the top with a knife.
- Bake for 35 – 40 minutes or until the loaf sounds hollow when tapped. Transfer the bread to a wire rack and leave to cool.

PREPARATION TIME 2 HOURS 30 MINUTES

COOKING TIME 35-40 MINUTES

INGREDIENTS

200 g / 7 oz / 1 ⅓ cup strong white bread flour, plus extra for dusting
200 g / 7 oz / 1 ⅓ cup malted granary flour
½ tsp easy blend dried yeast
1 tbsp caster (superfine) sugar
1 tsp fine sea salt
100 g / 3 ½ oz / 1 cup rolled porridge oats
55 g / 2 oz / ½ cup golden linseeds
55 g / 2 oz / ½ cup help seeds
1 tbsp sunflower oil

Oat, Seed and Almond Bread

 786

- Replace 55 g / 2 oz of the malted granary flour with the same weight of ground almonds for an added nut texture and flavour.

787

MAKES 1 LOAF Potato Bread

PREPARATION TIME 2 HOURS
30 MINUTES

COOKING TIME 35-40 MINUTES

INGREDIENTS

400 g / 14 oz / 2 ⅔ cups strong white
bread flour, plus extra for dusting
½ tsp easy blend dried yeast
1 tbsp caster (superfine) sugar
1 tsp fine sea salt
1 tbsp olive oil
150 g / 5 ½ oz / ⅔ cup mashed potato

- Mix together the flours, yeast, sugar and salt. Stir the oil and 150 ml of warm water into the mashed potato.
- Stir the liquid into the dry ingredients then knead on a lightly oiled surface for 10 minutes or until the dough is smooth and elastic.
- Leave the dough to rest, covered with oiled clingfilm, for 1 – 2 hours or until doubled in size.
- Knead the dough for 2 more minutes, then shape it into a long loaf.
- Transfer the loaf to a greased baking tray and cover again with oiled clingfilm. Leave to prove for 1 hour or until doubled in size.
- Meanwhile, preheat the oven to 220°C (200° fan), 430F, gas 7.
- When the dough has risen, slash the top with a knife.
- Transfer the tray to the top shelf of the oven then quickly throw a small cupful of water onto the floor of the oven and close the door.
- Bake for 35 – 40 minutes or until the loaf sounds hollow when tapped. Transfer the bread to a wire rack and leave to cool.

788

MAKES 24 Parmesan and Black Pepper Shortbread

PREPARATION TIME 20 MINUTES

COOKING TIME 12-15 MINUTES

INGREDIENTS

150g / 5 oz / ⅔ cup butter, cubed
230g / 8 oz / 1 ½ cup plain (all purpose) flour
50 g / 1 ¾ oz / ½ cup Parmesan, grated
2 tsp cracked black pepper

- Preheat the oven to 180°C (160° fan), 355F, gas 4 and line a baking tray with greaseproof paper.
- Rub the butter into the flour and stir in the Parmesan and black pepper.
- Knead gently until the mixture forms a smooth dough then roll out on a lightly floured surface to 5 mm thick.
- Use a cookie cutter to cut out circles and transfer them to the baking tray.
- Bake the biscuits for 12 - 15 minutes, turning the tray round halfway through.
- Transfer the biscuits to a wire rack and leave to cool.

MAKES 36 · 789

Pecan Snap Biscuits

- Preheat the oven to 180°C (160° fan), 355F, gas 4 and line 2 baking sheets with greaseproof paper.
- Melt the butter and golden syrup together in a saucepan.
- Mix the flour, sugar and pecans together then stir in the melted butter mixture and the beaten egg.
- Use a teaspoon to portion the mixture onto the baking trays, leaving plenty of room for the biscuits to spread.
- Bake in batches for 12 – 15 minutes or until golden brown.
- Transfer the biscuits to a wire rack and leave to cool and harden.

PREPARATION TIME 10 MINUTES

COOKING TIME 12-15 MINUTES

INGREDIENTS

75 g / 2 ½ oz / ⅓ cup butter, softened
100 g / 3 ½ oz / ⅓ cup golden syrup
225 g / 8 oz / 1 ½ cups self-raising flour
100 g / 3 ½ oz / ½ cup caster (superfine) sugar
75 g / 2 ½ oz / ⅔ cup pecan nuts, finely chopped
1 large egg, beaten

---

790 · **MAKES 36**

Waffle Biscuits

PREPARATION TIME 10 MINUTES

COOKING TIME 1 MINUTE

INGREDIENTS

110 g / 4 oz / ½ cup butter, softened
3 large eggs, beaten
150 g / 5 ½ oz / ⅔ cup caster (superfine) sugar

2 tsp baking powder
225 g / 8 oz / 1 ½ cups self-raising flour
1 tsp ground star anise

- Beat all the ingredients together until smooth.
- Heat a pizzelle iron on the hob until very hot, then add a heaped teaspoon of batter to each waffle indent and close the two halves together.
- Cook the waffles for 30 seconds to 1 minute or until cooked through.
- Repeat with the rest of the mixture, allowing the waffles to cool and crisp on a wire rack.

---

791 · **MAKES 20**

Pine Nut Crescent Biscuits

PREPARATION TIME 20 MINUTES

COOKING TIME 15-20 MINUTES

INGREDIENTS

175 g / 6 oz / 1 ¼ cup plain (all purpose) flour
55 g / 2 oz / ½ cup ground almonds

75 g / 2 ½ oz / ½ cup light brown sugar
150 g / 5 oz / ⅔ cup butter, cubed
100 g / 3 ½ oz / ¾ cup pine nuts

- Preheat the oven to 180°C (160° fan), 355F, gas 4 and line a baking tray with greaseproof paper.
- Mix together the flour, ground almonds and caster (superfine) sugar in a bowl, then rub in the butter.
- Knead gently with the pine nuts until the mixture forms a smooth dough.
- Divide the dough into 20 balls and then roll them into a sausage shape and curve round into crescents.
- Bake the biscuits for 15 - 20 minutes, turning the tray round halfway through.
- Transfer the biscuits to a wire rack and leave to cool.

792

MAKES 24

Raspberry Viennese Shortbread

PREPARATION TIME 10 MINUTES

COOKING TIME 15-20 MINUTES

INGREDIENTS

175 g / 6 oz / ¾ cup butter, softened
50 g / 1 ¾ oz / ¼ cup caster (superfine) sugar
4 tbsp raspberry syrup
175 g / 6 oz / 1 ¼ cup self-raising flour

- Preheat the oven to 170°C (150° fan), 340F, gas 3 and line 2 baking trays with non-stick baking mats.
- Cream the butter, sugar and raspberry syrup together with an electric whisk until pale and well whipped then stir in the flour.
- Spoon the mixture into a piping bag fitted with a large star nozzle and pipe 12 swirls onto each tray.
- Bake the biscuits for 15 – 20 minutes or until they are lightly golden.
- Transfer the biscuits to a wire rack and leave to cool completely.

Almond Viennese Shortbread

793

- Replace the raspberry syrup in the recipe with almond syrup for a nutty hint to these shortbreads.

794

MAKES 24

Pistachio Cookies

PREPARATION TIME 15 MINUTES

COOKING TIME 20-25 MINUTES

INGREDIENTS

125 g / 4 ½ oz / ½ cup butter, cubed
125 g / 4 ½ oz / ¾ cup plain (all purpose) flour
125 g / 4 ½ oz / ½ cup caster (superfine) sugar
3 large egg yolks
200 g / 7 oz / 1 ⅔ cup pistachio nuts, finely chopped

- Preheat the oven to 180°C (160° fan), 355F, gas 4 and line a baking tray with greaseproof paper.
- Rub the butter into the flour with a pinch of salt then stir in the sugar.
- Beat the egg yolks and stir them into the dry ingredients
- Bring the mixture together into a soft dough and space tablespoons of the mixture out on the baking tray. Sprinkle the biscuits liberally with chopped pistachios.
- Bake the biscuits for 20 – 25 minutes or until golden brown.
- Transfer the biscuits to a wire rack and leave to cool.

Pistachio White Chocolate Cookies

795

- Replace 100 g / 3 ½ oz of the pistachios with the same weight of chopped white chocolate for another flavour and texture to these cookies.

796

MAKES 12 # Raisin Rock Cookies

Raisin, Sultana and Currant Rock Cookies

 797

- Replace 55 g / 2 oz of the raisins with 30 g / 1 oz each of currants and sultanas for added flavour and texture.

Raisin Marshmallow Rock Cookies

798

- Replace 55 g / 2 oz of the raisins with the same weight of mini marshmallow for an additional chewy texture.

PREPARATION TIME 15 MINUTES

COOKING TIME 10-12 MINUTES

....

INGREDIENTS

100 g / 3 ½ oz / ½ cup butter
200 g / 7 oz / 1 ⅓ cup self-raising flour
100 g / 3 ½ oz / ½ cup caster (superfine) sugar
100 g / 3 ½ oz / 1 ⅔ cup raisins
1 large egg
2 tbsp whole milk

- Preheat the oven to 200°C (180° fan), 390F, gas 6 and grease a large baking tray.
- Rub the butter into the flour until the mixture resembles fine breadcrumbs then stir in the sugar and raisins.
- Beat the egg with the milk and stir it into the dry ingredients to make a sticky dough.
- Use a dessert spoon to portion the mixture onto the baking tray, flattening the cookies a bit with the back of the spoon but leaving the surface quite rough.
- Bake the cookies for 15 minutes then transfer them to a wire rack and leave to cool.

799

MAKES 1

Poppy Seed Twist Bread

PREPARATION TIME 2 HOURS
30 MINUTES

COOKING TIME 25-30 MINUTES

....

INGREDIENTS

400 g / 14 oz / 2 ⅔ cups strong white
bread flour, plus extra for dusting
½ tsp easy blend dried yeast
1 tbsp caster (superfine) sugar
1 tsp fine sea salt
1 tbsp olive oil
1 egg, beaten
4 tbsp poppy seeds

- Mix together the flour, yeast, sugar and salt. Stir in the oil and 280 ml of warm water.
- Knead the mixture on a lightly oiled surface for 10 minutes or until smooth and elastic.
- Leave the dough to rest, covered with oiled clingfilm, for 1 – 2 hours or until doubled in size.
- Knead the dough again then divide it into two batons.
- Twist them together and transfer to a greased baking tray. Cover with oiled clingfilm and leave to prove for 1 hour or until doubled in size.
- Preheat the oven to 220°C (200° fan), 430F, gas 7.
- Brush the loaf with egg and sprinkle with poppy seeds.
- Bake for 25 – 30 minutes or until the loaf sounds hollow when you tap it underneath.
- Transfer to a wire rack and leave to cool.

Two Poppy Seed Bread

800

- Use a mixture of white and black poppy seeds on the bread for an additional colour and flavour contrast.

801

MAKES 16

Parmesan and Prosciutto Palmiers

PREPARATION TIME 10 MINUTES

COOKING TIME 15-20 MINUTES

....

INGREDIENTS

250 g / 9 oz all-butter puff pastry
1 egg, beaten
8 slices prosciutto
60 g / 2 oz / ½ cup Parmesan, finely grated
2 tbsp poppy seeds

- Preheat the oven to 220°C (200° fan), 430F, gas 7 and line a baking tray with non-stick baking paper.
- Roll out the pastry on a floured surface into a large rectangle.
- Brush the surface with egg and lay out the ham slices so that they overlap each other slightly.
- Sprinkle over the grated Parmesan then, starting at one long edge, roll the pastry up into a tight sausage, stopping when you get to the centre.
- Roll up the other side of the pastry to meet the first in the middle then use a sharp knife to cut the roll into 1 cm thick slices and spread them out on the baking tray.
- Brush the palmiers with egg and sprinkle with poppy seeds then bake in the oven for 15 – 20 minutes or until golden brown and cooked through.
- Transfer the pastries to a wire rack to cool a little and serve warm.

Parmesan and Sundried Tomato Palmiers

802

- Replace the prosciutto with 55 g / 2 oz finely chopped sundried tomatoes for a Mediterranean-feeling flavour to these Palmiers.

MAKES 16 Poppy Seed and Hazelnut Shortbread

- Preheat the oven to 180°C (160° fan), 355F, gas 4 and line a baking tray with greaseproof paper.
- Mix together the flour and caster (superfine) sugar in a bowl, then rub in the butter.
- Knead gently with the poppy seeds and hazelnuts until the mixture forms a smooth dough then roll it into a log, 7 cm in diameter.
- Cut the log into 1cm slices and spread the shortbread out on the baking tray.
- Bake the biscuits for 15-20 minutes, turning the tray round halfway through.
- Transfer the biscuits to a wire rack and leave to cool.

PREPARATION TIME 20 MINUTES

COOKING TIME 15-20 MINUTES

INGREDIENTS

230 g / 8 oz / 1 ½ cup plain (all purpose) flour
75 g / 2 ½ oz / ⅓ cup caster (superfine) sugar
150 g / 5 oz / ⅔ cup butter, cubed
4 tbsp poppy seeds
50 g / 1 ¾ oz / ½ cup hazelnuts, finely chopped

Poppy Seed and Hazelnut Shortbread Biscuits 804

- Use 30 g / 1 oz finely chopped almonds in place of 30 g / 1 oz of the chopped hazelnuts for two different nut flavours.

MAKES 1 Wholemeal Poppy Seed Bread

- Mix together the flours, yeast, sugar and salt. Stir in the oil and 280 ml of warm water.
- Knead the mixture on a lightly oiled surface with your hands for 10 minutes or until smooth and elastic.
- Leave the dough to rest in a lightly oiled bowl, covered with oiled clingfilm, for 1 – 2 hours.
- Knead it for 2 more minutes, then shape into a round loaf on a greased baking tray.
- Cover with oiled clingfilm and leave to prove for 1 hour or until doubled in size.
- Preheat the oven to 220°C (200° fan), 430F, gas 7.
- Sprinkle the loaf with poppy seeds.
- Transfer the tray to the top shelf of the oven then quickly throw a small cupful of water onto the oven floor and close the door.
- Bake for 35 - 40 minutes or until the loaf sounds hollow when you tap it underneath.

PREPARATION TIME 2 HOURS
30 MINUTES

COOKING TIME 35-40 MINUTES

INGREDIENTS

300 g / 10 ½ oz / 2 cup stoneground wholemeal flour
100 g / 3 ½ oz / ⅔ cup strong white bread flour, plus extra for dusting
½ tsp easy blend dried yeast
2 tbsp caster (superfine) sugar
1 tsp fine sea salt
1 tbsp olive oil
3 tbsp poppy seeds

Wholemeal Sesame Seed Bread 806

- Replace the poppy seeds in the recipe with white sesame seeds for a different look and flavour to the bread.

807

MAKES 1 LOAF # Wholemeal Honey and Nut Bread

Honey and Nut Bread **808**

- Replace the stoneground wholemeal flour in the recipe with an additional 200 g / 7 oz of strong white bread flour for a white version of this bread.

Wholemeal Honey Oat Bread **809**

- Instead of using nuts for the topping, use 30 g / 1 oz rolled porridge oats for a softer texture to the topping.

PREPARATION TIME 2 HOURS 30 MINUTES

COOKING TIME 35-40 MINUTES

INGREDIENTS

200 g / 7 oz / 1 ⅓ cup strong white bread flour, plus extra for dusting
200 g / 7 oz / 1 ⅓ cup stoneground wholemeal flour
½ tsp easy blend dried yeast
4 tbsp runny honey
1 tsp fine sea salt
1 tbsp olive oil

FOR THE TOPPING
3 tbsp runny honey
2 tbsp sunflower seeds
25 g / 1 oz / ¼ cup blanched almonds
25 g / 1 oz / ¼ cup walnuts, chopped

- Mix together the flours, yeast, sugar and salt.
- Stir in the oil into 280 ml warm water, then mix with the dry ingredients.
- Knead the mixture on a lightly oiled surface for 10 minutes or until smooth and elastic.
- Leave the dough to rest in an oiled bowl for 1 – 2 hours or until doubled in size.
- Roll the dough with your hands into a fat sausage, then turn it 90⁰ and roll it tightly the other way. Tuck the ends under and transfer the dough to the tin, keeping the seam underneath.
- Cover the tin loosely with oiled clingfilm and leave to prove for 45 minutes.
- Preheat the oven to 220⁰C (200⁰ fan), 430F, gas 7.
- Bake for 35 – 40 minutes or until the loaf sounds hollow when you tap it underneath.
- Mix the honey with the seed and nuts and spoon it over the loaf.
- Transfer the bread to a wire rack and leave to cool completely before slicing.

810

MAKES 36 # Raisin Cookies

- Preheat the oven to 170°C (150° fan), 340F, gas 3 and line 2 baking sheets with greaseproof paper.
- Cream together the two sugars, butter and vanilla extract until pale and well whipped then beat in the egg and yolk, followed by the flour and raisins.
- Drop tablespoons of the mixture onto the prepared trays, leaving plenty of room to spread.
- Bake the cookies in batches for 12 – 15 minutes or until the edges are starting to brown, but the centres are still chewy.
- Transfer to a wire rack and leave to cool.

PREPARATION TIME 10 MINUTES

COOKING TIME 12-15 MINUTES

INGREDIENTS

175 g / 6 oz / ¾ cup butter, melted
225 g / 8 oz / 1 ⅓ cups light brown sugar
100 g / 3 ½ oz / ½ cup caster (superfine) sugar
1 tsp vanilla extract
1 egg, plus 1 egg yolk
250 g / 9 oz / 1 ⅔ cups self-raising flour
100 g / 3 ½ oz / ½ cup raisins

Sultana Cherry Cookies

811

- Replace the raisins in the recipe with 75 g / 3 oz of sultanas and 30 g / 1 oz of chopped cocktail cherries.

812

MAKES 12 # Raspberry Rock Cookies

- Preheat the oven to 200°C (180° fan), 390F, gas 6 and grease a large baking tray.
- Rub the butter into the flour until the mixture resembles fine breadcrumbs then stir in the sugar and raspberries.
- Beat the egg with the milk and stir it into the dry ingredients to make a sticky dough.
- Use a dessert spoon to portion the mixture onto the baking tray, flattening the cookies a bit with the back of the spoon but leaving the surface quite rough.
- Bake the cookies for 15 minutes then transfer them to a wire rack and leave to cool.

PREPARATION TIME 15 MINUTES

COOKING TIME 15 MINUTES

INGREDIENTS

100 g / 3 ½ oz / ½ cup butter
200 g / 7 oz / 1 ⅓ cup self-raising flour
100 g / 3 ½ oz / ½ cup caster (superfine) sugar
100 g / 3 ½ oz / ⅔ cup raspberries
1 large egg
2 tbsp whole milk

Mixed Berry Rock Cookies

813

- Use 100 g / 3 ½ oz frozen mixed berries that have been thawed instead of the raspberries for a more complex tasting rock cookies.

814

MAKES 1 LOAF Rice Bread

PREPARATION TIME 2 HOURS
30 MINUTES

COOKING TIME 35-40 MINUTES

INGREDIENTS

300 g / 10 ½ oz / 2 cup strong white
bread flour, plus extra for dusting
½ tsp easy blend dried yeast
1 tbsp caster (superfine) sugar
1 tsp fine sea salt
300 g / 10 ½ oz / 1 ¾ cup cooked
white rice, cooled
1 tbsp olive oil

- Mix together the flour, yeast, sugar, and salt. Stir the rice and oil into 280 ml of warm water and mix with the dry ingredients.
- Knead the dough on a lightly oiled surface for 10 minutes or until smooth and elastic.
- Leave the dough to rest, covered with oiled clingfilm, for 1 – 2 hours or until doubled in size.
- Roll the dough into a fat sausage. Turn it 90° and roll it tightly the other way then tuck the ends under and transfer the dough to a greased loaf tin, keeping the seam underneath.
- Cover the tin and leave to prove for 1 hour.
- Preheat the oven to 220°C (200° fan), 430F, gas 7.
- Bake for 35 – 40 minutes or until the loaf sounds hollow when you tap it underneath.

Rice and Soy Bread 815

- Add 30 ml / 1 fl. oz to the water before incorporating into the dry ingredients for an added savoury, Japanese flavour to the bread.

816

SERVES 8 Vanilla Swiss Roll

PREPARATION TIME 45 MINUTES

COOKING TIME 15-20 MINUTES

INGREDIENTS

100 g / 3 ½ oz / ⅔ cup self-raising
flour
1 tsp baking powder
100 g / 3 ½ oz / ½ cup caster
(superfine) sugar
100 g / 3 ½ oz / ½ cup butter
2 large eggs
1 tsp vanilla extract

TO DECORATE

300 ml / 10 ½ fl. oz / 1 ¼ cups double
cream
2 tbsp icing (confectioners) sugar
1 tsp vanilla extract
28 g / 1 oz dark chocolate (minimum
60 % cocoa solids)

- Preheat the oven to 180°C (160° fan), 355F, gas 4 and grease and line a Swiss roll tin.
- Put all of the cake ingredients in a large mixing bowl and whisk them together with an electric whisk for 4 minutes or until pale and well whipped.
- Spoon the mixture into the tin.
- Bake for 15 - 20 minutes.
- Turn the cake out onto greaseproof paper and roll up the cake whilst warm, using the greaseproof paper to help you.
- Leave the cake to cool.
- Whip the cream with the icing (confectioners) sugar and vanilla extract. Carefully unroll the cake and spread it with cream before rerolling.
- Melt the chocolate in a microwave or bain marie then use it to fill a small paper piping bag.
- Pipe lines across the width of the cake and leave to set.

Vanilla Strawberry Swiss Roll 817

- Instead of using melted chocolate to decorate this Swiss roll, use strawberry sauce instead for an added colour and flavour.

818

MAKES 1 LOAF Dried Fig and Honey Bread

- Mix together the flours, yeast, honey, figs and salt. Stir the oil into 280 ml of warm water.
- Stir the liquid into the dry ingredients then knead on a lightly oiled surface for 10 minutes or until the dough is smooth and elastic.
- Leave the dough to rest, covered with oiled clingfilm, for 1 – 2 hours or until doubled in size.
- Knead the dough for 2 more minutes, then shape it into a round loaf.
- Transfer the loaf to a greased baking tray and cover again with oiled clingfilm. Leave to prove for 1 hour.
- Preheat the oven to 220°C (200° fan), 430F, gas 7.
- When the dough has risen, slash the top with a knife and dust with flour.
- Bake for 35 – 40 minutes. Transfer the bread to a wire rack and leave to cool.

PREPARATION TIME 2 HOURS 30 MINUTES

COOKING TIME 35-40 MINUTES

INGREDIENTS

400 g / 14 oz / 2 ⅔ cups strong white bread flour, plus extra for dusting
½ tsp easy blend dried yeast
3 tbsp runny honey
100 g / 3 ½ oz / ½ cup dried figs, quartered
1 tsp fine sea salt
1 tbsp olive oil

Raisin and Honey Bread
819

- Instead of using fig in the bread, use 75 g / 3 oz raisins incorporating them well into the dough before kneading.

820

MAKES 1 Wholemeal Sesame Bread

- Mix together the flours, yeast, sugar, half of the sesame seeds and the salt. Stir the oil into 280 ml of warm water then stir it into the dry ingredients.
- Knead the mixture on a lightly oiled surface with your hands for 10 minutes or until smooth and elastic.
- Leave the dough to rest in a lightly oiled bowl, covered with oiled clingfilm, for 1 – 2 hours.
- Knead it for 2 more minutes, then shape into a long loaf on a greased baking tray.
- Cover with oiled clingfilm and leave to prove for 1 hour.
- Preheat the oven to 220°C (200° fan), 430F, gas 7.
- Sprinkle the bread with sesame seeds then slash the top with a knife.
- Bake for 25 - 30 minutes or until the loaf sounds hollow when you tap it underneath.
- Transfer to a wire rack and leave to cool.

PREPARATION TIME 2 HOURS 30 MINUTES

COOKING TIME 25-30 MINUTES

INGREDIENTS

300 g / 10 ½ oz / 2 cup stoneground wholemeal flour
100 g / 3 ½ oz / ⅔ cup strong white bread flour, plus extra for dusting
½ tsp easy blend dried yeast
2 tbsp caster (superfine) sugar
50 g / 1 ¾ oz / ½ cup sesame seeds
1 tsp fine sea salt
1 tbsp sesame oil
1 egg, beaten

Sesame and Orange Bread

821

- Incorporate 1 tbsp orange flower water and the finely grated zest of 1 orange into the dough before kneading for a citrus take on this bread.

822

MAKES 16

Lemon and Semolina Shortbread

PREPARATION TIME 20 MINUTES

COOKING TIME 15-20 MINUTES

INGREDIENTS

175 g / 6 oz / 1 ¼ cupplain (all purpose) flour
55 g / 2 oz / ½ cup fine semolina
75 g / 2 ½ oz / ⅓ cup caster (superfine) sugar
150 g / 5 oz / ⅔ cup butter, cubed
1 lemon, zest finely grated

- Preheat the oven to 180°C (160° fan), 355F, gas 4 and line a baking tray with greaseproof paper.
- Mix together the flour, semolina and caster (superfine) sugar in a bowl, then rub in the butter and lemon zest.
- Knead gently until the mixture forms a smooth dough then form into cylinder 6 cm in diameter.
- Slice the roll into 1 cm thick slices and spread them out on the baking tray.
- Bake the biscuits for 15 - 20 minutes, turning the tray round halfway through.
- Transfer the biscuits to a wire rack and leave to cool.

Orange Polenta Shortbread

823

- Replace the lemon in the recipe with the same amount of orange zest and use polenta instead of semolina for a crunchier texture.

824

MAKES 16

Sultana Shortbread Biscuits

PREPARATION TIME 20 MINUTES

COOKING TIME 15-20 MINUTES

INGREDIENTS

230 g / 8 oz / 1 ½ cup plain (all purpose) flour
75 g / 2 ½ oz / ⅓ cup caster (superfine) sugar
150 g / 5 oz / ⅔ cup butter, cubed
50 g / 1 ¾ oz / ¼ cup sultanas

- Preheat the oven to 180°C (160° fan), 355F, gas 4 and line a baking tray with greaseproof paper.
- Mix together the flour and caster (superfine) sugar in a bowl, then rub in the butter.
- Knead gently with the sultanas until the mixture forms a smooth dough then form into a cylinder 6 cm in diameter.
- Slice the roll into 1 cm thick slices and spread them out on the baking tray.
- Bake the biscuits for 15 - 20 minutes, turning the tray round halfway through.
- Transfer the biscuits to a wire rack and leave to cool.

Sultana Cherry Shortbread Biscuits

825

- Replace half of the sultanas with the same weight of chopped cocktail cherries.

826

MAKES 36

Nutmeg Cross Biscuits

Cinnamon Cross Biscuits

827

- Use 1 tsp of ground cinnamon in the icing instead of the nutmeg for an alternative spiced flavour.

Ginger Cross Biscuits

828

- Use 1 tsp of ground ginger in the icing instead of the nutmeg for a spicy, warming flavour.

PREPARATION TIME 10 MINUTES

COOKING TIME 12-15 MINUTES

INGREDIENTS

75 g / 2 ½ oz / ⅓ cup butter, softened
100 g / 3 ½ oz / ⅓ cup golden syrup
225 g / 8 oz / 1 ½ cups self-raising flour
100 g / 3 ½ oz / ½ cup caster (superfine) sugar
1 tsp nutmeg, freshly grated
1 large egg, beaten

TO DECORATE
4 tbsp icing (confectioners) sugar
1 tsp nutmeg, freshly grated

- Preheat the oven to 180°C (160° fan), 355F, gas 4 and line 2 baking sheets with greaseproof paper.
- Melt the butter and golden syrup together in a saucepan.
- Mix the flour, sugar and nutmeg together then stir in the melted butter mixture and the beaten egg.
- Use a teaspoon to portion the mixture onto the baking trays, leaving plenty of room for the biscuits to spread.
- Bake in batches for 12 – 15 minutes or until golden brown.
- Transfer the biscuits to a wire rack and leave to cool and harden.
- To make the icing, mix the icing (confectioners) sugar and nutmeg together then add enough water, drop by drop, to form a thick icing. Spoon it into a piping bag and pie a cross onto each biscuit.

MAKES 1 LOAF # Hedgehog Rye Bread

PREPARATION TIME 2 HOURS
30 MINUTES

COOKING TIME 35-40 MINUTES

INGREDIENTS

200 g / 7 oz / 1 ⅓ cup strong white
bread flour, plus extra for dusting
200 g / 7 oz / 1 ⅓ cups rye flour
½ tsp easy blend dried yeast
1 tbsp caster (superfine) sugar
1 tsp fine sea salt
1 tbsp olive oil

- Mix together the flours, yeast, sugar and salt. Stir in the oil and 280 ml of warm water.
- Knead on a lightly oiled surface for 10 minutes or until the dough is smooth and elastic.
- Leave the dough to rest, covered with oiled clingfilm, for 1 – 2 hours or until doubled in size.
- Knead the dough for 2 more minutes, then shape it into a round loaf.
- Transfer the loaf to a greased baking tray and cover again with oiled clingfilm. Leave to prove for 1 hour.
- Preheat the oven to 220⁰C (200⁰ fan), 430F, gas 7.
- When the dough has risen, use a pair of oiled scissors to snip the top into points.
- Bake for 35 – 40 minutes or until the loaf sounds hollow when tapped. Transfer the bread to a wire rack and leave to cool.

Hedgehog Granary Bread 830

- Instead of using rye flour, use the same weight of malted granary flour for an alternative flour and texture to the bread.

831

MAKES 1 LOAF # Cinnamon and Walnut Bread

PREPARATION TIME 2 HOURS
30 MINUTES

COOKING TIME 35-40 MINUTES

INGREDIENTS

200 g / 7 oz / 1 ⅓ cup strong white
bread flour, plus extra for dusting
200 g / 7 oz / 1 ⅓ cup stoneground
wholemeal flour
½ tsp easy blend dried yeast
1 tbsp caster (superfine) sugar
2 tsp ground cinnamon
1 tsp fine sea salt
100 g / 3 ½ oz / ¾ cup walnuts,
chopped
1 tbsp walnut oil

- Mix together the flours, yeast, sugar, cinnamon, salt and walnuts. Stir the oil into 280 ml of warm water.
- Knead on a lightly oiled surface for 10 minutes or until the dough is smooth and elastic.
- Leave the dough to rest, covered with oiled clingfilm, for 1 – 2 hours or until doubled in size.
- Knead the dough for 2 more minutes, then shape it into a round loaf.
- Transfer the loaf to a greased baking tray and cover again with oiled clingfilm. Leave to prove for 1 hour.
- Preheat the oven to 220⁰C (200⁰ fan), 430F, gas 7.
- When the dough has risen, slash the top with a knife.
- Bake for 35 – 40 minutes or until the loaf sounds hollow when tapped. Transfer the bread to a wire rack and leave to cool.

Walnut Allspice Bread 832

- Use 1 tbsp ground allspice in place of the ground cinnamon for an alternative wintery flavour to the bread.

833
MAKES 1 LOAF Chestnut and Chorizo Bread

- Mix together the flours, yeast, sugar and salt. Stir the chorizo into 280 ml of warm water and stir it into the dry ingredients.
- Knead the mixture on a lightly oiled surface for 10 minutes or until the dough is smooth and elastic.
- Leave the dough to rest in a lightly oiled bowl, covered with oiled clingfilm, for 1 – 2 hours.
- Punch the dough with your fist to knock out the air then knead it for 2 more minutes.
- Transfer the dough to a greased baking tray and cover with oiled clingfilm. Leave to prove for 1 hour or until doubled in size.
- Preheat the oven to 220°C (200° fan), 430F, gas 7.
- Bake for 35 – 40 minutes or until the loaf sounds hollow when you tap it underneath. Transfer the bread to a wire rack and leave to cool completely before slicing.

Smoked Paprika Chorizo Bread 834

- Replace the chestnut flour with the same weight of strong white bread flour and add 1 tbsp of smoked paprika to the flour mixture before mixing for a smokey, Spanish flavour.

PREPARATION TIME 2 HOURS 30 MINUTES

COOKING TIME 35-40 MINUTES

INGREDIENTS

200 g / 7 oz / 1 ⅓ cup strong white bread flour, plus extra for dusting
200 g / 7 oz / 1 ⅓ cup chestnut flour
½ tsp easy blend dried yeast
1 tbsp caster (superfine) sugar
1 tsp fine sea salt
200 g / 7 oz cooking chorizo, cubed

835
MAKES 1 LOAF Rye Bread

- Mix together the flour, yeast, treacle, malt extract and salt. Stir the oil into 280 ml of warm water.
- Stir the liquid into the dry ingredients then knead on a lightly oiled surface for 10 minutes.
- Leave the dough to rest, covered with oiled clingfilm, for 1 – 2 hours or until doubled in size.
- Knead the dough for 2 more minutes, then shape it into a round loaf.
- Transfer the loaf to a greased baking tray and cover again with oiled clingfilm. Leave to prove for 1 hour or until doubled in size.
- Preheat the oven to 220°C (200° fan), 430F, gas 7.
- When the dough has risen, score the top with a knife and dust with flour.
- Bake for 35 – 40 minutes or until the loaf sounds hollow when tapped. Transfer the bread to a wire rack and leave to cool.

Rye Whisky Bread 836

- Add 30 ml / 1 fl. oz of whisky, preferably rye, to the wet ingredients for an added complex flavour to the bread.

PREPARATION TIME 2 HOURS 30 MINUTES

COOKING TIME 35-40 MINUTES

INGREDIENTS

400 g / 14 oz / 2 ⅔ cup rye flour, plus extra
for dusting
1 tsp easy blend dried yeast
1 tbsp treacle
1 tbsp malt extract
1 tsp fine sea salt
1 tbsp olive oil

837

MAKES 20

Orange Shortbread Hearts

Chocolate Shortbread Hearts

838

- Replace 30 g / 1 oz of the plain (all purpose) flour with 30 g / 1 oz of good-quality cocoa powder for a chocolate take on these shortbread hearts.

Lemon Shortbread Hearts

839

- Replace the orange zest with lemon zest and add 1 tsp lemon essence for an added boost of lemon flavour to the shortbread hearts.

PREPARATION TIME 20 MINUTES

COOKING TIME 12-15 MINUTES

INGREDIENTS

175 g / 6 oz / 1 ¼ cups plain (all purpose) flour
1 orange, zest finely grated
75g / 2 ½ oz / ⅓ cup caster (superfine) sugar
150g / 5 oz / ⅔ cup butter, cubed

- Preheat the oven to 180°C (160° fan), 355F, gas 4 and line a baking tray with greaseproof paper.
- Mix together the flour, orange zest and caster (superfine) sugar in a bowl, then rub in the butter.
- Knead gently until the mixture forms a smooth dough then roll out on a lightly floured surface to 5 mm thick.
- Use a heart-shaped cookie cutter to cut out the biscuits and spread them out on the baking tray.
- Bake the biscuits for 12 - 15 minutes, turning the tray round halfway through.
- Transfer the biscuits to a wire rack and leave to cool.

840
MAKES 16 Jam Shortbread Biscuits

- Preheat the oven to 180°C (160° fan), 355F, gas 4 and line a baking tray with greaseproof paper.
- Mix together the flour and caster (superfine) sugar in a bowl, then rub in the butter.
- Knead gently until the mixture forms a smooth dough then form into a cylinder 6 cm in diameter.
- Slice the roll into 1 cm thick slices and spread them out on the baking tray.
- Make a hollow in the centre of the biscuits with your thumb then add a spoonful of jam to each one.
- Bake the biscuits for 15 - 20 minutes, turning the tray round halfway through.
- Transfer the biscuits to a wire rack and leave to cool.

PREPARATION TIME 20 MINUTES

COOKING TIME 15-20 MINUTES

INGREDIENTS

230 g / 8 oz / 1 ½ cup plain (all purpose) flour
75 g / 2 ½ oz / ⅓ cup caster (superfine) sugar
150 g / 5 oz / ⅔ cup butter, cubed
4 tsp strawberry jam
4 tsp raspberry jam
4 tsp apricot jam
4 tsp plum jam

Marmalade Shortbread Biscuits 841

- Use good-quality orange marmalade instead of jam to fill these biscuits for a citrus take on them.

842
MAKES 20 Iced Almond Shortbread Biscuits

- Preheat the oven to 180°C (160° fan), 355F, gas 4 and line a baking tray with greaseproof paper.
- Mix together the flour, ground almonds and caster (superfine) sugar in a bowl, then rub in the butter.
- Knead gently until the mixture forms a smooth dough.
- Divide the dough into 20 balls and shape them into short fingers.
- Bake the biscuits for 15 - 20 minutes, turning the tray round halfway through.
- Transfer the biscuits to a wire rack and leave to cool.
- Mix the icing (confectioners) sugar with just enough water to form a thick icing. Spoon it into a piping bag and pipe a zigzag pattern on top of each biscuit.

PREPARATION TIME 20 MINUTES

COOKING TIME 15-20 MINUTES

INGREDIENTS

175 g / 6 oz / 1 ¼ cups plain (all purpose) flour
55 g / 2 oz / ½ cup ground almonds
75 g / 2 ½ oz / ⅓ cup caster (superfine) sugar
150 g / 5 oz / ⅔ cup butter, cubed
4 tbsp icing (confectioners) sugar

Cherry Almond Shortbread Biscuits 843

- Add 75 g / 3 oz chopped cocktail cherries to the biscuit dough before baking. Leave the biscuits un-iced before serving.

844

MAKES 1 LOAF # Rye and Caraway Seed Bread

**PREPARATION TIME 2 HOURS
30 MINUTES**

COOKING TIME 35-40 MINUTES

INGREDIENTS

200 g / 7 oz / 1 ⅓ cup strong white
bread flour, plus extra for dusting
200 g / 7 oz / 1 ⅓ cups rye flour
½ tsp easy blend dried yeast
1 tbsp caster (superfine) sugar
1 tbsp caraway seeds
1 tsp fine sea salt
1 tbsp olive oil

- Mix together the flours, yeast, sugar, caraway and salt. Stir in the oil and 280 ml of warm water.
- Knead on a lightly oiled surface for 10 minutes or until the dough is smooth and elastic.
- Leave the dough to rest, covered with oiled clingfilm, for 1 – 2 hours or until doubled in size.
- Knead the dough for 2 more minutes, then shape it into a round loaf.
- Transfer the loaf to a greased baking tray and cover again with oiled clingfilm. Leave to prove for 1 hour.
- Preheat the oven to 220°C (200° fan), 430F, gas 7.
- When the dough has risen, dust the top with flour.
- Bake for 35 – 40 minutes or until the loaf sounds hollow when tapped. Transfer the bread to a wire rack and leave to cool.

Rye, Cumin and Onion Seed Bread — 845

- Replace the caraway seeds in the recipe with an even mixture of cumin and onion seeds before shaping and baking.

846

SERVES 8 # Poppy Seed Loaf Cake

PREPARATION TIME 10 MINUTES

COOKING TIME 35-40 MINUTES

INGREDIENTS

150 g / 5 ½ oz / 1 cup self-raising
flour
150 g / 5 ½ oz / ⅔ cup caster
(superfine) sugar
150 g / 5 ½ oz / ⅔ cup butter
3 eggs
1 tsp baking powder
1 tsp vanilla extract

TO DECORATE
2 tbsp poppy seeds

- Preheat the oven to 180°C (160° fan), 355F, gas 4 and grease and line a small loaf tin.
- Put all of the cake ingredients in a large mixing bowl and whisk them together with an electric whisk for 4 minutes or until pale and well whipped.
- Scrape the mixture into the tin and level the top with a spatula then sprinkle with the poppy seeds.
- Bake for 35 - 40 minutes. The cake is ready when a toothpick inserted in the centre comes out clean.
- Transfer the cake to a wire rack to cool completely.

Poppy Seed Lemon Loaf Cake — 847

- Combine the juice of 2 lemons with 200g of icing sugar and warm gently, stirring until smooth. Puncture the loaf cake all over before drizzling over the cake.

SERVES 10 Pine Nut, Raisin and Pumpkin Seed Loaf

- Preheat the oven to 180°C (160° fan), 355F, gas 4 and grease and line a small loaf tin.
- Put the flour, sugar, butter, eggs and baking powder in a large mixing bowl and whisk them together with an electric whisk for 4 minutes or until pale and well whipped.
- Fold in the pine nuts and raisins then scrape the mixture into the tin and level the top with a spatula.
- Sprinkle with the pumpkins seeds and demerara sugar then bake for 35 - 40 minutes.
- The cake is ready when a toothpick inserted comes out clean.
- Transfer the cake to a wire rack to cool completely.

PREPARATION TIME 20 MINUTES

COOKING TIME 35-40 MINUTES

....

INGREDIENTS

150 g / 5 ½ oz / 1 cup self-raising flour
150 g / 5 ½ oz / ⅔ cup caster (superfine) sugar
150 g / 5 ½ oz / ⅔ cup butter
3 large eggs
1 tsp baking powder
75 g / 2 ½ oz / ⅔ cup pine nuts
75 g / 2 ½ oz / ⅓ cup raisins

TO DECORATE

3 tbsp pumpkin seeds
2 tbsp demerara sugar

Pine Nut, Chocolate and Pumpkin Seed Loaf

849

- Instead of using raisins in the dough, use 100 g / 3 ½ oz chopped chocolate for a sweet hit to this bread.

SERVES 8 Sunflower and Black Sesame Cake Bread

- Preheat the oven to 170°C (150° fan), 340F, gas 3 and line a round cake tin with greaseproof paper.
- Sieve the flour and baking powder into a mixing bowl and add the butter and eggs.
- Beat the mixture with an electric whisk for 4 minutes or until smooth and well whipped.
- Scrape the mixture into the tin and sprinkle with sunflower seeds and black sesame seeds.
- Bake for 35 minutes or until a skewer inserted comes out clean.
- Transfer the cake to a wire rack and leave to cool completely before serving.

PREPARATION TIME 10 MINUTES

COOKING TIME 35 MINUTES

....

INGREDIENTS

300 g / 10 ½ oz / 1 cup self-raising flour
2 tsp baking powder
250 g / 9 oz / 1 ¼ cup butter, softened
4 large eggs
50 g / 1 ¾ oz / ½ cup sunflower seeds
25 g / 1 oz / ¼ cup black sesame seeds

Apricot and Black Sesame Cake Bread

 851

- Omit the sunflower seeds from the recipe and add 55 g / 2 oz apricot jam to the batter, swirling it in the tin, before baking.

852

SERVES 8

Fig, Rosemary and Prosciutto Loaf Cake

PREPARATION TIME 10 MINUTES

COOKING TIME 55 MINUTES

INGREDIENTS

300 g / 10 ½ oz / 2 cup self-raising flour
2 tsp baking powder
250 g / 9 oz / 1 ¼ cup butter, softened
5 large eggs
100 g 3 ½ oz / ½ cup dried figs, chopped
6 slices prosciutto, chopped
2 tbsp fresh rosemary, chopped

- Preheat the oven to 170°C (150° fan), 340F, gas 3 and line a large loaf tin with non-stick baking paper.
- Sieve the flour and baking powder into a mixing bowl and add the butter and eggs.
- Beat the mixture with an electric whisk for 4 minutes or until smooth and well whipped.
- Fold in the figs, prosciutto and rosemary then scrape the mixture into the loaf tin.
- Bake for 55 minutes or until a skewer inserted in the centre comes out clean.
- Transfer the cake to a wire rack and leave to cool completely before serving.

853

MAKES 8

Seeded Rolls

PREPARATION TIME 2 HOURS 30 MINUTES

COOKING TIME 10-12 MINUTES

INGREDIENTS

200 g / 7 oz / 1 ⅓ cup strong white bread flour, plus extra for dusting
200 g / 7 oz / 1 ⅓ cup stoneground wholemeal flour
½ tsp easy blend dried yeast
1 tbsp caster (superfine) sugar
1 tsp fine sea salt
1 tbsp olive oil

FOR THE SEED MIX
2 tbsp sunflower seeds
2 tbsp hemp seeds
3 tbsp sesame seeds
3 tbsp poppy seeds

- Mix together the flours, yeast, sugar and salt. Stir the oil into 280 ml of warm water then stir the liquid into the dry ingredients.
- Knead the mixture with half of the seed mix on a lightly oiled surface for 10 minutes or until smooth and elastic.
- Leave the dough to rest, covered with oiled clingfilm, for 1 – 2 hours or until doubled in size.
- Divide the dough into 8 evenly-sized pieces and shape into rolls on a greased baking tray.
- Cover the rolls with oiled clingfilm and leave to prove for 1 hour or until doubled in size.
- Preheat the oven to 220°C (200° fan), 430F, gas 7.
- When the rolls have risen, sprinkle with the rest of the seeds.
- Transfer the tray to the top shelf of the oven then quickly throw a small cupful of water onto the floor of the oven and close the door.
- Bake for 10 - 12 minutes or until the rolls sound hollow when you tap them underneath.

854

MAKES 12 Olive and Parmesan Rolls

- Mix together the flour, yeast, sugar, salt, olives and Parmesan. Stir in the oil and 280 ml of warm water.
- Knead the mixture on a lightly oiled surface for 10 minutes or until smooth and elastic.
- Leave the dough to rest, covered with oiled clingfilm, for 1 – 2 hours or until doubled in size.
- Shape the dough into 2 flat round loaves then cut each one into 6 wedges.
- Transfer the rolls to a greased baking tray and cover with oiled clingfilm. Leave to prove for 1 hour.
- Meanwhile, preheat the oven to 220°C(200° fan), gas 7.
- Bake for 15 – 20 minutes or until the rolls sound hollow when you tap them underneath.
- Transfer to a wire rack and leave to cool.

PREPARATION TIME 2 HOURS
30 MINUTES

COOKING TIME 15-20 MINUTES

INGREDIENTS

400 g / 14 oz / 2 ⅔ cups strong white bread flour, plus extra for dusting
½ tsp easy blend dried yeast
1 tbsp caster (superfine) sugar
1 tsp fine sea salt
75 g / 2 ½ oz / ½ cup green olives, pitted and chopped
75 g / 2 ½ oz / ¾ cup Parmesan, finely grated
1 tbsp olive oil

855

MAKES 12

Muesli Rolls

PREPARATION TIME 2 HOURS
30 MINUTES

COOKING TIME 15-20 MINUTES

INGREDIENTS

350 g / 12 ½ oz / 2 ⅓ cup strong white bread flour, plus extra for dusting
50 g / 1 ¾ oz / ⅓ cup stoneground

wholemeal flour
75 g / 2 ½ oz / ¾ cup muesli
½ tsp easy blend dried yeast
1 tbsp caster (superfine) sugar
1 tsp fine sea salt
1 tbsp olive oil

- Mix together the flours, muesli, yeast, sugar and salt. Stir in the oil and 280 ml of warm water. Knead the mixture on a lightly oiled surface for 10 minutes.
- Leave the dough to rest, covered with oiled clingfilm, for 1 – 2 hours.
- Knead it for 2 more minutes then split it into 12 even pieces and shape into rolls.
- Transfer the rolls to a greased baking tray and cover with oiled clingfilm. Leave to prove for 1 hour or until doubled in size.
- Preheat the oven to 220°C (200° fan), 430F, gas 7.
- Dust the rolls with flour and slash the tops with a knife.
- Bake for 15 – 20 minutes or until the rolls sound hollow when you tap them underneath.
- Transfer to a wire rack and leave to cool.

856

MAKES 12

Treacle and Raisin Rolls

PREPARATION TIME 2 HOURS
30 MINUTES

COOKING TIME 15-20 MINUTES

INGREDIENTS

350 g / 12 ½ oz / 2 ⅓ cup strong white bread flour, plus extra for dusting
50 g / 1 ¾ oz / ⅓ cup stoneground

wholemeal flour
75 g / 2 ½ oz / ⅓ cup raisins
½ tsp easy blend dried yeast
1 tbsp caster (superfine) sugar
1 tsp fine sea salt
1 tbsp olive oil
4 tbsp treacle

- Mix together the flours, muesli, yeast, sugar and salt. Stir in the oil, treacle and 280 ml of warm water.
- Knead the mixture on a lightly oiled surface for 10 minutes.
- Leave the dough to rest, covered with oiled clingfilm, for 1 – 2 hours.
- Knead it for 2 more minutes then split it into 12 even pieces and shape into rolls.
- Transfer the rolls to a greased baking tray and cover with oiled clingfilm. Leave to prove for 1 hour.
- Preheat the oven to 220°C (200° fan), 430F, gas 7.
- Bake for 15 – 20 minutes or until the rolls sound hollow when you tap them underneath.
- Transfer to a wire rack and leave to cool.

MAKES 36

Chocolate Chip and Cinnamon Cookies

857

PREPARATION TIME 10 MINUTES

COOKING TIME 12-15 MINUTES

INGREDIENTS

175 g / 6 oz / ¾ cup butter, melted
225 g / 8 oz / 1 ⅓ cups light brown sugar
100 g / 3 ½ oz / ½ cup caster (superfine) sugar
2 tsp vanilla extract
1 egg, plus 1 egg yolk
250 g / 9 oz / 1 ⅔ cups self-raising flour
2 tsp ground cinnamon

- Preheat the oven to 170°C (150° fan), 340F, gas 3 and line 2 baking sheets with greaseproof paper.
- Cream together the two sugars, butter and vanilla extract until pale and well whipped then beat in the egg and yolk, followed by the flour and cinnamon.
- Drop tablespoons of the mixture onto the prepared trays, leaving plenty of room to spread.
- Bake the cookies in batches for 12 – 15 minutes or until the edges are starting to brown, but the centres are still chewy.
- Transfer to a wire rack and leave to cool.

Coconut and Cinnamon Cookies   858

- Instead of using chocolate chips, add 110 g / 4 oz desiccated coconut to the cookie dough before shaping and baking for a tropical taste.

MAKES 24

Coconut Kisses

859

PREPARATION TIME 10 MINUTES

COOKING TIME 10-15 MINUTES

INGREDIENTS

2 large egg whites
110 g / 4 oz caster / ½ cup (superfine) sugar
250 g / 9 oz / 2 ½ cup unsweetened shredded coconut

- Preheat the oven to 170°C (150° fan), 325F, gas 3 and oil and line a large baking sheet with baking parchment.
- Whisk the egg whites to stiff peaks in a very clean bowl then carefully fold in the sugar and coconut.
- Spoon the mixture into a piping bag fitted with a large star nozzle and pipe small rosettes onto the prepared baking tray.
- Bake for 10 – 15 minutes or until they start to turn golden on top.
- Transfer to a wire rack to cool.

Coconut Cherry Kisses   860

- Substitute 75 g / 3 oz of the shredded coconut for the same weight of chopped glacé cherries for a fruity addition to the kisses.

861

MAKES 16

Milk Rolls

Herb Milk Rolls

862

- Add 1 tbsp chopped mixed herbs to the dough before kneading for an additional colour and flavour to these rolls.

Raisin Milk Rolls

863

- Add 100 g / 3 ½ oz raisins to the dough before kneading for a fruity addition to the rolls.

PREPARATION TIME 2 HOURS
30 MINUTES

COOKING TIME 15-20 MINUTES

INGREDIENTS

400 g / 7 oz / 2 ⅔ cup strong white bread flour, plus extra for dusting
½ tsp easy blend dried yeast
1 tbsp caster (superfine) sugar
1 tsp fine sea salt
280 ml / 10 fl.oz / 1 ¼ cups whole milk, warmed

- Mix together the flours, yeast, sugar and salt then stir in the warm milk.
- Knead the mixture on a lightly oiled surface with your hands for 10 minutes or until smooth and elastic.
- Leave the dough to rest in a lightly oiled bowl, covered with oiled clingfilm, for 1 – 2 hours or until doubled in size.
- Knead it for 2 more minutes then split it into 16 even pieces and shape into rolls
- Transfer the rolls to a greased baking tray and cover with oiled clingfilm. Leave to prove for 1 hour or until doubled in size.
- Meanwhile, preheat the oven to 220⁰C (200⁰ fan), gas 7.
- Transfer the tray to the top shelf of the oven then quickly throw a small cupful of water onto the oven floor and close the door.
- Bake for 15 – 20 minutes or until the rolls sound hollow when you tap them underneath.
- Transfer to a wire rack and leave to cool.

SAVOURIES

864

SERVES 8

Cep and Prosciutto Loaf Cake

Truffled Cep Loaf Cake   865

- Omit the pancetta and add ½ tsp of truffle oil to the cake mixture before whisking.

Cep and Rosemary Loaf Cake   866

- Omit the pancetta and add 1 tbsp of finely chopped fresh rosemary.

PREPARATION TIME 20 MINUTES

COOKING TIME 55 MINUTES

INGREDIENTS

200 g / 7 oz ceps, sliced
250 g / 9 oz / 1 ¼ cup butter, softened
300 g / 10 ½ oz / 2 cup self-raising flour
2 tsp baking powder
5 large eggs
100 g / 3 ½ oz prosciutto, chopped

- Preheat the oven to 170°C (150° fan), gas 3 and line a large loaf tin with non-stick baking paper.
- Fry the ceps in 1 tablespoon of the butter for 10 minutes or until all the liquid that comes out of them has evaporated and they start to brown. Leave to cool.
- Sieve the flour and baking powder into a mixing bowl and add the eggs and the rest of the butter.
- Beat the mixture with an electric whisk for 4 minutes or until smooth and well whipped.
- Fold in the cooled ceps and the prosciutto then scrape the mixture into the loaf tin.
- Bake for 55 minutes or until a skewer inserted in the centre comes out clean.
- Transfer the cake to a wire rack and leave to cool completely before serving.

867

SERVES 8

Olive, Ham and Roasted Pepper Loaf

- Preheat the oven to 170°C (150° fan), gas 3 and line a large loaf tin with non-stick baking paper.
- Sieve the flour and baking powder into a mixing bowl and add the butter and eggs.
- Beat the mixture with an electric whisk for 4 minutes or until smooth and well whipped.
- Fold in the olives, peppers and ham then scrape the mixture into the loaf tin.
- Bake for 55 minutes or until a skewer inserted in the centre comes out clean.
- Transfer the cake to a wire rack and leave to cool completely before serving.

PREPARATION TIME 10 MINUTES

COOKING TIME 55 MINUTES

INGREDIENTS

300 g / 10 ½ oz / 2 cup self-raising flour
2 tsp baking powder
250 g / 9 oz / 1 ¼ cup butter, softened
5 large eggs
75 g / 2 ½ oz / ½ cup green olives, pitted and halved
75 g / 2 ½ oz / ⅓ cup chopped roasted peppers in oil, drained
75 g / 2 ½ oz ham, cubed

Olive, Ham and Pepper Muffins
868

- Bake the mixture in a 12-hole silicone muffin tray and reduce the cooking time to 30 minutes.

869

SERVES 8

Parsley and Feta Loaf Cake

- Preheat the oven to 170°C (150° fan), gas 3 and line a large loaf tin with non-stick baking paper.
- Sieve the flour and baking powder into a mixing bowl and add the butter and eggs.
- Beat the mixture with an electric whisk for 4 minutes or until smooth and well whipped.
- Fold in the feta and parsley then scrape the mixture into the loaf tin.
- Bake for 55 minutes or until a skewer inserted in the centre comes out clean.
- Transfer the cake to a wire rack and leave to cool completely before serving.

PREPARATION TIME 10 MINUTES

COOKING TIME 55 MINUTES

INGREDIENTS

300 g / 10 ½ oz / 2 cup self-raising flour
2 tsp baking powder
250 g / 9 oz / 1 ¼ cup butter, softened
5 large eggs
150 g / 5 oz feta, cubed
3 tbsp flat leaf parsley, chopped

Dill and Feta Loaf Cake
870

- Replace the parsley with chopped fresh dill.

871

MAKES 12

Sundried Tomato and Basil Muffins

PREPARATION TIME 25 MINUTES

COOKING TIME 20-25 MINUTES

INGREDIENTS

2 large eggs
120 ml / 4 fl. oz / ½ cup sunflower oil
180 ml / 6 fl. oz / ⅔ cup Greek yoghurt
110 g / 4 oz / 1 cup Parmesan, grated
75 g / 2 ½ oz / ⅓ cup sundried tomatoes, chopped
2 tbsp basil leaves, shredded
225 g / 8 oz / 1 ½ cup plain (all purpose) flour
2 tsp baking powder
½ tsp bicarbonate of soda
½ tsp salt

- Preheat the oven to 180°C (160° fan), gas 4 and line a 12-hole muffin tin with paper cases.
- Beat the egg in a jug with the oil, yoghurt and cheese until well mixed.
- Mix the sundried tomatoes, basil, flour, raising agents and salt in a bowl, then pour in the egg mixture and stir just enough to combine.
- Divide the mixture between the paper cases, then bake in the oven for 20 – 25 minutes.
- Test with a wooden toothpick, if it comes out clean, the muffins are done.
- Transfer the muffins to a wire rack and leave to cool completely.

Sundried Tomato and Caper Muffins

 872

- Add 2 tbsp of capers to the cake mixture.

873

SERVES 8

Artichoke and Pine Nut Loaf Cake

PREPARATION TIME 10 MINUTES

COOKING TIME 55 MINUTES

INGREDIENTS

300 g / 10 ½ oz / 2 cup self-raising flour
2 tsp baking powder
250 g / 9 oz / 1 ¼ cup butter, softened
4 large eggs
75 g / 2 ½ oz / ¾ cup Parmesan, grated
300 g / 11 oz / 1 ½ cup artichoke hearts in oil, drained & sliced
75 g / 2 ½ oz / ⅔ cup pine nuts

- Preheat the oven to 170°C (150° fan), gas 3 and line a large loaf tin with non-stick baking paper.
- Sieve the flour and baking powder into a mixing bowl and add the butter, eggs and Parmesan.
- Beat the mixture with an electric whisk for 4 minutes or until smooth and well whipped.
- Fold in the sliced artichokes and pine nuts then scrape the mixture into the loaf tin.
- Bake for 55 minutes or until a skewer inserted in the centre comes out clean.
- Transfer the cake to a wire rack and leave to cool completely before serving.

Artichoke and Pesto Loaf Cake

874

- Add 4 tbsp of pesto to the cake mixture.

Smoked Bacon and Feta Loaf Cake

875

SERVES 8

- Preheat the oven to 170°C (150° fan), gas 3 and line a large loaf tin with non-stick baking paper.
- Sieve the flour and baking powder into a mixing bowl and add the butter and eggs.
- Beat the mixture with an electric whisk for 4 minutes or until smooth and well whipped.
- Fold in the feta and smoked bacon then scrape the mixture into the loaf tin.
- Bake for 55 minutes or until a skewer inserted in the centre comes out clean.
- Transfer the cake to a wire rack and leave to cool completely before serving.

PREPARATION TIME 10 MINUTES

COOKING TIME 55 MINUTES

INGREDIENTS

300 g / 10 ½ oz / 2 cup self-raising flour
2 tsp baking powder
250 g / 9 oz / 1 ¼ cup butter, softened
5 large eggs
150 g / 5 oz feta, cubed
150 g / 5 oz smoked streaky bacon, cubed

Bacon and Egg Loaf Cake

876

- Soft-boil and peel 4 eggs. Spoon half the cake mixture into the tin, then arrange the eggs in a line down the centre of the tin before topping with the rest of the cake mixture and baking as before.

Chicken and Tarragon Loaf Cake

877

MAKES 12

- Preheat the oven to 180°C (160° fan), gas 4 and line a loaf tin with greaseproof paper.
- Fry the chicken breast pieces in the oil for 5 minutes or until cooked through. Leave to cool.
- Beat the eggs in a jug with the oil, yoghurt and cheese until well mixed.
- Mix the chicken, tarragon, flour, raising agents and salt in a bowl, then pour in the egg mixture and stir just enough to combine.
- Scrape the mixture into the tin, then bake in the oven for 20 – 25 minutes.
- Test with a wooden toothpick, if it comes out clean, the cake is done.
- Transfer the loaf to a wire rack and leave to cool completely.

PREPARATION TIME 25 MINUTES

COOKING TIME 20-25 MINUTES

INGREDIENTS

2 skinless chicken breasts, cubed
2 tbsp olive oil
2 large eggs
120 ml / 4 fl. oz / ½ cup sunflower oil
180 ml / 6 fl. oz / ⅔ cup Greek yoghurt
110 g / 4 oz / 1 cup Parmesan, grated
2 tbsp tarragon leaves, chopped
225 g / 8 oz / 1 ½ cup plain (all purpose) flour
2 tsp baking powder
½ tsp bicarbonate of soda
½ tsp salt

Chicken and Tarragon Muffins

878

- Bake the mixture in a 12-hole silicone muffin tray and reduce the cooking time to 30 minutes.

879

SERVES 8

Red Onion and Rosemary Loaf Cake

PREPARATION TIME 10 MINUTES

COOKING TIME 55 MINUTES

....

INGREDIENTS

2 red onions, sliced
2 tbsp olive oil
300 g / 10 ½ oz / 2 cup self-raising flour
2 tsp baking powder
250 g / 9 oz / 1 ¼ cup butter, softened
5 large eggs
2 tbsp rosemary leaves

- Preheat the oven to 170⁰C (150⁰ fan), gas 3 and line a loaf tin with a paper case.
- Fry the onions in the oil for 10 minutes or until softened and starting to caramelise. Leave to cool.
- Sieve the flour and baking powder into a mixing bowl and add the butter and eggs.
- Beat the mixture with an electric whisk for 4 minutes or until smooth and well whipped.
- Fold in the onions and rosemary then scrape the mixture into the loaf tin.
- Bake for 55 minutes or until a skewer inserted comes out clean.
- Transfer the cake to a wire rack and leave to cool completely before serving.

Red Onion and Thyme Loaf Cake   880

- Replace the rosemary with fresh thyme.

881

MAKES 1 LOAF

Chorizo Bread

PREPARATION TIME 2 HOURS
30 MINUTES

COOKING TIME 35-40 MINUTES

....

INGREDIENTS

400 g / 14 oz / 2 ⅔ cups strong white bread flour, plus extra for dusting
½ tsp easy blend dried yeast
1 tbsp caster (superfine) sugar
1 tsp fine sea salt
200 g / 7 oz chorizo slices, chopped

- In a large bowl, mix together the flour, yeast, sugar and salt. Stir in the chorizo and 280 ml of warm water.
- Knead the mixture on a lightly oiled surface with your hands for 10 minutes or until the dough is elastic.
- Leave the dough to rest in a lightly oiled bowl, covered with oiled clingfilm, for 1 – 2 hours.
- Punch the dough with your fist to knock out the air then knead it for 2 more minutes. Cup your hands around the dough and move it in a circular motion whilst pressing down to form a tight round loaf.
- Transfer the dough to a greased round cake tin and cover with oiled clingfilm. Leave to prove for 1 hour.
- Meanwhile, preheat the oven to 220⁰C (200⁰ fan), 430F, gas 7.
- Bake for 35 – 40 minutes or until the loaf sounds hollow when you tap it underneath. Transfer the bread to a wire rack and leave to cool completely before slicing.

Chorizo and Thyme Bread   882

- Add 2 tbsp of fresh thyme leaves to the flour before adding the water.

883

SERVES 8

Bacon and Chicory Tarte Tatin

Chicory and Stilton Tarte Tatin

884

- Replace the bacon with 100 g of Stilton, cut into small cubes.

Leek and Bacon Tarte Tatin

885

- Replace the chicory with 6 leeks. Remove the green part of the stem and cut each leek lengthways in half.

PREPARATION TIME 10 MINUTES

COOKING TIME 25 MINUTES

INGREDIENTS

2 tbsp olive oil
4 rashers streaky bacon, chopped
4 small heads chicory, halved
250 g / 9 oz all-butter puff pastry

- Preheat the oven to 220°C (200° fan), gas 7.
- Heat the oil in a large ovenproof frying pan and fry the bacon for 5 minutes or until browned. Remove it from the pan with a slotted spoon and reserve.
- Arrange the chicory in the pan, cut side up and cook over a medium heat for 5 minutes until it starts to soften.
- Turn the chicory over so it lays cut side down and sprinkle over the bacon pieces. Season with salt and pepper.
- Roll out the pastry on a floured surface and cut out a circle the same size as the frying pan.
- Lay the pastry over the chicory and tuck in the edges then transfer the pan to the oven and bake for 25 minutes or until the pastry is golden brown and cooked through.
- Using oven gloves, put a large plate on top of the frying pan and turn them both over in one smooth movement to unmould the tart.

886

MAKES 24

Chorizo and Olive Canapés

PREPARATION TIME 10 MINUTES

COOKING TIME 10-15 MINUTES

....

INGREDIENTS

250 g / 9 oz all-butter puff pastry
1 egg, beaten
8 slices chorizo, finely chopped
10 green olives, pitted and sliced
60 g / 2 oz / ½ cup Parmesan, finely grated

- Preheat the oven to 220°C (200° fan), 430F, gas 7 and line a baking tray with non-stick baking paper.
- Roll out the pastry on a floured surface until 3 mm thick.
- Use a round cookie cutter to cut out discs of the pastry and transfer them to the prepared baking tray.
- Brush the surface with egg and scatter over the chorizo and olives.
- Sprinkle over the grated Parmesan then bake for 10 – 15 minutes or until golden brown and cooked through.
- Transfer the pastries to a wire rack to cool a little and serve warm.

Pine Nut and Sundried Tomato Canapés   887

- Replace the chorizo and olives with pine nuts and finely chopped sundried tomatoes.

888

MAKES 1 LOAF

Bacon and Black Olive Bread

PREPARATION TIME 2 HOURS
30 MINUTES

COOKING TIME 35-40 MINUTES

....

INGREDIENTS

400 g / 14 oz / 2 ⅔ cups strong white bread flour, plus extra for dusting
½ tsp easy blend dried yeast
1 tbsp caster (superfine) sugar
1 tsp fine sea salt
100 g / 3 ½ oz streaky bacon, chopped
100 g / 3 ½ oz / ⅔ cup black olives, pitted and sliced

- Mix together the flour, yeast, sugar and salt. Stir in the bacon, olives and 280 ml of warm water.
- Knead the mixture on a lightly oiled surface for 10 minutes or until the dough is smooth and elastic.
- Leave the dough to rest in a lightly oiled bowl, covered with oiled clingfilm, for 1 – 2 hours.
- Knead the dough for 2 more minutes then roll it into a fat sausage. Turn it 90° and roll it tightly the other way then tuck the ends under and transfer the dough to the tin, keeping the seam underneath.
- Cover the tin loosely with oiled clingfilm and leave to prove for 45 minutes.
- Preheat the oven to 220°C (200° fan), 430F, gas 7.
- Bake for 35 – 40 minutes or until the underneath sounds hollow when tapped.
- Leave to cool completely on a wire rack before slicing.

Bacon and Artichoke Bread   889

- Replace the olives with preserved artichokes in oil, roughly chopped.

890

MAKES 1 LOAF Courgette and Feta Loaf Cake

- Preheat the oven to 170°C (150° fan), 340F, gas 3 and either line a loaf tin with non-stick baking paper or grease a 12-hole silicone muffin mould.
- Sieve the flour and baking powder into a mixing bowl and add the butter and eggs.
- Beat the mixture with an electric whisk for 4 minutes or until smooth and well whipped.
- Fold in the feta and courgette then scrape the mixture into the loaf tin or muffin mould.
- Bake for 55 minutes for the loaf or 25 minutes for the muffins, or until a skewer inserted in the centre comes out clean.
- Transfer the cake to a wire rack and leave to cool completely before serving.

PREPARATION TIME 10 MINUTES

COOKING TIME 55 MINUTES

INGREDIENTS

300 g / 10 ½ oz / 2 cup self-raising flour
2 tsp baking powder
250 g / 9 oz / 1 ¼ cup butter, softened
5 large eggs
150 g / 5 oz feta, cubed
1 courgette (zucchini), grated

Courgette and Caraway Loaf Cake

891

- Omit the feta and add 1 tsp of caraway seeds to the flour.

892

SERVES 8 Aubergine, Feta and Pesto Loaf Cake

- Preheat the oven to 180°C (160° fan), 355F, gas 4 and line a loaf tin with greaseproof paper.
- Brush the aubergines with oil and spread out on a baking tray. Sprinkle with salt and pepper then roast for 15 minutes or until softened. Leave to cool.
- Beat the eggs in a jug with the oil, yoghurt and pesto until well mixed.
- Mix the feta, aubergine, flour, raising agents and salt in a bowl, then pour in the egg mixture and stir just enough to combine.
- Scrape the mixture into the tin, then bake in the oven for 20 – 25 minutes.
- Test with a wooden toothpick, if it comes out clean, the cake is done.
- Transfer the loaf to a wire rack and leave to cool completely.

PREPARATION TIME 25 MINUTES

COOKING TIME 20-25 MINUTES

INGREDIENTS

1 aubergine (eggplant), quartered and sliced
2 tbsp olive oil
2 large eggs
120 ml / 4 fl. oz / ½ cup sunflower oil
180 ml / 6 fl. oz / ⅔ cup Greek yoghurt
110 g / 4 oz / ⅓ cup pesto
110 g / 4 oz feta, cubed
225 g / 8 oz / 1 ½ cup plain (all purpose) flour
2 tsp baking powder
½ tsp bicarbonate of soda
½ tsp salt

Aubergine and Tapenade Loaf Cake

893

- Replace the pesto with an equal quantity of green olive tapenade.

894

SERVES 8

Courgette, Cheese and Salmon Loaf

Courgette and Smoked Mackerel Loaf Cake

895

- Replace the smoked salmon with flaked smoked mackerel.

Asparagus and Smoked Salmon Loaf Cake

896

- Use a vegetable peeler to cut 100 g of asparagus into long strips and use in place of the courgette.

PREPARATION TIME 25 MINUTES

COOKING TIME 20-25 MINUTES

INGREDIENTS

2 small courgettes
2 large eggs
120 ml / 4 fl. oz / ½ cup sunflower oil
180 ml / 6 fl. oz / ⅔ cup Greek yoghurt
110 g / 4 oz / ⅓ cup cottage cheese
110 g / 4 oz / 1 ½ cup smoked salmon, chopped
225 g / 8 oz / 1 ½ cup plain (all purpose) flour
2 tsp baking powder
½ tsp bicarbonate of soda
½ tsp salt

- Preheat the oven to 180°C (160° fan), 355F, gas 4 and line a loaf tin with greaseproof paper.
- Use a vegetable peeler to make the courgettes into long thin strips.
- Beat the eggs in a jug with the oil, yoghurt and cottage cheese until well mixed.
- Mix the salmon, courgette strips, flour, raising agents and salt in a bowl, then pour in the egg mixture and stir just enough to combine.
- Scrape the mixture into the tin, then bake in the oven for 20 – 25 minutes.
- Test with a wooden toothpick, if it comes out clean, the cake is done.
- Transfer the loaf to a wire rack and leave to cool completely.

897
SERVES 8

Cheese and Chive Loaf Cake

- Preheat the oven to 180°C (160° fan), 355F, gas 4 and line a loaf tin with greaseproof paper.
- Beat the eggs in a jug with the oil, yoghurt, Cheddar and chives until well mixed.
- Mix the flour, raising agents and salt in a bowl, then pour in the egg mixture and stir just enough to combine.
- Scrape the mixture into the tin, then bake in the oven for 20 – 25 minutes.
- Test with a wooden toothpick, if it comes out clean, the cake is done.
- Transfer the loaf to a wire rack and leave to cool completely.

PREPARATION TIME 25 MINUTES

COOKING TIME 20-25 MINUTES

INGREDIENTS

2 large eggs
120 ml / 4 fl. oz / ½ cup sunflower oil
180 ml / 6 fl. oz / ⅔ cup Greek yoghurt
110 g / 4 oz / 1 cup Cheddar, grated
3 tbsp chives, finely chopped
225 g / 8 oz / 1 ½ cup plain (all purpose) flour
2 tsp baking powder
½ tsp bicarbonate of soda
½ tsp salt

Cheese and Spring Onion Loaf Cake

898

- Replace the chives with 4 chopped spring onions.

899
SERVES 8

Herby Loaf Cake

- Preheat the oven to 170°C (150° fan), 340F, gas 3 and line a large loaf tin with non-stick baking paper.
- Sieve the flour and baking powder into a mixing bowl and add the butter and eggs.
- Beat the mixture with an electric whisk for 4 minutes or until smooth and well whipped.
- Fold in the herbs then scrape the mixture into the loaf tin.
- Bake for 55 minutes or until a skewer inserted in the centre comes out clean.
- Transfer the cake to a wire rack and leave to cool completely before serving.

PREPARATION TIME 10 MINUTES

COOKING TIME 55 MINUTES

INGREDIENTS

300 g / 10 ½ oz / 2 cup self-raising flour
2 tsp baking powder
250 g / 9 oz / 1 ¼ cup butter, softened
5 large eggs
2 tbsp flat leaf parsley, chopped
2 tbsp chives, chopped
2 tbsp tarragon, chopped

Herb and Spice Loaf Cake

900

- Add a finely chopped red chilli and ½ tsp each of crushed coriander seeds and crushed cumin seeds.

901

SERVES 8

Fig and Prosciutto Loaf

PREPARATION TIME 10 MINUTES

COOKING TIME 55 MINUTES

....

INGREDIENTS

300 g / 10 ½ oz / 2 cup self-raising
flour
2 tsp baking powder
250 g / 9 oz / 1 ¼ cup butter, softened
5 large eggs
4 fresh figs, cut into eighths
6 slices prosciutto, chopped
2 tbsp fresh thyme leaves

- Preheat the oven to 170°C (150° fan), 340F, gas 3 and line a large loaf tin with non-stick baking paper.
- Sieve the flour and baking powder into a mixing bowl and add the butter and eggs.
- Beat the mixture with an electric whisk for 4 minutes or until smooth and well whipped.
- Fold in the figs, prosciutto and thyme then scrape the mixture into the loaf tin.
- Bake for 55 minutes or until a skewer inserted in the centre comes out clean.
- Transfer the cake to a wire rack and leave to cool completely before serving.

Fig and Roquefort Loaf Cake

902

- Replace the prosciutto with 100 g of cubed Roquefort.

903

SERVES 8

Feta, Ham and Broccoli Loaf

PREPARATION TIME 10 MINUTES

COOKING TIME 55 MINUTES

....

INGREDIENTS

300 g / 10 ½ oz / 2 cup self-raising
flour
2 tsp baking powder
250 g / 9 oz / 1 ¼ cup butter, softened
5 large eggs
75 g / 2 ½ oz feta, cubed
4 slices ham, chopped
75 g / 2 ½ oz broccoli, finely chopped

- Preheat the oven to 170°C (150° fan), 340F, gas 3 and line a large loaf tin with non-stick baking paper.
- Sieve the flour and baking powder into a mixing bowl and add the butter and eggs.
- Beat the mixture with an electric whisk for 4 minutes or until smooth and well whipped.
- Fold in the feta, ham and broccoli then scrape the mixture into the loaf tin.
- Bake for 55 minutes or until a skewer inserted in the centre comes out clean.
- Transfer the cake to a wire rack and leave to cool completely before serving.

Feta, Ham and Broccoli Muffins

904

- Bake the mixture in a 12-hole muffin tin and reduce the cooking time to 35 minutes.

SERVES 8

Feta, Olive and Roasted Pepper Loaf

905

- Preheat the oven to 170⁰C (150⁰ fan), 340F, gas 3 and line a large loaf tin with non-stick baking paper.
- Sieve the flour and baking powder into a mixing bowl and add the butter and eggs.
- Beat the mixture with an electric whisk for 4 minutes or until smooth and well whipped.
- Fold in the olives, peppers and feta then scrape the mixture into the loaf tin.
- Bake for 55 minutes or until a skewer inserted in the centre comes out clean.
- Transfer the cake to a wire rack and leave to cool completely before serving.

PREPARATION TIME 10 MINUTES

COOKING TIME 55 MINUTES

INGREDIENTS

300 g / 10 ½ oz / 2 cup self-raising flour
2 tsp baking powder
250 g / 9 oz / 1 ¼ cup butter, softened
5 large eggs
75 g / 2 ½ oz black olives, pitted and sliced
75 g / 2 ½ oz chopped roasted peppers in oil, drained
75 g / 2 ½ oz feta, cubed

Wholemeal Mediterranean Loaf Cake

906

- Use wholemeal self-raising flour in place of the usual self raising flour.

SERVES 8

Gorgonzola, Rosemary and Honey Loaf

907

- Preheat the oven to 170⁰C (150⁰ fan), 340F, gas 3 and line a large loaf tin with non-stick baking paper.
- Sieve the flour and baking powder into a mixing bowl and add the rosemary, butter, eggs and honey.
- Beat the mixture with an electric whisk for 4 minutes or until smooth and well whipped.
- Spoon half of the mixture into the loaf tin and scatter over the Gorgonzola.
- Top with the remaining cake mixture and bake for 55 minutes or until a skewer inserted in the centre comes out clean.
- Transfer the cake to a wire rack and leave to cool completely before serving.

PREPARATION TIME 10 MINUTES

COOKING TIME 55 MINUTES

INGREDIENTS

300 g / 10 ½ oz / 2 cup self-raising flour
2 tsp baking powder
2 tbsp rosemary, finely chopped
250 g / 9 oz / 1 ¼ cup butter, softened
5 large eggs
4 tbsp runny honey
110 g / 4 oz Gorgonzola, cubed

Fig, Rosemary and Honey Loaf Cake

 908

- Replace the Gorgonzola with 4 finely chopped dried figs.

909

SERVES 8

Ham, French Bean and Carrot Loaf

PREPARATION TIME 10 MINUTES

COOKING TIME 55 MINUTES

INGREDIENTS

2 carrots, diced
100 g / 3 ½ oz French beans, chopped
300 g / 10 ½ oz / 2 cup self-raising flour
2 tsp baking powder
250 g / 9 oz / 1 ¼ cup butter, softened
5 large eggs
100 g / 3 ½ oz ham, chopped

- Preheat the oven to 170°C (150° fan), 340F, gas 3 and line a large loaf tin with non-stick baking paper.
- Blanch the carrots and beans in boiling salted water for 5 minutes then plunge into cold water and drain well.
- Sieve the flour and baking powder into a mixing bowl and add the butter and eggs.
- Beat the mixture with an electric whisk for 4 minutes or until smooth and well whipped.
- Fold in the vegetables and ham then scrape the mixture into the loaf tin.
- Bake for 55 minutes or until a skewer inserted in the centre comes out clean.
- Transfer the cake to a wire rack and leave to cool completely before serving.

Carrot, Bean and Chorizo Loaf Cake

910

- Replace the ham with 100 g of chorizo in small cubes.

911

SERVES 8

Bacon and Olive Loaf

PREPARATION TIME 25 MINUTES

COOKING TIME 20-25 MINUTES

INGREDIENTS

2 large eggs
120 ml / 4 fl. oz / ½ cup sunflower oil
180 ml / 6 fl. oz / ¾ cup Greek yoghurt
110 g / 4 oz streaky bacon, chopped
55 g / 2 oz / ⅓ cup green olives, pitted and sliced
55 g / 2 oz / ⅓ cup black olives, pitted and sliced
225 g / 8 oz / 1 ½ cup plain (all purpose) flour
2 tsp baking powder
½ tsp bicarbonate of soda
½ tsp salt

- Preheat the oven to 180°C (160° fan), 355F, gas 4 and line a loaf tin with greaseproof paper.
- Beat the eggs in a jug with the oil, yoghurt, bacon and olives until well mixed.
- Mix the flour, raising agents and salt in a bowl, then pour in the egg mixture and stir just enough to combine.
- Scrape the mixture into the tin, then bake in the oven for 20 – 25 minutes.
- Test with a wooden toothpick, if it comes out clean, the cake is done.
- Transfer the loaf to a wire rack and leave to cool completely.

Bacon and Basil Loaf Cake

912

- Omit the olives and stir 3 tbsp of shredded basil leaves into the cake mixture.

Cheese and Herb Loaf

913

SERVES 8

Cheese, Herb and Pine Nut Loaf Cake

914

- Add 2 tbsp toasted pine nuts to the cake mixture.

Cheese, Herb and Chestnut Loaf Cake

915

- Add 75 g of chopped, cooked chestnuts to the cake mixture.

PREPARATION TIME 10 MINUTES

COOKING TIME 55 MINUTES

INGREDIENTS

300 g / 10 ½ oz / 2 cup self-raising flour
2 tsp baking powder
250 g / 9 oz / 1 ¼ cup butter, softened
5 large eggs
100 g / 3 ½ oz / 1 cup Cheddar, grated
2 tbsp flat leaf parsley, chopped
2 tbsp chives, chopped

- Preheat the oven to 170°C (150° fan), 340F, gas 3 and line a large loaf tin with non-stick baking paper.
- Sieve the flour and baking powder into a mixing bowl and add the butter and eggs.
- Beat the mixture with an electric whisk for 4 minutes or until smooth and well whipped.
- Fold in the cheese and herbs then scrape the mixture into the loaf tin.
- Bake for 55 minutes or until a skewer inserted in the centre comes out clean.
- Transfer the cake to a wire rack and leave to cool completely before serving.

916

SERVES 10

Chicken, Olive and Sundried Tomato Loaf

PREPARATION TIME 25 MINUTES

COOKING TIME 20-25 MINUTES

INGREDIENTS

2 skinless chicken breasts, cubed
2 tbsp olive oil
2 large eggs
120 ml / 4 fl. oz / ½ cup sunflower oil
180 ml / 6 fl. oz / ¾ cup Greek yoghurt
110 g / 4 oz / 1 cup Parmesan, grated
75 g / 2 ½ oz / ⅓ cup sundried tomatoes in oil, drained
75 g / 2 ½ oz / ½ cup black olives, pitted and chopped
225 g / 8 oz / 1 ½ cup plain (all purpose) flour
2 tsp baking powder
½ tsp bicarbonate of soda
½ tsp salt

- Preheat the oven to 180°C (160° fan), gas 4 and line a long, thin loaf tin with greaseproof paper.
- Fry the chicken breast pieces in the oil for 5 minutes or until cooked through. Leave to cool.
- Beat the eggs in a jug with the oil, yoghurt and cheese until well mixed.
- Mix the chicken, tomatoes, olives, flour, raising agents and salt in a bowl, then pour in the egg mixture and stir just enough to combine.
- Scrape the mixture into the tin, then bake in the oven for 20 – 25 minutes.
- Test with a wooden toothpick, if it comes out clean, the cake is done.
- Transfer the loaf to a wire rack and leave to cool completely before slicing.

Chicken and Artichoke Loaf Cake   **917**

- Replace the olives and sundried tomatoes with 150 g of preserved artichokes in oil, roughly chopped.

918

SERVES 8

Ham and Mushroom Slice

PREPARATION TIME 10 MINUTES

COOKING TIME 20-25 MINUTES

INGREDIENTS

500 ml / 17 ½ fl. oz / 2 cups milk
35 g / 1 ¼ oz butter
2 tbsp plain (all purpose) flour
100 g / 3 ½ oz button mushrooms, chopped
100 g / 3 ½ oz ham, cubed
450 g / 1 lb all-butter puff pastry
1 egg, beaten

- Preheat the oven to 220°C (200° fan), 430F, gas 7.
- Heat the milk to simmering point and set aside.
- Heat the butter in a small saucepan and stir in the flour. Slowly add the hot milk, stirring constantly, and cook until the sauce is thick and smooth.
- Stir in the mushrooms and ham and season with salt and pepper, then leave to cool completely.
- Roll out the pastry and divide into 2 equal rectangles.
- Transfer one rectangle to a baking tray and spread over the filling, leaving a 2 cm border round the outside.
- Brush the edge of the pastry with beaten egg and lay the other pastry sheet on top. Squeeze the edges to seal and trim the pastry to neaten.
- Score a pattern on top with a sharp knife.
- Bake in the oven for 25 - 35 minutes or until the top is golden brown.

Chicken and Mushroom Slice   **919**

- Replace the ham with an equal weight of chopped cooked chicken breast.

920

SERVES 6-8

Onion and Thyme Quiche

- Rub the butter into the flour until the mixture resembles breadcrumbs, stir in enough cold water to bind; chill for 30 minutes.
- Preheat the oven to 190°C (170° fan), 375F, gas 5.
- Roll out the pastry and use it to line a square tart tin.
- Prick the pastry, line with clingfilm and fill with baking beans or rice. Bake for 10 minutes then remove the clingfilm and baking beans.
- Brush with beaten egg and bake for 8 minutes. Lower the oven to 150°C (130° fan), 300F, gas 2
- Fry the onions in the butter for 15 minutes. Add the garlic and cook for 2 more minutes.
- Whisk the eggs with the double cream then stir in the onions, thyme and half of the Gruyere. Season with salt and pepper.
- Pour the filling into the pastry case and scatter the rest of the cheese on top. Bake for 35 - 40 minutes.

Chorizo and Onion Quiche
921

- Add 100 g of chorizo in small cubes when you fry the garlic.

PREPARATION TIME 1 HOUR

COOKING TIME 35-40 MINUTES

INGREDIENTS

3 onions, thinly sliced
50 g / 1 ¾ oz / ¼ cup butter
2 cloves garlic, crushed
3 large eggs
225 ml / 8 fl. oz / ¾ cup double cream
2 tbsp thyme leaves
150 g / 5 ½ oz / 1 ½ cups Gruyere, grated

FOR THE PASTRY
100 g / 3 ½ oz / ½ cup butter, cubed
200 g / 7 oz / 1 ⅓ cups plain (all purpose) flour
1 large egg, beaten

922

SERVES 8

Pear and Roquefort Loaf

- Preheat the oven to 170°C (150° fan), 340F, gas 3 and line a large loaf tin with non-stick baking paper.
- Sieve the flour and baking powder into a mixing bowl and add the butter and eggs.
- Beat the mixture with an electric whisk for 4 minutes or until smooth and well whipped.
- Fold in the pear and Roquefort then scrape the mixture into the loaf tin.
- Bake for 55 minutes or until a skewer inserted in the centre comes out clean.
- Transfer the cake to a wire rack and leave to cool completely before serving.

Pear, Roquefort and Walnut Loaf Cake
 923

- Add 75 g of chopped walnuts to the cake mixture.

PREPARATION TIME 10 MINUTES

COOKING TIME 55 MINUTES

INGREDIENTS

300 g / 10 ½ oz / 2 cup self-raising flour
2 tsp baking powder
250 g / 9 oz / 1 ¼ cup butter, softened
5 large eggs
2 pears, peeled, cored and chopped
150 g / 5 ½ oz Roquefort, cubed

924

SERVES 8

Mushroom and Prosciutto Loaf

PREPARATION TIME 10 MINUTES

COOKING TIME 55 MINUTES

INGREDIENTS

300 g / 10 ½ oz / 2 cup self-raising flour
2 tsp baking powder
250 g / 9 oz / 1 ¼ cup butter, softened
5 large eggs
200 g / 7 oz button mushrooms, sliced
6 slices prosciutto, chopped

- Preheat the oven to 170°C (150° fan), 340F, gas 3 and line a large loaf tin with non-stick baking paper.
- Sieve the flour and baking powder into a mixing bowl and add the butter and eggs.
- Beat the mixture with an electric whisk for 4 minutes or until smooth and well whipped.
- Fold in the mushrooms and prosciutto then scrape the mixture into the loaf tin.
- Bake for 55 minutes or until a skewer inserted in the centre comes out clean.
- Transfer the cake to a wire rack and leave to cool completely before serving.

925

SERVES 8

Salmon, Dill and Goats' Cheese Loaf

PREPARATION TIME 15 MINUTES

COOKING TIME 30-35 MINUTES

INGREDIENTS

2 large eggs
120 ml / 4 fl. oz / ½ cup sunflower oil
180 ml / 6 fl. oz / ⅔ cup Greek yoghurt
110 g / 4 oz goats' cheese, cubed
110 g / 4 oz smoked salmon, chopped
2 tbsp dill, chopped
225 g / 8 oz / 1 ½ cup plain (all purpose) flour
2 tsp baking powder
½ tsp bicarbonate of soda
½ tsp salt

- Preheat the oven to 180°C (160° fan), 355F, gas 4 and line a loaf tin with greaseproof paper.
- Beat the eggs in a jug with the oil, yoghurt and goats' cheese until well mixed.
- Mix the salmon, dill, flour, raising agents and salt in a bowl, then pour in the egg mixture and stir just enough to combine.
- Scrape the mixture into the tin, then bake in the oven for 30 – 35 minutes.
- Test with a wooden toothpick, if it comes out clean, the cake is done.
- Transfer the loaf to a wire rack and leave to cool completely.

926

SERVES 8

Tuna and Cream Cheese Loaf Cake

- Preheat the oven to 180°C (160° fan), 355F, gas 4 and line a loaf tin with greaseproof paper.
- Beat the eggs in a jug with the oil, yoghurt and cream cheese until well mixed.
- Mix the tuna, flour, raising agents and salt in a bowl, then pour in the egg mixture and stir just enough to combine.
- Scrape the mixture into the tin, then bake in the oven for 30 – 35 minutes.
- Test with a wooden toothpick, if it comes out clean, the cake is done.
- Transfer the loaf to a wire rack and leave to cool completely.

PREPARATION TIME 10 MINUTES

COOKING TIME 30-35 MINUTES

INGREDIENTS

2 large eggs
120 ml / 4 fl. oz / ½ cup sunflower oil
180 ml / 6 fl. oz / ⅔ cup Greek yoghurt
3 tbsp cream cheese
300 g / 10 ½ oz canned tuna, drained
225 g / 8 oz / 1 ½ cup plain (all purpose) flour
2 tsp baking powder
½ tsp bicarbonate of soda
½ tsp salt

Pine Nut and Herb Loaf

927

SERVES 8

PREPARATION TIME 10 MINUTES

COOKING TIME 55 MINUTES

INGREDIENTS

300 g / 10 ½ oz / 2 cup self-raising flour
2 tsp baking powder
250 g / 9 oz / 1 ¼ cup butter, softened

5 large eggs
4 tbsp pine nuts
2 tbsp fresh thyme leaves
2 tbsp chives, chopped

- Preheat the oven to 170°C (150° fan), 340F, gas 3 and line a large loaf tin with non-stick baking paper.
- Sieve the flour and baking powder into a mixing bowl and add the butter and eggs.
- Beat the mixture with an electric whisk for 4 minutes or until smooth and well whipped.
- Fold in the pine nuts, thyme and chives then scrape the mixture into the loaf tin.
- Bake for 55 minutes or until a skewer inserted in the centre comes out clean.
- Transfer the cake to a wire rack and leave to cool completely before serving.

Courgette and Beetroot Loaf

928

SERVES 10

PREPARATION TIME 10 MINUTES

COOKING TIME 55 MINUTES

INGREDIENTS

300 g / 10 ½ oz / 2 cup self-raising flour
2 tsp baking powder
250 g / 9 oz / 1 ¼ cup butter, softened

5 large eggs
1 courgette (zucchini), quartered and sliced
2 tbsp thyme leaves
2 cooked beetroots, cubed

- Preheat the oven to 170°C (150° fan), 340F, gas 3 and line a loaf tin with non-stick baking paper.
- Sieve the flour and baking powder into a mixing bowl and add the butter and eggs.
- Beat the mixture with an electric whisk for 4 minutes or until smooth and well whipped.
- Fold in the courgette, thyme and beetroot then scrape the mixture into the loaf tin.
- Bake for 55 minutes or until a skewer inserted in the centre comes out clean.
- Transfer the cake to a wire rack and leave to cool completely before serving.

929

SERVES 8

Three Cheese Loaf Cake

PREPARATION TIME 10 MINUTES

COOKING TIME 20-25 MINUTES

INGREDIENTS

2 large eggs
120 ml / 4 fl. oz / ½ cup sunflower oil
180 ml / 6 fl. oz / ⅔ cup Greek yoghurt
110 g / 4 oz / 1 cup Cheddar, grated
110 g / 4 oz goat's cheese, cubed
110 g / 4 oz Roquefort, cubed
225 g / 8 oz / 1 ½ cup plain (all purpose) flour
2 tsp baking powder
½ tsp bicarbonate of soda
½ tsp salt

- Preheat the oven to 180°C (160° fan), 355F, gas 4 and line a loaf tin with greaseproof paper.
- Beat the eggs in a jug with the oil, yoghurt and cheeses until well mixed.
- Mix the flour, raising agents and salt in a bowl, then pour in the egg mixture and stir just enough to combine.
- Scrape the mixture into the tin, then bake in the oven for 20 – 25 minutes.
- Test with a wooden toothpick, if it comes out clean, the cake is done.
- Transfer the loaf to a wire rack and leave to cool completely.

Four Cheese Loaf Cake   930

- Spoon half the mixture into the tin then add a layer of sliced mozzarella before topping with the rest of the cake mixture.

931

SERVES 8

Cherry Tomato Loaf Cake

PREPARATION TIME 15 MINUTES

COOKING TIME 30-35 MINUTES

INGREDIENTS

2 large eggs
120 ml / 4 fl. oz / ½ cup sunflower oil
180 ml / 6 fl. oz / ⅔ cup Greek yoghurt
110 g / 4 oz / 1 cup Parmesan, grated
450 g / 1 lb cherry tomatoes
225 g / 8 oz / 1 ½ cup plain (all purpose) flour
2 tsp baking powder
½ tsp bicarbonate of soda
½ tsp salt

- Preheat the oven to 180°C (160° fan), 355F, gas 4 and line a loaf tin with greaseproof paper.
- Beat the eggs in a jug with the oil, yoghurt and Parmesan until well mixed.
- Mix the flour, raising agents and salt in a bowl, then pour in the egg mixture.
- Reserve 16 of the tomatoes and cut the rest into quarters. Add them to the bowl and stir everything just enough to combine.
- Scrape the mixture into the tin, and stud with the reserved tomatoes.
- Bake in the oven for 30 – 35 minutes.
- Test with a wooden toothpick, if it comes out clean, the cake is done.
- Transfer the loaf to a wire rack and leave to cool completely.

Tomato and Bacon Loaf Cake   932

- Add 100 g of smoked bacon lardons to the cake mixture.

933

MAKES 24

Olive and Rosemary Mini Muffins

Goat's Cheese and Rosemary Mini Muffins

934

- Replace the olives with 150 g of goat's cheese in small cubes.

Chorizo and Rosemary Mini Muffins

935

- Replace the olives with 100 g of chorizo in small cubes.

PREPARATION TIME 15 MINUTES

COOKING TIME 10-15 MINUTES

....

INGREDIENTS

2 large eggs
120 ml / 4 fl. oz / ½ cup sunflower oil
180 ml / 6 fl. oz / ⅔ cup Greek yoghurt
2 tbsp Parmesan, finely grated
225 g / 8 oz / 1 ½ cup plain (all purpose) flour
2 tsp baking powder
½ tsp bicarbonate of soda
½ tsp salt
75 g / 2 ½ oz / ½ cup black olives, stoned and chopped
2 tbsp fresh rosemary, chopped

- Preheat the oven to 180°C (160° fan), 350F, gas 4 and line a 24-hole mini muffin tin with paper cases.
- Beat the egg in a jug with the oil, yoghurt and cheese until well mixed.
- Mix the flour, raising agents, salt, olives and rosemary in a bowl, then pour in the egg mixture and stir just enough to combine.
- Divide the mixture between the paper cases, then bake in the oven for 10 – 15 minutes.
- Test with a wooden toothpick, if it comes out clean, the muffins are done.
- Serve warm.

936

SERVES 8

Cream Cheese and Salmon Loaf

PREPARATION TIME 15 MINUTES

COOKING TIME 30-35 MINUTES

INGREDIENTS

2 large eggs
120 ml / 4 fl. oz / ½ cup sunflower oil
180 ml / 6 fl. oz / ⅔ cup Greek yoghurt
3 tbsp cream cheese
110 g / 4 oz smoked salmon, chopped
2 tbsp dill, chopped
225 g / 8 oz / 1 ½ cup plain (all purpose) flour
2 tsp baking powder
½ tsp bicarbonate of soda
½ tsp salt

- Preheat the oven to 180°C (160° fan), 355F, gas 4 and line a loaf tin with greaseproof paper.
- Beat the eggs in a jug with the oil, yoghurt and cream cheese until well mixed.
- Mix the salmon, dill, flour, raising agents and salt in a bowl, then pour in the egg mixture and stir just enough to combine.
- Scrape the mixture into the tin, then bake in the oven for 30 – 35 minutes.
- Test with a wooden toothpick, if it comes out clean, the cake is done.
- Transfer the loaf to a wire rack and leave to cool completely.

Smoked Mackerel Loaf Cake　　937

- Replace the smoked salmon with 2 smoked mackerel fillets that have been skinned and flaked.

938

MAKES 12

Squash and Parmesan Mini Loaf Cakes

PREPARATION TIME 40 MINUTES

COOKING TIME 15-20 MINUTES

INGREDIENTS

200 g / 7 oz butternut squash, cubed
300 g / 10 ½ oz / 2 cup self-raising flour
2 tsp baking powder
250 g / 9 oz / 1 ¼ cup butter, softened
5 large eggs
75 g / 2 ½ oz / ¾ cup Parmesan, grated
2 tbsp chives, chopped

- Preheat the oven to 190°C (170° fan), 375F, gas 5 and oil a 12-hole silicone mini loaf cake mould.
- Put the squash in a roasting tin and cover with foil then bake for 20 minutes. Tip it into a sieve and leave to drain and cool completely.
- Sieve the flour and baking powder into a mixing bowl and add the butter, eggs and Parmesan.
- Beat the mixture with an electric whisk for 4 minutes or until smooth and well whipped.
- Fold in the squash and chives then spoon the mixture into the moulds.
- Bake for 15 - 20 minutes or until a skewer inserted in the centre comes out clean.
- Serve warm.

Squash and Stilton Mini Loaf Cakes　　939

- Replace the Parmesan with 100 g of Stilton in small cubes.

940

SERVES 8

Carrot and Roquefort Loaf

- Preheat the oven to 170°C (150° fan), 340F, gas 3 and line a large loaf tin with non-stick baking paper.
- Boil the carrots for 8 minutes or until tender then drain well and leave to cool.
- Sieve the flour and baking powder into a mixing bowl and add the butter and eggs.
- Beat the mixture with an electric whisk for 4 minutes or until smooth and well whipped.
- Fold in the carrots, Roquefort and Parmesan then scrape the mixture into the loaf tin.
- Bake for 55 minutes or until a skewer inserted in the centre comes out clean.
- Transfer the cake to a wire rack and leave to cool completely before serving.

PREPARATION TIME 10 MINUTES

COOKING TIME 55 MINUTES

INGREDIENTS

2 carrots, peeled and chopped
300 g / 10 ½ oz / 2 cup self-raising flour
2 tsp baking powder
250 g / 9 oz / 1 ¼ cup butter, softened
5 large eggs
150 g / 5 ½ oz Roquefort, cubed
75 g / 2 ½ oz / ¾ cup Parmesan, grated

Parsnip and Roquefort Loaf Cake   941

- Replace the carrots with parsnips and cook as before.

942

SERVES 8

Tomato, Sage and Mozzarella Loaf

- Preheat the oven to 170°C (150° fan), 340F, gas 3 and line a large loaf tin with non-stick baking paper.
- Sieve the flour and baking powder into a mixing bowl and add the butter, tomato puree and eggs.
- Beat the mixture with an electric whisk for 4 minutes or until smooth and well whipped.
- Fold in the mozzarella and sage then scrape the mixture into the loaf tin.
- Bake for 55 minutes or until a skewer inserted comes out clean.
- Transfer the cake to a wire rack and leave to cool completely before serving.

PREPARATION TIME 10 MINUTES

COOKING TIME 55 MINUTES

INGREDIENTS

300 g / 10 ½ oz / 2 cup self-raising flour
2 tsp baking powder
250 g / 9 oz / 1 ¼ cup butter, softened
2 tbsp tomato puree
4 large eggs
150 g / 5 ½ oz mozzarella, cubed
2 tbsp sage leaves, chopped

Tomato and Pesto Marbled Loaf Cake   943

- Divide the cake mixture in two and stir the tomato puree into one half. Stir 3 tbsp pesto into the other half then marble together in the tin.

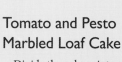

944

SERVES 8

Parmesan and Red Pepper Loaf Cake

Parmesan and Sundried Tomato Loaf Cake

945

- Replace the red pepper layer with sundried tomatoes.

Parmesan and Aubergine Loaf Cake

946

- Replace the red pepper layer with chargrilled aubergines in oil.

PREPARATION TIME 10 MINUTES

COOKING TIME 55 MINUTES

INGREDIENTS

300 g / 10 ½ oz / 2 cup self-raising flour
2 tsp baking powder
250 g / 9 oz / 1 ¼ cup butter, softened
150 g / 5 ½ oz Parmesan, grated
4 large eggs
1 jar roasted red peppers in oil, drained

- Preheat the oven to 170°C (150° fan), 340F, gas 3 and line a large loaf tin with non-stick baking paper.
- Sieve the flour and baking powder into a mixing bowl and add the butter, Parmesan and eggs.
- Beat the mixture with an electric whisk for 4 minutes or until smooth and well whipped.
- Spoon half of the mixture into the loaf tin and top with the red peppers.
- Top with the rest of the cake mixture and bake for 55 minutes or until a skewer inserted in the centre comes out clean.
- Transfer the cake to a wire rack and leave to cool completely before serving.

947

SERVES 8

Halloumi, Tomato and Basil Loaf Cake

- Preheat the oven to 180°C (160° fan), 355F, gas 4 and line a loaf tin with greaseproof paper.
- Beat the eggs in a jug with the oil, yoghurt and tomato puree until well mixed.
- Mix the Halloumi, tomatoes, basil, flour, raising agents and salt in a bowl, then pour in the egg mixture and stir everything just enough to combine.
- Scrape the mixture into the tin and bake for 30 – 35 minutes.
- Test with a wooden toothpick, if it comes out clean, the cake is done.
- Transfer the loaf to a wire rack and leave to cool completely.

PREPARATION TIME 15 MINUTES

COOKING TIME 30-35 MINUTES

INGREDIENTS

2 large eggs
120 ml / 4 fl. oz / ½ cup sunflower oil
180 ml / 6 fl. oz / ⅔ cup Greek yoghurt
2 tbsp tomato puree
225 g / 8 oz Halloumi, cubed
110 g / 8 oz cherry tomatoes, quartered
2 tbsp basil, finely chopped
225 g / 8 oz / 1 ½ cup plain (all purpose) flour
2 tsp baking powder
½ tsp bicarbonate of soda
½ tsp salt

Halloumi, Olive and Basil Loaf Cake

948

- Replace the cherry tomatoes with 75 g of chopped black olives.

949

SERVES 8

Asparagus and Bacon Loaf Cake

- Preheat the oven to 180°C (160° fan), 355F, gas 4 and line a loaf tin with greaseproof paper.
- Blanch the asparagus in boiling, salted water for 2 minutes then refresh in cold water and drain.
- Beat the eggs in a jug with the oil and yoghurt.
- Mix the bacon, flour, raising agents and salt in a bowl, then pour in the egg mixture and stir to combine.
- Scrape half of the mixture into the tin and lay all but 2 of the asparagus spears on top. Spoon over the rest of the cake mixture and level the top, then lay 2 pieces of asparagus diagonally on top.
- Bake the cake for 30 – 35 minutes.
- Test with a wooden toothpick, if it comes out clean, the cake is done.
- Transfer the loaf to a wire rack and leave to cool completely before slicing.

PREPARATION TIME 15 MINUTES

COOKING TIME 30-35 MINUTES

INGREDIENTS

8 asparagus spears, halved lengthways
2 large eggs
120 ml / 4 fl. oz / ½ cup sunflower oil
180 ml / 6 fl. oz / ⅔ cup Greek yoghurt
110 g / 4 oz streaky bacon, chopped
225 g / 8 oz / 1 ½ cup plain (all purpose) flour
2 tsp baking powder
½ tsp bicarbonate of soda
½ tsp salt

Asparagus and Pesto Loaf Cake

950

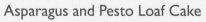

- Omit the bacon and stir 3 tbsp of pesto into the cake mixture.

951

SERVES 8

Stilton and Walnut Loaf

PREPARATION TIME 15 MINUTES

COOKING TIME 30-35 MINUTES

....

INGREDIENTS

2 large eggs
120 ml / 4 fl. oz / ½ cup sunflower oil
180 ml / 6 fl. oz / ⅔ cup Greek yoghurt
225 g / 8 oz Stilton, cubed
110 g / 3 ½ oz walnuts, chopped
225 g / 8 oz / 1 ½ cup plain (all purpose) flour
2 tsp baking powder
½ tsp bicarbonate of soda
½ tsp salt

- Preheat the oven to 180°C (160° fan), 355F, gas 4 and line a loaf tin with greaseproof paper.
- Beat the eggs in a jug with the oil and yoghurt until well mixed.
- Mix the Stilton, walnuts, flour, raising agents and salt in a bowl, then pour in the egg mixture and stir everything just enough to combine.
- Scrape the mixture into the tin and bake for 30 – 35 minutes.
- Test with a wooden toothpick, if it comes out clean, the cake is done.
- Transfer the loaf to a wire rack and leave to cool completely.

Stilton and Fig Loaf Cake

952

- Replace the walnuts with 4 finely chopped dried figs.

953

SERVES 8

Carrot, Gruyere and Poppy Seed Loaf

PREPARATION TIME 10 MINUTES

COOKING TIME 55 MINUTES

....

INGREDIENTS

300 g / 10 ½ oz / 2 cup self-raising flour
2 tsp baking powder
250 g / 9 oz / 1 ¼ cup butter, softened
5 large eggs
2 carrots, grated
150 g / 5 ½ oz / 1 ½ cups Gruyere, grated
2 tbsp poppy seeds

- Preheat the oven to 170°C (150° fan), 340F, gas 3 and line a large loaf tin with non-stick baking paper.
- Sieve the flour and baking powder into a mixing bowl and add the butter and eggs.
- Beat the mixture with an electric whisk for 4 minutes or until smooth and well whipped.
- Fold in the carrots, cheese and poppy seeds then scrape the mixture into the loaf tin.
- Bake for 55 minutes or until a skewer inserted in the centre comes out clean.
- Transfer the cake to a wire rack and leave to cool completely before serving.

Parsnip and Gruyere Loaf Cake

954

- Replace the carrot with grated parsnip.

955

SERVES 10

Roquefort, Pine Nut and Tomato Loaf

Wholemeal Roquefort Loaf Cake

956

- Replace the flour with wholemeal self-raising flour.

Roquefort and Dried Apple Loaf Cake

957

- Replace the sundried tomatoes with 75 g of chopped dried apple slices.

PREPARATION TIME 25 MINUTES

COOKING TIME 20-25 MINUTES

INGREDIENTS

2 large eggs
120 ml / 4 fl. oz / ½ cup sunflower oil
180 ml / 6 fl. oz / ⅔ cup Greek yoghurt
110 g / 4 oz Roquefort, cubed
75 g / 2 ½ oz / ⅓ cup sundried tomatoes in oil, drained
75 g / 2 ½ oz / ⅔ cup pine nuts
225 g / 8 oz / 1 ½ cup plain (all purpose) flour
2 tsp baking powder
½ tsp bicarbonate of soda
½ tsp salt

- Preheat the oven to 180°C (160° fan), gas 4 and line a long, thin loaf tin with greaseproof paper.
- Beat the eggs in a jug with the oil, yoghurt and cheese until well mixed.
- Mix the tomatoes, pine nuts, flour, raising agents and salt in a bowl, then pour in the egg mixture and stir just enough to combine.
- Scrape the mixture into the tin, then bake in the oven for 20 – 25 minutes.
- Test with a wooden toothpick, if it comes out clean, the cake is done.
- Transfer the loaf to a wire rack and leave to cool completely before slicing.

958

SERVES 36

Parmesan, Thyme and Peppercorn Cookies

PREPARATION TIME 15 MINUTES

COOKING TIME 10-15 MINUTES

INGREDIENTS

2 large eggs
110 ml / 4 fl. oz / ½ cup sunflower oi
110 ml / 4 fl. oz / ⅔ cup Greek
yoghurt
110 g / 4 oz / 1 cup Parmesan, grated
225 g / 8 oz / 1 ½ cup plain (all
purpose) flour
2 tsp baking powder
½ tsp bicarbonate of soda
½ tsp salt
2 tbsp fresh thyme leaves
1 tbsp pink peppercorns, crushed

- Preheat the oven to 180°C (160° fan), 355F, gas 4 and line 2 baking trays with greaseproof paper.
- Beat the eggs in a jug with the oil, yoghurt and Parmesan until well mixed.
- Mix the flour, raising agents, salt, thyme and peppercorns in a bowl, then pour in the egg mixture.
- Stir everything just enough to combine.
- Drop heaped teaspoons of the mixture spaced out on the baking trays and bake in batches for 10 – 15 minutes or until golden brown.
- Transfer to a wire rack and leave to cool.

Parmesan and Rosemary Cookies   959

- Replace the thyme with 2 tbsp of chopped fresh rosemary.

960

MAKES 6

Chicken and Almond Pastilla

PREPARATION TIME 25 MINUTES

COOKING TIME 25-30 MINUTES

INGREDIENTS

1 onion, finely chopped
2 tbsp olive oil
2 chicken breasts, finely chopped
2 cloves garlic, crushed
1 lemon, zest finely grated
100 g / 3 ½ oz / ¾ cup blanched
almonds, chopped
3 tbsp coriander (cilantro) leaves,
chopped
225 g / 8 oz filo pastry
100 g / 3 ½ oz / ½ cup butter, melted
icing (confectioners) sugar to dust

- Preheat the oven to 180°C (160° fan), 355F, gas 4 and grease a large baking tray.
- Fry the onion for 5 minutes then add the chicken and garlic and stir-fry for 3 minutes. Turn off the heat and stir in the lemon zest, almonds and coriander. Season with salt and pepper and leave to cool a little.
- Brush the pastry sheets with butter and layer them to create 6 separate stacks.
- Divide the chicken mixture between the filo stacks and fold in the edges.
- Turn the parcels over and transfer to the baking tray. Brush with a little extra butter then bake for 25 – 30 minutes or until the pastry is crisp and golden.
- Dust the pastillas with icing (confectioners) sugar before serving.
- To create the char marks, heat up a skewer with a blow torch or gas hob and burn lines in the icing sugar.

Pigeon and Almond Pastilla   961

- Replace the chicken breasts with 6 cubed pigeon breasts and add 1 tsp ground cinnamon when you add the lemon zest.

962

SERVES 8

Black Olive and Parsnip Loaf Cake

- Preheat the oven to 180°C (160° fan), 355F, gas 4 and butter a baking dish.
- Beat the eggs in a jug with the oil, yoghurt, parsnip and olives until well mixed.
- Mix the flour, raising agents and salt in a bowl, then pour in the egg mixture and stir just enough to combine.
- Scrape the mixture into the dish, then bake in the oven for 20 – 25 minutes.
- Test with a wooden toothpick, if it comes out clean, the cake is done.
- Serve warm.

PREPARATION TIME 25 MINUTES

COOKING TIME 20-25 MINUTES

INGREDIENTS

2 large eggs
120 ml / 4 fl. oz / ½ cup sunflower oil
180 ml / 6 fl. oz / ⅔ cup Greek yoghurt
110 g / 4 oz / ¾ cup parsnip, grated
110 g / 4 oz / ⅔ cup black olives, pitted and sliced
225 g / 8 oz / 1 ½ cup plain (all purpose) flour
2 tsp baking powder
½ tsp bicarbonate of soda
½ tsp salt

Black Olive and Sweetcorn Loaf Cake

963

- Replace the parsnip with 200 g of canned sweetcorn.

964

MAKES 1

Granary Corn Bread

- Mix together the flours, yeast, sugar and salt. Stir in the oil and 280 ml of warm water.
- Knead the mixture on a lightly oiled surface for 10 minutes or until smooth and elastic.
- Leave the dough to rest, covered with oiled clingfilm, for 1 – 2 hours or until doubled in size.
- Knead for 2 more minutes then roll the dough into a fat sausage. Roll it up the other way and drop it into a loaf tin with the seam underneath.
- Cover the tin with oiled clingfilm and leave for 1 hour.
- Preheat the oven to 220°C (200° fan), 430F, gas 7.
- Bake for 35 - 40 minutes or until the loaf sounds hollow when you tap it underneath.
- Transfer to a wire rack and leave to cool.

PREPARATION TIME 2 HOURS 30 MINUTES

COOKING TIME 35-40 MINUTES

INGREDIENTS

200 g / 7 oz / 1 ⅓ cup malted granary flour
200 g / 7 oz / 1 ⅓ cup fine corn meal
1 tsp easy blend dried yeast
2 tbsp caster (superfine) sugar
1 tsp fine sea salt
1 tbsp olive oil

Corn Bread Loaf

965

- Replace the malted granary flour with strong white bread flour.

966

MAKES 12

Crab and Herb Mini Loaf Cakes

Crab, Shallot and Lemon Mini Loaf Cakes

967

- Add a finely chopped shallot and the grated zest of a lemon to the cake mixture.

Crab and Chilli Loaf Cakes

968

- Add a finely chopped red chilli to the cake mixture and replace the tarragon with fresh coriander leaves.

PREPARATION TIME 15 MINUTES

COOKING TIME 10-15 MINUTES

INGREDIENTS

2 large eggs
120 ml / 4 fl. oz / ½ cup sunflower oil
180 ml / 6 fl. oz / ⅔ cup Greek yoghurt
2 tbsp Parmesan, finely grated
150 g / 5 ½ oz / ¾ cup fresh crab meat
2 tbsp flat leaf parsley, chopped
1 tbsp tarragon, chopped
1 tbsp chives, chopped
225 g / 8 oz / 1 ½ cup plain (all purpose) flour
2 tsp baking powder
½ tsp bicarbonate of soda
½ tsp salt

- Preheat the oven to 180°C (160° fan), 350F, gas 4 and line a 24 hole mini loaf tin with cases.
- Beat the egg in a jug with the oil, yoghurt, Parmesan, crab and herbs until well mixed.
- Mix the flour, raising agents and salt in a bowl, then pour in the egg mixture and stir just enough to combine.
- Divide the mixture between the cases, then bake in the oven for 10 – 15 minutes.
- Test with a wooden toothpick, if it comes out clean, the cakes are done.

969

SERVES 8

Chorizo and Olive Loaf Cake

- Preheat the oven to 180°C (160° fan), 355F, gas 4 and line a loaf tin with greaseproof paper.
- Beat the eggs in a jug with the oil, yoghurt, chorizo and olives until well mixed.
- Mix the flour, raising agents and salt in a bowl, then pour in the egg mixture and stir just enough to combine.
- Scrape the mixture into the tin, then bake in the oven for 20 – 25 minutes.
- Test with a wooden toothpick, if it comes out clean, the cake is done.
- Transfer the loaf to a wire rack and leave to cool completely.

PREPARATION TIME 25 MINUTES

COOKING TIME 20-25 MINUTES

INGREDIENTS

2 large eggs
120 ml / 4 fl. oz / ½ cup sunflower oil
180 ml / 6 fl. oz / ⅔ cup Greek yoghurt
110 g / 4 oz chorizo, cubed
110 g / 4 oz / ⅔ cup black olives, pitted and sliced
225 g / 8 oz / 1 ½ cup plain (all purpose) flour
2 tsp baking powder
½ tsp bicarbonate of soda
½ tsp salt

Chorizo and Caper Loaf Cake

970

- Replace the olives with capers.

971

SERVES 8

Courgette and Red Pepper Loaf

- Preheat the oven to 170°C (150° fan), 340F, gas 3 and line a loaf tin with greaseproof paper.
- Sieve the flour and baking powder into a mixing bowl and add the butter and eggs.
- Beat the mixture with an electric whisk for 4 minutes or until smooth and well whipped.
- Fold in the courgette, peppers and anchovies then scrape the mixture into the loaf tin.
- Bake the loaf for 55 minutes or until a skewer inserted comes out clean.
- Transfer the cake to a wire rack and leave to cool completely before serving.

PREPARATION TIME 10 MINUTES

COOKING TIME 55 MINUTES

INGREDIENTS

300 g / 10 ½ oz / 2 cup self-raising flour
2 tsp baking powder
250 g / 9 oz / 1 ¼ cup butter, softened
5 large eggs
1 courgette (zucchini), halved and sliced
150 g / 5 oz / ¾ cup roasted red peppers in oil, drained
10 anchovy fillets in oil, drained

Sundried Tomato and Anchovy Loaf Cake

972

- Replace the peppers with 100 g of chopped sundried tomatoes.

973

SERVES 8

Bacon and Caraway Loaf Cake

PREPARATION TIME 10 MINUTES

COOKING TIME 55 MINUTES

....

INGREDIENTS

300 g / 10 ½ oz / 2 cup self-raising
flour
2 tsp baking powder
250 g / 9 oz / 1 ¼ cup butter, softened
5 large eggs
150 g / 5 oz streaky bacon, cubed
2 tbsp caraway seeds

- Preheat the oven to 170⁰C (150⁰ fan), 340F, gas 3 and line a large loaf tin with non-stick baking paper.
- Sieve the flour and baking powder into a mixing bowl and add the butter and eggs.
- Beat the mixture with an electric whisk for 4 minutes or until smooth and well whipped.
- Fold in the bacon and half of the caraway seeds then scrape the mixture into the loaf tin.
- Sprinkle the top with the rest of the caraway and freshly ground black pepper.
- Bake for 55 minutes or until a skewer inserted in the centre comes out clean.
- Transfer the cake to a wire rack and leave to cool completely before serving.

Bacon and Fennel Loaf Cake

974

- Replace the caraway seeds with 1 tbsp of fennel seeds.

975

MAKES 1 LOAF

Chorizo and Thyme Bread

PREPARATION TIME 2 HOURS
30 MINUTES

COOKING TIME 35-40 MINUTES

....

INGREDIENTS

300 g / 10 ½ oz / 2 cup strong white
bread flour, plus extra for dusting
100 g / 3 ½ oz / ⅔ cup stoneground
wholemeal flour
½ tsp easy blend dried yeast
1 tbsp caster (superfine) sugar
1 tsp fine sea salt
100 g / 3 ½ oz chorizo, cubed
4 tbsp fresh thyme leaves

- Mix together the flours, yeast, sugar and salt. Stir in the chorizo, half of the thyme and 280 ml of warm water.
- Knead the mixture on a lightly oiled surface for 10 minutes or until the dough is smooth and elastic.
- Leave the dough to rest in a lightly oiled bowl, covered with oiled clingfilm, for 1 – 2 hours.
- Knead the dough for 2 more minutes then roll it into a fat sausage. Turn it 90⁰ and roll it tightly the other way then tuck the ends under and transfer the dough to the tin, keeping the seam underneath.
- Cover the tin with oiled clingfilm and leave for 45 minutes.
- Preheat the oven to 220⁰C (200⁰ fan), 430F, gas 7 and sprinkle the rest of the thyme over the loaf.
- Bake for 35 – 40 minutes or until the underneath sounds hollow when tapped.
- Leave to cool completely on a wire rack before slicing.

Fig and Chorizo Mini Loaf Cakes

976

MAKES 12

Fig and Walnut Mini Loaf Cakes

977

- Replace the chorizo with 75 g of chopped walnuts.

Double Fig Mini Loaf Cakes

978

- Replace the chorizo with 75 g of dried figs, cut into small pieces.

Fig and Stilton Mini Loaf Cakes

979

- Replace the chorizo with 100 g of Stilton in small cubes.

PREPARATION TIME 15 MINUTES

COOKING TIME 10-15 MINUTES

INGREDIENTS

2 large eggs
120 ml / 4 fl. oz / ½ cup sunflower oil
180 ml / 6 fl. oz / ¾ cup Greek yoghurt
2 tbsp Parmesan, finely grated
150 g / 5 ½ oz chorizo, cubed
4 fresh figs, chopped
225 g / 8 oz / 1 ½ cup plain (all purpose) flour
2 tsp baking powder
½ tsp bicarbonate of soda
½ tsp salt

- Preheat the oven to 180°C (160° fan), 350F, gas 4 and line a 24 hole mini loaf tin with greaseproof paper.
- Beat the egg in a jug with the oil, yoghurt, Parmesan, chorizo and figs until well mixed.
- Mix the flour, raising agents and salt in a bowl, then pour in the egg mixture and stir just enough to combine.
- Divide the mixture between the cases, then bake in the oven for 10 – 15 minutes.
- Test with a wooden toothpick, if it comes out clean, the cakes are done.

980

MAKES 24

Parmesan and Pistachio Mini Muffins

PREPARATION TIME 15 MINUTES

COOKING TIME 10-15 MINUTES

....

INGREDIENTS

2 large eggs
120 ml / 4 fl. oz / ½ cup sunflower oil
180 ml / 6 fl. oz / ¾ cup Greek yoghurt
100 g / 3 ½ oz / 1 cup Parmesan, grated
225 g / 8 oz / 1 ½ cup plain (all purpose) flour
2 tsp baking powder
½ tsp bicarbonate of soda
½ tsp salt
75 g / 2 ½ oz / ½ cup pistachio nuts

- Preheat the oven to 180°C (160° fan), 350F, gas 4 and line a 24-hole mini muffin tin with paper cases.
- Beat the egg in a jug with the oil, yoghurt and cheese until well mixed.
- Mix the flour, raising agents, salt and pistachios in a bowl, then pour in the egg mixture and stir just enough to combine.
- Divide the mixture between the paper cases, then bake in the oven for 10 – 15 minutes.
- Test with a wooden toothpick, if it comes out clean, the muffins are done.
- Serve warm.

Parmesan and Hazelnut Mini Muffins

981

- Replace the pistachios with hazelnuts.

982

SERVES 10

King Prawn and Sundried Tomato Loaf

PREPARATION TIME 25 MINUTES

COOKING TIME 20-25 MINUTES

....

INGREDIENTS

2 large eggs
120 ml / 4 fl. oz / ½ cup sunflower oil
180 ml / 6 fl. oz / ¾ cup Greek yoghurt
110 g / 4 oz / ½ cup king prawns (shrimp), cooked and peeled
75 g / 2 ½ oz / ⅓ cup sundried tomatoes in oil, drained
2 tbsp fresh thyme leaves
225 g / 8 oz / 1 ½ cup plain (all purpose) flour
2 tsp baking powder
½ tsp bicarbonate of soda
½ tsp salt

- Preheat the oven to 180°C (160° fan), gas 4 and line a long, thin loaf tin with greaseproof paper.
- Beat the eggs in a jug with the oil and yoghurt until well mixed.
- Mix the prawns, tomatoes, thyme, flour, raising agents and salt in a bowl, then pour in the egg mixture and stir just enough to combine.
- Scrape the mixture into the tin, then bake in the oven for 20 – 25 minutes.
- Test with a wooden toothpick, if it comes out clean, the cake is done.
- Transfer the loaf to a wire rack and leave to cool completely before slicing.

King Prawn and Pepper Loaf Cake

983

- Replace the sundried tomatoes with a jar of roasted red peppers in oil, drained.

984
SERVES 8 Vegetable and Goat's Cheese Loaf Cake

- Preheat the oven to 170°C (150° fan), 340F, gas 3 and line a large loaf tin with non-stick baking paper.
- Sieve the flour and baking powder into a mixing bowl and add the butter and eggs.
- Beat the mixture with an electric whisk for 4 minutes or until smooth and well whipped.
- Fold in the grated vegetables, goat's cheese and Parmesan then scrape the mixture into the loaf tin.
- Bake for 55 minutes or until a skewer inserted comes out clean.
- Transfer the cake to a wire rack and leave to cool completely before serving.

PREPARATION TIME 10 MINUTES

COOKING TIME 55 MINUTES

INGREDIENTS

300 g / 10 ½ oz / 2 cup self-raising flour
2 tsp baking powder
250 g / 9 oz / 1 ¼ cup butter, softened
5 large eggs
1 carrot, grated
1 parsnip, grated
1 courgette, grated
150 g / 5 ½ oz goat's cheese, cubed
75 g / 2 ½ oz / ¾ cup Parmesan, grated

Vegetable and Feta Loaf Cake   985

- Substitute feta for the goat's cheese.

986
MAKES 1 LOAF Goats' Cheese and Sage Bread

- Mix together the flour, yeast, sugar and salt. Stir in the goats' cheese, sage and 280 ml of warm water.
- Knead the mixture on a lightly oiled surface for 10 minutes or until the dough is smooth and elastic.
- Leave the dough to rest in a lightly oiled bowl, covered with oiled clingfilm, for 1 – 2 hours.
- Knead the dough for 2 more minutes then roll it into a fat sausage. Turn it 90° and roll it tightly the other way then tuck the ends under and transfer the dough to the tin, keeping the seam underneath.
- Cover the tin with oiled clingfilm and leave for 45 minutes.
- Preheat the oven to 220°C (200° fan), 430F, gas 7.
- Bake for 35 – 40 minutes or until the underneath sounds hollow when tapped.
- Leave to cool completely on a wire rack before slicing.

PREPARATION TIME 2 HOURS
30 MINUTES

COOKING TIME 35-40 MINUTES

INGREDIENTS

400 g / 14 oz / 2 ⅔ cup strong white bread flour
½ tsp easy blend dried yeast
1 tbsp caster (superfine) sugar
1 tsp fine sea salt
100 g / 3 ½ oz goat's cheese, cubed
2 tbsp sage leaves, chopped

Cheddar and Watercress Loaf Cake

SERVES 8

Cheddar and Spinach Loaf Cake

988

- Replace the watercress with chopped baby leaf spinach.

Goat's Cheese and Watercress Loaf Cake

989

- Replace the cheddar with 100 g of goat's cheese in small cubes.

Bacon and Watercress Loaf Cake

990

- Add 4 chopped rashers of smoked streaky bacon to the cake mixture.

PREPARATION TIME 25 MINUTES

COOKING TIME 20-25 MINUTES

INGREDIENTS

2 large eggs
120 ml / 4 fl. oz / ½ cup sunflower oil
180 ml / 6 fl. oz / ¾ cup Greek yoghurt
75 g / 2 ½ oz watercress, chopped
110 g / 4 oz / 1 cup Cheddar, grated
225 g / 8 oz / 1 ½ cup plain (all purpose) flour
2 tsp baking powder
½ tsp bicarbonate of soda
½ tsp salt

- Preheat the oven to 180°C (160° fan), 355F, gas 4 and line a loaf tin with greaseproof paper.
- Beat the eggs in a jug with the oil, yoghurt, watercress and half of the cheddar until well mixed.
- Mix the flour, raising agents and salt in a bowl, then pour in the egg mixture and stir just enough to combine.
- Scrape the mixture into the tin and sprinkle over the rest of the cheese, then bake in the oven for 20 – 25 minutes.
- Test with a wooden toothpick, if it comes out clean, the cake is done.
- Transfer the loaf to a wire rack and leave to cool completely.

991

SERVES 8-10 Almond and Greengage Jam Loaf Cake

- Preheat the oven to 180°C (160° fan), 355F, gas 4 and grease and line a wide loaf tin with greaseproof paper.
- Cream the butter and sugar together until well whipped then gradually whisk in the eggs, beating well after each addition.
- Fold in the flour and ground almonds then swirl through the greengage jam.
- Scrape the mixture into the tin and bake for 35 minutes or until a skewer inserted in the centre comes out clean.
- Turn the loaf out onto a wire rack and leave to cool before slicing.

PREPARATION TIME 10 MINUTES

COOKING TIME 35 MINUTES

....

INGREDIENTS

225 g / 8 oz / 1 cup butter, softened
225 g / 8 oz / 1 cup caster (superfine) sugar
4 large eggs, beaten
125 g / 4 ½ oz / ¾ cup self-raising flour
100 g / 3 ½ oz / 1 cup ground almonds
200 g / 7 oz / ⅔ cup greengage jam (jelly)

Almond and Cherry Jam Loaf Cake

992

- Replace the greengage jam with black cherry jam.

993

MAKES 12 Ham and Olive Sponge Squares

- Preheat the oven to 170°C (150° fan), 340F, gas 3 and line a square cake tin with greaseproof paper.
- Sieve the flour and baking powder into a mixing bowl and add the butter and eggs.
- Beat the mixture with an electric whisk for 4 minutes or until smooth and well whipped.
- Fold in the olives and ham then scrape the mixture into the loaf tin.
- Bake for 35 minutes or until a skewer inserted in the centre comes out clean.
- Transfer the cake to a wire rack and leave to cool completely before cutting into squares.

PREPARATION TIME 10 MINUTES

COOKING TIME 35 MINUTES

....

INGREDIENTS

300 g / 10 ½ oz / 2 cup self-raising flour
2 tsp baking powder
250 g / 9 oz / 1 ¼ cup butter, softened
5 large eggs
75 g / 2 ½ oz / ½ cup green olives, pitted and halved
75 g / 2 ½ oz ham, cubed

Tomato and Olive Sponge Squares

994

- Replace the ham with 4 finely chopped sundried tomatoes.

995

SERVES 8

Rocket and Parmesan Loaf Cake

PREPARATION TIME 10 MINUTES

COOKING TIME 55 MINUTES

....

INGREDIENTS

300 g / 10 ½ oz / 2 cup self-raising
flour
2 tsp baking powder
250 g / 9 oz / 1 ¼ cup butter, softened
150 g / 5 ½ oz / 1 ½ cup Parmesan,
grated
4 large eggs
50 g / 1 ¾ oz rocket leaves, chopped

- Preheat the oven to 170°C (150° fan), 340F, gas 3 and line a large loaf tin with greaseproof paper.
- Sieve the flour and baking powder into a mixing bowl and add the butter, Parmesan and eggs.
- Beat the mixture with an electric whisk for 4 minutes or until smooth and well whipped.
- Fold in the rocket and spoon into the tin.
- Bake for 55 minutes or until a skewer inserted in the centre comes out clean.
- Transfer the cake to a wire rack and leave to cool completely before serving.

996

MAKES 4

Pretzels

PREPARATION TIME 2 HOURS
30 MINUTES

COOKING TIME 10 MINUTES

....

INGREDIENTS

300 g / 10 ½ oz / 2 cups strong white
bread flour
½ tsp easy blend dried yeast
15 g butter, melted
1 tsp salt
1 egg, beaten
15 g sugar nibs

- Mix the flour, yeast, butter and salt together in a bowl and stir in 210ml of warm water.
- Bring the mixture into a dough with your hands and knead for 10 minutes.
- Leave to rest in a warm place for 1 hour or until doubled in size.
- Divide the dough into 4 even pieces and roll each one into a long sausage.
- Twist into a classic pretzel shape and transfer to an oiled baking tray.
- Prove for 45 minutes in a warm place.
- Preheat the oven to 220°C (200° fan), 425F, gas 7.
- When the pretzels are well risen, brush them with egg and sprinkle with sugar nibs then bake for 10 minutes or until golden brown and cooked through.

997

SERVES 8

Olive and Guacamole Loaf Cake

- Preheat the oven to 180°C (160° fan), 355F, gas 4 and line a loaf tin with greaseproof paper.
- Beat the eggs in a jug with the oil, yoghurt, avocado, chilli, spring onion and olives until well mixed.
- Mix the flour, raising agents and salt in a bowl, then pour in the egg mixture and stir just enough to combine.
- Scrape the mixture into the tin, then bake in the oven for 30 – 35 minutes.
- Test with a wooden toothpick, if it comes out clean, the cake is done.
- Transfer the loaf to a wire rack and leave to cool completely.

PREPARATION TIME 25 MINUTES

COOKING TIME 30-35 MINUTES

INGREDIENTS

2 large eggs
120 ml / 4 fl. oz / ½ cup sunflower oil
180 ml / 6 fl. oz / ¾ cup Greek yoghurt
2 avocados, peeled, stoned and diced
2 red chillies, finely chopped
2 spring onions, finely chopped
110 g / 4 oz / ⅔ cup mixed olives, pitted and sliced
225 g / 8 oz / 1 ½ cup plain (all purpose) flour
2 tsp baking powder
½ tsp bicarbonate of soda
½ tsp salt

Olive and Thyme Mini Loaf Cakes

998

MAKES 12

PREPARATION TIME 15 MINUTES

COOKING TIME 10-15 MINUTES

INGREDIENTS

2 large eggs
120 ml / 4 fl. oz / ½ cup sunflower oil
180 ml / 6 fl. oz / ¾ cup Greek yoghurt

2 tbsp Parmesan, finely grated
150 g / 5 ½ oz / 1 cup green olives, pitted
2 tbsp fresh thyme leaves
225 g / 8 oz / 1 ½ cup plain (all purpose) flour
2 tsp baking powder
½ tsp bicarbonate of soda
½ tsp salt

- Preheat the oven to 180°C (160° fan), 350F, gas 4 and oil a 24-hole silicone mini loaf mould.
- Beat the egg in a jug with the oil, yoghurt, Parmesan, olives and thyme until well mixed.
- Mix the flour, raising agents and salt in a bowl, then pour in the egg mixture and stir just enough to combine.
- Divide the mixture between the cases, then bake in the oven for 10 – 15 minutes.
- Test with a wooden toothpick, if it comes out clean, the cakes are done.

Ham, Sage and Onion Loaf Cake

999

SERVES 8

PREPARATION TIME 10 MINUTES

COOKING TIME 55 MINUTES

INGREDIENTS

2 onions, quartered and sliced
2 tbsp olive oil
300 g / 10 ½ oz / 2 cup self-raising flour

2 tsp baking powder
250 g / 9 oz / 1 ¼ cup butter, softened
5 large eggs
100 g / 3 ½ oz ham, cubed
2 tbsp fresh sage leaves, chopped

- Preheat the oven to 170°C (150° fan), gas 3 and line a loaf tin with greaseproof paper.
- Fry the onions in the oil for 10 minutes or until softened. Leave to cool.
- Sieve the flour and baking powder into a mixing bowl and add the butter and eggs.
- Beat the mixture with an electric whisk for 4 minutes or until smooth and well whipped.
- Fold in the onions, ham and sage then scrape the mixture into the loaf tin.
- Bake for 55 minutes or until a skewer inserted in the centre comes out clean.
- Transfer the cake to a wire rack and leave to cool completely before serving.

1000

SERVES 6-8 # Cheese and Bacon Quiche

PREPARATION TIME I HOUR

COOKING TIME 35-40 MINUTES

INGREDIENTS

225 g / 8 oz puff pastry
200 g / 7 oz smoked lardons
2 tbsp olive oil
3 large eggs, beaten
225 ml / 8 fl. oz / ¾ cup double cream
150 g / 5 ½ oz Gruyere, grated

- Preheat the oven to 190°C (170° fan), 375F, gas 5.
- Roll out the pastry on a floured surface and use it to line a 23 cm round tart tin.
- Prick the pastry with a fork, line with clingfilm and fill with baking beans or rice.
- Bake the case for 10 minutes then remove the clingfilm and baking beans.
- Brush the inside with beaten egg and return to the oven for 8 minutes to crisp.
- Lower the oven to 150°C (130° fan), 300F, gas 2
- Fry the lardons in the oil for 5 minutes.
- Whisk the eggs with the double cream until smoothly combined then stir in the lardons and half of the Gruyere. Pour the filling into the pastry case and scatter the rest of the cheese on top.
- Bake for 35 - 40 minutes or until just set in the centre.

1001

SERVES 8 # Roquefort and Walnut Loaf Cake

PREPARATION TIME 15 MINUTES

COOKING TIME 30-35 MINUTES

INGREDIENTS

2 large eggs
120 ml / 4 fl. oz / ½ cup sunflower oil
180 ml / 6 fl. oz / ¾ cup Greek yoghurt
225 g / 8 oz Roquefort, cubed
110 g / 3 ½ oz / ¾ cup walnuts, chopped
225 g / 8 oz / 1 ½ cup plain (all purpose) flour
2 tsp baking powder
½ tsp bicarbonate of soda
½ tsp salt

- Preheat the oven to 180°C (160° fan), 355F, gas 4 and line a loaf tin with greaseproof paper.
- Beat the eggs in a jug with the oil and yoghurt until well mixed.
- Mix the Roquefort, walnuts, flour, raising agents and salt in a bowl, then pour in the egg mixture and stir everything just enough to combine.
- Scrape the mixture into the tin and bake for 30 – 35 minutes.
- Test with a wooden toothpick, if it comes out clean, the cake is done.
- Transfer the loaf to a wire rack and leave to cool completely.

Goat's Cheese and Walnut Loaf Cake

1002

- Replace the Roquefort with an equal weight of goat's cheese in small cubes.

1003

MAKES 12 Crab, Chilli and Lime Muffins

- Preheat the oven to 180°C (160° fan), 350F, gas 4 and oil a 12-hole silicone muffin mould.
- Beat the egg in a jug with the oil, yoghurt, Parmesan, crab, chilli, lime and coriander until well mixed.
- Mix the flour, raising agents and salt in a bowl, then pour in the egg mixture and stir just enough to combine.
- Divide the mixture between the moulds, then bake in the oven for 20 – 25 minutes.
- Test with a wooden toothpick, if it comes out clean, the cakes are done.

PREPARATION TIME 15 MINUTES

COOKING TIME 20-25 MINUTES

INGREDIENTS

2 large eggs
120 ml / 4 fl. oz / ½ cup sunflower oil
180 ml / 6 fl. oz / ¾ cup Greek yoghurt
2 tbsp Parmesan, finely grated
150 g / 5 ½ oz / ¾ cup fresh crab meat
1 red chilli, finely chopped
1 lime, zest finely grated
1 tbsp coriander (cilantro) leaves, chopped
225 g / 8 oz / 1 ½ cup plain (all purpose) flour
2 tsp baking powder
½ tsp bicarbonate of soda
½ tsp salt

Shrimp, Chilli and Lime Muffins   1004

- Replace the crab meat with 150 g of peeled grey shrimp.

1005

MAKES 12 Roquefort Mini Loaf Cakes

- Preheat the oven to 180°C (160° fan), 350F, gas 4 and oil 12 mini loaf moulds.
- Beat the egg in a jug with the oil, yoghurt and Roquefort until well mixed.
- Mix the flour, raising agents and salt in a bowl, then pour in the egg mixture and stir just enough to combine.
- Divide the mixture between the cases, then bake in the oven for 10 – 15 minutes.
- Test with a wooden toothpick, if it comes out clean, the cakes are done.

PREPARATION TIME 15 MINUTES

COOKING TIME 10-15 MINUTES

INGREDIENTS

2 large eggs
120 ml / 4 fl. oz / ½ cup sunflower oil
180 ml / 6 fl. oz / ¾ cup Greek yoghurt
150 g / 5 ½ oz Roquefort, cubed
225 g / 8 oz / 1 ½ cup plain (all purpose) flour
2 tsp baking powder
½ tsp bicarbonate of soda
½ tsp salt

Bacon Mini Loaf Cakes   1006

- Replace the Roquefort with 100 g of smoked bacon lardons that have been fried in olive oil for 2 minutes.

1007

MAKES 2

Tuna and Black Olive Loaf Cake

Smoked Mackerel and Black Olive Loaf Cake

1008

- Replace the tuna with 2 fillets of smoked mackerel that have been skinned and flaked.

Tuna and Sweetcorn Loaf Cake

1009

- Replace the olives with 100 g of canned sweetcorn kernels.

PREPARATION TIME 10 MINUTES

COOKING TIME 30-35 MINUTES

INGREDIENTS

2 large eggs
120 ml / 4 fl. oz / ½ cup sunflower oil
180 ml / 6 fl. oz / ¾ cup Greek yoghurt
300 g / 10 ½ oz canned tuna, drained
100 g / 2 ½ oz / ⅔ cup black olives, pitted and sliced
225 g / 8 oz / 1 ½ cup plain (all purpose) flour
2 tsp baking powder
½ tsp bicarbonate of soda
½ tsp salt

- Preheat the oven to 180°C (160° fan), 355F, gas 4 and line 2 small loaf tins with greaseproof paper.
- Beat the eggs in a jug with the oil and yoghurt until well mixed.
- Mix the tuna, olives, flour, raising agents and salt in a bowl, then pour in the egg mixture and stir just enough to combine.
- Divide the mixture between the tins, then bake in the oven for 30 – 35 minutes.
- Test with a wooden toothpick, if it comes out clean, the cakes are done.
- Transfer the loaves to a wire rack and leave to cool completely.

1010

SERVES 10 Spinach and Pine Nut Loaf Cake

- Preheat the oven to 180°C (160° fan), gas 4 and line a loaf tin with greaseproof paper.
- Put the spinach in a saucepan with 2 tbsp water and cook with the lid on for 3 minutes. When cool enough to handle, squeeze out all the moisture and chop.
- Beat the eggs in a jug with the oil, yoghurt and chopped spinach until well mixed.
- Mix the pine nuts, flour, raising agents and salt in a bowl, then pour in the egg mixture and stir just enough to combine.
- Scrape the mixture into the tin, then bake in the oven for 20 – 25 minutes.
- Test with a wooden toothpick, if it comes out clean, the cake is done.
- Transfer the loaf to a wire rack and leave to cool completely before slicing.

PREPARATION TIME 25 MINUTES

COOKING TIME 20-25 MINUTES

INGREDIENTS

110 g / 4 oz spinach
2 large eggs
120 ml / 4 fl. oz / ½ cup sunflower oil
180 ml / 6 fl. oz / ¾ cup Greek yoghurt
75 g / 2 ½ oz / ⅔ cup pine nuts
225 g / 8 oz / 1 ½ cup plain (all purpose) flour
2 tsp baking powder
½ tsp bicarbonate of soda
½ tsp salt

Watercress and Pine Nut Loaf Cake

1011

- Replace the spinach with an equal weight of watercress and wilt as before.

1012

SERVES 8 Bacon and Black Olive Loaf Cake

- Preheat the oven to 180°C (160° fan), 355F, gas 4 and line a loaf tin with greaseproof paper.
- Beat the eggs in a jug with the oil, yoghurt, bacon and olives until well mixed.
- Mix the flour, raising agents and salt in a bowl, then pour in the egg mixture and stir just enough to combine.
- Scrape the mixture into the tin, then bake in the oven for 20 – 25 minutes.
- Test with a wooden toothpick, if it comes out clean, the cake is done.
- Transfer the loaf to a wire rack and leave to cool completely.

PREPARATION TIME 25 MINUTES

COOKING TIME 20-25 MINUTES

INGREDIENTS

2 large eggs
120 ml / 4 fl. oz / ½ cup sunflower oil
180 ml / 6 fl. oz / ¾ cup Greek yoghurt
110 g / 4 oz streaky bacon, chopped
110 g / 4 oz / ⅔ cup black olives, pitted and sliced
225 g / 8 oz / 1 ½ cup plain (all purpose) flour
2 tsp baking powder
½ tsp bicarbonate of soda
½ tsp salt

Bacon and Sage Loaf Cake

1013

- Omit the bacon and 2 tbsp of chopped fresh sage leaves to the cake mixture.

1014

SERVES 8

Gluten-Free Bacon and Black Olive Loaf

PREPARATION TIME 25 MINUTES

COOKING TIME 20-25 MINUTES

INGREDIENTS

2 large eggs
120 ml / 4 fl. oz / ½ cup sunflower oil
180 ml / 6 fl. oz / ¾ cup Greek yoghurt
110 g / 4 oz streaky bacon, chopped
110 g / 4 oz / ⅔ cup black olives, pitted and sliced
225 g / 8 oz / 1 ½ cup rice flour
2 tsp baking powder
½ tsp bicarbonate of soda
½ tsp salt

- Preheat the oven to 180°C (160° fan), 355F, gas 4 and line a loaf tin with greaseproof paper.
- Beat the eggs in a jug with the oil, yoghurt, bacon and olives until well mixed.
- Mix the flour, raising agents and salt in a bowl, then pour in the egg mixture and stir just enough to combine.
- Scrape the mixture into the tin, then bake in the oven for 20 – 25 minutes.
- Test with a wooden toothpick, if it comes out clean, the cake is done.
- Transfer the loaf to a wire rack and leave to cool completely.

Gluten-free Olive and Caper Loaf Cake

1015

- Omit the bacon and add 2 tbsp of capers to the cake mixture.

1016

SERVES 10

Caper and Sundried Tomato Loaf Cake

PREPARATION TIME 25 MINUTES

COOKING TIME 20-25 MINUTES

INGREDIENTS

2 large eggs
120 ml / 4 fl. oz / ½ cup sunflower oil
180 ml / 6 fl. oz / ¾ cup Greek yoghurt
3 tbsp capers, drained
75 g / 2 ½ oz / ⅓ cup sundried tomatoes in oil, drained
225 g / 8 oz / 1 ½ cup plain (all purpose) flour
2 tsp baking powder
½ tsp bicarbonate of soda
½ tsp salt

- Preheat the oven to 180°C (160° fan), gas 4 and butter a baking dish or loaf tin.
- Beat the eggs in a jug with the oil and yoghurt until well mixed.
- Mix the capers, tomatoes, flour, raising agents and salt in a bowl, then pour in the egg mixture and stir just enough to combine.
- Scrape the mixture into the dish, then bake in the oven for 20 – 25 minutes.
- Test with a wooden toothpick, if it comes out clean, the cake is done.
- Transfer the loaf to a wire rack and leave to cool completely before slicing.

Caper and Fresh Tomato Loaf Cake

1017

- Replace the sundried tomatoes with 100 g of cherry tomatoes, cut into quarters.

1018

MAKES 12 Roasted Pepper Rolls

- Mix together the flours, yeast, sugar and salt. Stir in the peppers and 280 ml of warm water.
- Knead the mixture on a lightly oiled surface with your hands for 10 minutes or until smooth and elastic.
- Leave the dough to rest in a lightly oiled bowl, covered with oiled clingfilm, for 1 – 2 hours.
- Knead it for 2 more minutes then split it into 12 even pieces and shape into rolls
- Transfer the rolls to a greased baking tray and cover with oiled clingfilm. Leave to prove for 1 hour.
- Preheat the oven to 220°C (200° fan), 430F, gas 7 and slash the tops of the rolls with a sharp knife.
- Bake for 15 – 20 minutes or until the rolls sound hollow when you tap them underneath.
- Transfer to a wire rack and leave to cool.

PREPARATION TIME 2 HOURS 30 MINUTES

COOKING TIME 25-40 MINUTES

INGREDIENTS

350 g / 12 ½ oz / 2 ⅓ cups strong white bread flour, plus extra for dusting
50 g / 1 ¾ oz / ⅓ cup stoneground wholemeal flour
½ tsp easy blend dried yeast
1 tbsp caster (superfine) sugar
1 tsp fine sea salt
1 jar mixed roasted peppers in oil, drained

Roasted Pepper and Parmesan Rolls   1019

- Five minutes before the end of cooking, sprinkle with Parmesan for a cheesy crust.

1020

SERVES 8 Cranberry and Flaked Almond Loaf Cake

- Preheat the oven to 180°C (160° fan), 355F, gas 4 and line a loaf tin with non-stick baking paper.
- Sieve the flour into a mixing bowl and rub in the butter until it resembles fine breadcrumbs then stir in the sugar and cranberries and almonds.
- Lightly beat the egg with the milk and stir it into the dry ingredients until just combined.
- Scrape the mixture into the loaf tin and bake for 55 minutes or until a skewer inserted in the centre comes out clean.
- Transfer the cake to a wire rack and leave to cool completely.

PREPARATION TIME 15 MINUTES

COOKING TIME 55 MINUTES

INGREDIENTS

225 g / 8oz / 1 ½ cups self raising flour
100 g / 3 ½ oz / ½ cup butter, cubed
85 g / 3oz / ⅓ cup caster (superfine) sugar
150 g / 5 ½ oz / ¾ cup dried cranberries
75 g / 2 ½ oz / 1 cup flaked (slivered) almonds
1 large egg
75 ml / 2 ½ fl. oz / ⅓ cup whole milk

Cranberry and Marzipan Loaf Cake   1022

- Add 150 g of marzipan in small cubes to the cake mixture with the cranberries.

Index

Index

Index

Index